THE MYSTERY OF EASTER ISLAND

Adventures Unlimited Press

The **Mystic Traveller Series:**
•IN SECRET TIBET by Theodore Illion (1937)
•DARKNESS OVER TIBET by Theodore Illion (1938)
•IN SECRET MONGOLIA by Henning Haslund (1934)
•MEN AND GODS IN MONGOLIA by Henning Haslund (1935)
•MYSTERY CITIES OF THE MAYA by Thomas Gann (1925)
•THE MYSTERY OF EASTER ISLAND by Katherine Routledge (1919)
•IN QUEST OF LOST WORLDS by Byron de Prorok (1937)

The **Lost Cities of the Pacific Series**:
•ANCIENT TONGA & THE LOST CITY OF MU'A
•ANCIENT MICRONESIA & THE LOST CITY OF NAN MADOL
•ANCIENT NEW ZEALAND & THE KAIMANAWA WALL
•ANCIENT RAPA NUI & THE LOST LAND OF HIVA
•ANCIENT TAHITI & THE LOST CITY OF HAVAI'IKI

The **Lost Cities Series**:
•LOST CITIES OF ATLANTIS, ANCIENT EUROPE
  & THE MEDITERRANEAN
•LOST CITIES OF NORTH & CENTRAL AMERICA
•LOST CITIES & ANCIENT MYSTERIES OF SOUTH AMERICA
•LOST CITIES OF ANCIENT LEMURIA & THE PACIFIC
•LOST CITIES & ANCIENT MYSTERIES OF AFRICA & ARABIA
•LOST CITIES OF CHINA, CENTRAL ASIA & INDIA

The **Atlantis Reprint Series:**
•RIDDLE OF THE PACIFIC by John MacMillan Brown (1924)
•THE HISTORY OF ATLANTIS by Lewis Spence (1926)
•ATLANTIS IN SPAIN by Elena Whishaw (1929)
•THE SHADOW OF ATLANTIS by Col. A. Braghine (1940)
•SECRET CITIES OF OLD SOUTH AMERICA by H. Wilkins (1952)

The **New Science Series**:
•THE FREE ENERGY DEVICE HANDBOOK
•THE FANTASTIC INVENTIONS OF NIKOLA TESLA
•THE ANTI-GRAVITY HANDBOOK
•ANTI-GRAVITY & THE WORLD GRID
•ANTI-GRAVITY & THE UNIFIED FIELD
•VIMANA AIRCRAFT OF ANCIENT INDIA & ATLANTIS

THE MYSTERY OF EASTER ISLAND

1919
Katherine Routledge

The Mystery of Easter Island
©Copyright 1919
Katherine Routledge

This edition

February 1998

ISBN 0-932813-48-8

Printed in the United States of America

Published by
Adventures Unlimited Press
One Adventure Place
Kempton, Illinois 60946 USA

THE MYSTERY OF
EASTER ISLAND

Katherine Routledge

PREFACE

As I sit down to write this preface there rises before me, not the other side of a London street, but the beautiful view over the harbour of St. Vincent, Cape Verde Islands, as seen from the British Consulate. It was a hot afternoon, but in that shady room I had found a fellow-woman and sympathetic listener. To her I had been pouring out, rather mercilessly as it seemed, the story of our interests and experiences, including the drowning of the tea in Las Palmas Harbour. When I had finished, she said quietly, "You are going to publish all this I suppose?" I hesitated, for the idea was new. "No," I replied, "we had not thought of doing so; of course, if we have any success at Easter Island we shall make it known, but this is all in the day's work." "I think," she said, "that there are many who lead quiet stay-at-home lives who would be interested." Times have changed since 1913, there are now few who have not had adventures, either in their own persons, or through those dear to them, compared with which ours were but pleasant play; but I still find that many of those who are good enough to care to hear what we did in those three years ask for personal details. After a lecture given to a learned society, which it had been an honour to be asked to address, I was accosted by a lady, invited for the occasion, with the remark, "I was disappointed in what you told us." My face fell. "You never said what you had to eat." This, and many similar experiences, are the apology for the trivialities of this work.

No attempt has been made to write any sort of a guide book to the varied places touched at by the yacht, neither space nor knowledge permitted; all that has been done either by pen or pencil is to try to give the main impression left on the mind of a passing dweller in their harbours and anchorages. It has, however, been found by experience that, in accounts of travel, the general reader loses much of the pleasure which has been experienced by the writer, through knowledge being assumed of the history of the places visited; a knowledge which the traveller himself has absorbed almost unconsciously. Without some acquaintance with past events the present cannot be understood; at the risk, therefore, of interrupting the narrative, a few notes of such history have been included.

In dealing with the main topic of the work, an endeavour has been made to give some idea of the problem of Easter Island as the expedition found it, and also of its work there. With regard to this part, some appeal is necessary to the understanding kindness of the reader, for it has not been an easy tale to tell, nor one which could be straightforwardly recounted. The story of Easter is as yet a tangled skein. The dim past, to which the megalithic works bear witness—the island as the early voyagers found it—its more recent history and present state, all of these are intermingled threads, none of which can be followed without reference to the remaining clues.

For those who would have preferred more scientific and fewer personal details, I can only humbly say wait, there is another volume in prospect with descriptions and dimensions of some two hundred and sixty burial-places on the island, thousands of measurements of statues, and other really absorbing matter. The numerical statements in the present book, dealing with archæological remains, must be considered approximate till it has been possible to go again through the large collection of notes.

It is fairly obvious why the writing of this story has fallen to the share of the sole feminine member of the expedition. I had also, what was, in spite of all things, the good fortune to be fourteen weeks longer on the island than my husband. They were fat weeks too, when the first lean ones, with their inevitable difficulties, were past ; and the unsettlement towards the end had not arrived. He has, I need hardly say, given me every assistance with this work. Generally speaking, all things which it is possible to touch and handle, buildings, weapons, and ornaments, were in his department ; while things of a less tangible description, such as religion, history, and folk-lore fell to my lot. Those who know him will recognise his touches throughout, and the account of the last part of the voyage, after my return to England, has been written by him.

The photographs, when not otherwise stated, are by members

of the Expedition. The drawings are from sketches made by the Author; those of the burial-places are from notebook outlines made in the course of work. The diagrams of the houses and burial-places are by my husband.

We are deeply grateful, both personally and on behalf of the Expedition, for all the aid, both public and private, extended to our work in the interests of science. We hesitate to allude to it in detail in connection with what may, it is to be feared, seem an unworthy book, but we cannot refrain from taking this, the earliest, opportunity of acknowledging our obligations. The Admiralty lent the Expedition a Lieutenant on full pay for navigation and survey. The Royal Society honoured it by bestowing a grant of £100, and the British Association by appointing a committee to further its interests accompanied by a small gift. Valuable scientific instruments were lent by both the Admiralty and Royal Geographical Society.

We are indebted to Sir Hercules Read and Captain T. A. Joyce, of the Ethnological Department of the British Museum, for the initial suggestion and much personal help. In our own University of Oxford the practical sympathy of Dr. Marett has been fully given from the time the project was first mooted till he read the proofs of the scientific part of this work; we owe more to such encouragement for any success attained than perhaps he himself realises. Mr. Henry Balfour has placed us, and all who are interested in the subject, under the greatest obligation for his work on our results which has thrown a flood of light on the culture of Easter Island, and has, in perhaps greater degree than anything else, made the Expedition seem "worth while." Dr. Rivers, of Cambridge, kindly undertook the position of Correspondent in connection with the committee of the British Association, and has put at our disposal his great knowledge of the Pacific. Dr. Haddon has also been good enough to allow us to avail ourselves of his intimate acquaintance with its problems. Dr. Corney has rendered constant and unique assistance with regard to the accounts of Easter Island as given by the early voyagers, a line of research most important in its bearings. Our thanks are due to Dr. Seligman for kind interest, to Professor Keith for his report on the two Pitcairn Islanders who returned with the yacht, and his examination of our osteological collection ; to Dr. Thomas of the Geological Survey for his report of the rocks brought back ; and not least to Mr. Sydney Ray, who has given most valuable time to our vocabularies of the language.

With regard to our journeyings and labours in the field, we are under great obligation to Mr. Edwards, the Chilean Minister in London, through whose representations his Government were good enough to grant us special facilities in their ports.   The Expedition owes much to Messrs. Balfour & Williamson of London, and the firms connected with them in Chile, California, and New York ; most especially to Messrs. Williamson & Balfour of Valparaiso for their permission to visit Easter Island and help throughout.   We are also very grateful to the manager of the ranch, Mr. Percy Edmunds, for his practical aid on the island ; since we left he has obtained for us a skin of the sacred bird which we had been unable to procure, and forwarded with it the negative of fig. 65, taken at our request.

It has been impossible in the compass of this book to express our gratitude to all those who gave help and hospitality on both the outward and homeward voyage.   We can only ask them to believe that we do not forget, and that the friendship of many is, we trust, a permanent possession.

For professional help in the production of this book it is a pleasure to acknowledge the skill and patience of Miss A. Hunter, who has assisted in preparing the sketches, and of Mr. Gear, President of the Royal Photographic Society, who has worked up the negatives ; also of Mr. F. Batchelor, of the Royal Geographical Society, who has drawn all the maps.

It has not, as will be readily understood, been always an easy matter to write of such different interests amidst the urgent claims and stupendous events since the time of our return ; but if any soul rendered sad by the war, or anxiously facing the problems of a new world, finds a few hours' rest surrounded by the blue of the sea or face to face with the everlasting calm of the great statues, then it will give very real happiness to

THE STEWARDESS OF THE *MANA*.

February 1919.

CONTENTS

PART I

THE VOYAGE TO EASTER ISLAND

CHAPTER I

xi

CONTENTS

PART III

THE HOMEWARD VOYAGE
EASTER ISLAND TO SAN FRANCISCO

CHAPTER XX

CONTENTS

PART IV

THE HOMEWARD VOYAGE—Continued
SAN FRANCISCO TO SOUTHAMPTON
BY S. R.

CHAPTER XXII

CHAPTER XXIII

CHAPTER XXIV

b

ILLUSTRATIONS

PART I

THE VOYAGE TO EASTER ISLAND

FIG. I.

M.A.N.1.

Charua Bay, Patagonian Channels.

CHAPTER I

Why we went to Easter Island—The Building and Equipping of the
Yacht—The Start from Southampton—Dartmouth—Falmouth.

" ALL the seashore is lined with numbers of stone idols, with
their backs turned towards the sea, which caused us no little
wonder, because we saw no tool of any kind for working these
figures." So wrote, a century and a half ago, one of the earliest
navigators to visit the Island of Easter in the South-east
Pacific. Ever since that day passing ships have found it incomprehensible that a few hundred natives should have been
able to make, move, and erect numbers of great stone monuments, some of which are over thirty feet in height; they have
marvelled and passed on. As the world's traffic has increased
Easter Island has still stood outside its routes, quiet and remote, with its story undeciphered. What were these statues
of which the present inhabitants know nothing ? Were they
made by their ancestors in forgotten times or by an earlier
race ? Whence came the people who reached this remote
spot ? Did they arrive from South America, 2,000 miles to the
eastward ? Or did they sail against the prevailing wind from the
distant islands to the west ? It has even been conjectured
that Easter Island is all that remains of a sunken continent.
Fifty years ago the problem was increased by the discovery on
this mysterious land of wooden tablets bearing an unknown
script; they too have refused to yield their secret.

When, therefore, we decided to see the Pacific before we
died, and asked the anthropological authorities at the British
Museum what work there remained to be done, the answer
was, " Easter Island." It was a much larger undertaking than
had been contemplated; we had doubts of our capacity for so

important a venture; and at first the decision was against it, but we hesitated and were lost. Then followed the problem how to reach the goal. The island belongs to Chile, and the only regular communication, if regular it can be called, was a small sailing vessel sent out by the Chilean Company, who use the island as a ranch; she went sometimes once a year, sometimes not so often, and only remained there sufficient time to bring off the wool crop. We felt that the work on Easter ought to be accompanied with the possibility of following up clues elsewhere in the islands, and that to charter any such vessel as could be obtained on the Pacific coast, for the length of time we required her, would be unsatisfactory, both from the pecuniary standpoint and from that of comfort. It was therefore decided, as Scoresby is a keen yachtsman, that it was worth while to procure in England a little ship of our own, adapted to the purpose, and to sail out in her. As the Panama Canal was not open, and the route by Suez would be longer, the way would lie through the Magellan Straits.

Search for a suitable vessel in England was fruitless, and it became clear that to get what we wanted we must build. The question of general size and arrangement had first to be settled, and then matters of detail. It is unfortunate that the precise knowledge which was acquired of the exact number of inches necessary to sleep on, to sit on, and to walk along is not again likely to be useful. The winter of 1910–11 was spent over this work, but the professional assistance obtained proved to be incompetent, and we had to begin again; the final architect of the little yacht was Mr. Charles Nicholson, of Gosport, and the plans were completed the following summer. They were for a vessel of schooner rig and auxiliary motor power. The length over all was 90 feet, and the water-line 72 feet; her beam was 20 feet. The gross tonnage was 91 and the yacht tonnage was 126.

The vessel was designed in four compartments, with a steel bulkhead between each of the divisions, so that in case of accident it would be possible to keep her afloat. Aft was the little chart-room, which was the pride of the ship. When we went on board magnificent yachts which could have carried our little vessel as a lifeboat, and found the navigation being done in the public rooms, we smiled with superiority. Out of the chart-room were the navigator's sleeping quarters, and in the overhang of the stern the sail-locker. The next compartment was given to the engines, and made into a galvanised iron box in case of fire. It contained a motor engine for such work as navigation in and out of harbour and traversing belts of calm. This was of 38 h.p. and run on paraffin, as petrol was disallowed by the insurance; it gave her 5½ knots. In the same compartment was the engine for the electric light : in addition the yacht had steam heating. The spaces between the walls of the engine-box and those of the ship were given to lamps, and to boatswain's stores.

Then came the centre of the ship, containing the quarters of our scientific party. The middle portion of this was raised three or four feet for the whole length, securing first a deck-house and then a heightened roof for the saloon below, an arrangement which was particularly advantageous, as no port-holes were allowed below decks, leaving us dependent on sky-lights and ventilators. Entering from without, two or three steps led down into the deck-house, which formed part of the saloon, but at a higher level ; it was my chief resort throughout the voyage. On each side was a settee, which was on the level of the deck, and thus commanded a view through port-holes and door of what was passing outside ; one of these settees served as a berth in hot weather. A small companion connected the deck-house with the saloon below: the latter ran across the width of the ship; it also had full-length settees both sides, and at the end of each was a chiffonier. On the port side was the dinner-table, which swung so beautifully that the fiddles were seldom used, and the thermos for the navigating officer could be left happily on it all night. Starboard was a smaller table, fitted for writing ; and a long bookshelf ran along the top of the for'ardside (fig. 1ᴬ).

On the afterside of the saloon a double cabin opened out of it, and a passage led to two single cabins and the bathroom. The cabins were rather larger than the ordinary staterooms of a mail steamer, and the arrangements of course more ample ; every available cranny was utilised for drawers and lockers, and in going ashore it was positive pain to see the waste of room under beds and sofas and behind washing-stands. My personal accommodation was a chest of drawers and hanging wardrobe, besides the drawers under the berth and various lockers. Returning to the saloon, a door for'ard opened into the pantry, which communicated with the galley above, situated on deck for the sake of coolness. For'ard again was a whole section given to stores, and beyond, in the bows, a roomy forecastle. The yacht had three boats—a lifeboat which contained a small motor engine, a cutter, and a dinghy; when we were at sea the two former were placed on deck, but the dinghy, except on one occasion only, was always carried in the davits, where she triumphantly survived all eventualities, a visible witness to the buoyancy of the ship.

While the plans were being completed, search was being made for a place where the vessel should be built; for though nominally a yacht, the finish and build of the Solent would have been out of place. It had been decided that she should be of wood, as easier to repair in case of accident where coral reefs and other unseen dangers abound; but the building of wooden walls is nearly extinct. The west country was visited, and an expedition made to Dundee and Aberdeen, but even there, the old home of whalers, ships are now built of steel; finally we fixed on Whitstable, from which place such vessels still ply round the coast. The keel was laid in the autumn of 1911; the following spring we took up our abode there to watch over her, and there in May 1912 she first took the water, being christened by the writer in approved fashion. " I name this ship *Mana*, and may the blessing of God go with her and all who sail in her "—a ceremony not to be performed without a lump in the throat. The choice of a name had been difficult ; we had wished to give her one borne by some ship of Dr. Scoresby, the Arctic explorer, a friend of my husband's family whose name he received, but none of them proved to be suitable. The object was to find something which was both simple and uncommon; all appellations that were easy to grasp seemed to have been already adopted, while those that were unique lent themselves to error. " How would it do in a cable? " was the regulation test. Finally we hit on *Mana*, which is a word well known to anthropologists, and has the advantage of being familiar throughout the South Seas. We generally translated it somewhat freely as "good luck." It means, more strictly, supernatural power: a Polynesian would, for instance, describe

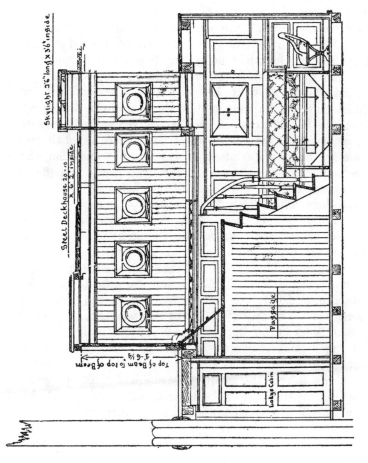

Skylight 3'6" long x 3'6" inside

Steel Deckhouse 20·10 X 6·2 inside

Top of Beam to top of Beam 3'-6 1/2"

Passage

Ladys Cabin

FIG. 1A.—MANA. SECTION OF DECKHOUSE AND SALOON.

the common idea of the effect of a horseshoe by saying that the shoe had "mana." From a scientific standpoint mana is probably the simplest form of religious conception. The yacht flew the burgee of the Royal Cruising Club.

From the time the prospective expedition became public we received a considerable amount of correspondence from strangers: some of it was from those who had special knowledge of the subject, and was highly valued; other letters had a comic element, being from various young men, who appeared to think that our few berths might be at the disposal of anyone who wanted to see the world. One letter, dated from a newspaper office, stated that its writer had no scientific attainments, but would be glad to get up any subject required in the time before sailing; the qualification of another for the post of steward was that he would be able to print the menus and ball programmes. The most quaint experience was in connection with a correspondent who gave a good name and address, and offered to put at our disposal some special knowledge on the subject of native lore, which he had collected as Governor of one of the South Sea islands. On learning our country address, he wrote that he was about to become the guest of some of our neighbours and would call upon us. It subsequently transpired that they knew nothing of him, but that he had written to them, giving our name. He did, in fact, turn up at our cottage during our absence, and obtained an excellent tea at the expense of the caretaker. The next we heard of him was from the keeper of a small hotel in the neighbourhood of Whitstable, where he had run up a large bill on the strength of a statement that he was one of our expedition, and we found later that he had shown a friend over the yacht while she was building, giving out he was a partner of my husband. We understand that after we started he appeared in the county court at the instance of the unfortunate innkeeper.

After much trouble we ultimately selected two colleagues from the older universities. The arrangement with one of these, an anthropologist, was, unfortunately, a failure, and ended at the Cape Verde Islands. The other, a geologist, Mr. Frederick Lowry-Corry, took up intermediate work in India, and subsequently joined us in South America. The Admiralty was good enough to place at our disposal a lieutenant on full pay for navigation, survey, and tidal observation. This post was ultimately filled by Lieutenant D. R. Ritchie, R.N.

With regard to the important matter of the crew, it was felt that neither merchant seamen nor yacht hands would be suitable, and a number of men were chosen from the Lowestoft fishing fleet. Subsequent delays, however, proved deleterious, the prospective " dangers " grew in size, and the only one who ultimately sailed with us was a boy, Charles C. Jeffery, who was throughout a loyal and valued member of the expedition. The places of the other men were supplied by a similar class from Brixham, who justified the selection. The mate, Preston, gave much valuable service, and one burly seaman in particular, Light by name, by his good-humour and intelligent criticism added largely to the amenity of the voyage. An engineer, who was also a photographer, was obtained from Glasgow. We were particularly fortunate in our sailing master, Mr. H. J. Gillam. He had seen, while in Japan, a notice of the expedition in a paper, and applied with keenness for the post; to his professional knowledge, loyalty, and pleasant companionship the successful achievement of the voyage is very largely due. The full complement of the yacht, in addition to the scientific members, consisted of the navigator, engineer, cook-steward, under-steward, and three men for each watch, making ten in all. S. was official master, and I received on the books the by no means honorary rank of stewardess.

Whitstable proved to be an unsuitable place for painting, so *Mana* made her first voyage round to Southampton Water, where she lay for a while in the Hamble River, and later at a yacht-builder's in Southampton. The steward on this trip took to his bed with seasickness; but as he was subsequently found surreptitiously eating the dinner which S. had been obliged to cook, we felt that he was not likely to prove a desirable shipmate, and he did not proceed further. We had hoped to sail in the autumn, but we had our full share of the troubles and delays which seem inevitably associated with yacht-building: the engine was months late in the installation, and then had to be rectified; the painting took twice as long as had been promised; and when we put out for trial trips there was trouble with the anchor which necessitated a return to harbour. The friends who had kindly assembled in July at the Hans Crescent

Hotel to bid us good speed began to ask if we were ever really going to depart. We spent the winter practically living on board, attending to these affairs and to the complicated matter of stowage.

The general question of space had of course been very carefully considered in the original designs. The allowance for water was unusually large, the tanks containing sufficient for two, or with strict economy for three months; the object in this was not only safety in long or delayed passages, but to avoid taking in supplies in doubtful harbours. Portions of the hold had to be reserved of course for coal, and also for the welded steel tanks which contained the oil. When these essentials had been disposed of, still more intricate questions arose with regard to the allotment of room ; it turned out to be greater than we had ventured to hope, but this in no way helped, as every department hastened to claim additional accommodation and to add something more to its stock. Nothing was more surprising all through the voyage than the yacht's elasticity: however much we took on board we got everything in, and however much we took out she was always quite full.

The outfit for the ship had of course been taken into consideration, but as departure drew near it seemed, from the standpoint of below decks, to surpass all reason ; there were sails for fine weather and sails for stormy weather, and spare sails, anchors, and sea-anchors, one-third of a mile of cable, and ropes of every size and description.

As commissariat officer, the Stewardess naturally felt that domestic stores were of the first importance. Many and intricate calculations had been made as to the amount a man ate in a month, and the cubic space to be allowed for the same. It had been also a study in itself to find out what must come from England and what could be obtained elsewhere; kind correspondents in Buenos Aires and Valparaiso had helped with advice, and we arranged for fresh consignments from home to meet us in those ports, of such articles as were not to be procured there or were inordinately expensive. The general amount of provisions on board was calculated for six months, but smaller articles, such as tea, were taken in sufficient quantities for the two years which it was at the time assumed would be the duration of the trip. We brought back on our return a considerable amount of biscuits, for it was found possible to bake on board much oftener than we had dared to hope. As a yacht we were not obliged to conform to the merchant service scale of provisions, our ship's articles guaranteeing "sufficiency and no waste." The merchant scale was constantly referred to, but it is, by universal agreement, excessive, and leads to much waste, as the men are liable to claim what they consider their right, whether they consume the ration or not; the result is that a harbour may not unfrequently be seen covered with floating pieces of bread, or even whole loaves. The quantity asked for by our men of any staple foods was always given, and there were the usual additions, but we subsisted on about three-fourths of the legal ration. We had only one case of illness requiring a doctor, and then it was diagnosed as "the result of over-eating." It was a source of satisfaction that we never throughout the voyage ran short of any essential commodity.

There were other matters in the household department for which it was even more difficult to estimate than for the actual food—how many cups and saucers, for example, should we break per month, and how many reams of paper and gallons of ink ought we to take. Our books had of course to be largely scientific, a sovereign's worth of cheap novels was a boon, but we often yearned unutterably for a new book. Will those who have friends at the ends of the earth remember the godsend to them of a few shillings so invested, as a means of bringing fresh thoughts and a sense of civilised companionship? For a library for the crew we were greatly indebted to the kindness of Lord Radstock and the Passmore Edwards Ocean Library. We were subsequently met at every available port by a supply of newspapers, comprising the weekly editions of the *Times* and *Daily Graphic*, the *Spectator*; and the papers of two Societies for Women's Suffrage.

In addition to the requirements for the voyage the whole equipment for landing had to be foreseen and stowed, comprising such things as tents, saddlery, beds, buckets, basins, and cooking-pots. We later regretted the space given to some of the enamelled iron utensils, as they can be quite well procured in Chile, while cotton and other goods which we had counted on procuring there for barter were practically unobtainable.

Some sacks of old clothes which we took out for gifts proved most valuable. Among late arrivals that clamoured for peculiar consideration were the scientific outfits, which attained to gigantic proportions. S., who had studied at one time at University College Hospital, was our doctor, and the medical and surgical stores were imposing: judging from the quantity of bandages, we were each relied on to break a leg once a month. Everybody had photographic gear; the geologist appeared with a huge pestle and other goods; there was anthropological material for the preserving of skulls; the surveying instruments looked as if they would require a ship to themselves; while cases of alarming size arrived from the Admiralty and Royal Geographical Society, containing sounding machines and other mysterious articles. The owners of all these treasures argued earnestly that they were of the essence of the expedition, and must be treated with respect accordingly. Then of course things turned up for which everyone had forgotten to allow room, such as spare electric lamps, also a trammel and seine, each of fifty fathoms, to secure fish in port. Before we finally sailed a large consignment appeared of bonded tobacco for the crew, and the principal hold was sealed by the Customs, necessitating a temporary sacrifice of the bathroom for last articles.

This packing of course all took time, especially as nothing could be allowed to get wet, and a rainy or stormy day hung up all operations. Finally, however, on the afternoon of February 28th, 1913, the anchor was weighed, and we went down Southampton Water under power. We were at last off for Easter Island!

We had a good passage down the Channel, stopped awhile at Dartmouth, for the Brixham men to say good-bye to their families, and arrived at Falmouth on March 6th. Here there was experienced a tiresome delay of nearly three weeks. The wind, which in March might surely have seen its way to be easterly, and had long been from that direction, turned round and blew a strong gale from the south-west. The harbour was white with little waves, and crowded with shipping of every description, from battleships to fishing craft. Occasionally a vessel would venture out to try to get round the Lizard, only to return beaten by the weather. We had while waiting the sad privilege of rendering a last tribute to our friend Dr. Thomas

Hodgkin, the author of *Italy and her Invaders*, who just before our arrival had passed where " tempests cease and surges swell no more." He rests among his own people in the quiet little Quaker burial-ground.

It was not till Lady Day, Tuesday, March 25th, that the wind changed sufficiently to allow of departure; then there was a last rush on shore to obtain sailing supplies of fresh meat, fruit, and vegetables, and to send off good-bye telegrams. Everything was triumphantly squeezed in somewhere and carefully secured, so that nothing should shift when the roll began. The only articles which found no home were two sacks of potatoes, which had to remain on the cabin floor, because the space assigned to them below hatches had, in my absence on shore, been nefariously appropriated by the Sailing-master for an additional supply of coal.

It was dark before all was ready, and we left Falmouth Harbour with the motor; then out into the ocean, the sails hoisted, the Lizard Light sighted, and good-bye to England !

" Two years," said our friends, " that is a long time to be away." " Oh no," we had replied; " we shall find when we come back that everything is just the same; it always is. You will still be talking of Militants, and Labour Troubles, and Home Rule; there will be a few new books to read, the children will be a little taller—that will be all." But the result was otherwise.

CHAPTER II

A Gale at Sea—Madeira—Canary Islands—Cape Verde Islands—
Across the Atlantic.

THE first day in open ocean was spent in shaking down ; on going on deck before turning in it was found to be a clear starlight night, and the man at the wheel prophesied smooth things.   It was a case of—

> " A little ship was on the sea,
>   It was a pretty sight,
>   It sailed along so pleasantly,
>   And all was calm and bright."

But, alas ! the storm did soon begin to rise ; by morning we were in troubled waters, and by noon we were battened down and hove to.   We had given up all idea of making progress and were riding out the gale as best we might.   All the saloon party were more or less laid low, including Mr. Ritchie, for the first time in his life.   The steward was not seen for two days ; and if it had not been that the under-steward, who shall be known as " Luke," rose to the occasion, the state of affairs would have been somewhat serious.   He not only contrived to satisfy the appetites of the crew, which were subsequently said to have been abnormally good, but also staggered round, with black hands and a tousled head, ministering with tea and bovril to our frailer needs.   The engineer, a landsman, was too incapacitated to do any work, and doubt arose as to whether we should not be left without electric light.   More alarming was the fact that the place smelt badly of paraffin, arousing anxiety as to the effect the excessive rolling of the ship might have had on our carefully tested tanks and barrels ; happily the odour proved to be due merely to a temporary overflow in the engine-room.

14

We now found the disadvantage of having abandoned, owing to our various delays, the trial runs in home waters which had at one time been planned. The skylights, which would have been adequate for ordinary yachting—which has been described as "going round and round the Isle of Wight"—proved unequal to the work expected of *Mana*, and the truth appeared of a dark saying of the Board of Trade surveyor that "skylights were not ventilation." Not only could they of course not be raised in bad weather, but those which, like mine, were arranged to open, admitted the sea to an unpleasant degree; such an amount of water had to be conveyed by means of dripping towels into canvas baths that it seemed at one time as if the Atlantic would be perceptibly emptier. When in the midst of the gale night fell on the lonely ship the sensation was eerie; every now and then the persistent rolling, which threw from side to side of the berth those fortunate enough to be below, was interrupted by a resounding crash in the darkness as a big wave broke against the vessel's side, followed by the rushing surge and gurgle of the water as it poured in a volume over the deck above. Then the hubbub entirely ceased, and for a perceptible time the vessel lay perfectly still in the trough of the wave, like a human creature dazed by a sudden blow, after a second or two to begin again her weary tossing. I wondered, as I lay there, which was the more weird experience, this night or one spent in camp in East Africa with no palisade, in a district swarming with lions, and again recalled the philosophy of one of our Swahili boys. "Frightened? No, he eats me, he does not eat me; it is all the will of Allah."

By morning the worst was over, and it was a comfort to hear Mr. Gillam singing cheerfully something about "In the Bay of Biscay O," a performance he varied with anathemas on the seasick steward. When I was able to get on deck, the waves were still descending on us—if not the proverbial mountains, at any rate hills high, looking as if they must certainly overwhelm us. It was wonderful to see, what later I took for granted, how the yacht rose to each, taking it as it were in her stride. It was reported to have been a "full gale, a hurricane, as bad as could be, with dangerous cross seas"; but the little vessel had proved herself a splendid sea-going boat, and "had ridden it out like a duck." For the next little while

I can only say in the words of the poet, "It was not night, it was not day"; neither the clothes people wore, nor the food they took, nor their times of downsitting and uprising had anything to do with the hours of light and darkness. By Saturday, however, the weather was better, meals were established, and things generally more civilised. We had another bad gale somewhere in the latitude of Finisterre, being hove to for thirty hours, but were subsequently very little troubled with seasickness. The second Sunday out, April 6th, we experienced a short interlude of calm, and I discovered that not only does a sailing ship not travel in bad weather, but that when it is really beautifully smooth she also has a bad habit of declining to go. Anyway, we held our first service, and " O God, our help " went, if not in Westminster Abbey form, at any rate quite creditably.

Mr. Ritchie had decided to take two sides of a triangle, first west and then south, rather than run any risk of being blown on to Ushant or Finisterre; a precaution which, in view of the proved powers of the boat to hold her own against a head wind, he subsequently thought to have been unnecessary. After we left the English shores we only saw two vessels till we were within sight of Madeira, and some of our Brixham men, who had never been far from their native shores or away from their fishing fleet, were much impressed with the size and loneliness of the ocean. "It was astonishing," said Light, "that there could be so much water without any land or ships," and he expressed an undisguised desire for " more company."

Somehow or other we had all come to the conclusion that we would put into Madeira, instead of going straight through to Las Palmas, for which we had cleared from Falmouth. The first land which we sighted was the outlying island of the group, Porto Santo. This was appropriate on a voyage to the New World, as Columbus resided there with his father-in-law, who was governor of the place; and it is said that from his observations there of driftwood, and other indications, he first conceived the idea of the land across the waters, to which he made his famous voyage in 1492. Our mate entertained us with a tale of how he had been shipwrecked on Porto Santo, the yacht on which he was serving having overrun her reckonings as she approached it from the west ; happily all on board were able to escape. The wind fell after we made the group, so that we did not get into the harbour of Funchal for another thirty-six hours, and then only with the help of the motor. It was most enjoyable cruising along the coast of Madeira, watching the great mountains, woods, ravines, and nestling villages, at whose existence the passengers on the deck of a Union-Castle liner can only vaguely guess. The day was Sunday, April 13th, and later it became a matter of remark how frequently we hit off this day of the week for getting into harbour, a most inconvenient one from the point of view of making the necessary arrangements. As we entered, a Portuguese liner, coming out of Funchal, dipped its flag in greeting to our blue ensign ; out came the harbour-master's tug to show us where to take up our position, down went the anchor with a comfortable rattle, and so ended the first stage of our journey.

The voyage had taken eighteen days, and averaged about sixty miles a day, as against the hundred miles on which we had calculated, and which later we sometimes exceeded. A man who crosses the ocean in a powerful steam-vessel, as one who travels by land in an express train, undoubtedly gains in speed, but he loses much else. He misses a thousand beauties, he has no contact with Nature, no sense of the exultation which comes from progress won step by step by putting forth his own powers to bend hers to his will. The late veteran seaman Lord Brassey is reported to have said that " when once an engine is put into a ship the charm of the sea is gone." All through our voyage also there was a fascinating sense of having put back the hands of time. This was the route and these in the main the conditions under which our ancestors, the early Empire builders, travelled to India ; later we were on the track of Drake, Anson, and others. Some of Drake's ships were apparently about the size of *Mana*.[1] The world has been shrinking of late, and to return to a simpler day is to restore much of its size and dignity.

[1] The *Pelican*, or *Golden Hinde*, was 120 tons ; the *Elizabeth* 80 tons, and three smaller ships were 50, 30, and 12 tons respectively. The crews all told were 160 men and boys.—Froude's *English Seamen*, p. 112.

FIG. 2.—PORTO SANTO.

MADEIRA

Madeira was settled by the Portuguese early in the fifteenth century. With the exception of an interlude in the Napoleonic wars, when it was taken by England, it has ever since been a possession of that country.

Funchal, with its sunshine and its smiling houses, is well known to all travellers to South Africa. The season was just over, but the weather was still pleasantly cool, and flowers covered the walls with great masses of colour. We were there three days, and occupied our time in the usual way by ascending the hill above the town in the funicular railway, but instead of descending in the picturesque toboggans we came down on foot. The walk took about two hours down a path which is paved the whole way, representing a very large amount of labour. We regretted that we were unable to stay longer and see something of the life in those lonely cottages among the mountains, which we had seen from the sea, where the women are said to add considerably to their income by the embroidery for which the island is famous. Since our visit Funchal, as belonging to one of the Allies, has suffered in the Great War through enemy action, having been shelled from the sea and the shipping in the harbour sunk by a German raid.

GRAND CANARY

The Canary group consists of some nine islands, of which the most important are Teneriffe and Grand Canary. They have been known from the earliest times, but European sovereignty did not begin till 1402, and it was the end of the century before all the islands became subject to the crown of Castile. This prolonged warfare was due to the very brave resistance offered by the original inhabitants, known as Guanches. These very interesting people, who are of Berber extraction, withstood the Spaniards till 1483, and the name of Grand Canary is said to have been obtained from their stubborn defence. The final defeat of the natives was largely due to the terror inspired by their first sight of a body of cavalry which the Spaniards had landed on the island. The Guanches of Teneriffe held out till 1496. The Canaries were thus subdued just in time to become a stepping-stone to the New World. The horses of the cavalry were carried to America, and formed part of the stock from which sprang the wild American mustang.

On quitting Madeira we caught the north-east trade wind at once, and had a capital run to the Grand Canary, doing the 197 miles in 51½ hours.

The aspect of our new harbour, Puerto de la Luz by name, was somewhat depressing. On its south side is the mainland of the island, which consists of sandhills, behind which are bleak, arid-looking mountains, whose summits during the whole of our three weeks' stay were continuously veiled in mist. The west side is formed by the promontory of Isleta, which would be an island save that it is connected with Grand Canary by a sand isthmus washed up by the sea, much after the manner that Gibraltar is united to the Spanish mainland. The remainder of the protection for the harbour consists of artificial breakwaters. The only spot on which the eye rests with pleasure is a distant view of a cluster of houses, above which rises a cathedral; this is the capital, Las Palmas, which lies two or three miles to the south. The effect made on the newcomer, especially after leaving luxuriant Madeira, is that of having been transported into the heart of Africa.

The port, if not attractive, is at any rate prosperous. The Canaries are still a stepping-stone to the New World, and in accordance with modern requirements have turned into a great coaling station. In Puerto de la Luz six or seven different firms compete for the work. The British Consul, Major Swanston, gave us a most interesting account of his duties during the

South African War in revictualling the transports which called here. Mention should not be omitted of the delightful new institute of the British and Foreign Sailors' Society, with billiard-room, reading-room, and arranged concerts, to which our men were very glad to resort ; but indeed we met similar kind provision in so many ports that it seems invidious to particularise.

This was my first experience of life in a foreign port as " stewardess," for our stay at Madeira was only an interlude. To passengers on a mail steamer the time so spent is generally concerned with changing into shore clothes, and making up parties for dinner on land to avoid the exigencies of coaling. To those in charge of a small boat its aspect is very different. Much of it is not a time of leisure, but to be an acting member of a British ship in a foreign port is distinctly exhilarating. It brings with it a sense both of being a humble represen-tative of one's own nationality, and also of belonging to the great busy fraternity of the sea. First, as land is approached, comes the running up of the ensign and burgee ; then the making of the ship's number, as the signal station is passed, which will in due course be reported to Lloyds ; next follows the entry into port, and the awaiting of the harbour-master, on whose fiat it hangs where the vessel shall take up her berth. He is succeeded by doctor and customs officer to examine the ship's papers ; and all these are matters not for some mysterious personages with gold braid, but of personal interest.

As soon as the yacht is safely berthed the Master goes on shore to visit the consul, and obtain the longed-for letters and newspapers. In the food department the important question of food at once arises. My hope had always been that we should have found a steward capable of taking over this re-sponsibility, but though we had various changes, and paid the highest wages, we were never able to get one sufficiently reliable, and the work therefore fell on the Stewardess. We at first used to go on shore and cater personally, which is no doubt the most satisfactory method, but in view of the time involved we sub-sequently relied on the " ships' chandlers," who are universal providers, to be found in all ports of any size, and who will bring fresh stores to the ship daily. A very careful examination and comparison of prices is necessary, for one of the annoying parts of owning a boat is that even the smallest yacht-owner is considered fair game for extortion and dishonest dealing. The variation in the cost of commodities in different harbours, requires a very elastic mind on the part of the housekeeper, both as to menus in port and purchases for the next stage of the voyage. It puts an extremely practical interest into the list of exports, which formed so dreary a part of geography as taught in one's own childhood. At Las Palmas prices were much as in pre-war England ; at our next port, in Cape Verde Islands, the best meat was sixpence a pound, and fish sufficient for four cost threepence, but the cost of bread was high. At Rio de Janeiro and elsewhere in South America, though most things were ruinous, we obtained enough coffee at very reasonable prices to carry us home; while in Buenos Aires, with mutton at fourpence a pound, it was a matter of regret that the hold was not twice as large.

On arriving in port after a long voyage, work is generally needed on the vessel or her engines: if so, the name of the right firm has to be obtained, the firm found, an estimate obtained and bargain made. Then the work has to be done and frequently redone, all of which causes delay it seems impossible to avoid ; a fortnight may thus easily be spent in getting a two days' job accomplished. In Las Palmas we were fortunate in finding a capable firm, who took in hand such alterations as our experience in the Bay had shown to be necessary. The offending skylights were fastened down, and ventilating shafts substituted, with the result that we had no more trouble. We had a good deal of extra work on board to do ourselves from a tiresome mishap. In inspecting the stove connected with the heating apparatus, it was noticed that there was water under the grating; this was at first thought to be due to skylight drip, but on lifting the grating there was seen to be quite deep water in the hold almost up to the outside sea-level. The pumps were at once rigged to get it down, but it was found still to be filling ; and it was then discovered that there was a serious leakage, due to the fact that the pipe through which the water came to cool the engine had been defectively jointed. It meant days of work to go through the stores affected. Happily nothing was lost except about twenty pounds of tea, and some sweets intended for gifts ; but if the accident, which was entirely due to careless workmanship, had happened at sea the results might have been disastrous.

We were glad when we were at last able to see something of the country.   If the harbour of Luz is not beautiful, the road from it into Las Palmas is still less so.   It runs between the sea and arid sandhills, and abounds in ruts and dust; as there is also no street lighting, "the rates," as S. remarked, "can hardly be high."   Half-way along this road there stand, for no very obvious reason, the English Church and Club, also a good hotel, the Santa Catalina, belonging to a steamship company; otherwise it is bordered by poor and unattractive houses of stucco, the inhabitants of which seem permanently seated at the windows to watch the passers-by.   Happily the distance is traversed by means of trams, owned by a company with English capital, which run frequently between the port and the city and do the journey in twenty minutes.

Las Palmas itself is not unpicturesque.   Its main feature is a stony river-bed, which runs down the centre of the city and is spanned by various bridges; it was empty when we saw it, but is no doubt at times, even in this waterless land, filled with a raging, boiling current from the mountains.   In the principal square, opposite the cathedral, is the museum, which contains an admirable anthropological collection, concerned mostly with relics of the Guanches.   When we were there the city was gay with bunting and grand stands for a *fiesta*, in celebration of the anniversary of the union of the islands with the crown of Castile; a flying man, a carnival, and an outdoor cinema entertainment were among the chief excitements.   At one of the hotels we discussed politics with the waiter, who was a native of the island.   He had been in England, but never in Spain; nevertheless, he seemed in touch with the situation in the ruling country.   There would, he declared, be great changes in Spain in the next fifteen years.   The King did his best in difficult circumstances, but anti-clerical feeling was too strong to allow of the continuation of the present state of things.   In Grand Canary there was, he said, the same feeling as in Spain against the constant exactions of the Church.   The women were still devout, but you might go into any village and talk against the Church and meet with sympathy from the men.   He himself was a socialist, and as such " had no country; countries were

FIG. 3.

LAS PALMAS, GRAND CANARY.

Katherine Routledge

for rich people who had something belonging to them, something to lose ; for those who had to work all countries were the same." He only lived in Canary, he said, because his people were there. We pointed out that the bond with one's own people was precisely what made one country home and not another, but the argument fell flat.

The great charm of the island lies in the mountainous character of the interior region. Three roads radiate from the capital, one along the coast to the north, another to the south, and the third inland. Along all these it is necessary to travel some distance before points of interest are reached, and we were at the disadvantage of never being able to be more than a night or two away from the ship without returning to see how the work on board was progressing. On all the main routes are run motor-buses, which are chiefly characterised by indications of impending dissolution, and inspire awe by the rapidity with which they turn corners without any preliminary easing down. The natives, however, appeared to think that the accidents were not unreasonably numerous.

In addition to motors there are local " coaches " drawn by horses, after the manner of covered wagonettes; they will no doubt be gradually superseded by the motors, but still command considerable custom. Both types of vehicles are delightfully vague in the hours which they keep, being just as likely to start too soon as too late, thus presupposing an indefinite amount of time for the passengers to spend at the starting-place.

Our first expedition was by the inland or middle road, which winds up by the bleak hillside till it reaches a beautiful and attractive country. To those unaccustomed to such latitudes, it comes as a surprise to see fertility increasing instead of diminishing with elevation, due to the more constant rain among the hills. Monte and Santa Brigida may be said to be residential neighbourhoods and have comfortable hotels and boarding-houses. There are two principal sights to be visited from there. One is the village of Atalaya, which consists of a zone of cave dwellings, almost encircling the summit of a dome-shaped hill. The eminence falls away on two sides to a deep ravine, over which it commands magnificent views, and is connected with the adjacent hills by a narrow coll. The rock

is of consolidated volcanic tuff, in which the dwellings are excavated. The fronts of the houses abut on the pathway, which
is about four feet wide, and are unequally placed, following
the contour of the ground. Each dwelling consists of two
apartments, both about twelve feet square, with rounded
angles and a domed roof, the surface of the walls shows the
chisel-marks. The front apartment is used as a bed-sitting-
room, the back one as a store; and in some cases a lean-to out-
house has been built of blocks of the same material, in which
cooking is done and the goats kept. Doors and window-sashes
are inserted into the solid stone. Both dwellings and surroundings are beautifully clean and neat; the first one exhibited
we imagined to be a " show " apartment, till others proved
equally neat and orderly. Flowers were planted in crannies of
the rock and around the doors and windows, being carefully
tended and watered. The industry of the village is making
pots by hand without a wheel, the sand being obtained in one
direction and the clay in another: the shapes coincide in
several instances with those taken from native burial-grounds
and now to be seen in the museum at Las Palmas. The occasion of our visit was unfortunately a *fiesta*, and regular work
was not going on: an old lady, however, made us a model
pot in a few minutes; it was fashioned out of one piece of clay,
with the addition of a little extra material if necessary: the
pottery is unglazed. Various specimens of the art were obtained
by the Expedition and are now in the Pitt-Rivers Museum at
Oxford.

About half a mile from these troglodyte abodes, and adjoining the coll, is an extraordinarily fine specimen of an extinct
crater or *caldero*. Its walls are almost vertical and unclad
by vegetation: about two-thirds of the circumference is igneous
rock, and the rest black volcanic ash, which exhibits the strati-
fication in the most marked manner. The crater is about 1,000
feet deep, the floor is flat and dry, and the visitor looks down
on a house at the bottom and cultivated fields.

We returned to *Mana* for a night or two, and then made an
expedition by motor along the north road, sleeping at the
picturesque village of Fergas, and from thence by mule over
the beautiful mountain-track to Santa Brigida. We changed
animals *en route*, and the price asked for a fresh beast was

outrageous. We were prepared under the circumstances to pay it, when the portly lady of the inn, who was obviously "a character," beckoned us mysteriously round a corner, and, though we had scarcely two words of any language in common, gave us emphatically to understand that we were on no account to be so swindled, she would see we got another. This, however, was not accomplished for another hour, with the result that the last part of the journey was traversed in total darkness, and the lights of the hotel were very welcome.

Mana being still in the hands of work-people, we made our next way by the south road to the town of Telde, near which is a mountain known as Montana de las Cuatro Puertas, where are a wonderful series of caves connected with the Guanches. The road from Las Palmas skirts the sea-coast for a large part of the way, being frequently cut into the cliff-face and in one place passing through a tunnel: the town lies on the lowland not far from the sea. We arrived late in the afternoon, and endeavoured to make a bargain for rooms with the burly landlord of the rather humble little inn. As difficulties supervened a man who spoke a little English was called in to act as interpreter. He turned out to be a vendor of ice-creams who had visited London, and to make the acquaintance of the exponent of such a trade in his native surroundings was naturally a most thrilling experience. He expressed a great desire to return to that land of wealth, England, though his knowledge of our language was so extremely limited he had obviously, when there, associated principally with his own countrymen.

We went for a stroll before dark, noticing the system of irrigation: the water is preserved in large tanks, from which it is distributed in all directions by small channels, and so valuable is it that these conduits are in many cases made of stone faced with Portland cement. They are now, however, in some instances being replaced by iron pipes, which have naturally the merit of saving loss by evaporation. Canary is a land where the owner of a spring has literally a gold-mine. This is the most celebrated district for oranges. After our evening meal we joined the company in the central *plaza* of the little town. The moon shone down through the trees; young men sat and smoked, and young girls, wearing white mantillas, strolled about in companies of four or five, chatting gaily. The elders belonged to the village club, which opened on to the square ; it was confined seemingly to one room, of which the whole space was occupied by a billiard-table; this, however, was immaterial, as the company spent a large part of the time in the *plaza*, an arrangement which doubtless had the merit of saving house rent. A little way down a side street the light streamed from the inn windows. Nearer at hand the church stood out against the sky; it was May, the month of the Virgin Mary, and a special service in her honour had just concluded. One felt a momentary expectation that Faust and Marguérite or other friends from stage-land would appear on the scene ; they may of course have been there unrecognised by us.

We discovered after much trouble that a motor-bus ran through the village early next morning, passing close to the mountain which we had come to visit, and could drop us on the way. We passed a fairly comfortable night, though not un-diversified by suspicions that our beds were occupied by earlier denizens; and had just begun breakfast when the bus appeared, some time before the earliest hour specified. We had to tear down and catch it, leaving the meal barely tasted; the kind attendant following us and pressing into our hand the deserted fried fish done up in a piece of newspaper. Such hurry, how-ever, proved to be quite unnecessary, as we had not got beyond the precincts of the small town before the vehicle came to an unpremeditated stop, through the fan which cools the radiator having broken. We waited half an hour or so in company with our fellow-passengers, who appeared stolidly resigned, and then, as there seemed no obvious prospect of continuing our journey, grew restless. Here again the ice-cream man acted as *deus ex machina*: he was standing about with the crowd which had assembled, blowing a horn at intervals, and distributing ices not infrequently to small infants, whose fond mammas provided the requisite penny ; he told us he generally made a sum equal to about one-and-sixpence a day in this manner. Grasping our difficulty, he delivered an impassioned address on our need to the assembled multitude, which after further delay resulted in the appearance of a wagonette and mules. The Montana de las Cuatro Puertas rises out of comparatively level ground near the coast and commands magnificent views. The top is honey-combed with caves, and one towards the north has the four

FIG. 5.

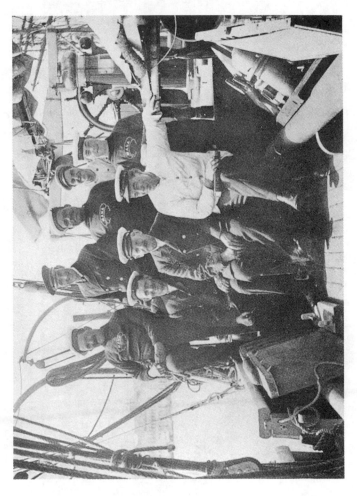

A GROUP ON DECK.

A. Light; Steward; B. Rosa; Under-Steward; C. Jeffery;
W. Marks; F. Preston (Mate); H. J. Gillam (Sailing-master).

32]

FIG. 4.

PORTO GRANDE, ST. VINCENT, CAPE VERDE ISLANDS.

27]

entrances from which the mountain takes its name. It is said to have been the site of funeral rites of the inhabitants. The place is both impressive and interesting, and would well repay more careful study than the superficial view which was all it was possible for us to give it.

We decided to return to Las Palmas in the local coach, as we had previously found travelling by this means both cheap and quite comfortable. This time, however, our luck was otherwise. The vehicle could have reasonably held eleven, but one passenger after another joined it along the route, one newcomer was constrained to find a seat on the pole, another stood on the step, and so forth, till we numbered twenty, of all ages and sexes. The day was hot, but the good-natured greeting, almost welcome, which was given to each arrival by the original passengers made us hesitate to show the feelings which consumed us. The sentiments of the horses are not recorded, but we gathered that they were more analogous to our own.

All on *Mana* was at length ready. There were the usual good-byes and parting duties: the bank had to be visited, all bills settled, and letters posted. Last of all a bill of health had to be obtained from the representative of the country to which the ship was bound, certifying that she came from a clean port and that all on board were well.

CAPE VERDE ISLANDS

The Cape Verde Islands are a collection of volcanic rocks, rising out of the Atlantic, some 500 miles from the African mainland. There are nine islands, with a total population (1911) of 142,000. The group was first discovered by Europeans in 1446, through the agency of one of the expeditions sent out by Prince Henry the Navigator. Unlike the Canaries, the Cape Verde Islands when found were uninhabited; but there were monolithic remains and other traces of earlier visitors, all of which have unfortunately now disappeared. The Portuguese settlers almost immediately imported negro labour, and the present population is a mixed race. For a long time the Leeward Islands, or southern portion of the group, attracted the most attention, and one of them, St. Jago by name, is still the seat of government. St. Vincent, however, which belongs to the Windward or northern section, and was at one time a convict settlement, is now the more important from a commercial point of view, as its magnificent harbour, Porto Grande, forms a coaling station for steamers bound to South America The British consul removed there from St. Jago during the middle of last century. It is also the centre for the East and West Cable Company.

The next stage of our outward voyage the conditions were again pleasant and satisfactory.

We left Las Palmas on Saturday, May 10th: the trade wind was still with us, the weather delightful, and we did the distance to St. Vincent, Cape Verde Islands, in seven days. We had heard nothing but evil of it. "An impossible place;" "another Aden;" "a mere cinder-heap." It was therefore a pleasant surprise to find ourselves in a most beautiful harbour. Rugged mountains of imposing height rise on three sides of the bay, Porto Grande, and the fourth is protected by the long high coast-line of the neighbouring island, San Antonio. Standing out in the entrance of the bay is the conical Birds' Rock, looking as if designed by nature for the lighthouse it carries. The colouring is indescribable: all the nearer mountains are what can only be termed a glowing red, which, as distance increases, softens into heliotrope. On the edge of the bay and at the foot of the eastern hills lies the town of Mindello. A building law, made with the object of avoiding glare, forbids any house to be painted white, and the resulting colour-washes, red, yellow, and blue, if sometimes a little crude, tone on the whole well into the landscape.

If beauty of form and strange weird colouring are the first things which strike the newcomer to St. Vincent, the next, it must be admitted, is the marvellous bleakness of the place. Hillsides and mountains stand out bare and rugged, without showing, on a cursory inspection at any rate, the least sign of vegetation. One of the characteristics also of the place is the constant tearing wind. During the whole of our visit of some ten days we were never able to find a day when it was calm enough for Mrs. Taylor, the wife of the British Consul, to face the short passage from the harbour and visit *Mana*. This wind is purely local and a short distance off dies away. How, one is inclined to ask, can it be possible for English men and women to endure life in a tropical glare, with a perpetual wind without any trees, any grass, any green on which to rest the eye? And yet we found over and over again that, though the comer from greener worlds is at first unhappy and restless in St. Vincent, those who had been there some time found life pleasant and enjoyable and had no desire to exchange it.

There are several coaling and other English firms, and local society rejoices in as many as thirty English ladies. The cable company has over a hundred employees, of whom the greater number are English. The unmarried members of the staff live together in the station, each having a bed-sitting-room and dining in a common hall. There is an English chaplain, and also a Baptist minister, who is the proprietor of the principal shop. The chaplain had the experience, which everyone must have felt would happen some time to someone, of being carried off involuntarily on an ocean-going steamer. He was saying good-bye to friends, missed the warning bell, and before he knew was *en route* for a port in South America, to which he had duly to proceed. For recreation St. Vincent possesses a tennis-court and cricket-field : the last is in a particularly arid spot some distance from the town, which is however already planned out on paper by the authorities with streets and houses for prospective needs ; in the design the pitch is left vacant and named in Portuguese " Game of Cricket," the remainder of the field being filled in anticipation with a grove of trees.

Some of the residents have villas among the hills or by one of the scarce oases. We made an excursion to one of these last resorts which is a famed beauty-spot, and found it a narrow gulch between two mountains, with a little stream and a few unhappy vegetables and woebegone trees. It was difficult to imagine, while traversing the road along one hillside after another, each covered with nothing but rocks and rubble, on what the few animals subsisted ; it was remarked that the milk could not need sterilising, as the cows fed only on stones. The rains occur in August, after which the hills are covered with a small green plant. We were told that some of the valleys higher up are comparatively fruitful, and certainly it is possible to obtain vegetables at a not unreasonable price. The women who live in the hills carry back quite usually, after a shopping expedition, loads of seventy to eighty pounds for a distance of perhaps three miles, with a rise of 900 feet, making the whole journey in two and a half hours.

The British Consul, Captain Taylor, R.N., has with much enterprise established a body of Boy Scouts among the youthful inhabitants. An attractive member of the corps, wearing a becoming and sensible uniform, accompanied us as guide on two occasions, when we made excursions on the island, giving the whole afternoon to us. He declined to accept any remuneration, as it was against the principles of his order to be paid for doing a good turn. Other youthful natives are less useful and more grasping. One small imp, with a swarthy complexion and head like an overgrown radish, became our constant follower. The acquaintance began one day when S. was carrying a large biscuit-tin from the post office, in which some goods had just arrived from England: he followed him down the pier, beseeching, " Oh, Captain Biscuit-Tin, give me one penny." Every time after this, when S. went on shore for business or pleasure, " Biscuit-Tin," as we in our turn named the boy, was there awaiting him. Once, in stepping out of the boat on to the rusty iron ladder of the jetty, his toe almost caught on a small round head as it emerged from the water uttering the cry, " Oh, Captain, where is that penny ? " A crowd had surrounded the landing-stage, so the boy had dived into the water as the easiest way of approach. He expressed the desire to come with us to Buenos Aires, undeterred by the information which S. gravely gave him that " all the boys on board were beaten every day, with an extra beating on Saturday." The avocation which he proposed to fill was that of cook's boy, as he " would have much to eat." He followed us for the whole of one expedition, eventually obtaining " that penny " as we shoved off from the pier for the last time, an hour before sailing. He clapped it into his cheek, as a monkey does a nut, and held out his hand to me for another; but I was already in the boat, and a coin was not forthcoming; so that the last which we saw of " Biscuit-Tin " he was still demanding " one penny."

We brought away from St. Vincent a permanent addition to our party, a Portuguese negro of fine build, by name Bartolomeo Rosa. The rest of the crew accepted his companionship without hesitation and naturally christened him " Tony." Later we found, with sympathy, that he was wearing goloshes, in a temperature when most of the party were only too happy to go shoeless, because Light, who had more particularly taken him under his wing, said " the sight of his black feet puts me off my food." Rosa remained with us to the end of the voyage. He learnt English slowly, and would never have risen to the rank of A.B., but was always quiet, steady, and dependable. He drew but little of his wages, and had therefore a considerable sum standing to his credit when we returned to Southampton. He proposed, he said, to go back to his old mother at St. Vincent and there set up with his earnings as a trader. He would get a shop, stock it, and marry a wife, and she would attend to the customers, while he would sit outside the door on the head of a barrel and smoke. When it was suggested that such a course would inevitably end in drink, he added a boat to the programme, in which he would sometimes go out and catch fish.

We were detained at St. Vincent awaiting the arrival of a spare piece of machinery, and occupied the time by watering the yacht at the bay of Tarafel in the island of San Antonio. A stream from the high ground there finds its way to the sea, and supplies the water for the town of Mindello. The lower part of its banks are fertile, forming a beautiful, if small, spot of verdure amid the arid surroundings. Light, with the green hills of Devonshire in mind, remarked, "It is very nice, ma'am, what there is of it—only there is so little."

When we brought up, the men went into the shallow water and shot the trammel in order to obtain some fresh fish. This brought on board an elderly gentleman, Señor Martinez, the official in charge of the place, who was not unnaturally indignant at what he imagined to be a foreign fishing vessel at work in territorial waters. We were able to explain matters, and were much interested in making his acquaintance. He had never visited England, but spoke English well, kept it up by means of magazines, and was greatly delighted with the gift of some literature. He welcomed us as the first English yacht which had been there since the visit of the *Sunbeam* in 1876, of which he spoke as if it had been yesterday.

Having got our package from England, we finally quitted the friendly harbour of Porto Grande on Thursday afternoon, May 29th, sailing forth once more, this time to cross the Atlantic, with the little shiver and thrill which it still gave some of us when we committed our bodies to the deep for a long and lonely voyage, even with every hope of a resurrection on the other side of the ocean. After we sighted St. Jago, the capital of the Cape Verde group, on the following day, we saw no trace of human life for thirteen days ; so that if mischance occurred there was nothing and no one to help in all the blue sea and sky.   The self-sufficiency needed by those who go down to the sea in ships is almost appalling.

Instead of making direct for Pernambuco, we steered first of all due south, carrying with us the north-east trade, in order to cross the Doldrums to the best advantage, and catch the south-east trade as soon as possible on the other side.   The calm belt may be expected just north of the Equator, but its position varies with climatic conditions, and it was therefore a matter of excitement to know how long we should keep the wind.   In the opinion of our authorities it might leave us on Sunday and could not be with us beyond Tuesday.   The engineer, whose duty had so far been light, had been chaffingly warned by the rest of the crew that his turn would come in the tropics, when he would have to work below for twenty-four hours on end.

On Sunday S. gave orders that the engine was to be started by day or night, whenever the officer in command of the watch thought it necessary; but still the north-east trade held good.   On Monday all hands were at work stowing the mainsail, for as soon as the calm came the squalls were expected which are typical of that part of the world.   On Tuesday evening, when according to calculation we should have been out of its zone, we were still travelling before the wind, and we began to congratulate ourselves with trembling, that our passage would be more rapid than we had ventured to hope.   All Wednesday, however, the breeze was very light, and we kept our finger on its pulse as on that of a sick man.   By Thursday it had faded and had died away, the sails hung slack, the gear rattled noisily, the motor was run.   The air was hot, damp, and sticky, with heavy squalls, and the nights were trying.   It is impossible to sleep on the deck of a small sailing ship, with so many strings about and someone always pulling at something, so we roamed from our berths to cabin floors and saloon settees and back again, "seeking rest and finding none."   The thermometer in the cabin never throughout the voyage rose to more than eighty-three degrees, but, as is well known, it is humidity and lack of air rather than the absolute height of temperature which determine comfort.   Friday afternoon increased air roused our hopes; but, alas! it soon subsided, and during the night we again relied on the engine.   Saturday morning was still squally, with a grey sea and heavy showers, but there was really a slight breeze. Was it or was it not, we asked under our breath, the beginning of the new wind ? By ten o'clock there was no longer room for doubt : the south-east trade was blowing strong and full, and the ship, like some living creature suddenly let loose, bounding away before it for very joy. It felt like nothing so much as a wonderful gallop over ridge and furrow after a long and anxious wait at covert-side.

We crossed the Equator in glorious weather about 9 p.m. on Monday, June 9th. None of the forecastle had been over before : Father Neptune did not feel equal to visiting them, but some addition to the fare was much appreciated. I was the doyen of the party, with now seven crossings to my credit. Flying-fish came at times on board from the shoals through which we passed, " Portuguese men-of-war" floated by the ship, and schools of porpoises played about her bows. The wind on the whole stood our friend for the rest of the way, and during the last week of the voyage the average daily run was 147 miles on our course, the highest record being 179 miles on June 14th. We continued, however, to have squalls and rain at intervals, as we were running into the rainy season ; and it was through a mist that on Sunday, June 15th, after a passage of seventeen days, we strained our eyes to see the South American coast. It dawned at last on our view, a flat and somewhat low land ; then came into sight the towers and coconut palms of Pernambuco, and the passage of the Atlantic was accomplished.

CHAPTER III

BRAZIL

Pernambuco—Bahia—Cabral Bay—Cape Frio—Rio de Janeiro—
Porto Bello—A Pampero.

After the discovery of the New World its possession was contested
by five sea-going nations of Western Europe—the Spanish, Portuguese, French, English, and Dutch. Of these the Spanish and
Portuguese were first in the field, and the Portuguese established
themselves in that part of the southern continent now known as
Brazil. Their acquisition of this particular territory was largely due
to accident : the Portuguese navigator Cabral, sailing in 1500 for
the East Indies, via the Cape of Good Hope, shaped his course so far
to the west, in order to avoid the calms off the African continent,
that he hit off this part of the coast. An important Portuguese
settlement grew up on the bay known as Bahia de Todos os Santos
(All Saints' Bay). Further south French Huguenots were the first
to discover and colonise the bay of Rio de Janeiro, but the Portuguese
finally succeeded in expelling them in 1567, when Rio became the
capital of the southern portion of their territory, Bahia retaining its
pre-eminence in the north.

In the seventeenth century Portugal, and consequently her overseas possessions, fell for a while under the dominion of Spain ; with
the result that the settlers acquired a new foe in the young power of
the Dutch, with whom the Spaniards were at war. The Dutch
West India Company was formed with the especial object of capturing Brazil : the first fleet, which sailed in 1623, gained for a time
possession of Bahia, and in 1629 the Dutch conquered Olinda and
the neighbouring town of Recife, or Pernambuco, where they established themselves under the able leadership of Prince Mauritz of
Nassau. In 1640, however, the Portuguese threw off the Spanish
yoke, and, as the quarrel of Holland had been with the latter, she
allowed herself to be bought out of her conquests in Brazil ; an
arrangement due in part to the intervention of Charles II of England,
who had married a Portuguese princess. There was an old alliance
between this country and Portugal, and when in 1739 war broke out
between England and Spain, occasioned by the wrongs of a certain
Captain Jenkins whose ear the Spaniards had cut off, Commander
Anson selected a Brazilian harbour in which to revictual his ships
on his way to harry the Spanish in the Pacific.

During the Napoleonic wars the history of Europe again affected
Brazil. In 1808, when the French were on the point of entering

Lisbon, the royal family escaped overseas, established their court at Rio de Janeiro, and made Brazil a kingdom. In 1820 King João VI returned to Portugal, leaving his son Pedro in command, and the mother country sought to reduce Brazil once more to the provincial status. This was resisted by the colonists, who had tasted the sweets of authority ; they declared themselves independent, and made Pedro, who was personally popular, into Emperor of Brazil. Pedro was succeeded by his son, who reigned till 1889 ; in that year a revolution occurred, due partly to defects of government, partly to the discontent caused by the emancipation of the slaves. Pedro II left for Europe, and Brazil was declared a republic.

PERNAMBUCO, or Recife, has been built on low land at the junction of two rivers, and has the advantage of a good harbour, protected by a natural reef, which has been improved by artificial means. The town has grandiosely, but not altogether inaptly, been called a " modern Venice " ; the business quarter, or Recife proper, is built on a peninsula formed by one of the rivers, while the windings of the other divide the remaining part of the town into sections, which have to be crossed and recrossed by bridges. Otherwise the place is not attractive, the site has originally been a quagmire, and the roads have been made by merely levelling the ground and covering it with rounded stones ; they now consist principally of shallow lakes and crevasses. The streets, with the exception of a few new thoroughfares, are little more than lanes and just wide enough for two vehicles to pass. Most of the traffic is done by mule trams, and any other vehicles, except when they can get on the tram lines, are obliged to move at a snail's pace. It is difficult to understand how the motors contrive to exist, but they are fairly numerous. The houses are of stucco and outrival those of St. Vincent in brilliancy of colouring. The authorities at the time of our visit had been seized with the laudable desire to reconstruct the town on a large and ambitious plan, the object being to rival the larger towns further south, and, in view of their growing prosperity, to keep a place also in the sun for Pernambuco. This form of civic patriotism plays a noticeable and unexpected part in various South American towns. The result at the moment was to make the place appear, in certain districts, as if it had suffered by fire or bombardment.

It is impossible not to be struck when walking the streets with the great varieties of type, and consequently of colouring, among the populace The original races have been the native

Indian, the European who conquered the land, and the Negro imported for his services, and there are now, in addition to their pure-blooded descendants, every shade and mixture of the three. The colour of a man's skin is however of little or no social concern, and there is an absence of race prejudice which to the Anglo-Saxon mind is very astonishing. We had the pleasure of visiting the opera on a gala night at the kind invitation of the British Consul and his sister, Mr. and Miss Dickie, and saw much mixture of colouring among the upper classes. The subject of the opera was romantic and dealt with the early Portuguese era, the heroine being carried off by Indian raiders. Women of all shades have a very proper idea of the consideration due to them, though there would seem to be no reason even to the most advanced of us why, as was said to be the case, a negress should consider it beneath her dignity to carry a message across the road.

The political situation is apparently liable to surprises. At the principal music-hall, just before our visit, an accident occurred to the driving-chain of the electric light, causing a certain amount of clatter; the audience immediately sprang to their feet, the women shrieked, and there was a general stampede. It had been immediately concluded that the noise was caused by pistol shots and heralded a revolution.

The economic standing of Pernambuco and the why and wherefore of its existence are a puzzle to the stranger. There is no appearance of any considerable quantity of trade or wealth, indeed, to judge by the notices displayed, the inhabitants live principally on mutual doctoring and pulling out each other's teeth. The cost of living is nevertheless very high, owing largely to the fact that everything seems to be brought from overseas. Stone for building is conveyed all the way from Northern Europe, and a Norwegian barque, which lay beside us, was busy unloading timber at the door of the forests of Brazil. Even the common articles in use are brought from the Old World, and the tables of the restaurants are crowded with imported products, in spite of almost prohibitive tariffs, which raise the price of a ham, for example, to four or five times its original value. In addition special prices are at times reserved for strangers: the yacht's steward was allowed to depart without purchasing a packet of cigarettes for which eightpence was asked ; Rosa, with his dark skin, got the identical article for a penny.

We followed one of the rivers in the launch almost as far as it is navigable, a distance of some nine miles. The banks are low, and were at first covered with mangrove ; later the land was cultivated after a fashion, and there were a certain number of country houses, but in a state of dilapidation and decay.

Anyone who wishes to leave the prosaic present and be transported back to the old times of colonisation should visit Olinda, the ancient seat of government, which lies three miles to the north of Pernambuco. The remains of it to-day are a little group of houses standing picturesquely on a wooded promontory, which rises high above the low-lying coast. The old street, winding up to the top of the semi-deserted city, along which must have passed gay cavalcades, sober monks, and captured Indians, is still the high way, but it is now carpeted with grass, kept short, not by traffic, but by the sheep which browse upon it. From the highest point, the view extends in one direction to the sea and in the other to the forests of the interior. The most arresting feature is the number of churches and religious houses: everywhere the eye turns these great buildings rise among the luxuriant foliage, from one standpoint we counted ten such edifices. Some are deserted; some are still inhabited. The Franciscan establishment, where a fraternity still occupy the conventual buildings, is said to have been the first of its kind in Brazil, but we could arrive at nothing more definite as to date from the brother who acted as guide than that the place was " three hundred years old." The church contained some particularly good Dutch tiles representing scenes from the life of the Virgin and St. Anne ; similar ones are to be seen in the cathedral, which was undergoing repair, and where no means were being taken to preserve them from injury at the hands of the workmen. These edifices were presumably rebuilt after the capture of the place by the Dutch; for Olinda is said to have been so utterly destroyed by the fighting, of which it was the centre, that Prince Maurice of Nassau gave his attention instead to the improvement of Recife.

Our regrets at leaving Pernambuco on Saturday, June 21st, after a stay of six days, were mitigated by the heat of the docks and by the fact that for some nights the mosquitoes had been unceasingly active. As soon as we left S. started an exterminating campaign, and killed sixty straight away in his own cabin and the saloon. For weeks afterwards, Mr. Gillam could be seen daily going on his rounds with a bottle of quinine tabloids, the lambs obediently swallowing the same. His medicinal doses were under all circumstances magnificently heroic, some of his remedies being kept in quart bottles, on the principle, as he explained, that it was "no use spoiling the ship for a halfpennyworth of tar." It was doubtful in this case if the enemy were really of the malaria-carrying type; they did not appear to stand on their heads in the correct manner—anyway, we all escaped contagion with one slight exception, though I myself had had a bad attack shortly before leaving England, brought on by influenza, after six years' complete immunity.

We had now before us a voyage of some 3,000 miles down the eastern coast of South America before the Magellan Straits were reached. It was marvellously impressive sailing day after day along the coast-line of a great continent, although at the moment the said coast was sandy and flat, the only diversity being occasional lights at night from some town on the shore. Bahia de Todos os Santos, more generally known simply as Bahia, was our next destination. Some fine Portuguese houses are said to survive from the days when it was the old capital, and it may be remembered as the locality where Robinson Crusoe was engaged in planting tobacco, when he was induced to go on the slave-raiding voyage which led to his best-known adventure. The bay, which runs north and south, extends for twenty-five miles, and the situation of the town on its east side is distinctly fine; part of it has been built on the shore, and part on the top of rising ground immediately above it. The funicular railway which connects the one with the other is to be seen from the sea.

This unfortunately is all that circumstances allow us to record. The anchor was dropped at midday, Wednesday, June 25th, and orders given for luncheon to be served at once, so that we might go on shore as soon as we had got our pratique. The health officer, when he came on board, was found to speak nothing but Portuguese, which made communication difficult; the same had been the case with the pilot at Pernambuco; and as half the vessels visiting those ports are English it might per-

FIG. 6.

BAHIA DE TODOS OS SANTOS.

haps be suggested, without insular pride, that a smattering of that language, or at least of French, might be desirable in such officials. We produced the bill of health from Pernambuco in ordinary course: this, however, did not satisfy the doctor. He asked for that from St. Vincent, then from Las Palmas, and finally from Falmouth, though we pointed out that, as this had been granted three months ago, it scarcely had a practical bearing on the case: the virgin health of Bahia must, we felt, indeed be immaculate to require such protection. Finally the bill was stamped and passed. Then the officer handed in a marvellous paper of directions given in English, which stated that " if the captain went on shore all boats' crews were to return immediately to the ship; that no one was to be on shore after 7 p.m.; no fruit was to be bought from hucksters, and none was to be eaten till it had been in a cool place for three days."

We felt that it had become our turn to inquire after the health of Bahia, and it was reluctantly admitted that yellow fever was raging. Upon hearing this we metaphorically gathered our skirts around us, and, although greatly disappointed to miss seeing the town, naturally decided that we would not land. A quaint position then arose, as the doctor, with an eye probably to the fee involved, stated that the ship could not leave unless S. went on shore and obtained a new bill of health, a proceeding at which, as may be supposed, he drew the line. As the official had no means of enforcing authority, victory remained with *Mana*, but even so we were left wondering whether the stain on our moral character of the Bahia endorsement of our certificate would secure us quarantine at our next port. We spent the night in the bay some distance from shore, in order that Mr. Ritchie might test the compass by swinging the vessel.

After we left Bahia the coast-line was at times broken by islands, and varied inland by hills which rose behind wooded banks and sandy shores. We had plenty of time to make notes of any features of interest, for the landmarks on the shore became quite old friends before we parted company. The weather became cooler, the cabin thermometer ranging from 75° to 80°; but we met with an unexpected and persistent head wind; long tacks seemed to bring us but little forward, and *Mana* presented the pathetic spectacle of a good ship struggling against adversity The log day after day gave the depressing chronicle of only some twenty to thirty miles of progress, and the 700 miles to Rio de Janeiro began to appear interminable. After some five days of this weary work, making eleven since we had left Pernambuco, S. decided that it would be in the interests of all to obtain a change by making the shore along which we were sailing. He therefore, after careful study of the sailing directions, selected a spot where health officers would not be found—Cabral Bay. Our Navigator thought the entrance somewhat risky, and requested written orders before going in: as, however, rashness is not one of my husband's sins I awaited the result with equanimity. It is the small bay where Cabral landed on April 24th, 1500, two days after discovering the continent. He erected a cross on the site of the present village, took possession of the land for the King of Portugal, and christened it Santa Cruz, a name which was changed in the middle of the sixteenth century to Brazil, from *brasa*, the term applied by the Portuguese to the brilliant red wood of its forests. The village and northern part of the bay continue, however, to bear the name of Santa Cruz, while the southern portion is called after the great navigator.

The land which forms the bay consists of a low ridge, two miles or so in length, covered with brushwood and undergrowth ; it is arrested suddenly to the north by the course of a river, which has here made a passage to the ocean, and ends abruptly in a steep white cliff. Between the cliff and the river nestles the small village of Santa Cruz, and on the height stands a church which forms the landmark for ships entering the bay. Up the hillside winds a little white path where the grass has been worn away by the feet of worshippers ascending to the house of prayer. At its southern end the ridge dies gradually away in a little promontory, on which stands a tall cross of wood with an inscription stating that it was erected by the Capuchins on the date 22.3.98, but whether that was yesterday, or one hundred, or two or three hundred years ago, there was nothing to show. In front of the bay is a coral reef, so that only baby waves break over the sandy beach, and hard by the cross is a stream, with low reaches and dark shady pools overhung by mangroves.

Here we spent two days, watered the ship from the stream, bathed, fished, and revelled in the wind and sunshine, feeling like prehistoric men, and at one with all creation, from amœbas to angels. The men from the village, dark and lithe, came to visit us in dug-out canoes, hollowed in true Robinson Crusoe fashion from the trunks of trees, and lent us a hand in our work, after which we had out the launch and gave them a tow back to the village. There we found the kindest welcome and walked up the little white path to the church. It was tattered and dirty; but old women with interesting faces, who came in to see the strangers, knelt devoutly at the altar-rails before putting out a hand to greet us. When we departed the inhabitants came to the river-side, where also stands a cross, though whether it is that erected by Cabral or not this history cannot say; they gave us presents, fired rockets, and waved us adieu to the last. Life might be hard at Santa Cruz, but at least it seemed quiet and peaceful. As *Mana* went out of the bay there was a stormy sunset over the church and a wonderful rainbow in the east; gradually the cross on the promontory faded away, the breaking waves on the coral reef could no longer be heard, and so, as John Bunyan would say, "we went on our way."

On leaving Cabral Bay we stood out to sea as the best chance of obtaining a fair wind, and the weather gradually became more favourable. One particularly clear evening, July 8th, at sunset, we were able to see a peak on the mainland which is just under 7,000 feet in height at a distance of ninety-six miles. Altogether it was a pleasant run, occupied by the Stewardess in reading geology and darning stockings. We had not been able completely to fill our water-tanks at Santa Cruz, and it was now decided to procure the remainder at Cape Frio, which was seventy miles this side of Rio de Janeiro, rather than risk the quality which might be obtainable in the city. As we returned to the coast we found that its low character had given way to a region of hills, cliffs, and islands. Cape Frio itself is a bold rocky promontory, or rather island, for it is separated from the mainland by a narrow passage, and shelters behind it a romantic basin consisting of a series of small coves. In places the surrounding mountains recede sufficiently to allow of little sandy beaches, elsewhere sheer cliffs covered with verdure come down to the margin, and trees and ferns overhang the water. We entered by moonlight, and the dark shadows and sparkling sand made a striking and effective contrast.

In one cove is a fishing village, with a church and small store.

Here for the first time oranges were valued as a native product, so far they had been no cheaper than in England, and at three-pence a dozen the forecastle and midships bought them by the bathful. The facilities for obtaining water next day proved not so good as had been hoped. I left S. superintending the crew, as they staggered through the surf to the cutter with bags of water from the village well, and ascended 300 or 400 feet to a signal station on the landward side of the gorge which cuts off the outlying island. This commanded a magnificent view of a wide stretch of blue Atlantic and the adjacent coast ; in the direction of Rio was a panorama of low lands and lagoons, bordered by ranges of rugged mountains which rose tier upon tier as far as the eye could reach. On the way down I gathered a spray of bougainvillea from a shrub in full bloom.

S. had meanwhile made acquaintance with the storekeeper and general village factotum, who we had already found, to our surprise, spoke English well. He turned out, as might have been expected, to be a German. The history of his life would probably be interesting. His experiences included at any rate residence at Bonn University and the post of steward on the yacht of the late Mr. Pierpont Morgan, but who or what had brought him to this spot did not transpire. He had at one time become naturalised as a citizen of Brazil, but had subsequently laid down his rights, preferring to keep out of public concerns, for, as he naïvely remarked, " they never talk politics here without killing a man."

The lore of Frio was as romantic as its appearance, and worthy of the pen of Stevenson. Not only have traces come to light on a neighbouring promontory of Indian burials consisting of bones and pottery, but more valuable treasure finds were of not infrequent occurrence; buried Spanish coins turned up at intervals, and an ingot of silver had lately been discovered. There was no doubt, in the opinion of the storekeeper, that con-siderable treasure was hidden among the islands along the coast, but hunting for it was forbidden by the government. Not far from the village itself there was a cave, which was obviously the work of man, and said to connect two coves, but no one dared to explore it. Nothing was known of its history, but, according to tradition, it was the work of the Jesuits : why a religious order should have made such a resort our informant was unable to explain, but he evidently considered that it would be quite in accord with their usual underground and mysterious methods of procedure. Thirty years ago he himself, with the owner of the cave and one other, had taken up a barrel of wine and had a drinking bout at its entrance, a scene which some old painter of the Dutch school would surely have found congenial: he had then penetrated some twenty or thirty yards into the interior; it was at first, he said, narrow, then became wider, but since that time no one had entered it.

S. was naturally fired with a desire to explore this hidden cavern; Mr. Gillam responded to the call for an assistant, and they set out for the place, accompanied by our informant. There proved to be some difficulty in discovering it, even with his assistance, owing to the dense vegetation which had arisen since it was last visited. Mr. Gillam's thoughts not unnaturally turned to snakes, and the information given in reply to a question on the subject lacked something in reassurance: there were a great many about, it was said, and of a dangerous kind, but they only struck when trodden upon, and as it was now getting late in the day it might be hoped that they had retired to their lairs. When the cave was at length found, bushes and undergrowth had to be cut down in order to effect an entrance, and a cloud of bats flew out of the darkness within. The walls were examined by the light of a ship's signalling lantern, and the statement that they had been artificially made was proved to be true. The party proceeded for ten or twelve yards, but then found that the way had been blocked by a comparatively recent fall of débris, and the enterprise had therefore to be abandoned. We commend it to fellow-voyagers and anthropologists.

We sailed the next morning at daybreak and our navigator, instead of taking the eastern road, by which we had come in, and going round the island, decided to attempt as a short cut the much narrower exit on the west, which lay between the precipitous cliffs that separated the cape proper from the mainland. By the soundings recorded on the chart there was everywhere sufficiency of water for our draught, but, while approaching the coast to take a direct course through the gorge, we were suddenly aware that the stern of the vessel had taken the ground. There was a moment of anxiety as to whether she had hit on an outlying rock, but happily she had only come in contact with a bank of drifted sand. We were, however, very near a rocky coast, and it was not far from high water. As much weight as possible was taken into the bows, a kedge was carried out astern, and she was hove off the way she came on.

The next morning we were at the entrance to Rio de Janeiro. There was, however, not a breath of wind, and the engine was giving trouble ; it refused to run more than a very short distance without becoming dangerously heated—a state of things subsequently found to be due entirely to improper installation. We sat, therefore, for twelve hours gazing at the tumbled mass of blue mountain-barrier, through the narrow opening in which the sea has found its way and formed the great sheet of water within. In front of us was the well-known conical form of the Sugar-loaf, to the west Corcovado, the Hunchback, with its strange effect of a peak which is bending forward, and beyond it Gavea with its table-top. The night fell, lights came out within, we still waited like a Peri at the gate of Paradise. The evening breeze, however, wafted us nearer, and at midnight we passed silently between the dark heights which guarded the entrance and dropped anchor in Botafogo Bay under the shelter of the Sugar-loaf, there to await the dawn.

It is an entrancing experience to wake on a sunny morning and find oneself for the first time among the soft and glowing beauty of Rio Harbour. We went up the bay in the early light, with a man posted at the flagstaff to exchange greetings with the Brazilian men-of-war which lay at anchor ; it was always our duty to dip first to warships, as it was the place of merchantmen to take the initiative with us. We finally took up our position some three miles higher up opposite to the old city.

It is the suicidal fate of each visitor to try to describe Rio de Janeiro, and fail in the attempt ; but with every warning to refrain the present chronicler must likewise rush on her doom. The first impression is that there is so much of it. It is not merely an enormous and beautiful bay, with a city upon it—it is a huge expanse of water, of which the whole margin, as far as the eye can reach, is used by man for his dwelling. To compare it with the bays of Naples or Palermo, or with the cities of Edinburgh or Athens, is, as far as size is concerned, to speak in the same breath of some picturesque manor-house and of Windsor

Castle. There are many places with wilder charm or more historic interest; but for what can only be termed "sleek beauty" Rio is incomparable. Every portion of the scenery is right, there are no parts of it which the eye consciously or unconsciously omits, and in whichever direction the gazer looks his æsthetic sense is satisfied. The shore-line disdains monotony and breaks itself into bays and islands. The great mountains, though they may lose in quiet dignity, range themselves in weird and striking shapes which attract the eye, while the verdure fulfils its purpose of showing off their beauty, here clothing a hillside with forest, there leaving bare a towering cliff. The white buildings which wander up hill and down dale are clean and prosperous, neither too new nor too old; they surround bays and stretch out to islands, not in oppressive continuity, but broken with the surface of the ground, while the gardens and boulevards with their tropical foliage know just how to intersperse themselves at the right intervals. The sun and air also appreciate their share in the situation, and flood mountain and water, verdure and the work of man, with wonderful transparent light, till the whole shines pure and soft, blue and green, like an opal. The night is not less beautiful; then the summits of the mountains show dark against the sky, myriads of lights outline the near bays, shine out from the islands and twinkle irregularly up the hillsides, while from the further shore another galaxy are reflected half-way across the still dark water. The whole gives the impression of some magic scene in the *Arabian Nights* lit up for a great *fiesta*. Rio is wonderful, marvellous; it leaves one like the Queen of Sheba; and yet—when I am dead I hope that I may return and visit the little bay of Santa Cruz, I know I shall pass by Rio de Janeiro.

The old part of the city is composed of narrow and noisy lanes, but the new boulevards are fine and broad. We did the usual sightseeing, with the details of which it is not proposed to trouble the reader. We had the pleasure of enjoying the hospitality of our Minister, Sir W. Haggard; but to my disappointment, for I had been looking forward for weeks to some feminine society, Lady Haggard was in England, and everyone else seemed to be a bachelor. By the most kind care of the British Consul, Mr. Hamblock, we had a memorable motor drive of some seventy miles through the mountains to the west of the bay, including the tract of forest reserved for the public by Dom Pedro. It has left us with a bewildered impression of roads winding below great crags, amongst tropical vegetation, and opening at intervals on vistas of rocky coast and deep blue sea. We visited the botanical gardens, admiring their marvellous avenue of palms: similar ones, and but little inferior, may be seen in many directions, rising amongst streets and houses like the pillars of a Greek temple. We ascended the Sugar-loaf by aerial railway, and gained a panoramic view of the harbour. Finally, a day was spent at Petropolis, a small place among the mountains at the head of the bay, which is reached by a railway with cogwheel gauge and is the special resort of the diplomatic colony. We lunched at an inn of which the walls were adorned impartially with portraits of the Hohenzollerns and French Presidents, the host turned out to be an Alsatian.

If at Rio every prospect pleases it is not altogether free from drawbacks: sanitary conditions have improved; but the pride the city takes in its public gardens and boulevards does not extend to the water of the harbour, which is repulsively dirty, and ships are warned in the Sailing Directions against using it even for washing their decks. When the American fleet visited Rio they consumed so much from the shore for that purpose, that there is said to have been almost a fresh-water famine in the city. When we left the bay our bill of health stated that the previous week there had been two cases of yellow fever, both dead, and two of bubonic plague, who were still alive. Even with our experience at Pernambuco the prices charged at Rio left us breathless: engineering work cost from four to five times as much as in England; even a poor man on the docks complained to our Sailing-master that he could not get a meal under 2s. 8d. One Englishman, professionally employed, calculated that the cost of his passage home every three years was met through the saving effected on buying his clothes in England. Finally, the Stewardess of the *Mana* was of the opinion that the limit was reached, when one shilling was charged for washing a pair of stockings.

The Brazilians of Rio appear to have more European blood than those who live further north, though a mixture of Indian or Negro is viewed with the same equanimity. The idea of government is democratic, and in theory at any rate the President will give an audience to the humblest Brazilian. The senators are paid £7 a day while sitting, so that an easy way of defraying debt is to prolong the session. The Central Railway belongs to the Government, and is regarded as giving billets for its supporters : engine-drivers, for example, are paid at a rate of from £700 per annum, the consequent large deficit on the working of the line being made good by the Treasury. There had been no political excitement very recently at Rio, but one old man was pointed out to us who, as governor of a northern state, had held his position by force and fraud until about a year previously, when he had been escorted by armed men on board ship and told that if he returned he would be shot.

We left Rio Harbour at daybreak on Wednesday, July 23rd, after a visit of nine days, and to our relief found a good sailing breeze outside. As Buenos Aires, at which we were bound to call for stores and letters, was still some 1,100 miles distant, it was decided to break the voyage, and the Sailing Directions were studied for some out-of-the-way stopping-place *en route.* We had found by experience that little anchorages were preferable : not only was there more confidence in the water supply than in the case of big towns, but there was no trouble with authorities, and bills of health, and the temptations of a big port were avoided. The smaller places also, if in some ways less interesting, were more attractive. The little bay of Porto Bello was selected, but when its neighbourhood was reached the following Sunday the weather had become rather thick and there was some difficulty in finding our way. At tea-time our Navigator came down somewhat amused to tell us that, during our afternoon siestas, *Mana* had wandered in and out of a wrong bay, about twenty miles north of our destination ; a small steamer in front of us had also obviously been in need of a signpost or kind policeman.

On Sunday afternoon we dropped anchor safely in a sheltered part of Porto Bello Bay known as Aco Cove. Our previous halts, the town of Pernambuco, the coral bay at Santa Cruz, the rocky basin of Cape Frio, and the world-famed harbour of Rio de Janeiro, bore little resemblance to each other, but they had one point in common, that they were all obviously South American. Porto Bello had nothing South American about it save its very unoriginal Spanish name ; it might, as far as

general appearance went, have been a loch imported straight
from the west coast of Scotland : the accent of our Glasgow
engineer became unconsciously more homelike, as he remarked
that it was " just like the scenery near Oban," and to add to the
illusion the weather, though warm, was a " wee bit saft," with
the nip in the air associated with Scotland in August.

The town of Porto Bello itself lies at the foot of the bay. It
will be found marked in the atlas of the infallible Stieler, but it is
nothing more than a hamlet, consisting of a few small houses,
with a church and one little store ; there was no inn visible, but
it is apparently connected with the outside world by telegraph
or telephone. Shanties, surrounded with banana groves, wandered up the hillsides or clustered round such sandy coves as
Aco ; some were made of wattle and daub, others of wooden
planks roofed with banana leaves or rough red tiles. We made
friends with a family who occupied a cottage near the stream
which supplied our water, and some of the party, a grandfather,
father, and small daughter, came off on their own initiative to
pay us a visit on board. They brought presents of eggs and
molasses, and three special shells as an offering for me. The
gifts which we on our side found were most appreciated, both
here and elsewhere, were tobacco, sweets, and ships' biscuits ;
the last were specially prized, being often preferred to money.
We showed our visitors over the vessel, and expected that such
fittings as electric light would produce a mild sensation, but it
was proved as usual that the eye can only take in what it has
sufficient knowledge to appreciate. The greatest success was
achieved by the supply of carpenters' tools, which excited much
admiration, while the pier-glass in my cabin came in a poor
second. A rather embarrassing situation arose when the old
man, who was getting a little imbecile, found the yacht so
attractive that he sat down in the deck-house and declined to
depart.

The quiet lives of these people, surrounded by agricultural
holdings with tropical produce, reminded us much of the existence of some of the natives in East Africa. They were
apparently not above the belief in charms, for opposite our friends'
door was a dried bush about four feet high, which had on the
extremity of each bough an eggshell, some fifteen in number ;
we never succeeded in finding out its precise meaning, for un-

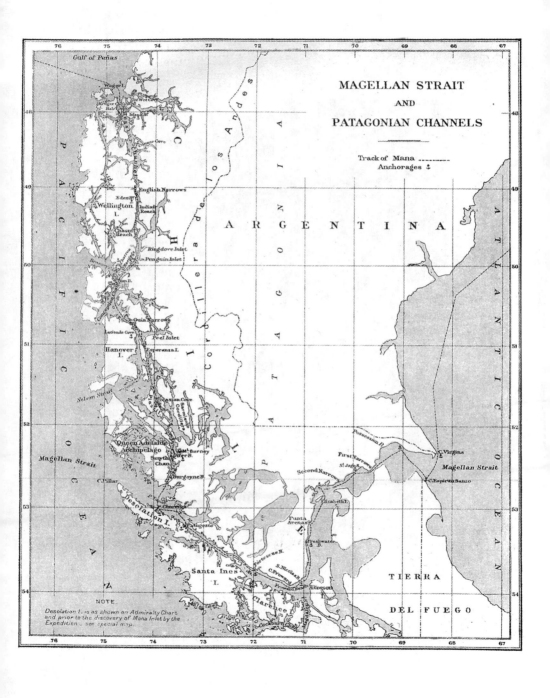

MAGELLAN STRAIT
AND
PATAGONIAN CHANNELS

Track of Mana ----------
Anchorages ‡

FIG. 7.

THE NATIVE CART, ACO COVE, PORTO BELLO.

fortunately our ignorance of the Portuguese language made any real conversation impossible. The appliances of life were simple : an ox-cart had solid wooden wheels, after the manner of an ancient British chariot, the noise made by which was portentous; and the anchors of the boats were of wood, the shank being formed of a frame of sticks, into which rocks were packed.

The business of watering the ship being ended, we tried to continue our journey, only to find that a dead calm reigned outside, and there was nothing to do but to return. Two or three days of detention passed very pleasantly exploring hill-tracks, photographing, and sketching. We were able to buy poultry, eggs, and oranges, and the men were very successful with the seine, getting quantities of delightful mullet. One afternoon we took our tea in the launch to the other side of the bay, but here for the only time we found the people a little suspicious and not quite friendly.

Saturday, August 2nd, we again made our way out of Porto Bello. Our course lay in the direction of the island of Sta. Catharina, some twenty miles to the southwards, and the whole of the next day we drifted along in sight of its beautiful mountainous coast-line. This was the rendezvous appointed by Anson for his fleet on his outward voyage, as it possessed an excellent reputation for stores. He sailed there direct from Madeira, arriving in December 1740 ; his voyage took forty-five days, as against our forty-eight days at sea to Porto Bello, by Cape Verde Islands and Pernambuco. Anson was, however, disappointed in his reception, as the governor proved himself unfriendly, and sent a messenger to communicate the presence of the squadron to the Spanish admiral, who lay with his ships in the River Plate. We occupied the time in endeavouring to check from the yacht the sketches given of the coast in the contemporary account of his voyage. Later on we more than once found ourselves on Anson's track.

The following days afforded great variety of weather, but it grew rapidly colder, and warm clothes which had been stowed since Madeira had to be brought out. The wind, which for a time was strong and fair, later veered round to the south-east and subsequently to the south-west. Our navigators were early anxious about the indications, fearing a *pampero*, the name by which the particular gales are known which sweep down from

4

the Andes over the *pampas* or great plains of the mainland, and on Monday, August 4th, the mainsail was stowed. Thursday we had a strong wind, accompanied by a most extraordinary display of lightning ; from midnight till 5 a.m. the place was lighted up almost without intermission, and there were reported to be at times as many as five to eight flashes visible at once ; at first there was no thunder, but subsequently it became audible. The next two days we beat against a head wind.

On Saturday evening we were placidly seated at dinner when the cry came, "All hands on deck." Suddenly, without at the last a moment's warning, the *pampero* was upon us. A half-finished meal was left to hurry up the companion and join in stowing sails. All night long the gale raged, straining at the rigging, tossing the ship from side to side, rattling everything in her above and below. The waves swept over the deck until it seemed as if their force might at any moment carry away the boats or burst in the door of the deck-house ; notwithstanding the heavy storm-boards with which it was always barricaded at such times. There was no sleep for anyone on board. The steward was up all night making cocoa for those on deck, for it was bitterly cold. As to the watch below, "a man," as Mr. Gillam said, "who could care so little what was going on above as to be able to sleep on such a night, simply because he was off duty, was no sailor worth the name." Four a.m. found two of us engaged in meditating on the "wet sea boy" who managed to have his eyelids sealed on the giddy mast during "the visitation of the wind," wondering whether he was an Elizabethan product or if we only owe his creation to the fact that Shakespeare was a landsman. I believe, from continued observation, that a good crew really like a gale, it has the "joy of battle." As to the Stewardess, her journal, which is not given to soliloquising, runs, I find, as follows in connection with the *pampero* : "It has been made painfully clear to me that my presence on deck when things are bad is an added anxiety ; this is humiliating, and will not, I trust, apply to the next generation of females."

When I came up next morning the wind was still raging fiercely, but there was a pale blue sky flecked with white clouds, and bright sunshine sparkled on the countless white crests of foam which covered a dark blue sea. I looked, with an instinct

which during all these months had become second nature, to see
who was at the wheel, and found, with a shock, that it was
deserted—the helm was lashed ! It felt for a moment as if the
ship were some dead thing, with all power of spontaneous movement, all volition gone. For the time being she was vanquished
by the elements, or at least reduced to armed truce ; we were
hove to and drifting slowly eastward, undoing all the work of
the last two days. " Rough on us, ma'am," as Light said with
a jovial laugh. At noon we had lost ground by 24 miles, and
were now 373 miles from Buenos Aires instead of 349.

Monday, 7 a.m., we began to sail, beating against the wind,
but by midday we had lost still further, being now 402 miles away
from the haven where we would be. We envied the cape pigeons,
twenty or thirty of which followed the vessel, as she was towing
bags of heavy oil to windward to prevent the waves from breaking, and the smoother water made it easier for them to see the
small fish below. They seemed to enjoy the gale, and swept
round the yacht gracefully, showing off their white bodies and
dark wings barred with white. They trod the water at intervals
as they ran along it on the tips of their feet, and rode in the
troughs of the waves securely sheltered from the wind. On
August 12th we signalised the day by making a bag, one gull,
but it came as a guest and was entitled to hospitality. It was
apparently tired out, and perched on one of the boats ; but when
S. began throwing some meat overboard, with the object of
attracting and photographing the cape pigeons, it joined in the
scramble. The pigeons, however, would have none of the stranger,
and set upon it, whereupon, worsted in the fray, the gull again
sought refuge on the vessel : there it stayed all night, sleeping
quite low down in the folds of some canvas and allowing itself
to be stroked and fed by any passer-by. With the morning,
being rested and refreshed, it flew away.

CHAPTER IV

ARGENTINA

The River Plate—Buenos Aires, its Trade and People

The Argentine Republic is the modern representative of the Spanish colonies on the east coast of South America, as Brazil is that of the Portuguese. Fifteen years after the landing of Cabral, Spanish sailors first sighted the entrance to the Rio Plata, and in 1535 Mendoza established a settlement on the site which later was Buenos Aires. No gold or silver, however, was to be found, and the Spaniards looked on their holdings on the South Atlantic merely as a back door to their richer possessions on the Pacific. Till the eighteenth century all their South American territories were under the Viceroy of Peru, and in order to suit the convenience of that colony no ship was allowed to trade direct with Buenos Aires ; all the merchandise from Europe had to be fetched over the Andes. It was not till the first richness of the mines was exhausted that attention was drawn to the grass-covered plains of the east.

The Napoleonic wars, which turned Brazil from a colony to an empire, ultimately led to the establishment of republican rule in the Spanish colonies. Pitt, however, made a mistake in judging in 1806 that the discontent felt by the younger nation with the rule of their mother-country would make them unite in the war against her. He sent an armed force to the River Plate, but his full expectation that there would be a local rising was grievously disappointed ; Buenos Aires was captured, but the British were subsequently heavily defeated and obliged to return home. The anniversary of the " reconquest " is yearly celebrated, and the newly arrived Briton, who probably never heard of the occurrence, finds that in Argentina his country is regarded as a defeated nation.

The loyalty of the colonists to the Crown of Spain was not, how-ever, of long duration. Seeing that in the old country all authority was in the melting-pot, a secret society was formed in Buenos Aires, of which Belgrano was a leading member, to work for representative government ; popular desire for freedom became too strong to be resisted, and on May 25th, 1810, the viceroy resigned. From that date the independence of Argentina is officially reckoned. The Argentines then successfully assisted the revolutionaries of Chile. Disputes subsequently arose as to the boundary between the two countries ; these differences were referred, at the beginning of this century, to the Crown of England, which appointed a commission to deal with the matter, and a treaty was agreed upon in accordance with its recommendations.

On Friday morning, August 15th, land became visible, and by 2 o'clock we were off Flores Island, the entrance to Rio Plata, where we took up a pilot for its navigation. The river is there about a hundred miles across, but narrows rapidly, and two hours later we were opposite Monte Video, where it is only half that width. Of Monte Video itself we could see only the outline. We proposed visiting it later by one of the steamers which run there every night from Buenos Aires, but were discouraged from doing so by the report that there was nothing whatever to see except an inferior Buenos Aires, and that the seaside resorts in the neighbourhood, which were filled in the summer by the Argentines, would be closed at that time of year. The Plate River is dull and dreary, having the charm neither of a river nor of the open sea ; it consists of a vast expanse of turbid yellow water, marked by buoys and the wrecks of ships which have gone aground on its dangerous shoals. The western bank only was visible, and that was low-lying, with a suspicion—was it only a suspicion ?—of tall chimneys. We felt that as far as beauty went we might as well be at the mouth of some English mercantile river, and certainly, as was remarked, we had much better have been there from the point of view of getting the needed work done on the ship. A number of insects of all sorts appeared on the yacht when we were at least four miles from the shore, suggesting that, if so many could land on one small ship, many millions must be blown out to sea.

At noon the following day we anchored for a short time, as the current was too strong for us, and at evening anchored again, apparently in the middle of nowhere, though with twelve large vessels as neighbours. We were in reality at the entrance to the Dredged Channel, where artificial means have had to be employed to make the river navigable for ships of large draft. Here it is necessary to pass the quarantine authorities and obtain a fresh pilot, which formalities being duly complied with, we proceeded next day on our journey. As it nears the city the Dredged Channel divides into two ; one branch leads to the basin at the north end of the docks, the other to that at the south end. The docks at Buenos Aires, instead of being stowed away as an

undesirable excrescence in some remote part of the town, as
is the case in most large seaports, form a frontage of some
three miles to the most important part of the city, and appeal
strongly to both the eye and the imagination.   There, in ordered
sequence, not by units—as, for example, at Southampton or
Marseilles—but by hundreds, lie great vessels of all descriptions
from almost every country in Europe ; the outward sign of the
great carrying trade between the old country and the new.
They have brought their human freight and cargo of manufactured goods, and are waiting to return with a food-supply of
livestock and grain.   Even these docks are not equal to cope
with the demand for accommodation, for in the grain season as
many as a hundred may be seen in the outer roadstead awaiting
admission, and large extensions were in progress.   Argentina is
one of those new lands which stand in the position of rural
estate to older and manufacturing Europe ; the supply of food,
which in the earliest stages of the world's development lay next
each man's dwelling, and then outside the towns, is now brought
across 7,000 miles of ocean.

Little *Mana* was most kindly welcomed by the port authority,
and awarded a place of honour by the entrance to the North
Basin, which is generally reserved for men-of-war.   Here she
appeared elegant but minute, and not being a battleship felt her
position somewhat precarious.   The next berth was occupied by
a large emigrant ship, which was German, French, and Italian by
turns, and as the yacht was immediately under the stern it looked
as if, with the least motion, she would be crushed out of existence.
Every time a huge ship went out of the entrance to the harbour,
all on board rushed to the yacht's deck to see if her bowsprit was
about to be carried away.   The manœuvring of the big vessels
by tugs in a limited space is, however, wonderful, and though
we had one or two narrow escapes, either the position was not so
perilous as appeared, or we became accustomed to alarms, for
we finally lived there quite comfortably.   We landed either by
boat across the docks, or by scrambling up a wharf like a house-
side by means of a lengthy and somewhat shaky ladder.   I have
a vivid mental picture of His Majesty's Minister, Sir Reginald
Tower, when he was good enough to come and see us, standing
on the top with a little dog, and not unnaturally wondering how
on earth he was expected to descend.

We lay at Buenos Aires for over a month, refitting and stowing, before facing the next part of the voyage. We grudged the delay, but even with the kind help we received there is, as has already been explained, much time inevitably lost in a new port, and New Spain, like its European prototype, is essentially a country of *mañana*. In the end we had to leave without getting the trouble with the engine put right. The stores sent ahead from England arrived safely, and through the courtesy of the Legation we received them custom free, but on some articles, which were unluckily ordered to come by post—a serge suit, linen coat, and two washing blouses—we had to pay £4 duty. I spent a portion of the time in luxury at an hotel while *Mana* had a much-needed spring-cleaning. S. lived on board, and I found on my return had had a good many visitors, whom he appeared to have enjoyed showing over the yacht with her hatches up and the floor covered with packing-cases ; maintaining, in reply to my chagrined comments, that the public were shown over the *Terra Nova* in just such a condition.

In such time as could be spared from the work of the Expedition we saw what we could of the life of the country, and our observations are given for what they are worth. Unlike Pernambuco there is no doubt as to the economical *raisons d'être* of the Argentine ; they are, of course, grain and meat. The area under cultivation, which we did not see, is steadily increasing, but the grain export is still far below that of the United States. The greater part of the mutton supplied to Great Britain comes from Australia and New Zealand, but the Argentine provides 72 per cent. of the beef which we receive from abroad, and we were much interested in seeing something of the cattle industry. We visited, by the courtesy of the owner, Señor Pereyra, an *estancia* about an hour's journey from Buenos Aires. The train traversed first the suburbs of a great town, then low country often under water, and we alighted at a little railway station, from which we immediately entered the park of the *estancia*. The estate was large, though there are others which exceed it ; it covers fifteen square miles, a portion of which is, however, undrained. It has been in the occupation of the same family for about ninety years, during which time continual planting has been going on. The road which led through the park to the house passed under several fine avenues ; the eucalyptus trees of older growth were most beautiful, and a revelation of what that tree can attain, to those who have only seen it in temperate climates or in the villages and towns of South Africa.

The dwelling of the owner proved to be a most charming country house. The dining-room was panelled with oak, displaying the magnificent collection of silver cups gained by the stock of the *estancia*. Our host was in the proud position of having just won at the cattle show, then being held at Buenos Aires, the highest awards for both Herefords and Shorthorns. The competition for such prizes lies in the Argentine between a limited number of noted breeders, and it is felt well to bring in a judge from the outside. That year an English gentleman, well known in connection with the Royal and other shows, had been requested to act. Eighty thousand Argentine dollars, or over £7,000 sterling, were paid at this show for a champion bull, being the highest price yet given for such an animal. After luncheon we inspected the large farm buildings where the most valuable of the stock were housed. The remainder of the cattle, some 7,000 in all, lived in different large enclosures in various parts of the estate, with a cottage near-by for the caretaker. The owner was assisted by an English and a French manager, and 260 *peons* or labourers, mostly Italian, were employed on the *estancia*. They earn £3 10s. a month, with practically no expenses, being housed in a row of buildings with a mess-room in common. There was no lack of labour, applicants having continually to be turned away.

Our education was continued by a visit to the market at Buenos Aires, where anything up to 5,000 head of cattle are disposed of daily. These are brought from all parts of the Argentine, and were formerly driven across country. Now, however, owing to the prevalence of wire fences, they are generally brought by train. They are confined in open pens, and sold by auction or otherwise. The cattle auctioneers are men of high position, and regard themselves as the aristocracy of the city. The animation of the scene is increased by the number of roughriders who career on spirited ponies up and down the alley-ways, looking after the stock and lassoing refractory beasts. No man connected with the " camp," as the open country is termed, ever thinks of walking at any time. The Argentine saddle has special characteristics, and consists of a pad each side of the spine of the horse, above and below which rugs are placed, the whole being covered with a piece of leather and kept in place by girths, thus forming a most comfortable cushion. The stirrup is so made that only the toe can go into it, and the whole is calculated to allow a man to fall clear if he is thrown, a wise precaution in a land of unbroken mounts. It has also the advantage of providing excellent bedding, but is of course adapted for a flat country only, and would be out of place in a mountainous one. A kind acquaintance, seeing the interest S. took in the saddle, made him a present of one, which proved invaluable in Easter Island.

The majority of the beasts sold at the cattle markets are for local consumption: those going to the freezing manufactories are generally bought by private treaty. We were taken over one of the largest of these *frigorificos*, as they are called, where some 1,200 cattle and 3,000 sheep are killed daily. Each animal is inspected from a sanitary point of view on arrival, and every beast is again examined after it has been killed. It is skinned and cleaned at the same time, and in fifteen minutes, from the moment of being slain, is ready in two sides to hang up in the chilling or freezing chamber. Each of the sides is subsequently enclosed in a muslin covering ready to be shipped. The hides are, of course, also a most valuable commodity, and the fat is subjected to pressure, the oil being used for cooking purposes and the solid residue for candle-making. The unused portion of the beast is turned into guano. Some of the meat is reserved for canning, and the tinned goods are particularly attractive. Each tin is closed save for one small hole at the top, and is then passed into a vacuum pump, which extracts the air and closes the hole with an electric needle.

A very determined set was being made to bring all the Argentine *frigorificos* into the American meat trust; those which, like the one we visited, are determined to resist have to fight hard to hold their position. There was a loud outcry with regard to the increase in the price of meat, which had gone up retail to about sevenpence a pound; but buying through a ship's chandler, who could obtain it for wholesale prices, we were able to purchase at a lower rate. The prices for tinned meat were much the same as in England. Salt meat we were warned to avoid, as it could not be guaranteed for more than two months, though the remainder of our stock that had been put on board in England, ten months before, was still in excellent condition. Every attempt, we were told, had been made to discover the reason for this failure, which is common to all meat south of the Equator ; the services of experts from Europe had been requisitioned, the method, the meat, the salt, and the water had all been carefully examined, but so far without result.

The city of Buenos Aires itself, of which the docks have already been described, is simply a glorified port for this trade, and for the produce of a wealthy hinterland. The old part of the town, in which all business is transacted and which most impresses itself on the memory, is a labyrinth, or rather chess-board, of terribly narrow streets. The thoroughfares are at right angles, and the houses, which are in regular blocks, are all precisely similar in appearance ; nothing, therefore, but an exact knowledge of the names and orders of the numerous streets as they lie in each direction of the chess-board can enable a stranger to find his way. The same street extends for miles, and he who forgets the number of his destination may as well give up the search. So narrow are these thoroughfares that two persons can only just pass on the pavement, and there is imminent danger of being pushed under the trams which run within fifteen inches of the curb. Traffic is only allowed in one direction.

In a town which has never been walled, and where space was no object, such a state of things is surprising ; the original construction is said to have been due to the desire to obtain a maximum of shade, and any alteration now is of course fraught with much difficulty. Great efforts are, however, being made to render the Argentine capital worthy of its wealth and position. An imposing avenue, with the House of Congress at one end, has been cleared at great cost. The more recent portion of the town boasts good squares and parks, for the network of streets is but the hub of a huge and quickly growing city. Underground railways are being constructed, but so rapid is the extension of Buenos Aires that it is said they will only relieve the traffic for eleven years. The general impression of a bustling sea port with a southern element recalls Marseilles, but it has not the same beauty of situation. Buenos Aires has been called " a horrible travesty of Paris," but perhaps the most correct description is that which styles it " a mixture of Paris and New York."

Of what description are the people in whose hands lie the development of this country, with its growing influence on the destinies of the world ? The new-comer arriving from the north is at once struck with the distinction between Brazil and the Argentine. Rio, with its strain of dark descent living in the midst of a dream of sleepy beauty, is still perhaps partly mediæval and undoubtedly tropical ; Buenos Aires, on its flat plain and dreary river, is awake, twentieth century, and wholly European; but it is to the south of Europe that the Argentine is akin and not to the north. A Latin race was the first to colonise the new land, and successive waves of the same are still reaching its shores. In 1911 the immigrants from Spain, Italy, and France numbered nearly 2,000,000, as against 13,000 from Britain and 7,000 from Germany. Many Italians, it is true, come only for one harvest, or possibly for two, returning for the busy season in their own homes. The wages earned are such that the more idle are in a position to disdain all other work, and a crowd of loiterers round the docks, who appeared to us to be unemployed of the usual character, turned out to be agricultural workers living on their own resources till the next harvest. Many, however, of these immigrants settle in the new land, by the law of which every child born in the country becomes *ipso facto* an Argentine subject. It is perhaps because of this comparatively uniform origin that an Argentine type seems to be already developing. It is fundamentally that of Southern Europe, but it is moulded by a new environment, is wide-awake and energetic, with an absence of all mystery and tradition, but alive to the finger-tips. The practical aspect of life is the dominant note, whether for the native or temporary resident. "We are all here to make money," the stranger is frankly informed, "and we talk of nothing else." No apology shall therefore be made for once more referring to the question of pounds, shillings, and pence, for in South America it is impossible to get away from it.

The cost of living in Buenos Aires is two or three times as high as that of London in normal times. At the best hotel, usually frequented by European travellers, the smallest bedroom cannot be obtained under eighteen shillings a night, and even at the less dear hotels, resorted to by those to whom expense is an object, the ordinary price for dinner is five dollars or 8s. 9d.

" One thinks a good deal in England of a £5 note," was the remark to us of one Argentine; "here one never goes out without a fifty-dollar note (between £4 and £5) in one's pocket." Rents are enormous, and a would-be purchaser told us ruefully that he could not obtain in the suburbs a house with three sitting and four bedrooms, on a plot of ground some thirty yards square, under £15,000. All this falls hardly on the visitor or foreign official, but it affects the resident but little; an 8 per cent. investment is looked upon as reasonable and cautious, and for the working classes wages are proportionately high. The temporary immigrant who wishes to go back to Europe saves most of the money by living under very meagre conditions; thus two or three Italians frequently join together in one room at about half the rate paid by less thrifty workmen. Most visitors to Southern Europe are acquainted with the little mansions, built in the villages of their birth, by natives who have returned with modest fortunes from the Argentine, and this is the process by which that wealth is accumulated. More rapid roads are occasionally found to success. Our Sailing-master was acquainted with a former gaol-warder who went out as an emigrant from Southampton; his wife joined him, but came back before long, saying little but that her husband was also returning. In less than two years the man was back with a competency for the rest of his days, the source of which continued to be veiled in mystery.

Science, literature, and art do not as yet thrive very largely in Argentina, though exception must be made for the very interesting museum at La Plata, whose director was most kind in affording information to the Expedition. The great recreation is racing, in addition to which the inhabitants are all born gamblers. Sir Reginald Tower, to whose kind arrangements for us we owe much of the interest of our time in Buenos Aires, was good enough to take us to a race meeting, and we were greatly impressed with the lavish arrangements for the comforts of the spectators. It was also most pleasant to be spared all cries of the bookmakers—the betting system is that of the *pari mutuel*. The jockey club is the most important social club, and with an entrance fee of nearly £300 is naturally extremely wealthy; its existing premises are palatial, and even so the removal to larger ones was under consideration. We were kindly entertained there by a distinguished representative of the early Spanish stock, Señor Calvo, to whom we were introduced while he was practising his profession of auctioneer at the cattle-market. His ancestor was a viceroy of the Court of Spain, and he is by descent on both sides a pure Spaniard; the cosmopolitan influences of to-day have, however, been too strong for the continuance of this tradition in the family, and he himself and other members of it have allied with outside nationalities. His father, who was responsible for the conduct of a public journal, had his life attempted three times by his political enemies, and finally sought refuge in England. There the son was born and educated, but later on, going out to the Argentine, he too entered public life and became a member of Congress, whose buildings it was most interesting to see under his guidance.

The life of Argentine women is almost that of the East. The men go their own way, make their own acquaintances, live their own life. They ask strangers but little to their homes, and it is possible to be on quite intimate terms with an Argentine and unaware whether he is married or single. Country-house hospitality scarcely exists, and even on the large *estancias* in the neighbourhood of Buenos Aires, a week-end party is unknown. A lady does not walk out alone, and never, even in her own home, receives a male guest without the presence of her husband. We have been credibly informed of a wife who boasted that during her husband's absence in Europe, of over a year, she never went out of the house. There is no higher education for women except for those training professionally, and the interests of the majority, like those of a certain set at home in pre-war days, consist mainly in bridge and dress. Forty years ago all women wore the mantilla, but to-day fabulous sums are spent on clothes. One charming Argentine lady told me that £30 was quite a usual sum to give for a smart but simple hat. At the seaside resorts the expenditure on clothes is so lavish, that it is cheaper to take the trip to Europe than to procure the necessary garments in which to be seen among your friends. In appearance the women are pretty and effective, but spoilt to the eyes of a European by the inordinate amount of powder. I was told by one present at the dinner-party in question of an amusing scene witnessed in the ladies' cloak-room; a daughter arriving with her mother called out, "Oh, mother, you have not nearly enough powder on," and made a dash for the powder-puff to remedy with two or three large splashes the supposed defect. It is said that the wave of female emancipation is reaching South America, but doubt was expressed by a keen observer whether it would necessarily take its European form of a demand for political and legal rights, or whether the Argentine woman would not begin by desiring the same social and matrimonial liberty as is assumed by her husband. At present, unfortunately, with the vicious circle in which such customs move, much of the precaution taken to guard women appears to be necessary, and I was sadly informed by more than one English girl employed in the business houses of Buenos Aires, that the freedom with which young women can move and conduct themselves at home was not only conventionally but actually impossible in their new surroundings.[1]

Argentina, as the depository of much that is undesirable from other nations, can hardly hope to escape the blackguard element. Assassination is the only thing which is cheap in the South American continent. The head of one of the seamen's missions at Buenos Aires told S. that it was possible at any time to procure the murder of a man by paying five dollars, not quite ten shillings, in the right quarters: this was somewhat less than at Rio, where the price was stated to be thirteen shillings and fourpence. The scenes which occur nightly about the docks are incredible; hence returning to *Mana* after dark was always a matter of some anxiety. Our steward received a typewritten letter saying that he had been mentioned as a suitable man for a desirable situation, and giving an appointment after dark at a certain house in a certain street. On inquiry the address turned out to be that of a low street in the new part of the town, where much land is still waste, and there was no house yet built of the number given. With regard to the said steward, one Sunday evening he left the yacht and never returned. All anxiety about his fate was set at rest by the fact that he had cleared his cabin of all his goods. He may have been homesick and arranged to work his passage back, or he may have been enticed by a more substantial offer, a very usual occurrence where

---

[1] Lady Grogan informs me that one of the main reasons for the position of women in Argentina is that there is no Married Women's Property Act, and that even an heiress is therefore in ordinary course entirely dependent on her husband.

trained servants are difficult to obtain. As he had of course signed the ship's articles for the trip, his desertion was reported to the consulate and the police, but we were told that to get him back would be practically an impossibility ; while, scruples apart, nothing would have been gained by the simpler method of assassination. The man himself we did not regret, but after the manner of his kind he had waited till we were on the point of sailing, and therefore left us in the lurch.

In spite of the fact that personal safety still leaves a good deal to be desired, the Government of Argentina is one of the purest in South America ; the result, it is said, of the wealth of her officials. She is already proudly conscious of her strength, and, in some quarters at any rate, is anxious to rely upon it alone for her position among nations rather than on any such external aid as the Monroe doctrine. Throughout the whole continent it is necessary in speaking of the citizens of the United States to term them carefully " North Americans," avoiding the usual and more abbreviated form.

Religion is not a powerful factor in Argentina either in public or private life. Roman Catholicism is officially recognised, but it does not strive to be a political force, and meets therefore with general toleration ; even when it is not practised it is neither hated nor feared. Many women and some men are devout, but the majority of men simply ignore it.

A Briton in leaving Argentina not unnaturally asks what is the share of his own countrymen in the development of the new republic. Our connection with it through trade is considerable. The railways are in British hands, and 61 per cent. of the shipping flies the Union Jack. In addition to young men who may wish to take up life in " the camp," or country, a certain number of Englishmen are employed in offices and professional positions, while in connection with retail trade, it is homelike to see the shops and advertisements of such firms as Harrod and Maple. A pleasing bond exists throughout the British colony in Freemasonry, which is a most living force, with many adherents, amongst whom our Minister is included. S. being one of the elect, we had, through the kindness of Mr. Chevalier Boutell, the Deputy Grand Master for South America, the pleasure of being present at a ladies' banquet, which proved a very brilliant and enjoyable entertainment.

While the English commercial position is still good, it is said that forty years ago our proportion of the trade was even greater. An old inhabitant told us that he knew personally of not less than twenty-five British firms who had gone under during that period, owing to the dogged incapacity of the Englishman to supply what his customer wanted, instead of what he himself chose to provide. Such failures leave, of course, the door open for German penetration. A reputation for the same want of adaptability, and also for being given to drink, makes Englishmen unpopular as employes. With regard to our women kind, certain posts in the town which are open to English girls are well paid, but they should be taken up in every case with the greatest caution, and the remuneration offered carefully compared with the increased cost of living. A woman who marries on to an *estancia* is necessarily comparatively isolated, and accounts differed as to the amount of help she is able to obtain in domestic labour. The 30,000 British subjects who form the whole of those resident in Argentina are, in any case, but a drop in the ocean, and they but seldom identify themselves with the country of their abode. It is not unusual for parents to arrange that their children shall be born in England, in order that they may avoid registration as citizens of the Republic, with its consequent liability to military service. It has been proposed in high quarters that suitable accommodation might be provided in the Falkland Islands, as nearer and more convenient British soil. Failing some such arrangement it is possible to register a child of British parentage which is born in Argentina, at the national consulate, and it is then *ipso facto* a British subject, except when actually in the land where it first saw the light. Whatever share Britain may have in developing the wealth of Argentina, that country never has been, and never will be, connected with us by blood; for that bond with new lands we must look to our own dominions over the seas.

CHAPTER V

Port Desire—Eastern Magellan Straits—Punta Arenas—Western
Magellan Straits—Patagonian Channels

The most southerly portion of the South American continent,
called Patagonia, first became known in the endeavour to find a new
way into the Pacific. Magellan was commissioned by Charles of
Spain to try to find by the south that ocean passage to the Indies
which Columbus had sought in vain further north. He sailed in
August 1519, and began his search along the coast at the River
Plate ; on October 21st, the day of the Eleven Thousand Virgins,
he came in sight of a large channel opening out to the west : the
promontory to the north of this channel still bears the name he
bestowed of Cape Virgins. He proceeded cautiously, sending boats
ahead to explore, and on November 28th entered the Pacific. When
he saw the open sea he is said to have wept for joy, and christened
the last cape " Deseado," or the " Desired."

The sea power of England, which had been negligible in the time
of the first voyages to the New World, was growing in strength ; and,
though she had attempted no settlement on the southern continent,
she saw no reason to acquiesce in the edicts of the King of Spain,
shutting her off from all trade with the New World. In 1578 Drake
took Magellan's route, with the object of intercepting galleons on
the Pacific coast, and passed through the Straits in sixteen days.
On entering the Pacific he was blown backward towards Cape Horn,
and was the first to realise that there was another waterway, yet
further south, from the Atlantic to the Pacific. Up till this time the
land had been supposed to extend to the Antarctic.

A hundred years later Charles II of England sent an expedition
under Sir John Narborough to explore this part of the world and
trade with the Indians, which wintered on the eastern coast of
Patagonia.

Anson's squadron avoided the Straits, taking the way by the Horn.

The Chilean and Argentine Boundary Commission divided Patagonia between the two countries, giving the west and south to Chile
and bisecting Tierra del Fuego, 1902.

WE left Buenos Aires on September 19th, achieving the descent
of the river without a pilot, and for the next fortnight had a
varying share of fair winds, contrary winds, and calms. Our
chief interest was the man who had taken the place of the

5   65

absconding steward, who shall be known as " Freeman " ; we heard of him through a seamen's home, and arranged that he should go with us to Punta Arenas, to which place he wished for a passage. He was a clean-looking " Britisher," who for the last seven years had been knocking about South America. He brought with him a gramophone, and a Parabellum automatic pistol, with which he proved an excellent shot, and he made it a *sine qua non* that we should find room on board for his saddle ; thus was my knowledge increased of the necessary equipment of an indoor servant. We paid him at the rate of £100 a year, and though we found that he could neither boil a suet pudding nor lay a table, so enlightening were his accounts of up-country life that we did not grudge him the money.

We flatter ourselves our experience in detecting mendacity would qualify us as police-court magistrates, but we never saw any reason to doubt the substantial accuracy of Freeman's stories. His experience dated back to the time when mares of two or three years old were sold for ten shillings, or were boiled down for fat, as, after the Spanish fashion, no man would demean himself by riding one. He had at one time ridden across the continent from the Patagonian to the Chilean coast, a journey of six weeks, half of which time he never saw a human being ; he was followed all the way by a dog, though the poor animal was once two or three days without water ; it got left behind at times, but always managed to pick up his trail. He was most candid about the means by which he had made money when at one time employed on the railway, for honesty was not in his opinion the way that the game was played in South America, and therefore no individual could afford to make it part of his programme : it did happen to be one of the rules on *Mana*, and we never knew him break it. He was once running away after some drunken escapade, when a policeman appeared and took pot-shots at him with a rifle. Freeman turned and dropped him with his revolver ; he did it the more reluctantly as he knew and liked the man. Happily the shot was not fatal, and he felt convinced that he himself had not been recognised.

After, therefore, carefully arranging an alibi elsewhere he returned, condoled with the victim on the lawless deed, and gave him what assistance he could ; he felt, however, that that part of the country had become not very " healthy," and subsequently moved on. Even our experiences of the ports had scarcely prepared us for the cynical indifference to human life which his experiences incidentally revealed as an everyday affair in " the camp." In sparsely inhabited districts, with their very recent population, the factors are absent through which primitive societies generally secure justice, clans do not exist, families are the exception, and in almost every case a man is simply a unit. The more advanced methods of keeping the peace have either not been formed or are not effective, for crime is often connived at by the authorities themselves. The result is that the era of vendetta and private revenge seems civilised in comparison with a state of things where no notice is taken of murder, and the victim who falls in a brawl or by fouler means simply disappears unknown and unmissed, while the murderer goes scot-free to repeat his crime on the next occasion.

Freeman had, *inter alia*, been employed on one of the farms in Patagonia, along the coast of which we were sailing, and told tales of the pumas, or South American lions, which abounded in a certain neighbourhood. This district had railway connection with a little anchorage known as Port Desire, and as one of our intervals in harbour was now due S. arranged to turn in here, and go up-country with him to try to get a shot at the animals. We therefore put into the port on October 3rd. It is a small inlet, of which the surrounding country is covered with grass, but flat and dreary in the extreme, the only relief being a distant vision of blue hills. Sir John Narborough, who spent part of the winter here in 1670, said he never saw in the country " a stick of wood large enough to make the handle of a hatchet."

The human dwellings are a few tin shanties. In a walk on shore we were able to see in a gully, a few remains of the walls of the old Spanish settlement. As to the puma, fortunately from its point of view, the railway service left a good deal to be desired. We arrived on Friday, and there turned out to be no train till the following Tuesday, so it lived to be shot another day—unless indeed it met a more ignominious end, for the South American lion is so unworthy of its name that it is sometimes killed by being ridden down and brained with a stirrup-iron. We took three sheep on board, as mutton at twopence a pound appealed to the housekeeping mind, and were able to secure some water, which is brought down by rail; it was a relief to have our tanks well supplied, as the ports further down the coast are defended by bars, and would have been difficult of access in bad weather. Drake, on whose course we were now entering, selected St. Julian, the next bay to the southward, for his port of call before entering the Straits of Magellan; it was there he had trouble with his crew, and was obliged to hang Doughty.

We sailed from Port Desire on Monday morning, but were not to say good-bye to it so speedily. We soon encountered a strong head-wind, with the result that Wednesday evening found us fifteen miles backwards on a return journey to Buenos Aires, and the whole of Thursday saw us still within sight of it. We amused ourselves by discussing the voyage, which had now lasted more than seven months. One of the company declared that he had lost all sense of time and felt like a native or an animal: things just went on from day to day; there was neither before nor after, neither early nor late. It did not, he said, seem very long since we left Falmouth, but on the other hand our stay at Pernambuco was certainly in the remote past, and so with everything else. We had now, in fact, done about three-quarters of the distance from Buenos Aires towards the Straits of Magellan, and had 300 miles left before we reached their entrance at Cape Virgins.

Ever since the Expedition was originally projected the passage of the Straits had been spoken of in somewhat hushed tones; but now, when with a more favourable wind we began to approach them, instead of going into Arctic regions, as some of us had anticipated, the weather improved, the sun went south faster than we did, and the days lengthened rapidly. Our numerous delays had at least one fortunate result—they secured us a much better time of year in the Straits than we had expected would fall to our lot. The feeling in the air was that of an English April, bright and sunny, but fresh; we kept the saloon cold on principle during the daytime, living in big coats; in the evening we had on the hot-water apparatus, so as to go warm to bed. It was quite possible to write on deck, and the sea was almost too beautifully calm. We had a great many ocean callers, who seemed attracted by the vessel: porpoises tumbled about the bows till we could nearly stroke them, a whale would go round and round the yacht, coming up to blow at intervals, while seals reared their heads and shoulders out of the waters and looked at us in a way that was positively bewitching ; once a whale and seal paid us a visit at the same time. One night S., who was keeping a watch for one of the officers who was indisposed, was interested in watching the gulls still feeding during the dark hours.

At 10 p.m. on October 15th the light of Cape Virgins was sighted, and we woke to find ourselves actually in the Straits of Magellan. The Magellan route, as compared with that by the Horn, is not only a short road from the Atlantic to the Pacific, cutting off the islands to the south of the continent, but ensures calm waters, instead of the stupendous seas of the Antarctic Ocean. For a sailing-ship, however, the difficulties are great ; the prevailing wind is from the west, and there is no space for a large vessel to beat up against it, nor does she gain the advantage that can be derived from any slight shift of wind ; outside the gale may vary a point or two, but within the channel it always blows straight down as in a gully. The early mariners could overcome these obstacles through the strength of their crews ; in case of necessity they lowered their boats and towed the ship, but the vessels of the present no longer carry sufficient men to make such a proceeding possible. Sailing-ships therefore take to-day the Cape Horn route, in spite of its well-known delays, trials, and hardships. When later the German cruiser turned up at Easter Island with her captured crews, the great regret of the latter was that they had been taken just too late, after they had gone through the unpleasantness of the passage round the Horn.

The first sight of Tierra del Fuego is certainly disappointing. The word calls up visions of desolate snowy mountains inhabited by giants ; what is seen are low cliffs, behind which are rolling downs, sunny and smiling, divided up into prosaic sheep farms. A reasonably careful study of the map would of course have shown what was to be expected, as on the Atlantic coast the plains continue to the extreme south of the continent, while the chain of the Andes looks only on to the Pacific. Nevertheless, if not thrilling, it was at least enjoyable to be in a stretch of smooth water, with Patagonia on the north and Tierra del Fuego on the south. The land on either hand is excellent pasture for sheep, and there is said to be sometimes as much as 97 per cent. increase in a flock. The largest owners are one or two Chilean firms, but the shepherds employed are almost all Scotsmen, and indeed the scenery recalls some of the less beautiful districts in the Highlands. When sheep-farming was established, the Indians, not unnaturally from their point of view, made raids on the new animals, with the result that the representatives of the company were consumed with wrath at seeing their stock eaten by lazy natives ; they started a campaign of extermination, shooting at sight and offering a reward for Indian tongues. Our friend Freeman had worked on one of the farms, which had a stock of 200,000 sheep, and the information he gave on this head was fully confirmed later in conversations at Punta Arenas. The destruction of the Indians was spoken of there as a matter for regret, but as rendered inevitable by circumstances.

The navigation through the straits of a craft like ours makes it necessary to anchor in the dark hours : the first night we spent off the Fuegian coast, in sight of one of the pillars which define the boundary of Chile and Patagonia ; the second we lay in Possession Bay, which is on the Patagonian side. We had time at the latter anchorage to examine the pathetic wreck of a steamer, which had gone aground. She was a paddle-boat, which was being towed presumably from one lake or river area to another, and had to be cut adrift. Even in such an unheroic vessel it was touching to see the sign of departed and luxurious life cast away on this lonely shore, stained-glass doors bearing the inscription of " smoking " or " dining-room," and good mahogany fittings such as washing-stands still in place. It is said that the outer coast is strewn with wrecks containing valuable articles which it is worth no one's while to remove. S. walked up to the neighbouring lighthouse, and was presented with three rhea eggs.

The next morning we were under way at 5 o'clock, in order to pass with the correct tide through what are known as the First Narrows. The current here is so strong that it would have been impossible for us to make headway against it ; as it was, the wind sank soon after we started, and we only just accomplished the passage, anchoring in St. Jago Bay. The following day, Sunday, we negotiated successfully the Second Narrows. From our next anchorage we saw from the yacht several rhea, or South American ostriches, on a small promontory. S. went ashore on the point and shot two of them, while Mr. Ritchie and Mr. Gillam, who had landed on the neck of the promontory,

FIG. 8.

IN THE MAGELLAN STRAITS.

S. and an ostrich.

endeavoured to cut off the retreat of the two remaining birds. The one marked by Mr. Ritchie went through some water and escaped him; the onlookers then viewed with much interest a duel between Mr. Gillam on the one hand, running about in sea-boots armed with a revolver, and the last ostrich on the other, vigorously using its legs and wings and on its own ground. Victory remained with the bird, which reached the mainland triumphantly, or at least disappeared behind a bush and was no more seen. Seven miles south-west of the Second Narrows lies Elizabeth Island, so named by Drake. We took the passage known as Queen's Road on the Fuegian side of the island, and reached Punta Arenas next afternoon, Monday, October 20th. We had intended to be there for two or three days only, but fate willed otherwise, and we sat for weeks in a tearing wind among small crests of foam, gazing at a little checkered pattern of houses on the open hillside opposite.

It will be remembered that the motor engine, to our great chagrin, was practically useless through heated bearings, and that all our endeavours at Buenos Aires to diagnose and remedy its ailment had been ineffectual. We had consequently to rely on passing through the Straits either under sail, or, as the late Lord Crawford had suggested to us before starting, through getting a tow from some passing tramp by means of a £50 cheque to the skipper, a transaction which would probably not appear in their log. However, in mentioning our disappointment to the British Consul, who was one of an engineering firm, he and his partner hazarded the suggestion that the defect lay, not in the engine, where it had been sought, but in the installation; that the shaft was probably not " true." They bravely undertook the job of overhauling it on the principle of " no cure, no pay," and were entirely justified by the result. The alteration was to have been finished in ten days, but there were the usual delays, one of which was a strike at the " shops," when a piece of work could only be continued by inducing one man to ply his trade behind closed doors while S. turned the lathe. It was six weeks before the anxious moment finally came for the eight hours' trial, which had been part of the bargain, but the motor did it triumphantly without turning a hair. We found what consolation for the delay was possible in the reflection that we had at least done all in our power to guard against such misfortune. The engine had been purchased from a first-class firm who had done the installation; the work had been supervised on our behalf by a private firm and passed by Lloyds; nevertheless it was peculiarly aggravating, for not only did it involve great money loss, but it sacrificed some of the strictly limited time of our navigator and geologist. We had the pleasure at this time of welcoming the said geologist, Mr. Lowry-Corry, who now joined the Expedition after successfully completing his work in India.

Punta Arenas, with which we became so well acquainted, is a new and unpretentious little town, but it is the centre of the sheep-grazing districts, and its shops are remarkably good. Any-thing in reason can be purchased there, and on the whole at more moderate prices than elsewhere in South America. The beautiful part of the Straits is not yet reached, and save for some distant views the place is ugly, but it gives a sensation of cleanliness and fresh air, and our detention might have been worse. There is indeed, on occasion, too much air, for it was at times impossible to get from the ship to the shore or *vice versa*, and if members of the party were on land when the wind sprang up they had to spend the night at the little hotel; the waves were not big, but the gales were too strong for the men to pull against them. I was with reluctance obliged to give up some promising Spanish lessons, with which I had hoped to occupy the time, for it was impossible to be sure of keeping any appointment from the yacht. Punta Arenas boasts an English chaplain, and Boy Scouts are in evidence. The chief celebrity is an Arctic spider-crab, which multiplies in the channels and is delicious eating, but we never discovered anything of much local interest.

I made one day a vain attempt to find the graves of the officers and crew of H.M.S. *Dotterel*, which was blown up off Sandy Point some thirty years ago. The cemetery overlooked the Straits; it was desolate and dreary, the ground being un-levelled and the tufted grass, with which it was covered, unkept and unmown. Most of the graves were humble enclosures, some of which gave the impression of greenhouses, being covered with erections of wood and glass; but here and there were small mausoleums, the property of rich families or corporations. It is the custom with some Chileans so to preserve the remains that the faces continue visible; an Englishman at Santiago told us that after a funeral which he had attended, the mourners expressed a desire to " see Aunt Maria," whereupon the coffin of a formerly deceased relative was taken down from its niche for her features to be inspected. The police of Punta Arenas had their home together in a large vault, which was apparently being prepared for a new occupant ; while the veterans of '79 (the war between Chile and Peru) slept as they had fought, side by side. There was apparently no Protestant corner, for the graves of English, Germans, and Norwegians were intermingled with those of Chileans. The resting-places of all, rich and poor alike, were lovingly decorated with the metal wreaths so prevalent in Latin countries, but unattractive to the English eye. Whilst I wandered among the tombs a storm burst, which had been gathering for some time amongst distant mountains, and chilly flakes of snow swept down in force, with biting wind and hail. I sheltered in the lee of a mausoleum, on whose roof balanced a large figure of the angel of peace bearing the palm-branch of victory, and the inscription on which showed it to be the property of a wealthy family, whose name report specially connected with the poisoning of Indians. The landscape was temporarily obscured by the driving storm, not a soul was in sight, and the iron wreaths on hundreds of graves rattled with a weird and ghostly sound. Presently, however, the tempest passed and the sun shone out, while over the Straits, towards the Fuegian land, there came out in the sky a wonderful arc of light edged by the colours of the rainbow, which turned the sea at its foot into a translucent and sparkling green.

But if there was not much occupation on shore, the unexpected length of our stay provided us unpleasantly with domestic employment. We had on arrival parted from our friend Freeman, his object in coming to Punta Arenas was, it transpired, to collect the remainder of a sum due to him in connection with the sale of a skating-rink, which he had at one time started there and run with considerable success : we were proud to think that service on an English scientific vessel would now be added to his experiences. Life below deck was then in the hands of Luke, the under-steward, who, as will be remembered by careful readers, had been the salvation of the inner man during our first gale in the North Atlantic. We had engaged him at Southampton on the strength of a character from a liner on which he had served in some subordinate capacity, and he signed on for the voyage of three years at the rate of £2 10s. a month. Though never what registry offices would call "clean in person and work," he plodded through somehow, and again in the Freeman episode rescued the ship from starvation ; we accordingly doubled his wages as a testimonial of esteem. My feelings can therefore be imagined when one morning, after we had been some weeks at Punta Arenas, I was told that Luke was not on board and his cabin was cleared. He had somehow in the early morning eluded the anchor watch and had gone off in a strange boat. A deserter forfeits of course his accumulated wages, which, by a probably wise regulation, are payable to Government and not to the owner ; but there is nothing to prevent a man who is leaving a vessel recouping himself by means of any little articles that he may judge will come in handy in his new career. The one that I grudged most to Luke was my cookery book, to which he had become much attached, and which was never seen again after his departure ; it was really a mean theft, from which I suffered much in the future.

S. offered, through the police, a reward for his detention, and enlarged his knowledge of the town by going personally through every low haunt, but without success. A rumour subsequently reached us that a muffled figure had been seen going on board one of the little steamers which plied backwards and forwards to the ports in Tierra del Fuego, and we heard, when it was too late, that Luke had been enticed to a sheep farm there,. with the promise of permanent employment at £10 a month, with £2 bonus during shearing-time, which was then in progress. The temptation was enormous, and I have to this day a sneaking kindliness for Luke, but for those who tempted him no pardon at all. The condition in which the successive defaulters had left their quarters is better pictured than described, and so stringent is the line of ship's etiquette between work on deck and below, that, as the simplest way and for the honour of the yacht, the Stewardess did the job of cleaning out cabin and pantry herself. The moral for shipowners is—do not dally in South American ports.

Now began a strange hunt in the middle of nowhere for anything that could call itself a cook or steward. The beach-combers who applied were marvellous; one persistent applicant

FIG. 9.

PUNTA ARENAS.

was the pianist at the local cinema; our expedition, as already
discovered, had a certain romantic sound, which was apt to
attract those who had by no means always counted the cost.
Mail steamers pass Punta Arenas every fortnight, once a month
in each direction, and these we now boarded with the tale of our
woes. Both captain and purser were most kind in allowing us
to ask for a volunteer among the stewards, but the attempt was
only temporarily successful; the routine work of a big vessel
under constant supervision proved not the right training for such
a post as ours.

Finally, we were told of a British cook who had been left
in hospital by a merchant ship passing through the Straits.
The cause of his detention was a broken arm, obtained in fighting
on board; this hardly seemed promising, but the captain was
reported to have said that he was " sorry to lose him," and we
were only too thankful to get hold of anything with some sort of
recommendation. On the whole Bailey was a success. He too
had knocked about the world; at one time he had made money
over a coffee-and-cake stall in Australia, and then thrown it away.
We had our differences of course; he once, for instance, told me
that as cook he took " a superior position on the ship's books
to the stewardess," but his moments of temper soon blew over.
I shall always cherish pleasant memories of the way in which
he and I stood by one another for weeks and months in a
position of loneliness and difficulty; but this is anticipating.

As departure drew near, provisioning for the next stage became
a serious business, as, with the exception of a few depots for ship-
wrecked mariners, there was no possibility of obtaining anything
after we sailed, before we reached our Chilean destination of
Talcahuano. S.'s work was more simple, as he had only to fill
up to the greatest extent with coal and oil, knowing that at the
worst the channels provide plenty of wood and water.

The next few weeks, when we traversed the remainder of
the Magellan Straits and the Patagonian Channels, were the
most fascinating part of the voyage. The whole of this portion
of South America is a bewildering labyrinth of waterways and
islands; fresh passages open up from every point of view, till
the voyager longs to see what is round the corner, not in one
direction, but in all. It has, too, much of the charm of the
unknown; such charts as exist have been made principally by

four English men-of-war at different periods, the earliest being
that of the *Beagle*, in the celebrated voyage in which Darwin
took part. A large portion of the ways and inlets are, however,
entirely unexplored. The effect of both straits and channels
is best imagined by picturing a Switzerland into whose valleys
and gorges the sea has been let in ; above tower snow-clad
peaks; while below precipices, clothed with beautiful verdure, go
straight down to the water's edge. The simile of a sea-invaded
Alps is indeed fairly accurate, for this is the tail of the Andes
which has been partially submerged. The mountains do not
rise above 5,000 feet, but the full benefit of the height is
obtained as they are seen from the sea-level. The permanent
snow line is at about 1,200 feet. The depths are very great,
being in some places as much as 4,000 feet, and the only places
where it is possible to anchor are in certain little harbours
where there is a break in the wall of rock. These anchorages
lie anything from five miles to twenty or thirty miles apart,
and as it was impossible to travel at night it was essential to
reach one of them before dark. If for any reason it did not
prove feasible to accomplish the necessary distance, there was
no option but to turn back in time to reach the last resting-place
before daylight failed, and start again on the next suitable day.
On the other hand, when things were propitious, we were able on
occasion to reach an even further harbour than the one which
had been planned.

The proceeding amusingly resembled a game, played in the
days of one's youth, with dice on a numbered board, and
entitled "Willie's Walk to Grandmamma" : the player might not
start till he had thrown the right number, and even when he
had begun his journey he might, by an unlucky cast, find that
he was "stopping to play marbles" and lose a turn, or be obliged
to go back to the beginning; if, however, he were fortunate he
might pass, like an express train, through several intermediate
stopping-places,, and outdistance all competitors. The two
other sailing yachts with whose record we competed were
the *Sunbeam* in 1876 and the *Nyanza* in 1888: the match was
scarcely a fair one, as the *Sunbeam* had strong steam power and
soon left us out of sight, while the *Nyanza*, though a much bigger
vessel, had no motor, and we halved her record.

It will be seen that it was of first-rate importance to make the most of the hours of daylight, which were now at their longest, and to effect as early a start as possible, so that in case of accident or delay we should have plenty of time in hand before dark. We therefore, long before such became fashionable, passed a summer-time bill of a most extended character, the clock being put five hours forward. Breakfast was really at 3 a.m., and we were under way an hour later, when it was broad daylight; but as the hours were called eight and nine everyone felt quite comfortable and as usual, it was a great success. The difficulty lay in retiring proportionately early. Stevenson's words continually rose to mind: "In summer quite the other way—I have to go to bed by day." The greatest drawback was the loss of sunset effects; we should, theoretically, have had the sunrise instead, but the mornings were often grey and misty, and it did not clear till later in the day.

One of the charms of the channels, is the smoothness of the water: we were able to carry our cutter in the davits as well as the dinghy. It also suited the motor, which proved of the greatest use, entirely redeeming its character, there is no doubt however, that to become accustomed to sailing is to be spoilt for any other method of progression. The photographers accomplished something, but the scenery scarcely lends itself to the camera and the light was seldom good. The water-colour scribbles with which I occupied myself serve their purpose as a personal diary.

We speculated from time to time whether these parts will ultimately turn into the "playground of South America," when that continent becomes densely populated after the manner of Europe, and amused ourselves by selecting sites for fashionable hotels: golf-courses no mortal power will ever make. On the whole the probability seems the other way, for the climate is against it; it is too near to the Antarctic to be warm even under the most favourable conditions, and the Andes will always intercept the rain-clouds of the Pacific. One of the survey-ships chronicled an average of eleven hours of rain in the twenty-four, all through the summer months. We ourselves were fortunate both in the time of year and in the weather. It resembled in our experience a cold and wet October at home; but there were few days, I cannot recall more than two, when we lost the greater part of the view through fog and rain. On the rare occasions when it was sunny and clear the effect was disappointing, and less impressive than when the mountains were seen partially veiled in mist and with driving cloud. The last hundred miles before the Gulf of Peñas it became markedly warmer, and the steam-heating was no longer necessary.

It was far from our thoughts that exactly one year later these same channels would witness a game of deadly hide-and-seek in a great naval war between Germany and England. In them the German ship *Dresden* lay hidden, after making her escape from the battle of the Falkland Islands, while for two and a half months English ships looked for her in vain. They explored in the search more than 7,000 miles of waterway, not only taking the risks of these uncharted passages, but expecting round every corner to come upon the enemy with all her guns trained on the spot where they must appear.

We left Punta Arenas on Saturday, November 29th, 1913, spending the night in Freshwater Bay, and the next afternoon anchored in St. Nicholas Bay, which is on the mainland. Opposite to it, on the other side of the Straits, is Dawson Island, and separating Dawson from the next island to the westward is Magdalen Sound, which leads into Cockburn Channel ; it was in this last that the *Dresden* found her first hiding-place after escaping from Sturdee's squadron and obtaining an illicit supply of coal at Punta Arenas. St. Nicholas Bay forms the mouth of a considerable river, the banks of which are clothed with forests which come down to the sea ; near the estuary is a little island, and on it there is a conspicuous tree. Mr. Corry and I went out in the boat, and found affixed to the tree a number of boards with the names of vessels which had visited the place. Jeffery scrambled up and added *Mana's* card to those already there. This was our first introduction to a plan frequently encountered later in out-of-the-way holes and corners, and which subsequently played a part in the war. At the outbreak of hostilities the *Dresden* was in the Atlantic, and had to creep round the Horn to join the squadron of Von Spee in the Pacific. She put into Orange Bay, one of the furthest anchorages to the south ; there she found that many months before the *Bremen* had left her name on a similar board. Moved by habit someone on the cruiser wrote below it " *Dresden*, September 11th, 1914 " ; then caution supervened, and the record was partially, but only partially, obliterated ;

FIG. 10.

RIVER SCENE, ST. NICHOLAS BAY.

79]

there it was shortly afterwards read by the British ships *Glasgow* and *Monmouth*, and formed a record of the proceedings of the enemy.

On Monday, December 1st, we started at daylight and made our way with motor and sail as far as Cape Froward, the most southerly point of the Straits; but the sea was running too high to proceed. We had to retrace our steps, and cast anchor again in St. Nicholas Bay. This time S. and I were determined to explore the river, so, after an early luncheon, in order to get the benefit of the tide, we made our way up it in the cutter. It was most pleasant rowing between the banks of the quiet stream, and so warm and sheltered that we might almost have imagined ourselves on the Cherwell, if the illusion had not been dispelled by the strange vegetation which overhung the banks, amongst which were beautiful flowering azaleas. Every here and there also a bend in the course of the river gave magnificent views of snow-clad peaks above. A happy little family of teal, father, mother, and children, disported themselves in the water. Later in the voyage, as the mountains grew steeper, we had many waterfalls, but never again a river which was navigable to any distance. Some of the crew had been left to cut firewood, and we found on our return that they had achieved a splendid collection, which Mr. Ritchie and Mr. Corry had kindly been helping to chop. Burning wood was not popular in the galley, but we were anxious to save our supplies of coal.

Tuesday, December 2nd, we again left the bay, and this time were more fortunate. It was misty and sunless, but as we rounded Cape Froward it stood out grandly, with its foot in grey seas and with driving clouds above. We had now definitely entered on the western half of the Straits and were amongst the spurs of the Andes. As the day advanced the wind freshened, the clouds were swept away, and blue sky appeared, while the sea suddenly became dark blue and covered with a mass of foaming, tumbling waves; on each coast the white-capped mountains came out clear and strong. This part of the channel, which is known as Froward Reach, is a path of water, about five miles wide, lying between rocky walls; and up this track *Mana* beat to windward, rushing along as if she thoroughly enjoyed it. Every few minutes came the call " Ready about, lee oh ! " and over she went on a fresh tack, travelling perfectly steadily, but listed over until the water bubbled beneath the bulwarks on the lee side. It would have been a poor heart indeed that did not rejoice, and every soul on board responded to the excitement and thrill of the motion: that experience alone was worth many hundred miles of travel. As evening came the wind sank, and we were glad of the prosaic motor to see us into our haven at Fortescue Bay.

The next day the wind was too strong to attempt to leave the harbour, and we went to bed with the gale still raging, but during the night it disappeared, and before dawn we were under way. As light and colour gradually stole into the dim landscape, the grey trunks and brown foliage of trees on the near mountain-sides gave the effect of the most lovely misty brown velvet. Rain and mist subsequently obscured the view, but it cleared happily as we turned into the harbour of Angosto on the southern side of the channel. Rounding the corner of a narrow entrance, we found ourselves in a perfect little basin about a quarter of a mile across, surrounded with steep cliffs some 300 feet in height, on one side of which a waterfall tore down from the snows above. Our geologist reported it as a glacier tarn, which, as the land gradually sank, had been invaded by the sea. We left it with regret at daylight next morning.

The Straits became now broader and the scenery was more bleak, the great grey masses being scarcely touched with vegetation till they reached the water's edge. It was decided to spend the night at Port Churruca in Desolation Island, rather than at Port Tamar on the mainland opposite, which is generally frequented by vessels on entering and leaving the Straits. We passed through the entrance into a rocky basin, but when we were at the narrowest part between precipitous cliffs the motor stopped. It had been frequently pointed out, when we were wrestling with the engine, how perilous would be our position if anything went wrong with it in narrow waters. I confess that I held my breath. S. disappeared into the engine-room, the Navigator's eyes were glued to the compass, and the Sailing-master gave orders to stand by the boats in case it was necessary to run out a kedge anchor and attach the yacht to the shore. It was a distinct relief when the throb of the motor was once more heard; the difficulty had arisen from the lowness of the temperature, which had interfered with the flow of the oil. The ship, how-

FIG. II.

CAPE FROWARD, MAGELLAN STRAITS.

Looking East.

FIG. 12.

THE GLACIER GORGE, PORT CHURRUCA.

ever, was luckily well under control, with the wind at the moment
behind her.   In an inner basin soundings were taken, " twenty-
five fathoms no bottom, thirty fathoms no bottom," till, when
the bowsprit seemed almost touching the sheer wall of rock, the
Nassau Anchorage was found and down went the hook.

We grew well acquainted with Churruca, as we were detained
there for five days; Saturday through the overhauling of the
engine; Sunday, Monday, and Tuesday by bad weather; of
Wednesday more anon.   The position was not without a certain
eeriness: we lay in this remote niche in the mountains, while the
storm raged in the channel without and in the peaks above; at
night, after turning in, the gale could be heard tearing down from
above in each direction in turn, and the vessel's chain rattling
over the stony bottom as she swung round to meet it.   The
heavy rain turned every cliff-face into a multitude of waterfalls,
which vanished at times into the air as a gust of wind caught
the jet of water and converted it into a cloud of spray.   Although
the weather prevented our venturing outside, it was quite possible
to explore the port by means of the ship's boats.   It proved not
unlike Angosto, but on a larger and more complicated scale.
Beyond our inner anchorage, although invisible from it, was a
further extension known as the Lobo Arm, and there were also
other small creeks and inlets.

Even the prosaic Sailing Directions venture on the statement
that the scenery at Port Churruca is "scarcely surpassed,"
and one of the fiords must be described, although the attempt
seems almost profane.   In its narrow portion it was about
a mile in length and from 100 to 200 yards in width; the
sheer cliffs on either hand were clothed to the height of many
hundreds of feet with various forms of fern and most brilliant
moss. Above this belt of colour was bleak crag, and higher again
the snow-line.   The gorge ended in a precipice, above which was
a mountain-peak; a glacier descending from above had been
arrested in its descent by the precipice and now stood above it,
forming part of it, a sheer wall of ice and snow as if cut off by a
giant knife.   There was little life to be seen, but an occasional
gleam was caught from the white breast of a sea-bird against the
dark setting of the ravine.   In one part, high up on the cliff, where
the wind was deflected by a piece of overhanging rock, was a
little colony of nests; the mother birds and young broods sat

6

on the edge in perfect shelter, even when to venture off it was to be beaten down on to the surface of the water by the strength of the wind. Some of our party visited the fiord on a second occasion to try to obtain photographs; it was blowing at the time a severe gale, and the effect was magical. The squalls, known as " williwaws," rushed down the ravine in such force that the powerful little launch was brought to a standstill. They lashed the water into waves, and then turned the foaming crests into spray, till the whole surface presented the aspect of a fiercely boiling cauldron, through which glimpses could be caught from time to time of the dark cliffs above.

While S. and I were visiting the glacier gorge, the two other members of the party were exploring the last portion of the inlet named on the chart the Lobo Arm. It terminated on low ground, on which stood the frame of an Indian hut, and pieces of timber had been laid down to form a portage for canoes. A few steps showed that the low ground extended only for some 160 yards, while beyond this was another piece of water which had the appearance of an inland lake, some three miles long and a mile wide. The portage end of the water was vaguely shown on the chart of Port Churruca, but there was no indication of anything of the kind on the general map of Desolation Island. Our curiosity was mildly excited, and we all visited the place ; one of our number remarked that " the water was slightly salt," another that there " were tidal indications," a third that " from higher ground the valley seemed to go on indefinitely." At last the map was again and more seriously examined, and it was seen that, while there were no signs of this water, there were on the opposite side of the island the commencements of two inlets from the open sea, neither of which had been followed up : the more northerly of these was immediately opposite Port Churruca. " If," we all agreed, " our lake is not a lake at all, but a fiord "—and to this every appearance pointed—" it is in all probability the termination of this northern inlet, and Desolation Island is cut in two except for the small isthmus with the portage." Then a great ardour of exploration seized us, Mr. Corry fell a victim to it, Mr. Gillam fell likewise, and we refused to be depressed by Mr. Ritchie's dictum that it had " nothing to do with serious navigation." We wrestled with a conscientious conviction that it had certainly nothing to do with Easter Island,

and we ought to go forward at the earliest possible moment, but the exploration fever conquered. We discussed the possibility of getting the motor-launch over the portage, and were obliged reluctantly to abandon it as too heavy, but it was concluded that it would be quite feasible with the cutter.

The next day proved too wet to attempt anything, but Wednesday dawned reasonably fine, though with squalls at intervals. Great were the preparations, from compasses, note-books, and log-lines, to tinned beef and dry boots. At last at 11.30 (or 6.30 a.m. by true time) we sallied forth. The launch towed us down the Lobo Arm, and then came the work of passing the boat across the isthmus, at which all hands assisted. It was the prettiest sight imaginable; the portage, which had been cut through the thick forest undergrowth, had the appearance of a long and brilliant tunnel between the two waters, it was carpeted with bright moss and overhung by trees which were covered with lichen (fig. 13). The bottom was soft and boggy, and I at one time became so firmly embedded that I could not get out without assistance. In less than half an hour the boat was launched on the other side, and Mr. Corry, Mr. Gillam, our two selves, and two seamen set forth on our voyage. Soon after starting the creek divided, part going to the north-west and part to the south-east. We decided to follow the latter as apparently the main channel.

We rowed for an hour and a quarter, taking our rate of speed by the log. The mountains on each side were of granite, showing very distinct traces of ice action. At 2 p.m. we landed on the left bank for luncheon. It was, it must be admitted, a somewhat wet performance; the soaked wood proved too much even for our expert campers-out, who had been confident that they could make a fire under all circumstances, and had disdainfully declined my proffered thermos. Enthusiasm was, however, undamped. Mr. Corry ascended to high ground and discovered that there was another similar creek on the other side of the strip of ground on which we had landed, which converged towards that along which we were travelling. After rowing for an hour and a half we reached the point where the two creeks joined; here we landed and scrambled up through some brushwood to the top of a low eminence. Looking backwards we could see up both pieces of water, while looking forward the two fiords, now one, passed at right angles, after some four miles, into a larger piece of water. This was where we had expected to find the open sea, and some distant blue mountains on the far horizon were somewhat of an enigma. As we had to row back against a head wind, it was useless to think of going further, unless we were prepared to camp out, so all we could do was to make as exact sketches as possible to work out at home.

The return journey was easier than had been expected, for the wind dropped; we kept this time to the right bank, and stopped for " tea " by some rocks, which added mussels to the repast for the taking. The portage was gained four hours after the time that the rest of the crew had been told to meet us there ; and it was a relief to find that they had possessed their souls with patience. *Mana* was finally reached at 11 p.m. It was found by calculating the speed at which we had travelled and its direction, that our creek had led into the more southerly of the unsurveyed inlets, and not as we had expected into that to the northward. The distant blue hills were islands. Like all great explorers, from Christopher Columbus downwards, our results were therefore not precisely those we had looked for, but we had undoubtedly proved our contention that Desolation Island is in two halves, united only by the 160 yards covered by the portage on the Lobo Isthmus.

A knowledge of the existence of this channel, connecting the Pacific Ocean with the Magellan Straits, might be of high importance to the crew of a vessel lost to the south of Cape Pillar, when making for the entrance to the Straits. Instead of trying to round that Cape against wind at sea, her boats should run to the southward until the entrance to the inlet is reached; they can then enter the Magellan Straits without difficulty at Port Churruca. With the consent of the Royal Geographical Society, it has been christened " Mana Inlet." [1]

The next morning, December 1st, we left Churruca with a fair wind, so that the engine was only needed at the beginning and end of the day; but the weather was drizzling and unpleasant, so

---

[1] We were subsequently interested to learn from a private diary kept on board *The Challenger* that they had also taken their boat over into this water; they had, however, neither explored it nor marked it on the map

that we could see little of Cape Pillar,[1] where the Magellan Straits enter the Pacific Ocean. Our own course was up the waterways between the western coast of Patagonia and the islands which lie off the coast. It is a route that is little taken, owing to the dangers of navigation. Not only is much of it uncharted and unsurveyed, but it is also unlighted, and its passage is

FIG. 13

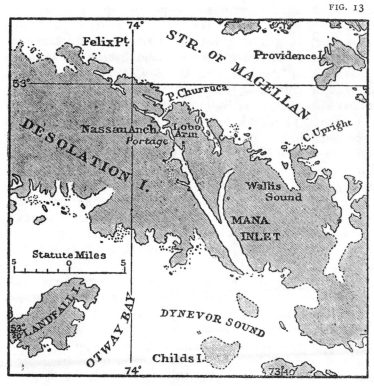

MANA INLET.

excluded by the ordinary insurance terms of merchant ships; they consequently pass out at once into the open sea at Cape Pillar. We turned north at Smyth's Channel, the first of these

[1] Cape Pillar is the name which has been given to Magellan's "Cape Deseado" since the days of Sir John Narborough; it has two peaks, of which the western one is like a pillar. The point which on the chart is named Deseado lies two miles to the south-west and could not possibly have been seen by Magellan: see *Early Spanish Voyages and the Straits of Magellan*, edited by Sir C. Markham, Hakluyt Series II. vol. xxviii

waterways, and made such good progress that, instead of anchoring as we had intended at Burgoyne's Bay, we were able to reach Otter Bay. It is situated amid a mass of islands, and the sad vision of a ship with her back broken emphasised the need for caution. The general character of the Patagonian Channels is of the same nature as the Magellan Straits, but particularly beautiful views of the Andes are obtained to the eastward. The next day Mount Burney was an impressive spectacle, although only glimpses of the top could be obtained through fleeting mists; and the glistening heights of the Sarmiento Cordillera came out clear and strong. We anchored that night at Occasion Cove on Piazzi Island; and on Saturday, December 13th, had a twelve hours' run, using the engine all the way. Here there was a succession of comparatively monotonous hills and mountains, so absolutely rounded by ice action as to give the impression of apple dumplings made for giants. The lines show always, as would be expected, that the ice-flow has been from the south. Later a ravine on Esperanza Island was particularly remarkable; its mysterious windings, which it would have been a joy to explore, were alternately hidden by driving cloud or radiant with gleams of sun. Glimpses up Peel Inlet gave pleasant views, and two snowy peaks on Hanover Island, unnamed as usual, were absorbing our attention when we turned into Latitude Cove.

On December 14th the landscape was absolutely grey and colourless, so that Guia Narrows were not seen to advantage. Later the channel was wider and the possibility of sailing debated, but abandoned in view of the head wind. We had been struck with the absence of life and fewness of birds, but we now saw some albatrosses. In slacking away the anchor preparatory to letting go in Tom Bay, in a depth stated to be seventeen fathoms, it hit an uncharted rock at eleven fathoms. It was still raining as we left Tom Bay, but when we turned up Brassey Pass, which lies off the regular channel, the clouds began to lift, and Hastings Fiord and Charrua Bay were grand beyond description. From time to time the mists rose for an instant, and revealed the immediate presence of reach beyond reach of wooded precipices; or a dark summit appeared without warning, towering overhead at so great a height that, severed by cloud from its base, it seemed scarcely to belong to the earth.

FIG. 14.

CANOE CORDUROY PORTAGE BETWEEN PORT CHURRUCA AND
MANA INLET.

FIG. 15.

PATAGONIAN WATERWAYS.

Showing water near the land smoothed by growing kelp.

Then as suddenly the whole panorama was cut off, and we were alone once more with a grey sea and sky.

As we approached Charrua, we caught sight among the trees on a neighbouring island of something which was both white and nebulous; it might, of course, be only an isolated wreath of mist, but after watching it for a while we came to the conclusion that it was undoubtedly a cloud of smoke. Our hopes of seeing Indians, which had grown faint, began to revive. As soon as we were anchored, orders were given that immediately after dinner the launch should be ready for us to inspect what we hoped might prove a camping-ground. This turned out to be unnecessary, as the neighbours made the first call. In an hour's time S. came to inform me that two canoes were approaching full of natives " just like the picture-books," whereon the anthropologists felt inclined to adapt the words of the immortal Snark-hunters and exclaim :

> " We have sailed many weeks, we have sailed many days,
>   Seven days to the week I allow,
> But an Indian on whom we might lovingly gaze
>   We have never beheld until now."

The crew, however, were fully convinced that the hour had arrived when they would have to defend themselves against ferocious savages. They had been carefully primed in every detail by disciples of Ananias at Buenos Aires, and by the blood-curdling accounts of a certain mariner named Slocum, who claimed to have sailed the Straits single-handed and to have protected himself from native onslaught by means of tin-tacks sprinkled on the deck of his ship. The canoes were about 23 feet in length, with beam of 4 to 6 feet and a depth of 2 feet. Six Indians were in one and seven in the other; all were young with the exception of one older man, and each boat contained a mother and baby. Their skins were a dark olive, which was relieved in the case of the women and children by a beautiful tinge of pink in the cheeks, and they had very good teeth. Their hair was long and straight, and a fillet was habitually worn round the brow; the top was cut *à la brosse*, giving the impression of a monk's tonsure which had been allowed to grow. The height of the men was about 5 feet 4 inches. Most of the party were clad in old European garments, but a few wore capes of skins, and some seemed still more at home in a state of nature. They had brought nothing for sale, but begged for biscuits and old clothes. I parted with a wrench from a useful piece of calico, in the interests of one of the infants, which was still in its primitive condition ; it was accepted, but with a howl of derision, which I humbly felt was well merited when it was seen that the rival baby was already wrapped in an old waistcoat given by the cook. One of the Indians talked a little Spanish, and was understood to say he was a Christian.

After dealing with them for a while we offered to tow them home, an offer readily understood, and accepted without hesitation. It was a strange procession amid weird surroundings; the sun had shown signs of coming out, but had thought better of it and retreated, and we made our way over a grey sea, between half-obscure cliffs in drizzling rain, taking keen note of our route for fear of losing our way back. Truly we seemed to have reached the uttermost ends of the earth. The lead was taken by that recent product of civilisation a motor-launch, containing our two selves and our Glasgow socialist engineer ; then at the end of a rope came the dinghy, to be used for landing, the broad back of one of our Devonshire seamen making a marked object as he stood up in it to superintend the towing of the craft behind. The two canoes followed, full of these most primitive specimens of humanity, while the rear was brought up by a seal, which swam after us for a mile or so, putting up its head at intervals to gaze curiously at the scene. S. had brought his gun, and as we approached the camp thought it well to shoot a sea-bird, for the double reason of showing that he was armed and giving a present to our new friends. The encampment was situated in a little cove, and nothing could have been more picturesque. In front was a shingly beach, on which the two canoes were presently drawn up, flanked by low rocks covered with bright seaweed. In the background was a mass of trees, shrubs, and creepers, which almost concealed two wigwams, from one of which had issued the smoke which attracted our notice (fig. 16).

We returned next morning to photograph and study the scene. The size of the shelters, or tents, was about 12 feet by 9 feet, with a height of some 5 feet. They were formed by a framework of rods set up in oval form, the tops of which were brought together and interwoven, and strengthened by rods laid horizontally and tied in place: the opening was at the side and towards the sea. Over this structure seals' skins were thrown, which kept in place by their own weight, as the encampments are always made in sheltered positions in dense forests. With the exception that they do not possess a ridge-pole, the tents, which are always the same in size and make, closely resemble those of English gipsies, the skins taking the place of the blankets used by those people. No attempt was made to level the floor, the fire was in the middle, and in one the sole occupant was a naked sprawling baby, who occupied the place of honour on the floor beside it. In some of the old encampments, which we saw subsequently, there were as many as six huts, but it was doubtful if they had all been occupied at the same time. The middens are outside and generally near the door. Some of the Indians were quite friendly, but others were not very cordial, the old women in particular making it clear to the men of the party that their presence was not welcome. The old man, whose picture appears (fig. 17), was apparently the patriarch of the party, and quite amiable, though he firmly declined to part with his symbol of authority in the shape of his club ; in order to keep him quiet while his photograph was taken he was fed on biscuits, which he was taught to catch after the manner of a pet dog. The staff of life is mussels and limpets, and we saw in addition small quantities of berries. A lump of seal fat weighing perhaps 10 lb. was being gnawed like an apple, and a portion was offered to our party. The dogs are smooth-haired black-and-tan terriers, like small heavy lurchers; they are, it is said, taught to assist their masters in the catching of fish.[1]

The company presently showed signs of unusual activity, and began to shift camp; the movement was not connected, as far as we could tell, with our presence, and, judging by the odour of the place, the time for it had certainly arrived. It was interesting to see their chattels brought down one by one to the canoes. Amongst them were receptacles resembling large pillboxes, about 12 inches across, made of birchwood, which was split thin and sewn with tendons. In these were kept running nooses made of whalebone for capturing wild geese, and also

---

[1] " The Indians had taught their dogs to drive the fish into a corner of some pond or lake, from whence they were easily taken out by the skill and address of these savages."—*Narrative of Hon. J. Byron*, ed. 1768, p. 56.

harpoon-lines cut out of sealskin : at one extremity of these last was a barbed head made of bone ; this head, when in use, fits into the extremity of a long wooden shaft, to which it is then attached by the leather thong. The possessions included an adze-like tool for making canoes, the use of which was demonstrated, and resembled that of a plane ; also an awl about 2 inches long, in form like a dumb-bell, with a protruding spike at one end. There were small pots made of birch bark for baling the boats, and some European axes. We did not see any form of cooking utensil. When all the objects, including the sealskin coverings of the huts, had been stowed in the canoes, the company all embarked and rowed off towards the open sea.

On leaving Charrua and returning to the main channel we obtained magnificent views of the Andes. Penguin Inlet leading inland opened up a marvellous panorama of snowy peaks, which can be visible only on a clear day such as we were fortunate in possessing ; this range received at least one vote, in the final comparing of notes, as to the most beautiful thing seen between Punta Arenas and the Gulf of Peñas. A white line across the water showed where the ice terminated, while small pieces which reached the main channel, looked, as they floated past us, like stray waterlilies on the surface of the sea. We anchored at Ring Dove Inlet, and went on next day through Chasm Reach, where the channel is only from five hundred to a thousand yards in width. Our expectations, which had been greatly raised, were on the whole disappointed, but here again no doubt it was a question of lighting ; the usually gloomy gorge was illuminated with the full radiance of the summer sun, leaving nothing to the imagination.

Chasm Reach leads into Indian Reach, in which sea, mountain, and sky formed a perfect harmony in varying shades of blue, with touches of white from high snow-clad peaks. Suddenly, in the middle of this vista, as if made to fit into the scene, appeared a dark Indian canoe with its living freight, evidently making for the vessel. We stopped the engine, threw them a line, and towed them to our anchorage in Eden Harbour. The weather had suddenly become much warmer, and the thermometer in the saloon had now risen to the comfortable but scarcely excessive height of 64° ; the crew of the canoe, however, were so overcome with the heat that they spent the time pouring

FIG. 16.

ENCAMPMENT OF PATAGONIAN INDIANS, BRASSEY PASS.

From sketch and photos.

FIG. 17.

INDIANS OF BRASSEY PASS.

FIG. 18.

CANOE IN INDIAN REACH.

what must have been very chilly sea-water over their naked bodies.[1]

The party was conducted by two young men; a very old woman without a stitch of clothing crouched in the bow; while in the middle of the boat, in the midst of ashes, mussel-shells, and other débris, a charming girl mother sat in graceful attitude. She was, perhaps, seventeen, and wore an old coat draped round her waist, while her baby, of some eighteen months, in the attire of nature, occupied itself from time to time in trying to stand on its ten toes. A younger girl of about fourteen sat demurely in the stern with her folded arms resting on a paddle which lay athwart the canoe, beneath which two shapely little brown legs were just visible. Her rich colouring, and the faded green drapery which she wore, made against the dark background of the canoe a perfect study for an artist, but the moment an attempt was made to photograph her she hid her face in her hands. The party was completed by a couple of dogs and a family of fat tan puppies, who were held up from time to time, but whether for our admiration or purchase was not evident.

The belongings were similar to those seen at the encampment and there were also baskets on board. The young mother had a necklace which looked like a charm, and therefore particularly excited our desires: in response to our gestures she handed to us a similar one worn by the baby, which was duly paid for in matches. When we were still unsatisfied she beckoned to the young girl to sell hers, but stuck steadfastly to her own, till finally a mixed bribe of matches and biscuits proved too much, and the cherished ornament passed into our keeping. The young men readily came on deck of the yacht, but the women were obviously frightened, and kept saying *mala, mala* in spite of our efforts to reassure them. After we had cast anchor, the party went with our crew to show them the best spot in which to shoot the net, and on their return ran up the square sail of their canoe, the halyard passing over a mast like a small clothes-prop with a Y-shaped extremity, got out their paddles, and vanished down-stream.

[1] " We were well clothed, and though sitting close to the fire were far from too warm ; yet these naked savages (Fuegians), though further off, were observed, to our great surprise, to be streaming with perspiration."—*Voyage of H.M.S. " Beagle "* (Darwin), ed. 1870, p. 220.

At Eden Harbour a wreck was lying in mid-stream, where she had evidently struck on an uncharted rock when trying to enter the bay, a danger from which no possible foresight can guard those who go down to the sea in ships. English Narrows, which was next reached, is considered the most difficult piece of navigation in the channels: a small island lies in the middle of the fairway, leaving only a narrow passage on either side, down which, under certain conditions, the tide runs at a terrific rate. It was exciting, as the yacht approached her course between the island and opposing cliff which are separated by only some 360 yards, to hear Mr. Ritchie ask Mr. Gillam to take the helm himself, and the latter give the order to " stand by the anchor " in case of mishap; but we had hit it off correctly at slack water and got through without difficulty. From there our route passed through Messier Channel, which has all the appearance of a broad processional avenue, out of which we presently turned to the right and found ourselves in Connor Cove. The harbour terminates in a precipitous gorge, down which a little river makes its way into the inlet. We endeavoured to row up it, but could not get further than 100 or 200 yards; even that distance was achieved with difficulty, owing to the number of fallen trees which lay picturesquely across the stream.

The plant life, which had always been most beautiful, became even more glorious with the rather milder climate, which we had now reached. When the trees were stunted it was from lack of soil, not from atmospheric conditions. Tree-ferns abounded, and flowering plants wandered up moss-grown stems; among the most beautiful of these blooms were one with a red bell and another one which almost resembled a snowdrop.[1] The impression of the luxuriant *mêlé* was rather that of a tropical forest than of an almost Antarctic world, while the intrusion of rocks and falling water added peculiar charm. Butterflies were seen occasionally, and sometimes humming-birds.

Since our detention at Churruca we had been favoured with unvarying good fortune, and the crew were beginning to say that thirteen, which we had counted on board since Mr. Corry joined us, was proving our lucky number. Now, however, our fate changed; twice did we set forth from this harbour only to be

---

[1] *Philesia buxifolia* and *Luzuriaga erecta.*

obliged to return and start afresh, till we began to feel that getting under way from Connor Cove was rapidly becoming a habit. On the first occasion the weather became so thick that in the opinion of our Navigator it was not safe to proceed : the second time the wind was against us. We tried both engine and sails, but though we could make a certain amount of headway under either it was obviously impossible, at the rate of progression, to reach the next haven before nightfall ; when, therefore, we were already half-way to our goal we once more found it necessary to turn round. It was peculiarly tantalising to reflect that there were, in all probability, numerous little creeks on the way in which we could have sheltered for the night, but as none of them had been surveyed there was no alternative but to go back to our previous anchorage. Residence there had the redeeming point that it proved an excellent fishing-ground. On each of the three nights the trammel was shot at a short distance from the spot where the stream entered the bay, and we obtained in all some 200 mullet. They formed an acceptable change of diet, and those not immediately needed were salted. From that time till we left the channels we were never without fresh fish, catching, in addition to mullet, bream, gurnet, and a kind of whiting ; they formed part of the menu at every meal, till the more ribald persons suggested that they themselves would shortly begin to swim.

Our third effort to leave Connor Cove was crowned with greater success, and we safely reached Island Harbour, which, as its name suggests, is sheltered by outlying islands. This bay and the neighbouring anchorage of Hale Cove are the last two havens in the channels before the Gulf of Peñas is reached, and in either of them a vessel can lie with comfort and await suitable weather for putting out to sea It is essential for a sailing vessel to obtain a fair wind, for not only has she to clear the gulf, but must, for the sake of safety, put 200 miles between herself and the land ; otherwise, should a westerly gale arise, she might be driven back on to the inhospitable Patagonian coast. In Island Harbour we filled our tanks, adorned the ship for'ard with drying clothes and fish, and for three days waited in readiness to set forth. At the end of that time it was still impossible to leave the channels, but we decided to move on the short distance to Hale Cove, which we reached on December 24th. Christmas Eve was spent by three of our party, Mr. Ritchie, Mr. Corry, and Mr. Gillam, on a small rock "taking stars" till 2 a.m. The rock, which had been selected at low tide, grew by degrees unexpectedly small, and to keep carefully balanced on a diminishing platform out of reach of the rising water, while at the same time being continuously bitten by insects, was, they ruefully felt, to make scientific observations under difficulties. On Christmas Day it poured without intermission, but it was a peaceful if not an exciting day. It is, I believe, the correct thing to give the menu on these occasions: the following was ours.

SCHOONER YACHT *MANA*, R.C.C.

CHRISTMAS DAY, 1913.

Potages aux légumes a l'Anglais.
Mulets d'eaux Patagonia.
Bœuf rôti d'Argentine. Pommes de terre de Punta Arenas.
Petits Pois à l'Angleterre.
Pouding Noël de Army & Navy Stores, garni " Holly Antarctic."
Fromage Gouda, Beurre, Pain de Mana, Biscuits Matelote.
Bonbons Peppermint à la School-girl.
Café de Rio de Janeiro.

The forecastle was visited after dinner and each man given a half-pound tin of tobacco. Boxing Day was comparatively fine, and a laundry was organised on shore with great success ; a fire was made, old kerosene tins turned into boilers, and the articles washed in camp-baths with water from a streamlet. It is one thing, however, to wet clothes in the Patagonian Channels ; it is quite another to dry them. For days afterwards the rain descended in torrents, while the wind blew persistently from the north-west ; with one short intermission we lay in Hale Cove weather-bound for thirteen days, till, as some one remarked, " it was a pity that we had not given it as a postal address." It was tiresome of course, but an interval of rest for all on board after the strenuous passage of the channels was not without advantage ; for ourselves journals were written up, flowers pressed, and photographs developed.

Hale Cove was fortunately one of those few ports in which it was possible to get a little exercise, which the denseness of the undergrowth generally rendered impossible. The cliffs, at the foot of which *Mana* lay, were precipitous and clothed with vegetation to the sky-line, they thus scarcely lent themselves to exploration. There was, however, across the small bay a southern spur, on the top of which for some reason trees had not flourished and which was comparatively clear; this it was possible to reach by landing on a little beach and scrambling along an old track which had been cut through an intermediate belt of wood. We could in this way get some sort of a walk, at the cost of course of becoming soaked through from bogs and dripping vegetation.

Not far from the cove there were traces of a small frame house, and near it flourished European wheat and grass, which had obviously taken root from stray seed. Its history was difficult to guess. Why had a white man lived there, and on what had he subsisted ? The only solution suggested was that it might at one time have been a port of call for a line of steamers, and a woodman had been employed to cut fuel. Another dwelling, but made of material found on the spot, had obviously been destroyed by fire, and on its abandoned site native wigwams had been erected. The place was evidently the resort of Indians; when, therefore, we noted near the old track, and not far from the water-course, part of two rough boards protruding from the earth, we hoped that we had chanced on an Indian burial-ground, which would naturally have been of much anthropological interest. The soil which had originally covered the boards had been partially washed away by the rain, and on moving them we found, as had been guessed, that just below were human bones ; they were so deeply encrusted with roots and earth that it was only by much digging with our fingers we could get them out at all. Then they proved to be in much confusion, two parts of the skull even were in different places, and it was difficult at first to say whether the body, which was that of a man in middle life, had been buried full length or in the folded attitude so common among primitive peoples. It was my first experience in scientific body-snatching, a proceeding to which later I became fairly well inured, and it felt not a little weird being thus in contact with the dead in his lonely resting-place. A great tree-fern kept guard over the grave on one side, a gnarled trunk bent over it from the other, and the sun gleamed at intervals through the thick branches of surrounding cedars. At last it became obvious that the body had been outstretched, and the grave lined as well as covered with boards, in addition to which there had been a wrapping of some woven material; it seemed therefore evident that the corpse had been that of a civilised man. Who was he ? the lumberman, the remains of whose hut we had seen ? one of the crew of some vessel which had put in here ? or possibly a ship-wrecked mariner ? for there were traces of an ill-fated vessel in a quantity of coal washed up on the beach. Why, though he had been buried with considerable care, was the grave so shallow, and why had it been left unmarked ? We buried him again reverently, and though he was very possibly an unpleasant person when alive, the thoughts of one of us at least, who is naturally mid-Victorian, turned to the mother who had once borne and tended him somewhere and who could so little have pictured where he would lie.

> " One midst the forest of the west
>   By a dark stream is laid;
> The Indian knows his place of rest,
>   Far in the cedar shade."
>
> MRS. HEMANS.

We discussed marking the spot, but came to the conclusion that the best way to prevent its again being disturbed was to obliterate all traces of it ; so there the nameless man rests on in his hidden grave.

The wind still being contrary, charts and sailing directions were ransacked for change of scene, and on New Year's Eve we shifted our quarters, proceeding up Krüger Channel, and anchoring in a little cove called after De Wet : as Joubert was also in the neighbourhood, officials of the Chilean Government who had surveyed the district had apparently been of pro-Boer sympathies. On January 1st, 1914, we went out into the Gulf of Peñas, only to find that it was useless to attempt to put to sea, and we returned again to Hale Cove. The *Challenger* had, we found, anchored in the same spot on New Year's Day, 1876. During the next few days Mr. Ritchie, with the help of Mr. Corry, occupied himself at my husband's request in surveying a small cove as a possible anchorage for lesser craft.

A shooting expedition also took place after kelp-geese, which are large birds about the size of Aylesbury ducks. When cruising in the launch we saw at some distance a couple of them swimming in the sea; we circled round them in the endeavour to get a shot, till we were about a hundred yards

FIG. 19.

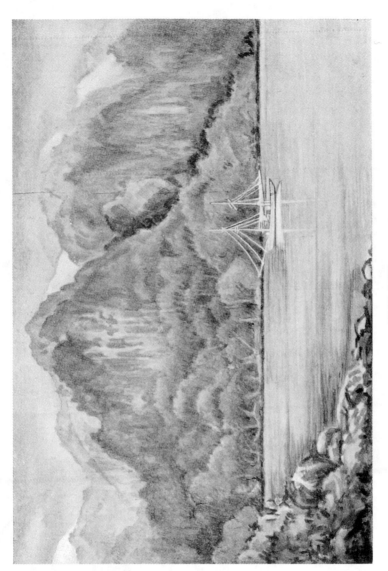

HALE COVE.

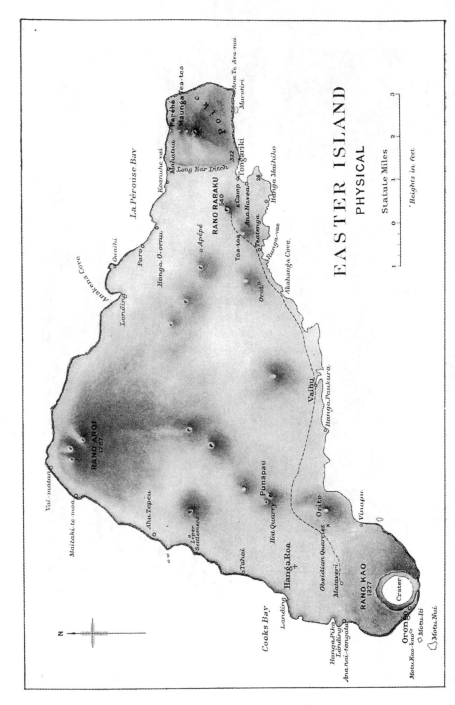

N

EASTER ISLAND
PHYSICAL

Statute Miles

Heights in Feet

Cooks Bay

La Pérouse Bay

Anakena Cove

Vai-mataa

Maitaki-te-moa

Ahu-Tepeu

Lower
Settlement

Tahai

Landing

HangaRoa

Flat Quarry

Obsidian Quarries

Mataveri

HangaPiko
Landing
Ana-rai-tongata

Motu-Kao-kao
Motu-Iti
Motu-Nui

Orongo

RANO KAO
1327

Crater

Vinapu

Orito

Punapau

RANO AROI
1767

Vaihu

Hanga Paukura

Oroi

Akahanga Cove

Runga-vae

Teretenga

Hanga Maihiko

Ildaga Maihiko

Ana Havea

Camp

RANO RARAKU
540

26

322

Tongariki

Long Ear Ditch

Koanuha vai

Ahitatua

Hanga-O-onui

Paro

Owaihi

Landing

Apepe

Toa-toa

POIKE

Parehe

Maunga Tea-tea

Ana-Te-Ava-nui

Maroriri

140A]

distant, when they took the alarm and made off. They are unable to fly, but when, as in this case, they anticipate danger scuttle along on the top of the water, lashing it up with their webbed feet. The surface was smooth as a mirror, and the boat went about seven miles an hour, but for some two miles we were unable to overhaul them. Presently they dived and separated, and on their reappearance we continued to follow one of them. During the whole of the pursuit, whenever the wobbling of the boat and the antics of the bird permitted the fore and back sights to be brought in line, a ·275 mauser bullet was sent somewhere in the neighbourhood of the fleeing object. The goose apparently came to the conclusion that the white launch, with its spluttering motor, was a peculiarly formidable sea-beast, and the safest place would be on land; he therefore went on shore, climbed up some rocks, and looked at it ; a bullet between his feet, however, unsettled his mind on the subject, and he once more took to the water, where he finally met his doom. Light, who happened to be with us, witnessed the chase with intense delight, and constantly referred to it afterwards as the most exciting recollection of the voyage. As was not astonishing in the case of such an athletic bird, no part of him proved to be eatable except his liver, which was excellent.[1]

On Tuesday, January 6th, we at last got our favourable wind and said good-bye to Hale Cove. It is the usual resort for vessels entering and leaving the channels, but we had lain there for nearly a fortnight in the height of the season without seeing a trace of a ship, a fact which shows how little these waterways are frequented. As we passed out of the Gulf of Peñas we gazed with interest on the unfriendly and barren peaks of Wager Island, where Anson's store-ship of that name was lost on May 14th, 1740, after the squadron had rounded the Horn. The members of the crew who survived the wreck, one hundred and forty-five in number, were there for five months, at the end of which time they had been reduced by about one-third, chiefly through starvation. Seventy or eighty of the remainder then took to the longboat and cutter, of whom thirty finally reached the coast of Brazil via

---

[1] "Among the birds we generally shot was a bird much larger than a goose, which we called the Racehorse, from the velocity with which it moved upon the surface of the water in a sort of half-flying, half-running motion."—*The Narrative of the Hon. John Byron*, ed. 1768, p. 50.

7

the Magellan Straits.   The rest of the survivors, a party of twenty, including the captain and an officer named Byron, a great-uncle of the poet, made their way northward, and through the aid of Indians four of them managed to reach the Spanish settlements in Chile.   The graphic account given by Byron of their surroundings on the island would be equally applicable to-day, and has already been quoted in these pages.

CHAPTER VI

CHILE

Refitting at Talcahuano—Trip to Santiago and across the Summit of
the Andes—Valparaiso—To Juan Fernandez—Typhoid on
Board—Back to Chile—Juan Fernandez again.

The principal Spanish colonies in South America were, as has been
seen, on the western side of the continent. Balbao crossed the
isthmus of Panama in 1513. In 1531 Pizarro landed in Peru, where
he encountered and overthrew the empire of the Incas. Valdivia,
one of his ablest lieutenants, made his way still further south, and
in 1541 founded Santiago, the present capital of Chile, on the fruitful
plain between the Andes and the sea. His further progress was
checked by the Araucanians, a warlike tribe of Indians, who offered
a much stronger resistance than the Incas. They were never
entirely conquered, and the Spaniards in Chile were engaged in
perpetual struggle with them, while at the same time open to attacks
on the coast from European powers who were at enmity with Spain.
When the revolutionary waves swept the continent the Chilean
patriots were at first compelled to withdraw across the Andes. The
most famous of them was Bernardo O'Higgins ; his father, originally
a bare-footed Irish boy, was one of the last viceroys of Peru, and
the son became one of the first presidents of the new republic.
Argentina had at this time accomplished her own freedom, and was
able to send help to Chile. General San Martin crossed the Andes,
and inflicted a crushing defeat on the Spaniards at Maipu in 1818.
The revolutionary army then passed north, the Viceroy evacuated
Lima, and at Guayaquil San Martin met the liberator Bolivar, who
had marched down from the north. Meanwhile Admiral Cochrane,
who had reorganised the Chilean and Peruvian navies, had been
engaged in freeing the Pacific from Spanish ships. South America
thus was finally cleared from the domination of the Spaniard.

Disputes, however, arose between the new republics as to their
respective boundaries : Chile fought Peru in 1879 over the possession
of the nitrate-fields, and issued victorious from the struggle. The
long series of difficulties between Chile and Argentina was ended,
as has been recorded, through British arbitration, in 1902.

IT is hard not to believe that the " roaring forties " have a
personality: a polytheist who goes thither in ships ought to
sacrifice to the spirit of that unquiet belt. As soon as we had
passed the magic limit of degrees the weather changed and

became beautifully balmy, and the rest of our passage was excellent. When we again came in sight of land it was in strong contrast to that which we had left, being brown, dried up, and somewhat low: all visions of snow-clad Andes had disappeared; neither here nor at Talcahuano was anything to be seen that could justify the name of a coast range. Talcahuano, the Chilean naval port, stands on a magnificently sheltered bay and was an ideal spot for our purpose of refitting. It is much to be preferred, from the shipping point of view, to the bay of Valparaiso, some 260 miles further up the coast, which lies exposed to the northerly winds and is crowded with shipping. Through the kindness of Mr. Edwards, the Chilean minister in London, a naval order had been promulgated some time before our arrival giving instructions that the Expedition was to be afforded all facilities. We accordingly met with every courtesy, and the yacht was almost at once placed in the floating dock to allow of the examination of her bottom, an essential proceeding, as it had not been overlooked, except by a diver at Punta Arenas, since we left England, now nearly twelve months ago. A floating dock consists of a huge tray, with an enormous tank on either side; when these tanks are filled with water the dock sinks, and the vessel floats on to the tray, being supported against its sides, the tanks are then emptied, and the tray rises, bearing the vessel clear out of the water; when the work is completed the process is reversed and the ship floats out once more.

After this overhauling, which took four days, came the work of examining and restowing the hold; this was expedited by all the contents being taken out and placed in a lighter alongside. It was the work of the Stewardess to check the stores in hand, and also those contained in ninety-five new packages from England which we found awaiting our arrival. On the representation of our Legation at Santiago, the Government had done us the favour to remit all duties on them except 5 per cent., which it would have required a special Act of Parliament to repeal. As some goods pay as much as 55 per cent. in customs we were greatly the gainers, in spite of the fact that an illicit levy had been taken of our butter and jam, which are among the most heavily taxed articles, to an amount equivalent to a supply of some weeks for the saloon party. We were happily able to make good the deficiency, which would otherwise have been somewhat maddening, by purchases of honey, which all down this part of the coast is good and cheap. Jam is ruinously expensive, if procurable at all, and our sympathy was extended to the skipper of an English merchant ship in the bay, whose stock was finished, but whose crew were in no way inclined to waive their Board of Trade rights, for Jack thinks potted strawberries and damsons quite as essential an article of diet as does Tommy. Our loss was less annoying, if also less amusing, than that of the owners of a lighter which was lying just outside the custom-house, and which was forcibly despoiled during the night. The thieves turned out to be the guards set by the custom-house, who apparently thinking the hours of darkness long had contrived thus to pass the time. We told this story to one of the inhabitants of another South American port. "Ah, yes," he said drily, "the custom-house here has now a bright electric light; it makes it easier for them to take out the nails without hurting their fingers."

We were now nearing the end of our outward voyage, and the provisions had to be divided between the respective sea and land parties. Easter Island affords no good anchorage, and our plan was that the yacht, after disembarking the scientific members and waiting awhile off the coast, should return to Talcahuano under charge of Mr. Gillam, to collect letters and goods and then come out again to the island. The stores, therefore, had to be divided into four lots, with much arithmetical calculation: firstly, the portion needed by the whole Expedition for the voyage out, which was expected to last about a month; secondly, that for the shore party for a period of six months; thirdly, a share for the crew alone for four months; and, fourthly, the remainder which was to be left at Talcahuano and gathered up later. The island allotment was the most difficult, as we had only a general idea of what it would be possible to procure on shore.

It was altogether, as will be seen, a considerable work, and we were hard at it for a fortnight, during which time, with the exception of two shopping expeditions to the neighbouring city of Concepcion, we had little opportunity to see the surrounding country. It felt at any rate dry and warm, in fact well aired, after the damp of the Patagonian Channels, and might have been even adjudged too dry and dusty. The most refreshing sight was a little garden which adjoined the custom-house steps, at which we landed almost daily, and which, in spite of difficulties, was invariably bright with geraniums and other flowers : Chile is much more a country of gardens, in the English sense, than any other land it has been my lot to visit. Talcahuano has about 13,000 inhabitants, and consists of little beside the dockyard, in which the chief posts are filled by Englishmen. Three English officers are also lent in peace time by our own navy to that of Chile; one of these, with whom we happened to have mutual acquaintances, was kind enough to entertain us on board the Chilean warship, whose name, being translated, was *Commander Pratt.*

A point anxiously debated at the moment, and not without some practical interest for us, was whether Chile could afford to keep the Dreadnoughts which were being built for her by Messrs. Armstrong. There was a financial crisis at the time, and the exchange was much against Chile; hence firms there which owed money to England were delaying meeting their liabilities, with the result that more than one English company had failed in consequence. The sale of a Dreadnought would of course greatly affect the rate ; even without that before we left the country it had materially risen, and the value received for a sovereign was, from our point of view, regrettably diminished.

An Englishman feels distinctly more at home in Chile than in either Brazil or Argentina. Some of the best-known firms are genuinely English, though the possession of an English name is in itself no guarantee of more than a remote British origin : a Mr. Brown may, for instance, marry a Miss Thompson, and neither be able to speak the English tongue.[1] Our language is the only one taught free in the schools ; it is presumably the most useful from the point of view of trade with ourselves and the United States. One of our countrymen resident in the Republic explained to us that " the Chileans hate all foreigners, but they hate the British rather less than the others." Those at least were our recorded impressions at this time ; on the subsequent visit of the yacht, after war broke out, the German influence was strong enough to affect her position adversely in the way of work and stores.

[1] Some of the Chileans with British names are said to be descended from the officers and men under command of Lord Cochrane.

At last the provision lists were finished and we felt entitled to take a holiday, leaving the remainder of the work on the ship in the competent hands of Mr. Gillam ; our special objects were to see the Easter Island collection in the museum at Santiago and get a glimpse of the Trans-Andine Railway. This part of our journeyings has nothing to do with the voyage of the *Mana*, and accounts of the ground covered have been given by much abler hands, notably by Lord Bryce in his *Impressions of South America*; it shall therefore be told in outline only. We left Talcahuano by the tri-weekly day express for Santiago; it took twelve hours to travel about 350 miles, but the Pullman car was luxurious, and we were able to see the country well. The line passes northward through the long fruitful plain between the Andes and the coast range, which constitutes the land of Chile, and crosses continually the streams which traverse it on their course from the mountains to the sea. The train stops from time to time at cheerful little towns, and finally at Santiago, which is a most attractive city, with a sense of quiet and yet cheerful dignity. There are but few streets at the end of which it is not possible to obtain a glimpse of the surrounding mountains, but they were scarcely either as near or impressive as descriptions had led us to expect.

The first night of our residence in the capital we experienced an earthquake. I was already asleep when about 10.30 I was awakened by the shock; the light when turned on showed the chandeliers and pictures swinging in opposite directions, and one of the latter was still oscillating when the current was switched off eight or ten minutes later. There was a slighter recurrence at 3 a.m. The shock was stated to be the worst since the great earthquake of 1906, and numbers of people had, we found, rushed out into the streets and squares. It was generally agreed that familiarity in the case of earthquakes breeds not contempt but the reverse, and that shocks of which the new-comer thinks but little, fill those who know their possibilities with nervous alarm. In this case no great damage was done; the only fatalities occurred at Talca, a little place about half-way along the line by which we had come. When we called at the Legation the next day to express our thanks to the British Minister for the trouble taken about our stores, we were shown the cracks in the walls which were the result of the previous earthquake and the fresh additions made to them the night before. We had the good fortune at Santiago to become acquainted with Sir Edward and Lady Grogan. Sir Edward filled the post of military attaché for six of our South American legations, and I had heard at Buenos Aires much of the work and interests of Lady Grogan. She was the almost last Englishwoman whom I met till my return to my native land two years later, when I had the pleasure of renewing the acquaintance this time in Cromwell Road in proximity to numerous bales for Serbian refugees. We visited the Museum of Antiquities, where we found the objects from Easter Island of which we were in search; and the beautiful new Museum of Fine Arts, which also contains articles from the island.

We left Santiago at noon on Saturday, January 31st, the line at first continuing northwards. The country through which we passed looked rainless and barren, and the journey was hot and tiring. The train was crowded with Saturday travellers, and purveyors of drinks and ices continually pushed their way down it, apparently finding a ready market for their wares. At the junction of Llay-Llay, the line which comes from Santiago on the south connects with that from Valparaiso on the west, and branches off also eastward over the Andes to the Argentine. Here on the platform sat rows of women with some of the delightful fruit in which Chile abounds: grapes can be bought at 5*d*. a pound and peaches and nectarines at 8*d*. or 9*d*. a dozen. The drawback, however, in the case of the two last mentioned, is that, partly owing to the exigencies of packing, the Chileans make a point of gathering and also eating them quite hard and flavourless. The conscientious British matron can scarcely see without distress children of the more prosperous classes, as young as five or six years, concluding a heavy evening meal at eight or half-past, by eating entirely unripe peaches. She ceases to wonder that infant mortality in Chile is said to be heavy.

At Llay-Llay we took the easterly line, which ascends a valley full of prosperous cultivation, till it reaches the little town of Los Andes, where the Chilean state railway ends and the Trans-Andine service begins. The two ends of this railway, the Chilean and Argentine, are in the hands of different companies, which naturally adds much to the difficulty of working the line. The trains run on alternate days in each direction. There is a comfortable hotel at Los Andes where passengers sleep the previous night in order to start the journey over the pass at 7 a.m. ; much of the revenue of the line, however, is derived, not from the passenger traffic, but from the cattle brought from the ranches of the Argentine to Chile. The Chilean company is an English one, and the manager, Mr. J. H. White, was good enough to arrange for us to travel with the French minister, who happened to be quitting Santiago, in an observation car at the end of the train ; we had, therefore, both pleasant company and most excellent views of the pass. The line winds up a valley, which grows ever narrower between precipitous mountain-sides, but as long as any green thing can find a footing the cultivation is intense ; where the incline is most steep a cog-wheel is employed. Presently every trace of vegetation is left behind, and the route enters on its grandest and wildest phase. Bleak rock-masses tower to the sky on every hand, and on their lower slopes rest masses of boulders, which have descended at some earlier stage in the world's history. When a great height has been attained a little lake is reached, which, with its colouring of gorgeous blue, resembles a perfect turquoise in a grey setting. At 10,000 feet the highest point is gained and the train enters the tunnel, which has been bored through the summit and which was opened for traffic in 1909. It here leaves Chile and issues on the Argentine side amidst similar but less striking scenery. The line now runs beneath a series of shelters for protection from snow ; they are of corrugated iron and provided with huge doors which can be closed in case of drift. The difficulties which arise in winter from such causes are very great, but at the time of our visit the snow was as a rule confined to occasional white patches near the summit of the mountains : the great peak of Aconcagua, 23,000 feet high, which was now to be seen seventeen miles to the northward, was principally remarkable for standing out as a huge white mass among its greyer fellows.

Inca Bridge is shortly reached, and here we left the train. It is somewhat astonishing to find a large and fashionable hotel in these surroundings; it is resorted to by the inhabitants of Buenos Aires when in search of cooler air or desirous of partaking of the iron waters for which the place is famous. We started at 8 o'clock next morning for the return journey, which we made by riding with mules over the part of the summit traversed by the tunnel, catching the train on the Chilean side. It is a delightful and easy expedition, which can be thoroughly recommended. The road runs at first parallel to the line, and when it leaves the valley rises by gradual zigzags: our guide dispensed with all corners by means of short cuts, but even so the ascent was not strenuous. As we mounted higher and higher the corrugated iron railway shelters looked like long, headless, grey caterpillars crawling along the valley beneath. We had been warned to expect high wind, but it only became unpleasant as we reached the actual summit, along which runs the boundary between Chile and Argentina. The celebrated statue of the Christ with uplifted hands blessing both countries, which commemorates the arbitration treaty, stands on the main road a little to the east of the track by which we crossed, which was, as usual, a short cut.

The descent fully justified the impression which we had formed from the train of the superior grandeur of the Chilean side; it must be even more impressive when more snow is visible. We regained the railway in plenty of time to see the Argentine train issue from the tunnel at 2 o'clock: the travellers had left Buenos Aires on the morning of the previous day, traversed the great Argentine plains, and spent the night *en route*. If the train is delayed and arrives at the summit too late to be conveyed down before dark, the Chilean officials refuse to take it over, as the descent would be too dangerous; the passengers under such circumstances have to spend the night in their carriages or find such hotel accommodation as is possible. They were indeed, as we saw then, a cosmopolitan crowd; the languages of France, Germany and Spain, also English, of both the European and American variety, were all being spoken in the crowded carriage in which we found places. Our nearest neighbours were two young couples from the United States, evidently making the journey for the first time; as we began the descent through the very finest part of the scenery, they produced packs of cards and became engrossed in a game of auction bridge. This is one of the things which must be seen to be believed, but we were subsequently told it was by no means a unique instance. We arrived at Los Andes, hot and dusty after our early start and long day, to find ourselves carried off to the manager's house and most kindly welcomed by Mrs. and Miss White to a refreshing tea amid the delight of a cool veranda and beautiful garden.

Next day we left for Valparaiso, retracing our steps as far as the junction of Llay-Llay, and then traversing the coast range. The huge bay of Valparaiso, filled with shipping, is an imposing sight, and the town climbs picturesquely up the mountains which surround it ; the higher parts are residential, and are reached by elevators, which are stationed at intervals in the main street, which runs parallel to the harbour. On the lower level there are well-built offices of leading firms, shipping lines, and banks, which give a pleasant sensation of wide interest and touch with the great world. Nevertheless, Valparaiso is scarcely as fine a city architecturally as would be expected from its importance, nor is the hotel accommodation worthy of a first-class port. Its inhabitants cheerily endorse the opinion of a visitor who is reported to have said, " There is one word only for Valparaiso, and that is ' shabby.' " The city has, however, profited through the rebuilding necessitated by the earthquake, and the improvement of the harbour and other works were in progress. The earthquake is still a very present memory ; one resident showed us the spot where one of his servants, escaping from the house at the same time as himself, was killed by falling masonry.

We called on Messrs. Williamson & Balfour ; the firm have a financial interest in Easter Island, and it was through their kind permission that we were visiting it. We saw Mr. Hope-Simpson, one of the managing partners; his power and expedition filled us with grateful awe. He sat at the end of a telephone and appeared to put through in a few minutes all our arrangements, whether with the Government, shipping, or docks, which would have taken us many days of weary trudging about the city to accomplish. I have often thought of that morning when confronted with the appalling delays in public offices at home. We were introduced by him to Señor Merlet, the chairman of the company for the Exploitation of Easter Island, who are the direct lessees; he had been there himself and was kind enough to give us all information in his power.

We returned to Talcahuano by sea as the easiest method. There were a few more days of preparation, and on Friday, February 13th, a date subsequently noted by the superstitious,

we were at length ready to depart. As the last things were
hurried on board it recalled our departure from Falmouth: this
time the deck had to accommodate paraffin tins full of cement
to make a dock for Mr. Ritchie's tidal observations; the passage
had to find room for a table for survey purposes; rolls of wire
for excavation sieves were strapped beneath beams of the saloon ;
while on the top of one was fastened a row of portentous jars,
the object of which was to hold the acid from the batteries when
we left the ship, as the electrical gear would be dismantled when
the engineer came on shore in his capacity of photographer.
Two zinc baths for laundry work in camp were looked at ruefully ;
there seemed to be no place for them in heaven or earth, certainly
not on *Mana*. But half our heavy task of stowage was accomplished when we were out of Talcahuano Harbour, the boat
began to roll prodigiously, and the work was finished somehow
with astonishing rapidity.

The next day found us all confined to our cabins, having,
after our time on land, temporarily lost our sea legs. By Sunday
we began to feel better, except Mr. Corry, who had a slight temperature and complained of feeling unwell. When on Monday we
arrived at Juan Fernandez, S. was down with dysentery and a
temperature of 103°, while Mr. Corry's rose, to our alarm, to
104° ; Tuesday and Wednesday he was still in high fever, and
by Wednesday evening it was obviously useless to hope that
his illness was either influenza or malaria: there was nothing
to be done but to act on the third possibility and assume that
it was typhoid fever ; we therefore turned the ship round and
ran for Valparaiso. The prospect of the passage back was
hardly cheerful ; I was out certainly for fresh experiences, but
not for the responsibility of nursing typhoid and dysentery at
the same time in a small boat in mid-Pacific. Each twelve hours,
however, was got through somehow, and better on the whole
than might have been expected. S. happily improved, and our
poor geologist himself was wonderfully cheerful and plucky ;
the sea was kind to us, and we reached Valparaiso on Sunday
morning with our invalid in a condition which we felt did us
credit. The difficulties of arriving in port with illness on board
proved to be not so great as I, at any rate, had feared ; the
authorities were most kind in allowing us to haul down our
yellow flag almost at once, and taking us to a Government

anchorage. The harbour doctor was found to give the necessary authority for landing a sick man, while arrangements were made with the hospital for a stretcher and ambulance, and by the middle of the afternoon the patient was comfortably on shore and in bed. The British hospital at Valparaiso is new, reserved almost entirely for paying patients, and much surpasses in comfort anything that we have either of us seen in England. Our diagnosis unfortunately proved to be accurate, but we had the comfort of knowing that the illness was well understood, as typhoid is, it appeared, very common in South America, especially among new-comers. It had been obviously contracted during the time at Talcahuano, when both Mr. Corry and Mr. Ritchie had had frequent meals on shore.

We waited in port for a week, communicating by cable with the friends of our patient, and then held a council of war. The doctor gave it as his opinion that there was no reason for delay, and it was obviously impossible in such an illness to wait pending recovery. We had, however, to face the position that there was a chance, although a slight one, of other cases occurring on board ; hospital records show a percentage of about 3 per cent. of doctors and nurses infected by patients, and of course our precautions had, through circumstances, been neither so timely nor so thorough ; with 2,000 miles of Pacific before us we felt that we could take no risk. On the other hand, we had no wish for further experiences in hanging about in South American ports, more especially as smallpox was at this time raging at Valparaiso. We therefore decided that we would run back again to Juan Fernandez, and put in a few days in a sort of quarantine, before finally leaving for our destination.

The episode was most disappointing for all concerned ; nevertheless our prevailing feeling was one of thankfulness both for the sufferer and ourselves, that, if the thing had to be, the illness had declared itself while we were still within reach of help ; the thought that we were within measurable distance of having a case of typhoid on Easter Island still makes us shudder. Hopes were cherished for a while that it might be possible for our geologist to join us, either when *Mana* returned or by the Chilean naval training ship, which it was said might shortly visit the island. Unfortunately the case proved not only severe, but was prolonged by relapses, and on recovery the doctor forbade any such roughing it. Mr. Corry therefore went back to England, from whence he sent us a report on the geology of the Patagonian Channels, and such information as he had gathered on the moot question of the submergence of a Pacific continent. When war broke out he was among the first to join His Majesty's forces, and, alas! laid down his life for his country in September 1915. When on our return to London my husband addressed the Geological Society on the results of the Expedition, our thoughts naturally turned with sadness to the one who, under other circumstances, should have had that honour; I sat next to one of the older Fellows, and he expressed his special sorrow at the scientific loss caused by the early death of our colleague. "Corry was," he said, "quite one of the most promising of the younger men in the geological world."

FIG. 20.—JUAN FERNANDEZ: AN IMPRESSION.

CHAPTER VII

JUAN FERNANDEZ

Juan Fernandez was discovered by the navigator of that name on a voyage from Peru to Chile in 1512. He rightly judged that the southerly wind, which impeded all navigation in that direction, might be adjacent only to the mainland ; he therefore stood out to the west in the hope of avoiding it, and so came across the island. His voyage was so short that he was accused of witchcraft, and suffered accordingly at the hands of the Inquisition ; he was rescued from its power by the Jesuits, to whom he ceded his rights in the newly discovered land. The Order founded a colony there, but it proved a failure. The abandoned island then became the resort of the buccaneers, who preyed on Spanish commerce, and who used it to refit their vessels, so that Spanish merchantmen had special orders to avoid it. The privateers turned down goats to provide meat, on which the Spaniards imported dogs to kill the goats ; these achieved their purpose on the low ground, but in the hills the goats held their own, and the battle was therefore a drawn one. It was from an English privateer that the Scotsman, Alexander Selkirk, was landed in 1704 ; while some of the incidents in the life of Robinson Crusoe, such as those connected with the goats, rats, and cats, were taken by Defoe from the experiences of Selkirk, he is, if looked upon as the prototype of the immortal hero, somewhat of a fraud. Not only is the scene of Crusoe's adventures laid in the West Indies, but Selkirk was put on shore at his own request, with such stores as he required, because he had an objection to the captain. He knew that sooner or later the place would be visited by some ship coming to refit, and he was only there altogether four years and four months. Selkirk reported that he had slit the ears of some of the goats and let them go ; a number of these animals so marked and of " venerable aspect " were found in 1741 by Anson's sailors when they arrived on the island after their passage of the Horn.

Anson's own ship, the *Centurion*, lay in Cumberland Bay for three

months, during which time two others of the squadron and the
victualler arrived at the rendezvous ; the *Gloucester* had a terrible
experience, being a month within sight of the island with her men
dying daily of scurvy, and unable through contrary winds to make
the anchorage.   The crews of the three men-of-war had numbered
on their departure from England 961 : only 335 of these were alive
when they left Fernandez.   The state of affairs is less surprising
considering that Anson was obliged to take a large consignment of
Chelsea pensioners ; the almost incredible age of some of the company
comes out incidentally in the statement that owing to scurvy the
wound of one man reopened which had been received in the battle
of the Boyne fifty years before.[1]   The island was subsequently
occupied by the Spanish, and after the independence of Chile it was
for a while used as a convict settlement.

OUR time in " quarantine " at Juan Fernandez proved most
enjoyable. We lay in Cumberland Bay, which is the only
anchorage ; being on the north side, it is sheltered from the south-
east trade wind. The island is volcanic, but the actual craters
have broken down in course of ages, and their form can no longer
be traced, at least by the superficial observer ; it is now a mass
of mountains of striking shapes, interspersed with wooded ravines.
We were able to see certain portions, mounted on ponies, but
much of the ground must be impossible to traverse. S. had a
day's goat-stalking, but saw only two animals, and those were
out of rifle shot ; the ponies, he said, scrambled about like cats,
putting their fore feet on the higher rocks and so dragging themselves up. The cattle which roam over the island are not infrequently killed by falling down the precipices. Our meat orders
were executed by four men in a boat armed with rifles, who went
round by sea to some spot where the beasts were likely to be
found, and having shot one cut it up and brought it back. The
result was rather a plethora of Sunday beef even for a yacht's
hungry crew.

A spot known as Selkirk's Look-out (fig. 20B), on the dividing
ridge of the island, commands glorious views of the other
side and the adjacent island of Santa Clara ; to gaze down
from the wooded heights on to the panorama of sea and
land 2,000 feet below seemed like a glimpse into an enchanted
land. The tablet which marks the spot was put up by H.M.S.
Topaze in 1868. We also visited a cave (D) which tradition points
out as Selkirk's first residence, rowing in the boat round cliffs

---

[1] See *Anson's Voyage Round the World*, quarto ed., 1748, p. 102

FIG. 21.

CUMBERLAND BAY, JUAN FERNANDEZ.

FIG. 22.

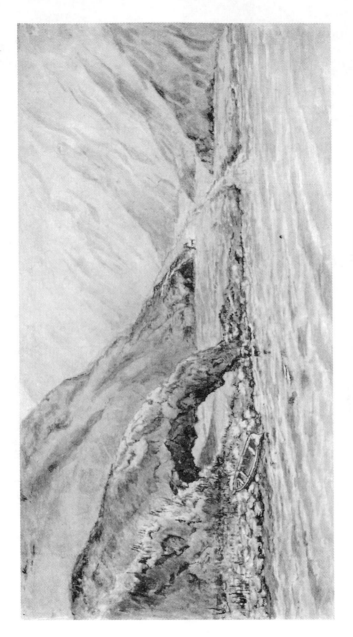

SELKIRK'S CAVE, JUAN FERNANDEZ.

113]

so steep that a stone dropped from the top would fall more than 1,000 feet clear into the sea ; flights of pigeons wheeled out from the rocks, looked at us, and went away again. The landing-place for the cave is somewhat dangerous from the view of safety to the ship's boats, being in a cove whose beach is composed of big boulders. Once on shore the way lies through a mountain-spur on the right, which has been worn by the force of the waves into an imposing natural arch. It leads on to a little lawn at the end of a valley running up into the mountains, down which flows a small stream. In the hillside is the cave opening on to the meadow and looking out to sea ; the fireplace is visible, also a shelf cut in the rock and niches to hold utensils. A prominent feature near the anchorage are six or eight large caves (c), like big halls, the roofs of which are adorned with drooping ferns, giving the effect of a beautiful greenhouse: if originally natural they have probably been much enlarged. They are said to have been used by the Spaniards for their prisoners. Someone had been digging in the floor for treasure, under the assumption that it had been left by pirates, presumably of an earlier day.

Juan Fernandez has at present some 300 inhabitants; its industry is lobster-canning. Lobsters are also taken alive in the tank of a motor-schooner to Valparaiso, their value growing *en route* from 2*d*. each in the island to 3*s*. 9*d*. in the city. The schooner was also the mail-carrier, and we took a mutual and friendly interest in one another, as she and *Mana* were about the same size. An old gentleman was in charge of the island as governor, supported by four gendarmes; serious offenders are exported to the mainland. The means of communication will shortly be more rapid, as a house was already built to be used for wireless installation (A).

On March 9th, 1915, one year precisely from the date we left the island, the German ship *Dresden* arrived in Cumberland Bay. She had been driven by want of coal out of her hiding-places in the southern channels and sought refuge at Juan Fernandez. Here after five days she was found by the *Glasgow* with her flag still flying. She had many times broken neutrality regulations, and the Chilean governor with his gendarmes could scarcely, as will have been seen, be expected to intern her. The *Glasgow* fired, the *Dresden* replied, tried to negotiate, and then

8

blew herself up.   The crew had all been landed, and the officers were conveyed to Chile with the mails and lobsters.   Thus in the twentieth century did Fernandez once again play its part as a place of resort in time of war.

After five days, no illness having appeared, we felt we might with safety depart, and we started therefore on our 2,000-mile voyage, the last stage of the outward journey.

CHAPTER VIII

LIFE ON BOARD

THIS is perhaps as good a time as any to attempt to give a general impression of life on board the yacht. In the first place it should be realised that no hardship was involved, and that the sense of safety, so far from being less, soon became infinitely greater than on a larger ship. Not only does a small boat ride over the waves like a cork, but there is the assurance that in case of accident everyone will know what to do, and orders will be received without delay ; there is plenty of room in the boats, and the lowering away is known to be a comparatively easy matter. On first going on board a big liner after being accustomed to *Mana*, it felt an alarmingly dangerous means of transit.

Existence on any ship has drawbacks in bad weather or extreme heat, but on the yacht the arrangement by which the saloon and cabins were connected with the deck-house made the circulation of air particularly good. A sailing ship is also without the universal and unpleasant draughts which are omnipresent in a steamer. In regard to the pleasure of movement there is of course no comparison between the two.

As to the food there cannot be the same variety where no refrigerators are possible, and preserved and salt meats are apt to become monotonous, but we always left port with as large a supply of fresh meat as possible, and a few hens and sometimes a sheep. Preserved vegetables are good, and potatoes could be carried throughout a voyage, also eggs, and some fruit such as bananas. With but few exceptions, in very bad weather, we had bread every day in the cabin and twice a week in the forecastle. The crew much preferred tinned milk and declined fresh even when it was available, and for the saloon the unsweetened variety was quite pleasant. In all other respects the meals were such as would obtain in any simple household at home.

The routine of ship's life turns on the watches, the alternate four hours on and four hours off of the crew. Only in case of urgency is it permissible to call the watch below, and hence any deck work, such as altering or shortening sails, when it is not immediately imperative, waits for the changes of the watch at 8, 12, and at 4, when all the crew are available; those also are meal hours for the forecastle, with which those of the cabin must not clash. The afternoon or dog watches are of two hours only, from 4 to 6 and 6 to 8, in order to secure that the same hours are not kept on two consecutive days by the same members of the crew. It is a strange life from the point of view of the landsman, especially in its bearing on the hours of sleep: eight hours on and eight hours off duty would have seemed preferable, but it is the general rule throughout the merchant service, and the men are accustomed to it.

My own daily round began with ordinary domestic duties, which were seldom accomplished before 11 o'clock. On Saturday the work took even longer, as, in addition to the usual business of life, the weekly stores were given out to the forecastle, and fresh boxes of provisions were fetched up from below and decanted into tins for shelves; if weather permitted the main hold was opened. Not only do a marvellous number of small things need attention on a boat, but every action takes much longer, owing to the constant movement of the vessel; each article, for example, has to be put down so that it cannot be overthrown by a sudden lurch. To my friends who were anxious as to what we did for exercise, I replied that to give out stores in a rolling boat, in imminent danger of having the whole contents of a shelf thrown at one's head, was an acrobatic performance which involved sufficient activity to last the twenty-four hours. The same is also true in degree of every muscular movement, so that the need was rarely felt for such artificial exercise as deck promenades. This was as well, for as both the lifeboat and cutter were carried in the waist of the ship when we were at sea, the space available for "constitutionals" was prescribed.

On certain passages when such a precaution seemed desirable, as for instance in crossing the Doldrums, the supply of water was rationed; a gallon per man per day is the allowance, of which the cook took the morning quota, or half of the whole amount; in the afternoon everyone produced a quart tin to be filled (about a fair-sized hot-water can), and this was the private reserve for washing and drinking. It is wonderful what can be done with it, and to use a full basin of water for the washing of hands and then throw it away seems even to-day wicked waste ; the Stewardess was given a double supply, and found it more than necessary. A new form of philanthropy came into play, when one member might be overheard saying to another, "Can I let you have some of my savings, I am really quite well off," the savings being *aqua pura*. When rain came every available utensil was utilised to catch it, and we all suddenly became millionaires. It must be borne in mind that for many things, such as bathing and scrubbing down, there was an unlimited supply of salt water, and a " salt-water soap " proved a great success.

When the household duties were over for the time being, the favourite resort, if the weather was bad or very hot, was in the deck-house, otherwise it was the after end or poop of the ship. This space, which was that above the chart-room, and of course the place of the helm, was raised as in old-fashioned ships, so that it was almost always dry even if the waist of the ship was slightly awash. There was no need, nor indeed space, for chairs ; cushions on the deck made satisfactory seats with the steering-gear casing for a back, or in stormy weather on the top of the box, with a rope to cling to if necessary. The position had to be changed of course from time to time if the vessel went over on the other tack.

A certain amount of writing and reading was accomplished, but not so much as had been expected, for any considerable roll made them a strain on the eyesight ; a monumental piece of embroidery, which was to have commemorated the voyage, was brought back practically untouched. Even when no fixed occupation was possible the hours evaporated marvellously, and for the first time on a voyage it was a pleasure to see the hands of the clock put back. There was usually something to observe going on on deck, and the speed at which the vessel was travelling was a perennial source of interest : four miles an hour was fair, six was good, and anything over eight was exciting. The speed was checked every watch by means of the patent log, a mechanical screw which trailed behind the vessel and whose evolutions registered its rapidity ; its reckoning, however, became more than once somewhat surprising, owing to the sharks which mistook it for something good to eat, and its bright copper surface was accordingly painted black. We once nearly secured a baby shark, which could be seen clearly in the green water following the salt meat which was being soaked by being towed overboard; the usual little pilot-fish was in attendance. It took a bait, but got away with the hook just as it was being hauled over the rail. This was almost the nearest we came to success in fishing from the deck, in which we were uniformly unfortunate, in spite of the fact that all on board were fishermen and the crew were professionals. Passing bird and marine life were frequently of interest. Above all the ever-changing ocean was an immediate neighbour, always claiming attention, whether it bore a calm blue surface, on which was traced the white line of the vessel's course, or resolved itself into a grey mass of tumbling billows, ever trying to break and again falling back, leaving little white crests to mark their vain attempt. It is presumably from this lazy frame of mind on the old sailing vessels that the idea arose of a voyage as a cure for overwrought nerves; the present mail steamer, with its hurly-burly of strangers, noisy children, deck sports, and sweeps on the log may or may not be a place of entertainment—it can hardly be considered one of rest.

When the ship's bell sounded eight bells, or noon, all the hands which could be spared went below to their dinner, a wonderful stillness reigned, and the deck was devoted to the solemn ceremonies of navigation. Three figures, those of the Navigating Lieutenant, the Sailing-master, and frequently that of S., might be seen balanced in various attitudes, sextant in hand, endeavouring to shoot the sun. The most exciting moment of the twenty-four hours was when the paper was handed in which stated the exact position of the vessel, and the amount she had done on her course in the last twenty-four hours. It was naturally preluded by guesses as to what the result would be, those who had kept themselves informed of the records of the patent log having an undue advantage.

The hours between luncheon and tea time were largely devoted to slumber, and the ship was kept as quiet as possible in order not to disturb the men who had kept the middle watch the preceding night; their rest was apparently much more affected by noise than is generally presumed to be the case with non-brain workers. The same sound varies in its effect on different persons; when it was necessary to use the engine the Sailing-master complained that he could never sleep with that " unnatural noise " going on. He altogether refused to allow that its regular beat might be considered less distracting than the spasmodic jibing of the ship, with its inevitable accompaniment of shouting of orders, stamping, and hauling of ropes ; those he maintained were absolutely " natural " sounds. This recalls the attitude of the cook to cabbage day, which, though beloved of the men, is, under certain conditions of the elements, the reverse of pleasant to others on a small vessel, so much so that on many yachts its recurrence is restricted by the ship's articles ; *Mana's* cook was of the opinion that the smell was " rather nice "; he evidently considered it a " natural " odour, which perhaps on the whole was fortunate.

The most pleasant time of all on deck was after tea; it was then cool, with the almost daily spectacle of a magnificent sunset. Sometimes the sinking globe went down amid a glory of clouds, which turned the sea into a blaze of red and gold; at others its descent could be traced inch by inch as the ball of fire sank below the horizon on its road to other lands, leaving behind it a track of light across the still waters. One evening in the Pacific the whole sky, east as well as west, was covered with pink clouds, which found their counterpart in the water below. It is at times such as sunset, when sky and sea form a joint panorama, that the dweller on the water truly comes into his own. In ordinary circumstances, contrary to what might be expected, the ocean appeals less to the imagination when seen from shipboard than when viewed from the land; without foreground or counterbalancing element its restless infinity seems bewildering to the comprehension. But when at sea the sky takes up the tale; then the waters below and the firmament above each find in the other their perfect complement and expression.

As soon as twilight reigned the gazer was recalled to the work-a-day world; the navigator came up from the chart-room to take the ship's position by the evening star, the junior member of the watch clambered up the fore-rigging to hang out the ship's lights, and so night fell.

One of the charms of a ship is that she never sleeps. In the hours of darkness the ordinary habitation relapses to a state of coma, and to the mental condition of the primitive jelly-fish; a vessel is always alive, always intelligent.   The larger the craft, the more the vital functions are withdrawn from the common gaze; in a small yacht they are always visible as an inseparable part of the whole.   In wakeful nights and from hot cabins, it is only necessary to stumble up the companion to find the cool freshness of deck and waking companionship.   Silhouetted against the sky, is the dark figure of the man at the wheel, somewhere in the gloom is the officer in charge, and for'ard, though invisible, is the watch on the look-out. The latest news of wind and progress are to be had for the asking; it is full of mystery and yet reassuringly practical.

The night *Mana* crossed the Equator is unforgettable; the yacht, borne along by the newly caught trade wind, raced through the water with the very poetry of motion.   The full moon made a silver pathway over the sea and lit up not only the foam from the vessel's bows, but also her white sails, which were faintly reflected in the dark sea; the masts and rigging stood out black against the deep blue sky, while over all was the Southern Cross.   What has been said of sunset from shipboard is still more true of moonlight and star-light nights.   Then ocean and sky become a whole of marvellous beauty, and of majesty beyond human ken ; always suggesting questions, always refusing the answer.

PART II
EASTER ISLAND

EASTER ISLAN

FIG. 23.

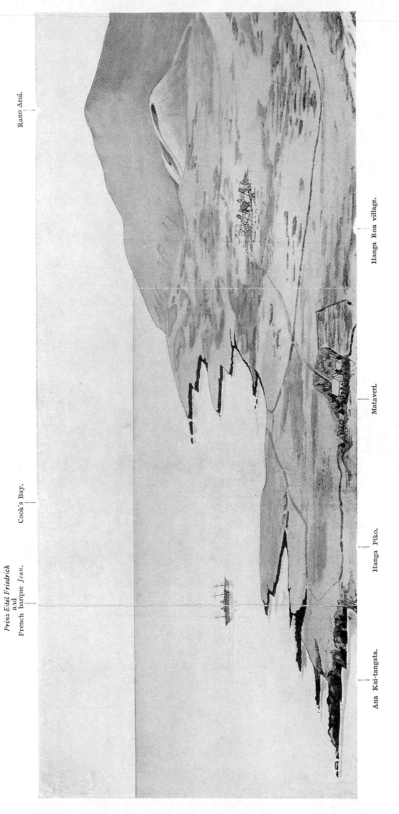

Rano Aroi.

Hanga Roa village.

Mataveri.

Cook's Bay.

Hanga Piko.

Prins Eitel Friedrich
and
French barque *Jean*.

Ana Kai-tangata.

FIG. 24.

Punapau, with broken crater.
(Hat Quarry further side
not visible.)

Eastern Headland.
        | Rano Raraku.

Orito.

Foreground, Rano Kao.

EASTER ISLAND.

Diagrammatic sketch from Rano Kao looking north and east.

Christmas Day, 1914.

GLOSSARY

OF NATIVE WORDS FREQUENTLY EMPLOYED

Ahu . A burial place
Aku-aku . Spirit
Ana . Cave
Ao . . The clan or clans celebrating bird rites
Ao . . A ceremonial paddle
Ariki . Chief
Atua . God

Hanga . Bay or foreshore
Haré . House
Hau . Hat
Hopu . Servant to fetch " First egg "

Iti . . Small
Ika . Fish
Ivi-atua . Person supernaturally gifted

Kai . Eat
Kaunga . Function in honour of a mother
Ko . . Definite article before proper nouns
Kohau rongo-rongo . Tablet with script
Koro . Function in honour of a father

Marama . Light (In Tahitian = moon)
Manu . Bird
Manu-tara The sacred bird (Sooty Tern)
Máta . Clan or group

Mataa . Obsidian spear-head
Maunga . Hill
Miro . Wood
Moai . An image
Motu . Islet

Nui . Big

Paina . A wooden figure, also the function connected with it
Péra . Taboo for the dead
Poki . A child
Raa . Sun
Ranga . Captivity
Rano . Crater lake, also the extinct volcano
Rapa . Small dancing-paddle
Roa . Long
Rongo-rongo Sacred words
Také . Ceremonial retreat
Tangata . Man
Tangata-ika A slain man
Tangata manu . The bird-man
Tangata rongo-rongo . Man learned in sacred words (generally the script)
Tatane . Spirit (from " Satan ")
Te . . Definite article before common noun
Tea . White

Words such as *nui, iti,* and *roa,* when they have become in themselves geographical names, are treated as proper nouns, otherwise as adjectives.

123

CHAPTER IX

ARRIVAL AT EASTER ISLAND

1722 .	.	Discovered by the Dutch Admiral Roggeveen.
1770 .	.	Visited by the Spaniards under Gonzalez.
1774 .	.	Visited by the English under Cook.
1786 .	.	Visited by the French under La Pérouse.
		Receives occasional visits from passing ships.
1862 Dec.	.	Peruvian slave-raiders carry off many inhabitants.
1864 Jan.	.	Arrival of first missionary from Valparaiso.
1867 (cir.)	.	Commercial exploitation begins — arrival of M. Dutrou Bornier from Tahiti.
1868 .	.	Visit of H.M.S. *Topaze*—removal of statues now in British Museum.
1888 .	.	Visit of U.S.A. warship *Mohican*.
1888 .	.	Chilean Government takes possession.
1897 .	.	Mr. Merlet of Valparaiso leases the greater part of the island, and subsequently forms a company for the " Exploitation of Easter Island."

For further historical details, see below, pp. 200–10.

EASTER Island at last ! It was in the misty dawn of Sunday, March 29th, 1914, that we first saw our destination, just one week in the year earlier than the Easter Day it was sighted by Roggeveen and his company of Dutchmen. We had been twenty days at sea since leaving Juan Fernandez, giving a wide berth to the few dangerous rocks which constitute Salo-y-Gomez and steering directly into the sunset. It was thirteen months since we had left Southampton, out of which time we had been 147 days under way, and here at last was our goal. As we approached the southern coast we gazed in almost awed silence at the long grey mass of land, broken into three great curves, and diversified by giant molehills (fig. 23). The whole looked an alarmingly big land in which to find hidden caves. The hush was broken by the despairing voice of Bailey, the ship's cook. " I don't know how I am to make a fire on that island, there is no wood ! " He spoke the truth; not a vestige of timber or even brushwood was to be seen. We swung round the western headland with its group of islets and dropped anchor in Cook's Bay. A few hundred yards from the shore is the village of Hanga Roa, the native name for Cook's Bay. This is the only part of the island which is inhabited, the two hundred and fifty natives, all that remain of the population, having been gathered together here in order to secure the safety of the livestock, to which the rest of the island is devoted. The yacht was soon surrounded by six or seven boat-loads of natives, clad in nondescript European garments, but wearing a head-covering of native straw, somewhat resembling in appearance the high hat of civilisation (fig. 83).

The Manager, Mr. Edmunds, shortly appeared, and to our relief, for we had not been sure how he would view such an invasion, gave us a very kind welcome. He is English, and was, to all intent, at the time of our arrival, the only white man on the island ; a French carpenter, who lived at Hanga Roa with a native wife, being always included in the village community. His house is at Mataveri (fig. 25), a spot about two miles to the south of the village, surrounded by modern plantations which are almost the only trees on the island; immediately behind it rises the swelling mass of the volcano Rano Kao. The first meal on Easter Island, taken here with Mr. Edmunds, remains a lasting memory. It was a large plain room with uncarpeted floor, scrupulously orderly; a dinner table, a few chairs, and two small book-cases formed the whole furniture. The door on to the veranda was open, for the night was hot, and the roar of breakers could be heard on the beach; while near at hand conversation was accompanied by a never-ceasing drone of mosquitoes. The light of the unshaded lamp was reflected from the clean rough-dried cloth of the table round which we sat, and lit up our host's features, the keen brown face of a man who had lived for some thirty years or more, most of it in the open air and under a tropical sun. He was telling us of events which one hardly thought existed outside magazines and books of adventure, but doing it so quietly that, with closed eyes, it might have been fancied that the entertainment was at some London restaurant, and we were still at the stage of discussing the latest play.

" This house," said our host, " was built some fifty years ago by Bornier, who was the first to exploit the island. He was murdered by the natives: they seized the moment when he was descending from a ladder; one spoke to him and another struck him down. They buried him on the hillock near the cliff just outside the plantation: you will see his grave, when the grass is not so long; it is marked by a circle of stones. A French warship arriving almost immediately afterwards, they explained that he had been killed by a fall from his horse, and this is the version still given in some of the accounts of the island, but murder will always out. After that another manager had trouble: it was over sheep-stealing. There were three or four white men here at the time, and they all rode down to the village to teach the natives a lesson, but the ponies turned restive at the sound of gun-fire, and the rifles themselves were defective, so the boot was on the other foot, and they had to retreat up here followed by the mob ; for months they lived in what was prac tically a state of siege, with one man always on guard for fear of attack.

" My latest guests were a crew of shipwrecked mariners, Americans, who landed on the island last June. A fortnight earlier the barometer here had been extraordinarily low, but we did not get much wind; further to the south, however, the gale was terrific, and the *El Dorado* was in the midst of it. The captain, who had been a whaler in his day, said that he had never seen anything approaching it, the sea was simply a seething mass of crested waves. The ship was a schooner, trading between Oregon and a Chilean port; she was a long way from land, as sailing vessels make a big semicircle to get the best wind. She had a deck load of timber, 15 feet high, which of course shifted in such a sea ; she sprang leaks in every direction, and it was obvious that she must soon break up. The crew took to their boat, not that they had much hope of saving their lives, but simply because there was nothing else to be done. They got some tins of milk and soup on board, and a box of biscuits, and a cask holding perhaps twenty gallons of water. The captain managed to secure his sextant, but when he went back for his chronometers, the chart-room was too deep in water for him to be able to reach them. They saw by the chart that the nearest land was this island: it was seven hundred miles off, and as they had no chronometer, and could take no risks, they would have to go north first in order to get their latitude, which would add on another two hundred. There was nothing for it, however, but to do the best they could ; they had more gales too, and only saved the boat from being swamped by making a sea-anchor of their blankets. The spray of course kept washing over them, and as the boat was only 20 feet long and there were eleven of them, there was no room for them to lie down. Each day they had between them a tin of the soup and one of milk, and an allowance of water, but the sea got into the water-cask and made it brackish, and before the end their sufferings from thirst were so great that one or two of them attempted to drink salt water; the mate stopped that by saying that he would shoot the first man who did it.

"After nine days they sighted this island, but then luck was against them, for the wind changed, and it was forty-eight hours, after they saw the coast, before they were able to beach the boat. They got on shore at the other end of the island, which is uninhabited. They were pretty much at the last stage of exhaustion, and their skin was in a terrible condition with salt water; their feet especially were so bad that they could hardly walk. One of them fell down again and again, but struggled on saying, 'I won't give up, I won't give up.' At last my man, who looks after the cattle over there, saw them and brought me word. The officers were put up here, you must really forgive the limitations of my wardrobe, for I had to give away nearly everything that I had in order to clothe them.

"The most curious part of the whole business was that after they had been here three or four months the captain took to the boat again. I believe that he was buying his house at home on the instalment plan, and that if he did not get in the last payment by the end of the year the whole would be forfeited; anyway, as soon as the fine weather came on he had out the boat and patched her up. He got two of his men to go with him. I lent him a watch for navigation purposes, and we did all we could for him in the way of food; there were no matches on the island, so he learnt how to make fire with two pieces of wood native fashion. Anyway, off he started last October for Mangareva, sixteen hundred miles from here; he must have got there safely, for you brought me an answer to a letter that I gave him to post.[1]

[1] Captain Benson and his crew made the voyage in the ship's boat to Mangareva in sixteen days, and after two days there left in the same manner for Tahiti, accomplishing the further nine hundred miles in eleven days. Mr. Richards, the British Consul at the latter place, told us later of his astonishment, when, in answer to his question whence the crew had come, he received the amazing reply, "Easter Island." For the whole account see *Captain Benson's Own Story* (The James H. Barry Co., San Francisco).

But," and here for the first time the eyes of our host grew animated, and he raised his voice slightly, " it is maddening to think of that cargo drifting about in the Pacific. I do trust that next time a ship breaks up with a deck-load of timber, she will have at least the commonsense to do so near Easter Island." Then, after a pause, " I wish you no ill, but the yacht would make a splendid wreck."

We kept *Mana* for nearly two months while learning our new surroundings. Not only were we anxious to find if we had the necessary camp gear and stores, but we were engaged in agonised endeavours to foresee the details of excavation and research, in case essential tools or equipment had been forgotten, which the yacht could fetch from Chile. The time, however, arrived when she must go. Mr. Ritchie was now on shore with us for survey work, but as his service with the Expedition was limited, the vessel had to return in time to take him back to civilisation by the correct date. Mr. Gillam had from this time sole charge of the navigation of *Mana*. Instructions for him had to be written, and correspondence grappled with ; business letters, epistles for friends, and reports to Societies were hurriedly dealt with ; and an article which had been promised to the *Spectator*, " First Impressions of Easter Island," was written in my tent, by the light of a hurricane-lamp, during the small hours of more than one morning.

When the mail-bag was finally sealed, there was great difficulty in getting hold of *Mana*. The position of a skipper of a boat off Easter Island, unless she has strong steam-power, is not a happy one. Mr. Gillam used to lie in his berth at Cook's Bay hearing the waves break on the jagged reaches of lava, and the longer he listened the less he liked it. The instant that the wind shows signs of going to the west, a ship must clear out. It is reported that on one occasion there were some anxious moments on board: a sudden change of wind and tide were setting the yacht steadily on the rocks ; the engineer was below in the engine-room, and Mr. Gillam shouted to him down the hatchway, " If you can't make that motor of yours go round in three minutes, you will know whether there is a God or not."

To get in touch with the yacht was like a game of hide-and-seek, for often by the time those on shore arrived at one side of

FIG. 25.

MANAGER'S HOUSE, MATAVERI.

Supported by foundation-stones of old native houses.

the island, the wind had shifted, and she had run round to the other. She was on the north coast when we managed to catch her, and to get back to Mataveri necessitated retracing our steps, as will be seen from the map, over the high central ground of the island, and down on the other side ; the track was rough, and the ride would ordinarily take from two to three hours. It was 4 p.m. before all work was done on board, the good-byes said, and we were put on shore ; the sandy cove, the horses and men, with *Mana* in the offing, formed a delightful picture in the evening light, but there the charms of the situation ended. There was only one pack-horse, and a formidable body of last collections sat looking at us in a pile on the grass. In addition we had not, in the general pressure, sufficiently taken into account that we were bringing off the engineer, now to be turned into photographer ; there he was, and not he alone but his goods and bedding. The sun set at five o'clock, and it would be dark at half-past five; it seemed hopeless to get back that night.

A neighbouring cave was first investigated as a possible abiding-place, but proved full of undesirable inhabitants, so everyone set to work and the amount stowed on that wretched pack-horse was wonderful. Then each attendant was slung round with some remaining object, S. took the additional member on his pony, and off we set. Before we got to the highest point all daylight had gone, and there was only just enough starlight to keep to the narrow track by each man following a dim vision of the one immediately in front. My own beast had been chosen as " so safe " that it was most difficult to keep him up with the others, let alone on his four legs. The pack-horse, too, began pointing out that he was not enjoying the journey; the load was readjusted more than once, but when we were on the down grade again he came to a full stop and we all dismounted. There in the creepy darkness we had a most weird picnic ; not far off was a burial-place, with a row of fallen statues, while the only light save that of the stars was the striking of an occasional match. S. produced a tin of meat, which he had brought from the yacht, and which was most acceptable, as he and I had had no substantial food, save a divided tin of sardines, since breakfast at 7 o'clock. He shared it out between the party amid cries from our retainers of " Good food, good Pappa," for we were, as in East Africa, known as " Pap-

9

pa " and " Mam-ma " to a large and promising family.   By some inducement the pack-horse was then deluded into proceeding, and we finally reached Mataveri at nine o'clock, relieved to find we had not been given up and that supper awaited us. So did we cut our last link with civilisation, and were left in mid-Pacific with statues and natives.

The next part of this story deals with the island, the conditions of life on it, and our experience during the sixteen months we were to spend there.   Such scientific work as the Expedition was able to accomplish will be recounted later.

CHAPTER X

CONDITIONS OF LIFE ON THE ISLAND

EASTER is a volcanic land, and in the earliest days of the world's history great lights and flowing lava must have gleamed across the expanse of water, then gradually lessened and died away, leaving their work to be moulded by wind and tide. The island, as the forces of nature have thus made it, is triangular in shape and curiously symmetrieal. The length of the base—that is, of the south, or strictly speaking south-east, coast—is about thirteen miles, and the greatest width about seven miles; the circumference, roughly speaking, is thirty-four miles. The apex, which is the highest ground, is a volcano over 1,700 feet in height whose summit is formed of a cluster of small craters; the eastern and western angles are each composed of a large extinct volcano. The place is geologically young, and the mountains, in contrast to those of Juan Fernandez, still preserve their original rounded shape; there are no ravines, no wooded precipices, no inaccessible heights, but round the whole coast erosion is at work, with the result that, while on the land side the slopes of all these three mountains are gradual, on the sea side—that is, in portions of the north, east, and west coasts respectively—they have been worn back by the power of the waves into imposing cliffs. In the lower districts the sheets of lava form a shore-line of some 50 to 100 feet in height, and extend into the sea in black, broken ridges. Against this coast of alternating high cliffs and jagged rocks the swell of the Pacific is always dashing, and in a high wind clouds of white spray first hide, and then reveal, the inhospitable shore.

The comparatively level and low-lying regions of the island, namely, those which are not covered by the three great vol. canoes, consist of the south coast, and of two tracts which run across the island on either side. The high ground which forms the apex of the triangle is thus divided from that of the eastern and western angles respectively. Another level strip, some quarter of a mile wide at its broadest, lies in an elevated and romantic position around the northern apex between the highest portion of the central mountain and the precipitous sea-cliff. This distribution of the level ground is, as will be later seen, reflected in the disposition of the various clans which formerly spread over the island (fig. 91).

In addition to the three large mountains, there are smaller elevations some hundreds of feet in height, generally in the form of cones with craters distinctly visible. These lesser volcanoes, with one or two exceptions, may be roughly said to lie in two lines which radiate irregularly from the northern eminence, spreading out from it like fingers and pointing respectively to the east and west ends of the south coast. The hills, which may be termed the root of the fingers, form part of the high ground, while those equivalent to the tips rise out of the low-lying portion, where the east and west transverse belts join the southern plain.

In some instances the crater of a mountain has become a lake: when this is the case the term " rano " is prefixed to its name. It is quaintly told that one visitor, considering the volcanic origin, hazarded the suggestion that " rano " was equivalent to fire, to which the natives indignantly replied that, on the contrary, it meant water. These lakes are almost the only water-supply of the island : there is a good rainfall, but no single running stream. Owing to the porous nature of the ground the water sinks beneath the surface, sometimes forming underground channels from which it flows into the sea below high-water mark : thus giving rise to the curious statement of early voyagers that the natives were able to drink salt water [1] (fig. 124). The lower portions of the island are composed of sheets of lava, in process of disintegration, across which walking is almost impossible and riding a very slow process ; the surface of the mountains and

---

[1] " I will only add this one word about the curious way in which they get fresh water on some of the coral islands, such as Nangone, where there is none on the surface. Two go out together to sea, and dive down at some spot where they know there is a fresh-water spring, and they alternately stand on one another's backs to keep down the one that is drinking at the bottom before the pure water mixes with the surrounding salt water."—" Notes on the Maoris and Melanesians," Bishop of Wellington : *The Journal of the Ethnological Society*, New Series, vol. i, session 1868–9.

hills is smoother, being volcanic ash. The whole is covered with grass, which sprouts up between the masses of lava and gives the hills a delightful down-like appearance. Forest growth has probably never consisted of more than brushwood and shrubs, and to-day even those have disappeared.

The best panorama of the island is obtained from the western volcano, by name Rano Kao (fig. 24). Below on the left lies Cook's Bay, with Mataveri and the village of Hanga Roa, and beyond them the high bleak central ground of the island, generally known by the name of one of its craters, Rano Aroi. On the right is the plain of the south coast, culminating in the eastern headland, a district the greater part of which is known as Poike. Just in front of the headland can be seen the two peaks of the mountain of Rano Raraku, from which the statues were hewn and which is the most interesting place in the island ; while on a clear day there can be obtained a glimpse of the northern coast and the sea beyond.

Such is Easter Island. It bears no resemblance to the ideal lotus-eating lands of the Pacific; rather, with its bleak grass-grown surface, its wild rocks and restless ocean, it recalls some of the Scilly Isles or the coast of Cornwall. It is not a beautiful country nor even a striking one, but it has a fascination of its own. All portions of it are accessible; from every part are seen marvellous views of rolling country; everywhere is the wind of heaven; around and above all are boundless sea and sky, infinite space and a great silence. The dweller there is ever listening for he knows not what, feeling unconsciously that he is in the antechamber to something yet more vast which is just beyond his ken.

The objects of antiquarian interest proved to be widely scattered. The statues have originally stood on a particular kind of burial-place, generally known as a " terrace " or " platform." These terraces surround the whole coast, and each one had of course to be studied. For those at the western end, and for certain stone remains on the volcano of Rano Kao, Mataveri was a most convenient centre; but the distance from there to the places of interest at the other end of the island was unduly great. We therefore decided to avail ourselves of the offer of the Manager and remain for a while at his establishment, where *Mana* left us, and later move camp. Survey and photography had of course to keep pace with research, and a general look-out to be kept for any caves which it might pay to explore. There was also the question of getting into touch with the natives and finding if any lore existed which threw light on the antiquities: this last, from what we had been told in England, was not a very hopeful quest; anyway, it seemed wiser to defer it for the moment till we knew something of the language and were more at home in our surroundings.

The Manager's house has six rooms, three of which are at the front, and three, having a separate entrance, at the back. These last, with a most useful attic, Mr. Edmunds kindly put at our disposal, and we supplemented the accommodation with tents pitched in the grounds. My own tent, for the sake of quietness, was on the western side of the plantation, about a hundred yards from the house. S. used to escort me down at night, with a camp lantern, by a little track through the eucalyptus trees, see that all was well, put down the light, and leave me with the mystery of the island. The site was one dedicated to cannibal feasts; immediately behind was the hillock with the grave of the murdered manager; while not far away the waves thundered against the cliffs, making in stormy weather the ground tremble as if with an earthquake. In the morning came the glory of the waking, of being at once *tête à tête* with air, sunshine, and dewy grass: to those who have not known the wonder of these things, it cannot be explained; to those who have experienced it, no words are needed.

Tent life is not all " beer and skittles " ; Easter is too windy for an ideal camping-ground; my pitch was sheltered, but even so it seemed at times as if the structure would be carried away bodily. To preserve a tent in place taut ropes are needed, but if rain descends these shrink, and either burst with the strain or tear the pegs out of the ground: the conscientious dweller under canvas will, under these conditions, arise from his warm bed, and in the pouring deluge race round the tent, slacking off the said ropes. Mine, like the stripes of St. Paul, numbered forty save one. Before the end we were able to make different arrangements.

When we had been some three and a half months at Mataveri— that is, in the middle of July 1914—we felt that the time had come to begin work on the other end of the island. It must be remembered that our original idea was that six months would probably suffice for the whole inquiry, and in any case we had no intention of staying beyond the period which would allow of *Mana's* making a second trip to Chile.

We therefore established ourselves at Rano Raraku as the most convenient site. It takes about two hours to ride there from Mataveri. The road is made, like all those in the island, by simply clearing away the stones, but it is wide enough to permit the passage of a wagon. It leads first across the island by the western transverse plain till, at Vaihu, the sea is reached, then runs along the south coast with its low rocks and continuous line of breaking surf. Every step of this part of the way is marked, for those who have eyes to see, with ruined burial-places ; many of them strewn with the remains of the statues which have once been erected upon them. As Raraku is approached, there lie by the roadside isolated figures of portentous size, abandoned, it has been thought, in the act of removal from the quarries to the terraces. We grew to know by heart this road, which led from what we termed our " town establishment," to our " country house," and have ridden it, together or separately, at all hours and in every weather. We were not infrequently detained by business, at one end or the other, till too late to save the daylight, and after dark it was not easy to keep to the track, even with the help afforded by the sound of the breakers. Our ponies gave us no assistance in the difficulty, for as foals they had run wild with their mothers, and were, therefore, equally happy wandering off among the fields of broken lava. As the " twilight of the dove " gradually changed to the " twilight of the raven," and the huge figures loomed larger than ever in the gathering gloom, it seemed that, if ever the spirits of the departed revisit their ancient haunts, the ghosts of the old image-makers must be all abroad about their works and places of burial.

Rano Raraku (fig. 45) stands by itself where the flat ground of the southern coast meets the eastern transverse plain, and forms the isolated tip of those lesser volcanoes which have been described as the eastern finger. About a mile to the eastward rises the high ground of Poike. Raraku scarcely deserves the name of mountain, being little more than a basin containing a crater lake; yet it curiously dominates the scene. There will be much to tell of it hereafter; for the moment suffice it to say that a large number of statues stand on its lower slopes, while above are the quarries from which, with very few exceptions, all the figures in the island have been obtained. The side nearest the sea is a sheer cliff, the extremities of which form the two peaks which are so characteristic of the mountain. Beneath the cliff is a flow of lava; here the French carpenter had managed to put up two iron huts which had been sent ahead from England; one was a store, the other formed my one-roomed villa residence. Their erection was somewhat of a triumph, as all the bolts had been stolen on the way. The rest of the camp, the tent for meals, that of S., and those for the servants, were pitched for protection about 50 feet lower down, on the further side of the lava flow; but even here, owing to the tearing wind which howled round the mountain, their canvas flies had to be tied back and walls erected around them. On our every hand were the remains of native life prior to the removal of the inhabitants to Hanga Roa, the most welcome being a single well-grown tree of the sort known in tropical countries as the " umbrella tree." It was the only example of its kind on the island, and was of an age that suggested it had been planted by the early missionaries.

The whole situation was not only one of striking beauty, but brought with it an indescribable sense of solemnity. Immediately above the camp towered the majestic cliff of Raraku, near at hand were its mysterious quarries and still erect statues; on the coast below us, quiet and still, lay the overturned images of the great platform of Tongariki, one fragment of which alone remains on its base, as a silent witness to the glory which has departed. The scene was most wonderful of all when the full moon made a track of light over the sea, against which the black mass of the terrace and the outline of the standing fragment were sharply defined; while the white beams turned the waving grass into shimmering silver and lit up every crevice in the mountain above.

Easter Island lies in the sub-tropics, and, if the question of wind be eliminated, the climate is as near perfection as possible in this world. There may be, especially in the winter months, a spell of three or four days of rain, or a wind from the Antarctic, when woollen clothes are welcome; and occasionally, in the summer, it is preferable to be indoors during the noontide hours;

but with these exceptions, it is one of those rare localities where it is possible to be warm the whole year round, and yet to utilise to the full the hours of daylight. There are, as might be expected, too many insects; cockroaches abound, out of doors and under statues as well as in houses and tents; when things were very bad they might even be seen on the dinner-table. I was calmly told, with masculine insensibility, that "if I had not naturally a taste for such things, the sooner that I acquired it the better"; the only consolation was that they were of a handsome red variety and not shiny black. Flies also are numerous; I have counted two hundred in a bowl of soapy water, and six or eight at once on my hand while busy writing; "their tameness was shocking to me." Mosquitoes, which have been imported, varied in their attentions; when they were at their worst it was necessary to wear head-gear and dine in gloves. There is said to be no fever in the islands; we had two or three attacks, but it may have been "original sin." Once we had a plague of little white moths, and occasionally, for a short while, visitations of a small flying beetle, whose instinct seemed to be to crawl into everything, making it safer to stuff one's ears with cotton-wool. On these occasions dinner had to be put earlier, owing to Bailey's pathetic complaint that, with a lamp burning in the kitchen, business was rendered impossible from the crowds which committed suicide in the soup.

The lack of firewood was met by using oil; when, later, we had to economise in that commodity, it was supplemented by collecting dried manure. The natives use brushwood or anything they can pick up; their manner of cooking, which is after Polynesian fashion by heating stones placed in the earth, requires very little fuel. The water difficulty was ever present. At the Mataveri establishment the supply collected from the roof was generally sufficient; we arrived, however, in a dry spell, and one morning the request for water was met by the information that the "tank was empty"; even *Mana*, one felt, had never fallen quite so low. It was consoling to be informed that "clothes could always be washed in the crater," a climb of 1,300 feet. At our Raraku camp all the water, except that which could be collected on the roof of a tin hut, had to be fetched from the crater lake; this rendered us tiresomely dependent on getting native labour. The rain-clouds are often intercepted by the high grounds at the south-western end of the island, in a manner which is most tantalising to the dweller in the eastern, if supplies happen to be low.

The ranch supported at this time about 12,000 sheep, 2,000 head of cattle, and other livestock ; we were generously supplied with milk and could purchase any quantity of mutton: beef was not often killed for so small a party. Chickens of a lean species were sometimes available. *Mana* later brought Mr. Edmunds some turkeys which did well. Bananas were useful, when in season. Fig-trees thrive, and we had a lavish and most acceptable supply at Raraku of this fruit from those planted by the natives prior to their removal to Hanga Roa. Vegetables were scarce, as the Manager took no interest in his garden, owing to the depredations of the natives, and we had no time for their cultivation. Groceries had, of course, been brought with us, and on our arrival they were deposited in the locked and strongly built wool-shed at Hanga Piko, a small-boat landing between Hanga Roa and Mataveri. Housekeeping was a much easier business than on the yacht, but S.'s share of practical work was considerably greater, for, beside the initial camp-pitching, all tent or kitchen gear that went wrong and every lamp which would not burn made demands on his time. In his department also came the stud ; we had been kindly provided with some of the island ponies, of which there are about five hundred; as export is impossible, the value of each animal is put at 5s. When not in use the steeds were put out to graze as best they might; and in addition to the care of the saddlery, every tethering rope which chafed through against the stones was brought for repair to the head of the Expedition. In judging of scientific work under such conditions, it must always be borne in mind how many hours and days are thus inevitably consumed in practical labour.

There was, luckily for us, the one skilled workman on the island, the French carpenter who had made his way from New Caledonia ; his name was Vincent, but he answered to the appellation of " Varta " (the figure in fig. 37) ; the difficulty was to obtain his services as he was constantly employed on the estate. One of our few retainers, Mahanga (fig. 89), was not a native of Easter, but had come from the Paumotu Islands ; he served faithfully for many months, the goal in view being the possession of one of the tin huts, which passed into his keeping when we left the island. It was related that having been at one time afflicted with some skin disease, he had taken the heroic remedy of plunging into a vat in which the sheep were being dipped, with painful but beneficial results. The native girls make quite tolerable servants, and I was fortunate in never being without one (fig. 29). They take a keen interest in their own clothes and some of them are surprisingly good needle-women ; in some of the houses there are even sewing-machines. But to obtain labour, whether for camp work or excavation, was always difficult, and for a while circumstances rendered it almost impossible.

CHAPTER XI

A NATIVE RISING

IT was stated a little while back that we were left on the island with statues and natives. The statues remained quiescent, the natives did not. The inhabitants, or Kanakas to give them their usual name [1] (fig. 26), are on the whole a handsome race, though their voices, particularly those of the women, are very harsh. They are fortunate also in possessing attractive manners, from which they get the full benefit in their intercourse with passing ships. The older people we found always kind and amiable, but the younger men have a high opinion of their own merits, and are often difficult to deal with. Their general morality, using the word in its limited sense, is, in common with that of all Polynesians, of a particularly low order ; it is true that the Europeans with whom they have come into contact did not initiate this condition, but they have seldom done anything to show that that of their own lands is in any way higher ; a fact which should be remembered when complaint is made that Kanakas "have no respect for white men." The native love of accuracy also leaves a good deal to be desired, and their lies are astonishingly fluent ; but lack of truthfulness is scarcely confined to Kanakas. In common with all residents in the South Seas, or indeed elsewhere, they exert themselves no more than is necessary to supply their wants ; unfortunately these, save in the matter of clothes, have scarcely increased since pre-Christian days. The food-supply of sweet potatoes and bananas, with a few pigs and fowls, can be obtained with a minimum of labour ; the keeping of sheep and cattle is not permitted by the Company, owing to the impossibility of discovering or tracing theft. Their old huts, which were made with sticks and grass, have been replaced by

---

[1] "Kanaka" is a name originally given by Europeans to the inhabitants of the South Seas, and is one form of the Polynesian word meaning "man."

FIG. 26.

A GROUP OF EASTER ISLANDERS OUTSIDE THE CHURCH DOOR.

FIG. 27.

HANGA ROA VILLAGE.
Native houses and church.   Rano Kao in the distance.

141]

small houses of wood or stone, but, except in a few cases, there is no furniture, and the inhabitants continue to sleep on the floor, in company with hens, which freely run in and out (fig. 27). There seems no desire to improve their condition; " Kanakas no like work, Kanakas like sit in house," was the ingenuous reply given by one of them, when my husband pointed out the good results which would accrue from planting some trees in village territory.

Perhaps the greatest barrier to native progress lies in the absence of security of property; they steal freely from one another, as well as from white men, so that all individual effort is rendered nugatory. At the same time they are curiously lacking in pugnacity, and if detected in theft quietly desist or return the property: as a typical instance our cook once met a man wearing one of his, Bailey's, ties; he looked steadily at him, the man's hand went up, he took off the tie and handed it back. Their own native organisation was peculiarly lax, no kind of justice being administered, and they have never had for any duration the civilising effect of religious instruction or civil power. The missionaries were replaced by a native lay reader; there is a large church where services are regularly held, which form important functions for the display of best clothes, but it is difficult to say how much they convey to the worshippers. The older ones, at any rate, have two names, both a native and Christian appellation. Mr. Edmunds had, on our arrival, the status of a Chilean official, and was both just and kind in his dealings, but he had no means of enforcing order; the two police- men who had been at one time on the island had been withdrawn owing to their own bad conduct. The marvel is not that the Kanakas are troublesome, but that they are as good as they are.

We had heard in Chile rumours of native unrest, owing to the action of a white man, who had been for a short while on the island, and who had done his best to undermine the authority of the Manager. We had before long unpleasant evidence that they were out of hand. The wool-shed, which contained our minutely calculated stores, was broken into, and a quantity of things stolen, the most lamented being three-fourths of the stock of soap; no redress or punishment was possible. On June 30th, while we were still at the Manager's, a curious development began which turned the history of the next five weeks into a

Gilbertian opera—a play, however, with an undercurrent of reality which made the time the most anxious in the story of the Expedition. On that date a semi-crippled old woman, named Angata (fig. 30), came up to the Manager's house accompanied by two men, and informed him that she had had a dream from God, according to which M. Merlet, the chairman of the Company, was " no more," and the island belonged to the Kanakas, who were to take the cattle and have a feast the following day.[1] Our party also was to be laid under contribution, which, it later transpired, was to take the form of my clothes. Later in the day the following declaration of war was formally handed in to Mr. Edmunds, written in Spanish as spoken on the island :

" *June 30th,* 1914.

" SENIOR EMA, MATAVERI,

" Now I declare to you, by-and-by we declare to you, which is the word we speak to-day, but we desire to take all the animals in the camp and all our possessions in your hands, now, for you know that all the animals and farm in the camp belong to us, our Bishop Tepano gave to us originally. He gave it to us in truth and justice. There is another thing, the few animals which are in front of you,[2] are for you to eat. There is also another thing, to-morrow we are going out into the camp to fetch some animals for a banquet. God for us, His truth and justice. There is also another business, but we did not receive who gave the animals to Merlet also who gave the earth to Merlet because it is a big robbery. They took this possession of ours, and they gave nothing for the earth, money or goods or anything else. They were never given to them. Now you know all that is necessary.

" Your friend,

" DANIEL ANTONIO,

" *Hangaroa.*"

If some of the arguments are probably without foundation, as, for example, that regarding native rights in the cattle, they were at least, as will be seen, of the same kind which have inspired

---

[1] The natives of Easter hold very firmly the primitive belief in dreams. If one of them dreamt, for example, that *Mana* was returning, it was retailed to us with all the assurance of a wireless message.

[2] The milch-cows.

risings in many lands and all ages. The delivery of the document was immediately followed by action. The Kanakas went into "the camp," eluding Mr. Edmunds, who had gone in another direction, and secured some ten head of cattle. The smoke from many fires was shortly to be seen ascending from the village, and one of our party was shown a beast which was to be offered to us in place of our stolen property, "God" having apparently reversed his message on the subject of our contribution to the new republic. The next few days there was little more news "from the front," save that Angata, the old woman, had had another dream, in which God had informed her that "He was very pleased that the Kanakas had eaten the meat and they were to eat some more." A week later, riding home through the village, I saw a group on the green engaged in dressing a girl's hair ; on inquiry it was found that she was to be married next day. Congratulations had hardly been expressed, when another young woman was pointed out who was also to change her state at the same time, and another and another, till the prospective brides totalled five in all. The idea, it seemed, was prevalent, that if punishment was subsequently inflicted for the raids, it was the single men who would be taken to Chile, hence this rush into matrimony, undeterred by the fact that Mr. Edmunds, in his capacity as Chilean official, had declined for the present to perform the civil part of the ceremony. The wedding feast was, of course, to be furnished by the sheep of the Company. Unfortunately, under such circumstances, it seemed hardly loyal to our host to attend the multiple wedding, which was duly solemnised in the church next day.

Meanwhile, the white residents had, of course, been considering their position, and in orthodox fashion, counting the number on which they could rely in an emergency. Beside Mr. Edmunds there were at this time in our party, myself and five men : S., Mr. Ritchie, the photographer, the cook, and a boy from Juan Fernandez. There were about half a dozen more or less reliable Kanakas, including the native Overseer and the village Headman, but everyone else was involved. Mr. Edmunds's position as custodian of the livestock was unenviable, and ours was not much more pleasant. After much thought we strongly dissuaded him from taking any action ; if he interfered, there would be an affray. The natives were said to have a rifle and some pistols; it was doubtful how many would go off, but there would anyway be stone-throwing: if he was then forced to shoot, the only deterrent possible, he would have to continue till resistance was entirely cowed, or all our lives would remain in danger. His personal safety was however another matter, and our party therefore accompanied him in an attempt to frustrate a raid, but this obviously could not be continued if our work was to be accomplished. We were strengthened in adopting a waiting policy by the fact that, most fortunately, a fortnight earlier a passing vessel had left us newspapers; they confirmed the news heard in Chile that the naval training-ship, the *Jeneral Baquedano*, whose visits occurred at intervals of anything from two to five years, was shortly leaving for Easter Island. We could only hope her arrival would be soon.

S. suggested that, being an unofficial person, he might meanwhile try the effect of negotiations; for the raids were continuing, and the head of cattle killed on one day had risen to fifty-six, including females and young. He therefore went down to the village, assembled the natives, and offered the company a present of two bullocks a week, if they would refrain from taking any more stock till the arrival of the warship, when the whole matter could be referred to the captain. The audience laughed the suggestion out of court, for " the whole of the cattle," they said, belonged to them, as God had told Angata, but they would let our party " have twenty" if we wished; as for Mr. Edmunds, " he is a Protestant, and therefore, of course, has no God."

When my husband returned saying he had accomplished nothing, I felt that it was " up to me." " This," I said, " is a matter requiring tact, and is therefore a woman's job; *I* will go and see the old lady." I had already received from her an embarrassing present of fowls, which, after referring the matter to our host, it had seemed better to accept. Not without inward trepidation, I rode down to the village, taking the Fernandez boy as interpreter, for many of the natives speak a smattering of Spanish. The place was a perfect shambles, joints of meat hanging from all the trees, and skins being pegged out to dry on every hand, but the raiders had been displaying energy in re-building the wall round the church. The Prophetess was with a group outside the house of the acting priest, who was her

FIG. 29.

EASTER ISLAND WOMEN.
Parapina standing.

FIG. 28

BAILEY, THE COOK, ON GUARD.

FIG. 30.

ANGATA, THE PROPHETESS.

son-in-law; she was a frail old woman with grey hair and expressive eyes, a distinctly attractive and magnetic personality. She wore suspended round her neck some sort of religious medallion, a red cross, I think, on a white ground, and her daughter who supported her carried a small picture of the Saviour in an Oxford frame. She held my hand most amiably during the interview, addressing me as " Caterina." I had brought her a gift and began by thanking for the fowls. She refused all payments, saying " Food comes from God, I wish for no money," and proceeded to offer me some of the meat. This gave an opening, and in declining I besought her not to let the Kanakas go out again after the animals, for Mr. Edmunds said he would shoot if they did, and there would be trouble for them when the *Baquedano* came. As I spoke of the raids her face hardened and her eyes took the look of a fanatic; she said something about " God " with the upward gesture which was her habit in speaking His name. I hastened to relieve the tension by saying that " We must all worship God," and was happy to find that I was allowed a share in the Deity. Her manner again softened, and looking up to heaven she declared, with an assured confidence, which was in its way sublime, " God will never let the Kanakas be either killed or hurt." The natives were, in fact, firmly persuaded that no bullet could injure them. As for myself, Angata would, she said, " pray " for me, adding, with a descent to the mundane, that if ever she had " chickens or potatoes," I should be the first to have them. It was impossible to reason further; we parted the best of friends, but the " tactful " mission had failed !

This was the state of affairs when we decided that we must transfer our work and consequently our belongings to the other end of the island. Our surveyor and photographer remained, however, at Mataveri, as the accommodation there was more convenient for their occupations, so Mr. Edmunds was not alone. Moving camp, levelling ground, and building walls, were not light matters, when the Kanakas had found such much more interesting employment, but at last it was accomplished, and then came the question of the stores, which after the robbery at the woolshed had been taken to Mataveri. After much consultation it was decided to remove them to Raraku, as on the whole safer than leaving them at the Manager's house, which might, by the look of things, be any day looted or burnt down. But when the ox-cart had been carefully loaded up with the numerous boxes and goods, the cash supply, consisting of £50 of English gold and some Chilean paper, being carefully hidden amongst them, a spell of bad weather set in. It was impossible to move the cart, and our possessions sat there day after day most handily arranged for the revolutionists if their desires should turn that way.

Our new camp we were often obliged to leave without defence save for the redoubtable Bailey, who had also served as guard at Mataveri (fig. 28). There had been no demonstration against us so far, but of course the future was unknown, and I never came in sight of our house, on returning from any distant work, without casting an anxious glance to see if it were still standing. We always went about armed, and the different ranges for rifle-shot were measured off from my house and marked by cairns, which will no doubt in future add yet one more to the mysteries of Easter Island.

One day I had just come back from a stroll, when the cry was raised " The Kanakas are coming," and a troop of horsemen, about thirty strong, appeared on the sky-line some four hundred yards distant. Fortunately S. was at hand, we hurried inside my house, shut the lower half of its door, which resembled that of a loose-box, and carelessly leant out. Any unpleasantness could then only be frontal ; at the same time all weapons were within easy grasp, though not visible from the outside.

It soon, however, became clear that the visitors were approaching at a walk only, from which it was gathered their intentions were friendly. Nevertheless it was a relief when, as they got nearer, they raised their hats and gave a cheer ; they then formed a semi-circle round the door and dismounted. The " priest " who was with them, and who carried a picture of the Virgin, read something, presumably a prayer, at which the company crossed themselves. He then gave greetings from Angata, and a message from her to say that *Mana* was returning safely with letters on board, and the men presented from their saddle-bows, eggs, potatoes, and about a dozen hens. The position was unwelcome, but as none of the goods were stolen, it seemed better to accept, and discharge the obligation as far as possible by giving in return what European food we could spare.

We subsequently informed Mr. Edmunds, and sent a message to the Prophetess that, as our camp was out of bounds, the Kanakas must not come without leave. The old lady herself, however, kept sending to us for anything she happened to want, and as the requests continually grew in magnitude the breaking-point seemed only a question of time. One of the earlier demands, to which Mr. Edmunds thought it advisable we should accede, was for material for a flag for the new Republic ; later, it floated proudly as a tricolour, made of a piece of white cotton, some red material from the photographic outfit, and a fragment of an old blue shirt.

Elsewhere things went from bad to worse, and it seemed as if the expected warship would never arrive. Word came that the Kanakas had ordered the native overseer to leave his house, the only one outside the village, and were taking away the servants of the Manager ; our photographer wrote that he " dared not come over as their lives were being threatened "; and finally, one afternoon we received a note from Mr. Edmunds, saying, that " he could not leave the place as the Kanakas were talking of coming up in a body to the house." They were also, as we later learnt, threatening to kill him if he resisted their taking possession. It was obvious that the crisis had arrived ; that we must risk leaving the camp and go into Mataveri. We talked over every conceivable plan of campaign, but it was too late to do anything that night, and I remember that, finally at dinner, to turn our thoughts, we discussed the curious manner in which some of the statues had fallen. In four cases which we had seen that day, while the body lay on its front, the head had broken off in mid air, turned a complete somersault, and rested on its back with the crown towards the neck. The next morning, August 5th, I awoke early and recorded in my journal the events of the day before. " Of course," I added, " if it were a stage play, just as the crisis arrived there would be cries of ' the *Baquedano* is here,' and the curtain would fall. But, alas ! it is not." Scarcely was the ink dry—only it was pencil—when a man rode up waving a note from Mr. Edmunds, and shouting, " A ship !—a ship ! " The previous afternoon, as the Kanakas were assembling in the village to go up to Mataveri, the *Baquedano* had been sighted, and four of the ringleaders were now in irons. I scarcely knew how great had been the long strain till the relief came.

Our rejoicings, however, we found to have been partly premature. The warship had unfortunately brought with her large gifts of clothes for the natives from well-wishers in Chile. Some little while before attention had been drawn to the inhabitants of Easter, by an Australian captain who had touched there on his homeward voyage. The natives had, as usual, come off to his ship in their oldest garments ; he had been impressed with their ragged condition and made a collection of clothes for them in Australia amounting to many bales, but on his next voyage to Chile he had been unable to touch again at the island and had left them at Valparaiso. We had been asked to bring these bales, but had declined on the score of space.[1] The Chileans disliked the idea of their protectorate being indebted to strangers, made a collection on their own account, and despatched them by the *Baquedano*. It seemed unthinkable that people, every one of whom for weeks had been consuming stolen goods, and who, two days before, had been on the verge of murder, should be immediately presented officially with the commodity they most prized. I therefore went on board the *Baquedano*, saw the Captain, and ventured to request that the goods should be handed over to us, promising personally to visit every house before our departure, ascertain the needs of the people, and distribute the articles. " Surely," he said, " you shall have them." Within a few hours they had been distributed by his officers on the beach. Some of the garments were useful, but an assortment of ball-slippers seemed a little out of place, and the greater part of the community, men and women, blossomed out into washing waistcoats. The stolen sheepskins, or some of them, were returned, but three of the four ringleaders were set at liberty, and no corporate punishment was inflicted ; indeed, the Captain had told me he considered that the natives had " behaved very well not to murder Mr. Edmunds " prior to our arrival.

Before the ship left the island, the Captain wrote officially to the " Head of the British Scientific Expedition " to the effect, that the action he had been obliged to take to restore order would probably have the result of rousing more feeling against

[1] Considerably later *Mana* was again approached on the subject of the Australian gifts, and Mr. Gillam consented to bring them ; it then transpired that they were no longer available, having " been given by the wife of the head of the Customs to the deserving poor of Valparaiso."

foreigners; he therefore could not guarantee our safety and offered us passages to Chile—an offer which, needless to say, we declined. So ended the Revolution ; we felt with interest that the confidence of the Prophetess had been justified, at any rate as far as 249 Kanakas were concerned out of the 250.

The old lady died six months later ; I attended her funeral. The coffin was pathetically tiny, and neatly covered with black and white calico. A service was first held in the church where, during the rising, she used to take part in the assemblies and address her adherents. There figured prominently in the ceremony a model of the building and also two prie-dieu, roughly made of boards, one of which she had used in private, the other in public worship. She was laid to rest beneath the great wooden cross, which marks the Kanaka burying-ground, between the village and the bay. I stood at a little distance watching gleams of sunshine on the great stones of the terrace of Hanga Roa and on the grey sea beyond, and musing on the strange life now closed, whose early days had been spent in a native hut beneath the standing images of Raraku. My attention was recalled by an evident hitch in the proceedings: difficulty had arisen in lowering the coffin, owing to the fact that the prie-dieu was also being fitted into the grave. When all had been finally adjusted and the interment was completed, a sound was heard, unusual in such circumstances—three English cheers—hip, hip, hooray ; the natives had learnt it from passing ships and esteemed it an essential part of a ceremony. The company was not large for the obsequies of one who had so recently been the heroine of the village, and on asking in particular why a certain near relative was absent, the answer received was that " there was to be a great feast of pigs, and he was busy preparing it " ; doubtless others were similarly detained.

During the remainder of our sojourn there were, as will be seen, additional white men on the island. The Kanakas were occupied in various ways and there was no further open demonstration, but their independence and demands increased daily. Since we left, a white employé of the Company has been murdered by them and thrown into the sea.

CHAPTER XII

MANA appeared on August 23rd, a week after the warship left, and not before we had become a little anxious about her. She had done the passage to the mainland in eighteen days, establishing a record, but had had bad luck on her return journey, the voyage having taken forty-one days. Even after her arrival there was the usual chase to get hold of her, and we did not receive the mail till late one night. We had had no letters since we left Talcahuano the preceding February, and read them eagerly during the small hours ; it was the greatest relief to find that all at home was well. The yacht had to put out again to sea before the newspapers could be landed, but we later received in them the accounts of the murder of the Austrian Archduke and Duchess ; even then, of course, Ireland and labour troubles loomed much more largely on the political horizon. As soon as the return mail was ready, on September 4th, we despatched *Mana* again, the instructions sent home being that everything was to be sent to Tahiti, as we expected to get off when she once more returned the following November.

The *Baquedano* had brought some additions to the community on the island : one or two Europeans to work on the estate and a German to plant tobacco. The fact that the presence of this last coincided with the declaration of the war, and the subsequent use of the island by his nation as a naval base, gave rise later to a good deal of comment ; it is certain that but little effort was made to grow tobacco. He left shortly before we did. A schoolmaster from Chile was also among the newcomers; he was sent by the Government, and brought an expensive school building. In this he entertained us all to celebrate the day of Chilean Independence, September 18th, when the natives gave some masque dances, a fashion imported from Tahiti. It was interesting to notice that the women always preferred to wear for best occasions their own distinctive dress, rather than the smart clothes of the *Baquedano*, or similar gifts, which were relegated to every-day service ; I have seen a really beautifully embroidered underskirt used for riding astride. The native garment is of any washing material, preferably white for Sundays. It falls straight and loosely down from a yoke, and is worn unreasonably long; the sleeves are made to the wrist, with puffs at the top (fig. 29). This fashion is said to be common throughout the South Seas, presumably dating from the first introduction of clothes by the missionaries.[1]

School was duly begun, but after a few days the children ceased to appear, the master declared he was "not an attendance officer," and from then till we left, nearly a year later, no school was held ; the last we saw of the blackboard and counting-frame, they were rotting in a field some two miles off, where they had been taken by the French marooned sailors for use in some carnival pony-races. The warship also brought an epidemic of bad colds: every ship except *Mana* left some such legacy.

Now that peace was in some measure restored, we set to work to excavate some of the statues which stood on the slope of the Raraku mountain. The natives were entirely indifferent whether they worked or not, but by paying high wages and giving any quantity of mutton, we were able at this time to get a certain amount of precarious labour for digging and camp work. The whole lot, including my maid-servant, went in for every week-end to the village, and it was always a matter of anxiety to know whether they would ever return. Our Sundays were spent peacefully, doing housework, taking the ponies to water in the crater, changing their pitches at due intervals, and similar jobs.

We had just begun the week's work on Monday, October 12th, when word was brought that some steamers had appeared. The whole of the native staff, of course, at once departed to see what could be begged from the ships. The vessels turned out to be

[1] Since writing the above, the following account has been found of dress at Tahiti in 1877 : " All the women, without exception, have their dresses cut on the pattern of the old English sacques worn by our grandmothers. . . . It is a matter of deep congratulation that the dress in fashion in Europe at the period when Tahiti adopted foreign garments should have been one so suitable."

" We may be thankful that Prince Alfred's strong commendation of the graceful sacque has caused it to triumph over all other varieties of changeful and unbecoming fashion which for a while found favour here."—*Cruise in a French Man-of-war*, Miss Gordon Cumming, pp. 299 and 284.

a German squadron, going, they said, "from the China station to Valparaiso." Some more turned up later, till there were twelve in all, four or five of the number being warships, and the remainder colliers or other smaller vessels. They kept entire silence on the European situation. We had not, of course, the slightest idea that war had broken out, still less that our lonely island was the meeting-place, cleverly arranged by Admiral von Spee, for his ships from Japan—the *Scharnhorst* and *Gneisenau*—with the other German warships in this region; the *Nürnberg* and *Leipzig* had turned up from the west coast of Mexico, and the *Dresden* from the other side of South America. A writer in the *Cornhill* (August 1917) states "there happened to be upon it [Easter Island] a British scientific expedition, but busied over the relics of the past, the single-minded men of science did not take the trouble to cross the island to look at the German ships." S. was, as a matter of fact, twice over at Mataveri while they were in Cook's Bay, but it is true of this "single-minded" woman, who felt she had something else to do than to ride for some four hours to gaze at the outside of German men-of-war. What did interest us was that presumably, after the usual manner of passing ships, the officers would come over to Raraku, and being intelligent Germans, would photograph our excavations. We therefore turned to, and with our own hands covered up our best things.

We seized the opportunity to write letters, which were posted on the ships, and one of our number went to see the doctor. To the credit of the enemy be it said, that almost all the letters subsequently arrived, a sad exception being a butterfly, addressed to Professor Poulton at Oxford, which, if, as may have been the case, it was retained as something valuable, presumably went down off the Falkland Islands. Mr. Edmunds, meanwhile, had not unnaturally rejoiced at having his market brought to his door, and sold the ships nearly £1,000 worth of meat. They offered to pay for it in gold, but it seemed common prudence to ask instead for an order, a decision which was later sadly lamented.

On Thursday some of our staff returned: the Germans were, it seemed, most unpopular; they did not come on shore and had given no food, clothes, or soap. Kanaka sentiment at this moment would have been certainly pro-Ally.

On Friday rumours reached us that there was something mysterious going on. Why, it was asked, did the Germans say they had no newspapers, so rarely come on shore, and go out at night without lights ? and why did one officer say that " in two months Germany would be at the top of the tree " ? We discussed the matter and passed it off as " bazaar talk." On Sunday, however, news came from Mataveri which we could no longer wholly discredit. The German tobacco planter had been on board, and the crew had disobeyed orders and disclosed to their countryman the fact that there was a great European war ; the combatants were correctly stated, but much detail was added. Two hundred thousand men were, it was said, waiting at Kiel to invade England ; the war had taken our country by surprise, and the German ships had already made a sudden raid and sunk eight or nine Dreadnoughts in the Thames ; the Emperor was nearly at Paris, though the French continued to fight on most bravely. It was a terrible war as neither side would show the white flag. An army had been sent from England to the assistance of the French, but it had been badly defeated. The English Labour Party had objected to troops being sent out of the country, in consequence of which the Asquith ministry had fallen, the House of Lords came in somehow ; anyway, England was now a Republic, and so were Canada and Australia ; India was in flames, and two troopships had been sunk on the way there from Australia.

We are still inclined to think that the Germans themselves believed all these things; they had so often been told, by those in authority, that such would occur on the outbreak of war with England, that wishes had become facts. As a small mercy we got the news of the loss of the German colonies, but the *Scharnhorst*, which had just come from the French possession of Tahiti, said that the natives there having risen and killed the Germans, the warships had therefore bombarded the town of Papeete, which was now " no more." The reason given for keeping us in the dark so long was, that hearing there were foreigners on the island, they thought that we might fight amongst ourselves. Von Spee made exact inquiries as to the number of whites in the place, and told the Kanakas that when he returned he would hold them responsible for our safety. The real reason of the silence maintained was most probably to prevent any question being raised of their use of the island as a naval base. When the news could no longer be concealed, the officers gave it as their opinion, that " when Germany had conquered France, peace would be made with England, in which case Britain would probably gain some territory as she had such good diplomatists," a compliment at least for Lord Grey. The reality of the war was brought home by the concrete fact that the ships were reliably reported to be in fighting trim, with no woodwork visible. That Sunday evening one of us saw the squadron going round in the dusk, the flagship leading. They had said that they would come again, but they never did. They went on their way to Coronel and the Falklands.

On Monday morning we met our photographer by arrangement on the road to Mataveri, in order to take some of the half-way terraces; he had brought two newspapers, which had at last been got hold of, and we sat down beneath a wall to read them. They were German ones, of September 15th and 17th, published in Chile, and contained little news; but we read between the lines that things were going better in France, for the Germans had made " a strategic retreat according to plan," and then the curtain fell on the great drama. The ground rocked for us, as it did at home in those first August days; it was just one week since we had covered up our diggings and it seemed centuries. How much to believe we did not know, but some of it sounded plausible, and when later we found that England was facing the struggle as a united whole, and that there was still a British Empire, we felt that the greatest nightmare of the war had passed.

From the personal point of view our thoughts turned, of course, to the yacht; she would no doubt remain in safety at Talcahuano, that was a comfort. At any other time it would have been a matter of anxiety that the crew should continue indefinitely without employment, and that there was no pecuniary arrangement there for so long a detention; as it was, we were so absolutely helpless that the futility of worrying was obvious. As regards ourselves, we could only cut down our use of such things as flour and tea, and wait; our experience of war rations thus came early. The most serious threatened shortage was that of paper. It was intensely strange to go back to digging out statues, when morning, noon, and night our hearts were over the seas; but that was "our job," there was at least no daily and hourly waiting for news, and in the peace of a plain duty and the absolute silence of the sea around us there was a certain kind of rest.

For the next few weeks life went on quietly, sheep-shearing absorbed the energies of the community, and the village was laid low by an attack of dysentery, from which in a short time there were eight deaths: the disease was either a legacy from the Germans, or the result of the distribution of some more *Baquedano* clothes which had been left with the schoolmaster. It seemed as if we might spend the rest of our lives on the island, when suddenly, as things always happened in mid-Pacific, on December 1st, six weeks after the departure of the German squadron, a little ship turned up. She was flying the Chilean flag, but had an English captain, and was to take back word to Valparaiso how things were going on the island. She brought good news on the whole, but also the regretted tidings of the sinking of the *Good Hope* and *Monmouth* on November 1st. Mr. Gillam wrote that the yacht was, as we had expected, detained at Talcahuano till the passage was considered safe. The point which immediately concerned us was the offer of passages in this vessel to Chile should we desire them; but she could only by her charter stay some five days, during which time it would have been quite impossible, even had our work been finished, to transport our goods from Raraku. There was no room for hesitation: S. must go and look after *Mana*, and insure her against war risks. Mr. Ritchie and the Fernandez boy had already sailed on the *Baquedano*, and as the photographer's work on the island was nearly done for the present, it seemed best he should accompany my husband and resume his post on the yacht. Bailey and I were therefore left to represent the Expedition on the island.

When the good-byes had been said, it was better not to have time to think, so we at once set to work, packed up such things as were necessary from our country house, and transferred the camp back to Mataveri. There I took up life once more in my tent by the grave of the murdered manager. Mr. Edmunds would, I knew, kindly give me assistance in case of necessity, and it was desirable to be near the village, for I proposed to spend the time till S. returned in interviews with such of the old people

as could remember traditions and customs, prior to the coming
of Christianity. This work was, however, not destined to
continue undisturbed.

On Wednesday morning, December 23rd, another German
ship came into Cook's Bay—the armed cruiser *Prinz Eitel
Friedrich*. The Manager went on board, and returned with the
information that the Captain had said he " would require thirty
or forty beasts, but that as the crew would be busy next day
they would not take them till after Christmas." They would
give no account of themselves, nor any news of the war. It was
a relief to realize that S. would not yet have had time to leave
Chile, and that he and the yacht were presumably safe in harbour.
That very afternoon, however, my writing was interrupted by
a cry of congratulation from the native girls at work in Mr.
Edmunds' kitchen, " *Mana* is coming." A woman, who had
been up on the high ground, had reported that she had seen the
little vessel off the south coast and that she was now sailing
round Rano Kao, hence making direct for Cook's Bay. It
might, of course, be a mistake, but it was, on the other hand,
just possible that Mr. Gillam had seized an opportunity to slip
across to the island without waiting for a reply to his letter.
The immediate question, supposing that it was indeed *Mana*,
was how she could be stopped walking straight into the jaws of
the enemy. Bailey saddled in haste, and rode up to the top of
the headland to try to warn her not to proceed. I armed myself
with a towel and coat to make a two-flag signal, which denotes
urgency, and fled down to the rocks on the coast below, selecting
a point from which it was possible to command the furthest
view, without being noticed from the cruiser. It was a very
forlorn hope, that it might be possible to attract the yacht's
attention before she was seen by the enemy, but it was obviously
out of the question to continue, under a tree, copying notes
while *Mana* might be at the moment meeting with a watery
grave.

My thoughts, while I sat there with eyes glued to the horizon,
went back to academic discussions with Admiral Fremantle
on board a P. & O. liner only a few years before, on the right
in war-time to capture private property at sea, and how
little it had then occurred to me that the matter would ever
become so vitally personal. I waited for two and a half hours,

not daring to leave, but with hope growing momentarily stronger that there was an error somewhere. Meanwhile, Bailey had seen the vessel from the mountain and was confident that it was the returning yacht, but had been unable to get into touch with her. He had come down and consulted with Mr. Edmunds, who had then most kindly ridden over to the south coast to see what could be done from there ; the nearer view had made clear that the alarm was a false one, the vessel was not *Mana* but some other passing schooner, and we breathed once more.

Everyone, however, seemed to take particular pleasure in talking to the Germans about the yacht and her movements, in a way which to me was more amusing than reassuring. As a scientific ship, she theoretically shared with Red Cross vessels immunity under the Hague Convention, but even in those days, as will have been seen, that did not bring complete confidence. One of the German officers had, I was told, given it as his opinion that his Captain would not touch her, but " it was," he remarked, " a matter for individual judgment, and other commanders might act differently." The same officer expressed his surprise that the Manager had ventured on the cruiser, as he " might have been made a prisoner, as a German had been on a French ship " ; whereupon Mr. Edmunds naturally resolved not to accept an informal invitation to attend theatricals to be held on board on Christmas Eve.

The reason for the occupation of the crew soon became obvious. The warship went out on the following morning and returned with a French barque, the *Jean*, which she had captured some time before, and which, being laden with coal, she had towed most of the way to the island. She laid the barque alongside her in Cook's Bay and proceeded to hoist out the cargo (fig. 24), finally shooting away the masts and spars in order that the French ship might not capsize as she gradually lost her ballast.

The cruiser, it transpired, had also on board it the crew of an English sailing-ship, the *Kildalton*, which she had captured and sunk near the Horn; but when an attempt was made to speak to the men, they were ordered below. The German officers and crew then landed daily, rode over the island, came up to the Manager's house, and generally behaved as if the whole place belonged to them. The officers were courteous and always saluted when we met, an attention with which one would have preferred to dispense ; one of the crew penetrated to our kitchen, which he was at once requested to leave, in spite of Bailey's evident fear that he and I would immediately be ordered out for execution ; the man hesitated, looked astonished, but obeyed. It must be remembered that there was no reason to suppose that it was otherwise than civilised warfare, the idea that anyone could or would injure non-combatants on neutral soil never seriously occurred to me : the story of Belgium was unknown.

Indignation was, however, roused by the fact that the Germans were remaining far beyond the twenty-four hours to which they were entitled in a neutral port, and obviously again using the island as a base. It grew to fever-heat when news came that a signal-station had been erected on Rano Aroi, the high central point, with an officer and men in charge, from which notice might be given to the cruiser below if an " enemy " ship was sighted. I took Juan, the headman of the village who was our usual escort, rode up to the point in question, and thus verified the fact of the station and men on watch. I remained at a short distance, but Juan went on and spoke to the Germans ; he came back to me saying impressively, " They do not like to see you here," to which sentiment the reply naturally was " I dislike still more to see them." Never would the white ensign have been more welcome ! To relieve my feelings, although with a sense of futility, I wrote a formal protest, under the grandiloquent title of " Acting Head of the British Scientific Expedition," pointing out for the benefit of the Chilean Govern-ment these abuses of neutrality. The schoolmaster had been, since his arrival, the formal representative of his country, and I went down to the village to give it to him ; its presentation was delayed by his having gone on board the cruiser for the Christmas theatricals, where he remained over the next day, but it was finally handed to him.

On New Year's Eve I was coming in from a business ride about 1 o'clock, and, having breakfasted at 6, was feeling not a little hungry, when the German ship was seen steaming from her anchorage, looking as she did so like a great blot on the radiant sea. The first impression was that she was leaving the island, but on observing more closely, her errand was apparent ; she was not alone, but had the graceful little barque with her, towing her side by side in a last Judas embrace. Naturally, one could go no farther, and for two and a half hours a little company, including the crew of the doomed ship, who had just been landed, sat spell-bound on the cliff watching the tragedy. When the cruiser had gone a short distance, but well within the three-mile limit, she cast the French vessel adrift, the small craft rolled helplessly, high out of the water, without ballast or cargo, and with only a mizzen-mast remaining. The warship then swooped round in great circles like an evil bird of prey, and every time that she came broadside on she fired at her victim. The first shot missed; the second went through the upper part of the barque into the sea the other side. The third shot obviously told, but the executioner fired once again and then ceased, satisfied with her work, for the little ship could be seen gradually regaining her water-line, though with an ominous list, and a ballast never designed by the builder. As she sank she drifted slowly southward, at the mercy of wind and current. The cruiser moved with her, keeping at an even distance and steadily watching her victim till suddenly the end came, and where there had been two vessels on the blue sea only one remained. Another gallant ship had joined the company of ghosts in the ocean Hades below.

When she had thus accomplished her work, the *Eitel Friedrich* departed, having taken on board stores, which would, she stated, with those already in hand, last her till the following April. She kept her prisoners on board till almost the last, in order to serve, it was said, as hostages should a British warship appear, and then deposited them all on shore. Our feelings on thus finding our island invaded, resembled, in some measure, the classical ones of Robinson Crusoe on a somewhat similar occasion ; the new-comers consisted of the captains and crews of both the English and French ships, forty-eight persons in all. They had been well treated on the cruiser, and were given on landing the remaining stores out of the sunken barque. A camp was made for them in the wool-shed, near the landing-place at Hanga Piko, and formed a great attraction to the natives who flocked there hourly to see what could be picked up. A room was found for the captain of the English ship in the Manager's house, where he made a pleasant addition to the party. The charms of Easter Island did not appeal to him, and he was naturally concerned for the anxiety which would be felt at home when his ship was reported "missing." His great occupation was to walk, many times a day, to the top of the knoll behind my tent, to try to catch sight of a sail, a hope which those of us who were better acquainted with the island felt to be somewhat forlorn.

Unfortunately, the epidemic of dysentery which had prevailed in the island since the previous October, laid low some of the sailors. This was a serious anxiety, as there was no doctor of any kind, and the only medical stores and books were those of the Expedition, which had to be routed out from our camp at the other end of the island. One young Englishman, named Campbell, to our great regret, succumbed to the disease ; he was "the only son of his mother, and she was a widow" ; a little white cross in the Easter Island burial-ground makes yet another memorial of the Great War. Captain Sharp's persistent look-out was rewarded sooner than might have been expected ; false hopes were raised by a vessel which went on without waiting, but when the marooned men had been with us some two months, a Swedish steamer appeared. She had come out of her way attracted by the fame of the antiquities, and it was a pleasure to show one or two of the officers what little could be seen of those statues near Cook's Bay. She kindly took on board the English crew and the greater part of the Frenchmen, but a few of the latter preferred to remain, on the ground that they had "sent word to the French Consul at Valparaiso, and must await his directions." It was said that, prior to leaving the *Eitel Friedrich*, they had signed an undertaking never to bear arms against Germany, and they were consequently not anxious to find themselves again in France, where their position might be invidious. One of them, who hailed from the French West Indies, subsequently married his hostess, a lady in the village. The wedding was celebrated in the church and largely attended ; during a great part of the service the couple sat on a low form before the altar, with the arm of the bridegroom round the waist of the bride; the ceremony was followed by a sumptuous and decorous repast.

Such an excitement as the German visit had of course upset my grown-up children, but we gradually resumed our talks. The ways, means, and result of those conversations will come more appropriately under the heading of the scientific work. It took, as a rule, about the same number of hours to copy out the rough notes of an interview as to get the substance; if, therefore, the morning had been given to talk, the afternoon was spent in writing. It soon became obvious that it was going to be a race against time to get all the information available before *Mana* returned, especially as the interviews involved a certain amount of strain, and it was better, in the interests of all, to diversify them with topographical and other work. In this sense every day was prized which the yacht delayed her return, and there was little opportunity for feeling lonely, at any rate during working hours. The time, however, began to grow long. January changed into February, and February turned into March, and there was still no news of her; everyone began to inquire if I were " not becoming very anxious," in a manner which was truly reassuring. And now, in approved fashion, we will turn and see what was happening to the other part of the Expedition.

After leaving the Raraku camp S. had ridden in to Cook's Bay, and there had difficulties about getting on board, for the Kanakas had made one bargain for the use of their boat, and then wanted double; during the delay rain came on, and he was obliged to shelter himself and his goods in the native boat-house by the landing. He at length, however, reached the ship, where the captain gave him his own cabin under the bridge. At tea-time the first officer, who was of German nationality, came out of his cabin and conversed in such a way that it was obvious that he was not altogether sober; the captain soon came along, rated him for drinking, told him the curse of the sea was alcohol, and he was to go at once on deck. Upon which the mate ascended to the bridge, groaning deeply. Now the said captain had, unfortunately, on board sixteen cases of whisky, which he had brought to trade at Easter, but which Mr. Edmunds had not allowed him to land. He himself shortly began to drink steadily, and went on till delirium tremens supervened, and he became obsessed with the idea that there was an affray going on between the sailors and stewards. By the arrangement of the vessel, the crew were berthed for'ard and the stewards aft, while the waist of the ship was filled by a stack of coal, which had been left on deck, to save the trouble of stowing it in the bunkers, and in the pious hope that no bad weather would supervene. On the top of this coal the captain now took his stand, declared that

II

he would have no fighting on his ship, and hurled pieces of coal first at an imaginary crew for'ard and then at supposititious stewards aft ; though all hands were in reality carefully lying low to keep out of his way.

S., meanwhile, was unfortunately confined to his cabin, having gone down, about the second day out, with a very severe attack of dysentery ; the epidemic on the island had never reached our camp ; he had presumably contracted it during the delay in starting. His position was anything but enviable : there was no steward, only a cabin-boy, well-meaning, but languid and very dirty. He could get no food which he could take, and lay there helpless with the rats eating his clothes ; if it had not been for the kindness of the chief engineer, who looked in occasionally, it seems doubtful if he would have lived to reach Chile. To this pleasing state was now added the apprehension that the captain. who was wandering about by day and night, might at any moment attack him for being in the cabin, in anticipation of which event S. kept a loaded revolver under his pillow. At last things got to such a state that the chief engineer came and asked his advice on the desirability of screwing up the skipper, Oxford fashion, and passing his food through the port. Before, however, this step could be taken, the offender had reached the stage of mental collapse, melted into tears and spent his time in protracted prayers, beseeching the engineer to put the accursed stuff overboard. S. naturally advised taking him at his word, when it was found that he had been drinking at the rate of nearly three bottles a day.

All this time the German mate had been obliged, to his great annoyance, to keep sober for the sake of his own safety, but as they approached Juan Fernandez there was much anxiety on board, for no one was very sure where it was, and they wanted to see it without hitting it ; by good luck it was fortunately sighted during the hours of daylight. They managed, somehow, to reach Valparaiso, and S. was at once taken to the same English hospital to which Mr. Corry had been removed. Here he lay for weeks, delighted to be well nursed and comfortable, and when convalescent, was most hospitably entertained by our friend Mr. Hope-Simpson, till he was equal to going down to Talcahuano to see after the yacht.

On February 20th, 1915, *Mana*, now duly insured, sallied

forth once more, having lain at Talcahuano for nearly five months. Von Spee's squadron had been annihilated off the Falkland Islands on December 8th, and though the exact whereabouts of his sole remaining ship, the *Dresden*, were still unknown, the coast was thought to be clear. As a matter of fact, the cruiser had crept out of her hiding-place in the Patagonian Channels sixteen days earlier, and was at this time not far from the entrance to the bay, where she was no doubt apprised by wireless from the shore of the movements of all shipping. Luckily the yacht's departure was delayed at the last by some parting arrangements, and she left port some hours later than had been intended ; in the interval, according to information subsequently received, another ship went by, the cruiser captured her and went off. Thus did *Mana* pass by in safety, and before she reached Easter Island the *Dresden* had met with her doom at Juan Fernandez.

March 15th was a joyful day, when the yacht at length turned up all safe and sound. We rapidly decided that the best thing we could do would be to let the British Representative in Chile know at once of the call of the *Eitel Friedrich*, and of the use made of the island by the Germans, more particularly as there were recent reports from more than one quarter that a vessel with two funnels had been seen off the island. A despatch was therefore written for our Minister at Santiago, and Mr. Gillam was instructed to hand it with a covering letter to the British Consul at Valparaiso. The enemy might turn up any day, and, in view of the gossip there had been about the yacht when they were here before, it was obviously desirable to maintain secrecy as to her whereabouts. No one save the Sailing-master, therefore, was informed of her destination; she lay for two nights off Hanga Roa, and on the third morning she was gone. On her arrival at Valparaiso the Consul requested Mr. Gillam to take the despatch himself to Santiago in order to answer any questions in his power ; this he did, and had a long interview with the British Minister. We have subsequently received kind acknowledgment from the Admiralty of our efforts to be useful. The yacht then returned to the island,[1] where we had been doing last things, including finishing off our excavations, in which we

---

[1] *Mana* made seven trips in all between Chile and Easter Island, traversing, in this part alor her voyage, over 14,000 miles on her course.

were very kindly assisted by some of the remaining members of the French crew; they worked for us at a rate of pay refused by the natives.   The packing-up of specimens alone was no light business.   There had turned out to be much more work to be done on the island than we had anticipated, and though our residence had been prolonged far beyond the time originally contemplated, we had, from the scientific point of view, been largely single-handed and had also been hindered by circumstances.   So far as research was concerned we would gladly have remained for another six months, to write up results and make good omissions; but England was at war, the three years our crew had signed-on for would shortly expire, our wonderful time was over, and we must go.

PREHISTORIC REMAINS

AHU OR BURIAL-PLACES

FIG. 31.

STATUE AT THE BRITISH MUSEUM.

(Back of statue, Fig. 106.)

CHAPTER XIII

PREHISTORIC REMAINS

AHU OR BURIAL-PLACES

Form of the Easter Island Image—Position and Number of the Ahu—Design and Construction of the Image Ahu—Reconstruction and Transformation—The Semi-pyramid Ahu—The Overthrow of the Images and Destruction of the Ahu.

In many places it is possible in the light of great monuments to reconstruct the past. In Easter Island the past is the present, it is impossible to escape from it ; the inhabitants of to-day are less real than the men who have gone ; the shadows of the departed builders still possess the land. Voluntarily or involuntarily the sojourner must hold commune with those old workers ; for the whole air vibrates with a vast purpose and energy which has been and is no more. What was it ? Why was it ? The great works are now in ruins, of many comparatively little remains ; but the impression infinitely exceeded anything which had been anticipated, and every day, as the power to see increased, brought with it a greater sense of wonder and marvel. " If we were to tell people at home these things," said our Sailing-master, after being shown the prostrate images on the great burial place of Tongariki, " they would not believe us."

The present natives take little interest in the remains. The statues are to them facts of every-day life in much the same way as stones or banana-trees. " Have you no *moai* " (as they are termed) " in England ? " was asked by one boy, in a tone in which surprise was slightly mingled with contempt ; to ask for the history of the great works is as successful as to try to get from an old woman selling bootlaces at Westminster the story of Cromwell or of the frock-coated worthies in Parliament Square. The information given in reply to questions is generally wildly mythical, and any real knowledge crops up only indirectly.

Anyone who is able to go to the British Museum can see a typical specimen of an Easter Island statue, in the large image which greets the approaching visitor from under the portico (fig. 31). The general form is unvarying, and with one exception, which will be alluded to hereafter, all appear to be the work of skilled hands, which suggests that the design was well known and evolved under other conditions. It represents a half-length figure, at the bottom of which the hands nearly meet in front of the body. The most remarkable features are the ears, of which the lobe is depicted to represent a fleshy rope (fig. 58), while in a few cases the disc which was worn in it is also indicated (fig. 59). The fashion of piercing and distending the lobe of the ear is found among various primitive races.[1] The tallest statues are over 30 feet, a few are only 6 feet, and even smaller specimens exist. Those which stood on the burial-places, now to be described, are usually from 12 to 20 feet in height, and were surmounted with a form of hat.[2]

Position and Number of Ahu.—In Easter Island the problem of the disposal of the dead was solved by neither earth-burial nor cremation, but by means of the omnipresent stones which were built up to make a last resting-place for the departed. Such burial-places are known as " ahu," and the name will henceforth be used, for it signifies a definite thing, or rather type of thing, for which we have no equivalent. They number in all some two hundred and sixty, and are principally found near the coast, but some thirty exist inland, sufficient to show that their erection on the sea-board was a matter of convenience, not of principle. With the exception of the great eastern and western headlands, where they are scarce, it is probably safe to say that, in riding round the island, it is impossible to go anywhere for more than a few hundred yards without coming across one of these abodes of the dead. They cluster most thickly on the little coves and their enclosing promontories, which were the principal centres of population. Some are two or three hundred yards away from the edge of the cliff, others stand on the verge ; in the lower land they are but little above the sea-level, while on the precipitous part of the coast the ocean breaks hundreds of feet below.

[1] For an illustrated description of the method of expanding the ear, see *With a Prehistoric People, the Akikuyu of British East Africa*, p. 32.
[2] A full description of the statues is given in chap. xiv.

AKAHANGA C(

FIG. 32.

URING AHU.

Portion of an image
still standing.

Rano Raraku, S.E. face.

(A modern wall.)

AHU TON

Bases of fallen images.

FIG. 33.

SIDE.

Head on its back.   Body of statue on its front.

AHU TON

Wi

FIG. 34.

Crown or hat.

Portion of an image
still standing.

Crown or hat.

) SIDE.

For distant view, see fig. 73.

Central portion.

FIG. 35.

Wing.

It was these burial-places, on which the images were then standing, which so strongly impressed the early voyagers and whose age and origin have remained an unsolved problem.

During the whole of our time on the island we worked on the ahu as way opened. Those which happened to lie near to either of our camps were naturally easy of access, but to reach the more distant ones, notably those on the north shore, involved a long expedition. Such a day began with perhaps an hour's ride ; at noon there was an interval for luncheon, when, in hot weather, the neighbourhood was scoured for miles to find the smallest atom of shade ; and the day ended with a journey home of not less than two hours, during which an anxious eye was kept on the sinking sun. The usual method, as each ahu was reached, was for S. to dismount, measure it and describe it, while I sat on my pony and scribbled down notes; but in some manner or other every part of the coast was by one or both of us ridden over several times, and a written statement made of the size, kind, condition, and name of each monument.

Unfortunately there is in existence no large-scale plan of the coast, a need we had to supply as best we could; map of Easter Island there is none, only the crude chart ; the efforts of our own surveyor were limited, by the time at his disposal, to making detailed plans of a few of the principal spots. The want is to be regretted geographically, but it does not materially affect the archæological result. We were always accompanied by native guides in order to learn local names and traditions, and it was soon found necessary to make a point of these being old men ; owing to the concentration of the remains of the population in one district, all names elsewhere, except those of the most important places, are speedily being forgotten. The memories of even the older men were sometimes shaky, and to get reasonably complete and accurate information the whole of a district had, in more than one case, to be gone over again with a second ancient who turned out to have lived in the neighbourhood in his youth and hence to be a better authority.

Original Design and Construction of Image Ahu.—The burial-places are not all of one type, nor all constructed to carry statues; some also are known to have been built comparatively recently, and will therefore be described under a later section. The image ahu are, however, all prehistoric. They number just under a hundred, or over one-third of the whole.[1]   The figures connected with them, of which traces still remain, were counted as 231, but as many are in fragments, this number is uncertain.

A typical image ahu (fig. 36) is composed of a long wall running parallel with the sea, which, in a large specimen, is as much as 15 feet in height and 300 feet in length ; it is buttressed on the land side with a great slope of masonry.   The wall is in three divisions.   The main or central portion projects in the form of a terrace on which the images stood, with their backs to the sea ; it is therefore broad enough to carry their oval bed-plates ; these measure up to about 10 feet in length by 8 feet or 9 feet in width, and are flush with the top of the wall.   On the great ahu of Tongariki there have been fifteen statues, but sometimes an ahu has carried one figure only.

The wall which forms the landward side of the terrace is continued on either hand in a straight line, thus adding a wing at each end of the central portion which stands somewhat farther back from the sea (fig. 41).   Images were sometimes placed on the wings, but it was not usual.   From this continuous wall the masonry slopes steeply till it reaches a containing wall, some 3 feet high, formed of finely wrought slabs of great size and of peculiar shape ; the workmanship put into this wall is usually the most highly finished of any part of the ahu.   Extending inland from the foot of this low wall is a large, raised, and smoothly paved expanse.   The upper surface of this, too, has an appreciable fall, or slope, inland, though it is almost horizontal, when compared with the glacis.

By the method of construction of this area, vault accommodation is obtained between its surface pavement and the sheet of volcanic rock below, on which the whole rests.   In the largest specimen the whole slope of masonry, measured that is from either the sea-wall of the wing or from the landward wall of the terrace to its farthest extent, is about 250 feet.   Beyond this the ground is sometimes levelled for another 50 or 60 yards, forming a smooth sward which much enhanced the appearance of the ahu.   In two cases the ahu is approached by a strip of narrow pavement formed of water-worn boulders laid flat, and bordered with the same kind of stone set on end ; one of these

[1] This excludes some fifteen which may have carried statues, but about which doubt exists.

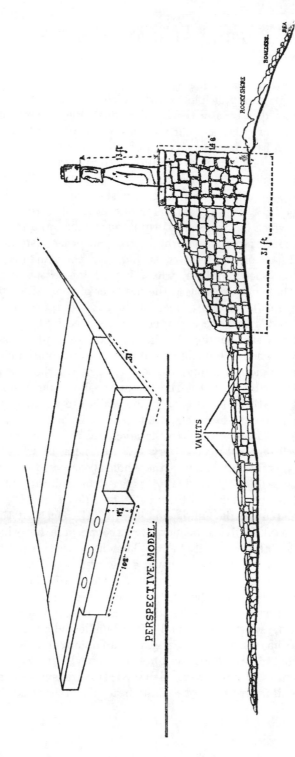

PERSPECTIVE. MODEL.

VAULTS

ROCKY SHORE

BOULDERS

SEA

FIG. 36. DIAGRAM OF IMAGE AHU.

pavements is 220 feet in length by 12 feet in width, the other is somewhat smaller (fig. 93).

The general principle on which the sea or main walls are constructed is usually the same, though the various ahu differ greatly in appearance: first comes a row of foundation blocks on which have been set upright the largest stones that could be found; the upper part of the wall is composed of smaller stones, and it is finished with a coping. The variety in effect is due to the difference in material used. In some cases, as at Tongariki (fig. 33), the most convenient stone available has consisted of basalt which has cooled in fairly regular cubes, and the rows are there comparatively uniform in size; in other instances, as at Ahu Tepeu on the west coast (fig. 37), the handiest material has been sheets of lava, which have hardened as strata, and when these have been used the first tier of the wall is composed of huge slabs up to 9 feet in height. Irregularities in the shape and size of the big stones are rectified by fitting in small pieces and surmounting the shorter slabs with additional stones until the whole is brought to a uniform level; on the top of this now even tier horizontal blocks are laid, till the whole is the desired height (fig. 42). The amount of finish put into the work varies greatly: in many ahu the walls are all constructed of rough material; in others, while the slabs are untouched, the stones which bring them to the level and the cubes on the top are well wrought; in a very few instances, of which Vinapu (fig. 35) is the best example, the whole is composed of beautifully finished work. Occasionally, as at Oroi, natural outcrops of rock have been adapted to carry statues (fig. 122).

The study of the ahu is simplified by the fact that they were being used in living memory for the purpose for which they were doubtless originally built. They have been termed " burial-places," but burial in its usual sense was not the only, nor in most cases their principal, object. On death the corpse was wrapped in a tapa blanket and enclosed in its mattress of reeds; fish-hooks, chisels, and other objects were sometimes included. It was then bound into a bundle and carried on staves to the ahu, where it was exposed on an oblong framework. This consisted of four corner uprights set up in the ground, the upper extremities of which were Y-shaped, two transverse bars rested in the bifurcated ends, one at the head, the other at the foot, and

FIG. 37.

AHU TEPEU.

Part of seaward wall showing large slabs—some of the stones forming upper courses
are wrought foundation-stones of canoe-shaped houses, pp. 215–16.

FIG. 38.

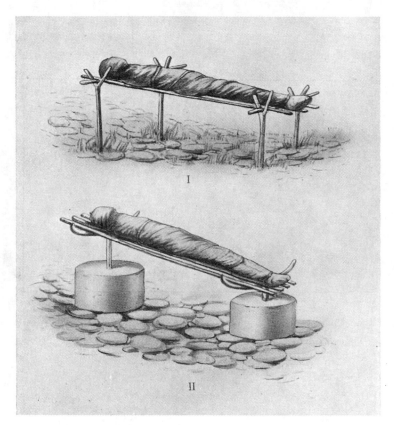

I

II

METHOD OF EXPOSING THE DEAD FROM ILLUSTRATED
DESCRIPTIONS.

on these transverse bars were placed the extremities of the bundle which wrapped the corpse. The description and sketch are based on a model framework, and a wrapped-up figure, one of the wooden images of the island, prepared by the natives to amplify their verbal description.[1] At times, instead of the four supports, two stones were used with a hole in each, into which a Y-shaped stick was placed (fig. 38). While the corpse remained on the ahu the district was marked off by the péra, or taboo, for the dead ; no fishing was allowed near, and fires and cooking were forbidden within certain marks—the smoke, at any rate, must be hidden or smothered with grass. Watch was kept by four relatives, and anyone breaking the regulations was liable to be brained. The mourning might last one, two, or even three years, by which time the whole thing had, of course, fallen to pieces. The bones were either left on the ahu, or collected and put into vaults of oblong shape, which were kept for the family, or they might be buried elsewhere. The end of the mourning was celebrated by a great feast, after which ceremony, as one recorder cheerfully concluded, " Pappa was finished."

Looked at from the landward side, we may, therefore, conceive an ahu as a vast theatre stage, of which the floor runs gradually upwards from the footlights. The back of the stage, which is thus the highest part, is occupied by a great terrace, on which are set up in line the giant images, each one well separated from his neighbour, and all facing the spectator. Irrespective of where he stands he will ever see them towering above him, clear cut out against a turquoise sky. In front of them are the remains of the departed. Unseen, on the farther side of the terrace, is the sea. The stone giants, and the faithful dead over whom they watch, are never without music, as countless waves launch their strength against the pebbled shore, showering on the figures a cloud of mist and spray.

Reconstruction and Transformation.—Those which have been described are ideal image ahu, but not one now remains in its original condition. It is by no means unusual to find, even in the oldest parts now existing, that is in walls erected to carry statues, pieces of still older images built into the stonework ; in one case a whole statue has been used as a slab for the sea-wall,

[1] The body was no doubt supported by staves, though they were dispensed with in the model, being unnecessary for the wooden figure.

showing that alteration has taken place even when the cult was alive (fig. 42). Again, a considerable number of ahu, some thirteen in all, after being destroyed and terminating their career as image-terraces, have been rebuilt after the fashion of others constructed originally on a different plan (fig. 39). This is a type for which no name was found : it is in form that of a semi-pyramid, and there are between fifty and sixty on the island, in addition to those which have been in the first place image-ahu (fig. 42). A few are comparatively well made, but most are very rough. They resemble a pyramid cut in two, so that the section forms a triangle ; this triangle is the sea-wall ; the flanking buttress on the land side is made of stones, and is widest at the apex or highest point, gradually diminishing to the angles or extremities. The greatest height, in the centre, varies from about 5 feet to 12 feet, and a large specimen may extend in length from 100 feet to 160 feet. They contain vaults. In a few instances they are ornamented by broken pieces of image-stone, and occasionally by a row of small cairns along the top, which recall the position of the statues on the image-platform; for these no very certain reason was forthcoming, they were varyingly reported to be signs of " péra " or as marking the respective right of families on the ahu. As image-terraces may be found reconstructed as pyramid ahu, the latter form of building must have been carried on longer than the former, and probably till recent times, but there is nothing to show whether or not the earliest specimens of pyramid ahu are contemporary with the great works, or even earlier.

Overthrow of the Images and Destruction of the Ahu.—The only piece of a statue which still remains on its bed-plate is the fragment already alluded to at Tongariki (fig. 34). In the best-preserved specimens the figures lie on their faces like a row of huge nine-pins; some are intact, but many are broken, the cleavage having generally occurred when the falling image has come in contact with the containing wall at the lower level. The curious way in which the heads have not infrequently turned a somersault while falling and now lie face uppermost is shown in the eighth figure from the western end on Tongariki ahu (fig. 34).

No one now living remembers a statue standing on an ahu ; and legend, though not of a very impressive character, has

FIG. 39.

A SEMI-PYRAMID AHU.

FIG. 40.

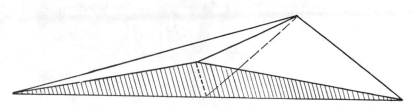

DIAGRAM OF SEMI-PYRAMID AHU.

FIG. 41.

AHU MAHATUA, SEAWARD SIDE.

Image ahu, with east wing clearly defined. Landward side and centre converted to semi-pyramid form.

already arisen to account for the fall of some of them. An old man arrived, it is said, in the neighbourhood of Tongariki, and as he was unable to speak, he made known by means of signs that he wished for chicken-heads to eat; these were not forth-coming. He slept, however, in one of the houses there, and during the night his hosts were aroused by a great noise, which he gave it to be understood was made by his feet tapping against the stone foundations of the house. In the morning it was found that the statues on the great ahu had all fallen: it was the revenge of the old man. Such lore is, however, mixed up with more tangible statements to the effect that the figures were overthrown in tribal warfare by means of a rope, or by taking away the small stones from underneath the bed-plates, and thus causing them to fall forward. That the latter method had been used had been concluded independently by studying the re-mains themselves. It will be seen later, that other statues which have been set up in earth were deliberately dug out, and it seems unnecessary to look, as some have done, to an earthquake to account for their collapse.

Moreover, the conclusion that the images owed their fall to deliberate vandalism during internecine warfare is confirmed by knowledge, which still survives, connected with the destruction of the last one. This image stood alone on an ahu on the north coast, called Paro, and is the tallest known to have been put up on a terrace, being 32 feet in height. The events occurred just before living memory, and, like most stories in Easter Island, it is connected with cannibalism. A woman of the western clans was eaten by men of the eastern; her son managed to trap thirty of the enemy in a cave and consumed them in revenge; and during the ensuing struggle this image was thrown down (fig. 78). The oldest man living when we were on the island said that he was an infant at the time; and another, a few years younger, stated that his father as a boy helped his grandfather in the fight. It is not, after all, only in Easter Island that pleasure has been taken during war-time in destroying the architectural treasures of the enemy.

While, therefore, the date of the erection of the earliest image ahu is lost in the mists of antiquity, nor are we yet in a posi-tion to say when the building stopped, we can give approxi-mately the time of the overthrow of the images. We know, from the accounts of the early voyagers, that the statues, or the greater number of them, were still in place in the eighteenth century; by the early part of the middle of the nineteenth century not one was standing.

The destruction of the ahu has continued in more modern days.   A manager, whose sheep had found the fresh-water springs below high water, thinking they were injuring themselves by drinking from the sea, erected a wall round a large part of the coast to keep them from it.   For this wall the ahu came in of course most conveniently; it was run through a great number and their material used for its construction.   One wing of Tongariki has been pulled down to form an enclosure for the livestock.   In addition to the damage wrought by man, the ocean is ever encroaching: in some cases part of an ahu has already fallen into the sea, and more is preparing to follow; statues may be found lying on their backs in process of descending into the waves (fig. 43).   One row of images, on the extreme western edge of the crater of Rano Kao, which were visible, although inaccessible, at the time of the visit of the U.S.A. ship *Mohican* in 1886, are now lying on the shore a thousand feet below.   As the result of these various causes the burial-places of Easter Island are, as has been seen, all in ruins, and many are scarcely recognisable; only their huge stones and prostrate figures show what they must once have been.

FIG. 42.

AHU MAITAKI-TE-MOA, SEAWARD SIDE.

An image ahu partially destroyed and changed to semi-pyramid type. A statue from Raraku lies in foreground; another statue of different stone forms part of the main wall.

FIG. 43.

AHU RUNGA-VAE, ON SOUTH COAST, UNDERMINED BY THE SEA.

Statue has fallen backwards.

PREHISTORIC REMAINS

STATUES AND CROWNS

174 B]
Opposite fig. 43.]

FIG. 44.

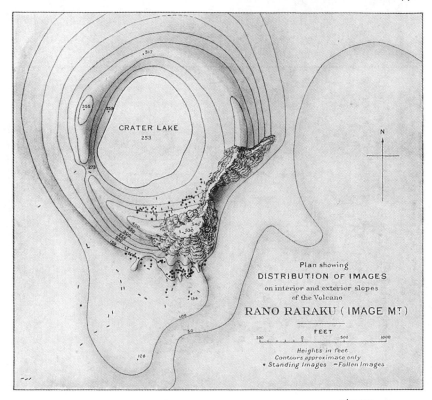

CRATER LAKE
253

N

Plan showing
DISTRIBUTION OF IMAGES
on interior and exterior slopes
of the Volcano

RANO RARAKU (IMAGE Mᵗ)

FEET

500   0   500   1000

Heights in feet
Contours approximate only
• Standing Images ⁻Fallen Images

1/14,000

45

FIG. 45.

RANO RARAKU FROM THE SEA.

RANO RARA
Images prostrate in fore

FIG. 46.

UTH-WEST.
ope ; quarries above.

FIG. 47.

CRATER.

on slope and in quarry

CHAPTER XIV

PREHISTORIC REMAINS (*continued*)

STATUES AND CROWNS

Rano Raraku, its Quarries and Standing Statues—the South-east Face of the Mountain—Isolated Statues—Roads—Stone Crowns of the Images.

STRANGE as it may appear, it is by no means easy to obtain a complete view of a statue on the island : most of the images which were formerly on the ahu lie on their faces, many are broken, and detail has largely been destroyed by weather. Happily, we are not dependent for our knowledge of the images on such information as we can gather from the ruins on the ahu, but are able to trace them to their origin, though even here excavation is necessary to see the entire figure. Rano Raraku is, as has already been explained, a volcanic cone containing a crater-lake. It resembles, to use an unromantic simile, one of the china drinking-vessels dedicated to the use of dogs, whose base is larger than their brim. Its sides are for the most part smooth and sloping, and several carriages could drive abreast on the northern rim of the crater, but towards the south-east it rises in height, and from this aspect it looks as if the circular mass had been sliced down with a giant knife forming it into a precipitous cliff. The cliff is lowest where the imaginary knife has come nearest to the central lake, thus causing the two ends to stand out as the peaks already mentioned (fig. 45).

The mountain is composed of compressed volcanic ash, which has been found in certain places to be particularly suitable for quarrying ; it has been worked on the southern exterior slope, and also inside the crater both on the south and south-eastern sides. With perhaps a dozen exceptions, the whole of the images in the island have been made from it, and they have been dragged from this point up hill and down dale to adorn the terraces round the coast-line of the island ; even the images on the ahu, which have fallen into the sea on the further extremity of the western volcano, are said to have been of the same stone. It is conspicuous in being a reddish brown colour, of which the smallest chips can be easily recognised. It is composite in character, and embedded in the ash are numerous lapilli of metamorphic rock. Owing to the nature of this rock the earliest European visitors came to the conclusion that the material was factitious and that the statues were built of clay and stones ; it was curious to find that the marooned prisoners of war of our own time fell into the same mistake of thinking that the figures were " made up."

The workable belt, generally speaking, forms a horizontal section about half-way up the side of the mountain. Below it, both on the exterior and within the crater, are banks of detritus, and on these statues have been set up ; most of them are still in place, but they have been buried in greater or less degree by the descent of earth from above (fig. 57). Mr. Ritchie made a survey of the mountain with the adjacent coast, but it was found impossible to record the results of our work without some sort of plan or diagram which was large enough to show every individual image. This was accomplished by first studying each quarry, note-book in hand, and then, with the aid of field-glasses, amalgamating the results from below ; the standing statues being inserted in their relation to the quarries above. It was a lengthy but enjoyable undertaking. Part of the diagram of the exterior has been redrawn with the help of photographs (fig. 60); the plan of the inside of the crater is shown in what is practically its original form (fig. 47).

Quarries of Rano Raraku.—Leaving on one side for the moment the figures on the lower slope, let us in imagination scramble up the grassy side, a steep climb of some one or two hundred feet to where the rock has been hewn away into a series of chambers and ledges. Here images lie by the score in all stages of evolution, just as they were left when, for some unknown reason, the workmen laid down their tools for the last time and the busy scene was still. Here, as elsewhere, the wonder of the place can only be appreciated as the eye becomes trained to see. In the

majority of cases the statues still form part of the rock, and are
frequently covered with lichen or overgrown with grass and
ferns ; and even in the illustrations, for which prominent figures
have naturally been chosen, the reader may find that he has to
look more than once in order to recognise the form. A con-

FIG. 48.

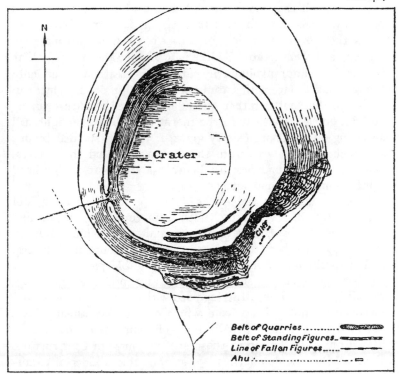

DIAGRAM OF RANO RARAKU.

spicuous one first strikes the beholder : as he gazes, he finds with
surprise that the walls on either hand are themselves being
wrought into figures, and that, resting in a niche above him, is
another giant ; he looks down, and realises with a start that his
foot is resting on a mighty face. To the end of our visit we
occasionally found a figure which had escaped observation.

The workings on the exterior of Raraku first attract atten-

12

tion ; here their size, and incidentally that of many of the statues, has largely been determined by fissures in the hillside, which run vertically and at distances of perhaps 40 feet. The quarries have been worked differently, and each has a character of its own. In some of them the principal figures lie in steps, with their length parallel to the hill's horizontal axis ; one of this type is reached through a narrow opening in the rock, and recalls the side-chapel of some old cathedral, save that nature's blue sky forms the only roof (no. 74, fig. 60) ; immediately opposite the doorway there lies, on a base of rock, in quiet majesty, a great recumbent figure. So like is it to some ancient effigy that the awed spectator involuntarily catches his breath, as if suddenly brought face to face with a tomb of the mighty dead. Once, on a visit to this spot, a rather quaint little touch of nature supervened : going there early in the morning, with the sunlight still sparkling on the floor of dewy grass, a wild-cat, startled by our approach, rushed away from the rock above, and the natives, clambering up, found nestling beneath a statue at a high level a little family of blind kittens.

In other instances the images have been carved lying, not horizontally, but vertically, with sometimes the head, and sometimes the base, toward the summit of the hill. But no exact system has been followed, the figures are found in all places, and all positions. When there was a suitable piece of rock it has been carved into a statue, without any special regard to surroundings or direction. Interspersed with embryo and completed images are empty niches from which others have already been removed ; and finished statues must, in some cases, have been passed out over the top of those still in course of construction. From all the outside quarries is seen the same wonderful panorama : immediately beneath are the statues which stand on the lower slopes; farther still lie the prostrate ones beside the approach ; while beyond is the whole stretch of the southern plain, with its white line of breaking surf ending in the western mountain of Rano Kao (fig. 54).

The quarries within the crater are on the same lines as those without, save that those on the south-eastern side form a more continuous whole. Here the most striking position is on the top of the seaward cliff, in the centre of which is a large finished image (no. 16, fig. 47) ; on one side the ground falls away more or

FIG. 49.

STATUE IN QUARRY, PARTIALLY SCULPTURED

[No. 41. Fig. 60.]

FIG. 50.

STATUE IN QUARRY

Attached to rock by " keel " only.   Top of head (flat surface) towards spectator.
[No. 61.   Fig. 60.]

FIG. 51.

STATUE IN QUARRY

Ready to be launched ; movement prevented by stone wedges.   Base towards spectator.
[No. 57.   Fig. 60.]

less steeply to the crater-lake, on the other a stone thrown down would reach the foot of the precipice; the view extends from sea to sea. Over all the most absolute stillness reigns.

The statues in the quarries number altogether over 150. Amongst this mass of material there is no difficulty in tracing the course of the work. The surface of the rock, which will form the figure, has generally been laid bare before work upon it began, but occasionally the image was wrought lying partially under a canopy (fig. 49). In a few cases the stone has been roughed out into preliminary blocks (no. 58, fig. 60), but this procedure is not universal, and seems to have been followed only where there was some doubt as to the quality of the material. When this was not the case the face and anterior aspect of the statue were first carved, and the block gradually became isolated as the material was removed in forming the head, base, and sides. A gutter or alley-way was thus made round the image (fig. 55), in which the niches where each man has stood or squatted to his work can be clearly seen; it is, therefore, possible to count how many were at work at each side of a figure.

When the front and sides were completed down to every detail of the hands, the undercutting commenced. The rock beneath was chipped away by degrees till the statue rested only on a narrow strip of stone running along the spine; those which have been left at this stage resemble precisely a boat on its keel, the back being curved in the same way as a ship's bottom (fig. 50). In the next stage shown the figure is completely detached from the rock, and chocked up by stones, looking as if an inadvertent touch would send it sliding down the hill into the plain below (fig. 56). In one instance the moving has evidently begun, the image having been shifted out of the straight. In another very interesting case the work has been abandoned when the statue was in the middle of its descent; it has been carved in a horizontal position in the highest part of the quarry, where its empty niche is visible, it has then been slewed round and was being launched, base forward, across some other empty niches at a lower level. The bottom now rests on the floor of the quarry, and the figure, which has broken in half, is supported in a standing fashion against the outer edge of the vacated shelves. The first impression was that it had met with an accident in transit, and been abandoned; but it is at least equally possible that for the purpose of bringing it down, a bank or causeway of earth had been built up to level the inequalities of the descent, and that it was resting on this when the work came to an end; the soil would then in time be washed away, and the figure fracture through loss of support.

In the quarry which is shown in fig. 54, the finished head can be seen lying across the opening, the body is missing, presumably broken off and buried; the bottom of the keel on which the figure at one time rested can be clearly traced in a projecting line of rock down the middle of its old bed, also the different

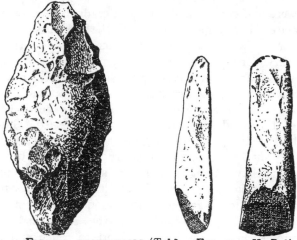

FIG. 52. STONE TOOLS (*Toki*).   FIG. 53.   *H. Balfour del.*

sections where the various men employed have chipped away the stone in undermining the statue. In the quarry wall the niches occupied by the sculptors are also visible, at more than one level, the higher ones being discarded when the upper portion of the work was finished and a lower station needed. The hand of the standing boy in fig. 51 rests on a small platform similarly abandoned.

The tools were found with which the work has been done. One type of these can be seen lying about in great abundance (fig. 52). They are of the same material as the lapilli in the statues, and made by flaking. Some specimens are pointed at both ends,

FIG. 54.

HEAD OF A STATUE AT MOUTH OF QUARRY FROM WHICH IT HAS BEEN HEWN

[No. 72. Fig. 63.]

FIG. 55.

UPPER PORTION OF LARGEST IMAGE IN QUARRY,
WITH ALLEY-WAY FOR WORKMEN.

[No. 64.   Fig. 50.]

others have one end more or less rounded. It is unlikely that they were hafted, and they were probably held in the hand when in use. They were apparently discarded as soon as the point became damaged. There is another tool much more carefully made, an adze blade, with the lower end bevelled off to form the cutting edge. In the specimen shown, the top is much abraded apparently from hammering with a maul or mallet (fig. 53). These are rarely found, the probability being that they were too precious to leave and were taken home by the workmen. The whole process was not necessarily very lengthy; a calculation of the number of men who could work at the stone at the same time, and the amount each could accomplish, gave the rather surprising result that a statue might be roughed out within the space of fifteen days. The most notable part of the work was the skill which kept the figure so perfect in design and balance that it was subsequently able to maintain its equilibrium in a standing position; to this it is difficult to pay too high a tribute.

It remains to account for the vast number of images to be found in the quarry. A certain number have, no doubt, been abandoned prior to the general cessation of the work; in some cases a flaw has been found in the rock and the original plan has had to be given up—in this case, part of the stone is sometimes used for either a smaller image or one cut at a different angle. In other instances the sculptors have been unlucky enough to come across at important points one or more of the hard nodules with which their tools could not deal, and as the work could not go down to posterity with a large wart on its nose or excrescence on its chin, it has had to be stopped. But when all these instances have been subtracted, the amount of figures remaining in the quarries is still startlingly large when compared with the number which have been taken out of it, and must have necessitated, if they were all in hand at once, a number of workers out of all proportion to any population which the island has ever been likely to have maintained. The theory naturally suggests itself that some were merely rock-carvings and not intended to be removed. It is one which needs to be adopted with caution, for more than once, where every appearance has pointed to its being correct, a similar neighbour has been found which was actually being removed ; on the whole, however, there can be little doubt that it is at any rate a partial solution of the problem. Some of the images are little more than embossed carvings on the face of the rock without surrounding alley-ways. In one instance, inside the crater, a piece of rock which has been left standing on the very summit of the cliff has been utilised in such a way that the figure lies on its side, while its back is formed by the outward precipice (fig. 56) ; this is contrary to all usual methods, and it seems improbable that it was intended to make it into a standing statue. Perhaps the strongest evidence is afforded by the size of some of the statues: the largest (fig. 55 ; no. 64, fig. 60) is 66 feet in length, whereas 36 feet is the extreme ever found outside the quarry; tradition, it is true, points out the ahu on the south coast for which this monster was designed, but it is difficult to believe it was ever intended to move such a mass. If this theory is correct, it would be interesting to know whether the stage of carving came first, and that of removal followed, as the workmen became more expert ; or whether it was the result of decadence when labour may have become scarce. It is, of course, possible that the two methods proceeded concurrently, rock-carvings being within the means of those who could not procure the labour necessary to move the statue.

Legendary lore throws no light on these matters, nor on the reasons which led to the desertion of this labyrinth of work ; it has invented a story which entirely satisfies the native mind and is repeated on every occasion. There was a certain old woman who lived at the southern corner of the mountain and filled the position of cook to the image-makers. She was the most important person of the establishment, and moved the images by supernatural power (*mana*), ordering them about at her will. One day, when she was away, the workers obtained a fine lobster, which had been caught on the west coast, and ate it up, leaving none for her ; unfortunately they forgot to conceal the remains, and when the cook returned and found how she had been treated, she arose in her wrath, told all the images to fall down, and thus brought the work to a standstill.

Standing Statues of Rano Raraku.—Descending from the quarries, we turn to the figures below. A few at the foot of the mountain have obviously been thrown down; one of these (no. 6, fig. 60) was wrecked in the same conflict as the one on Ahu Paro,

FIG. 56.

STATUE CARVED ON EDGE OF PRECIPICE.
INTERIOR OF CRATER.
[No. 27.   Fig. 47.]

FIG. 57.

No. 32.　　　　　　　　No. 33.　　　　　　　　No. 34.

STANDING STATUES ON EXTERIOR OF RANO RARAKU SHOWING PARTIAL BURIAL.

and one is shown where an attempt has been made to cut off the head. Another series of images have originally stood round the base on level ground (nos. 1, 2, 3, fig. 60), extending from the exterior of the entrance to the crater to the southern corner; these are all prostrate. On the slopes there are a few horizontal statues, but the great majority, both inside the crater and without, are still erect. Outside, some forty figures stand in an irregular belt, reaching from the corner nearest the sea to about half-way to the gap leading into the crater. The bottom of the mountain is here diversified by little hillocks and depressions ; these hillocks would have made commanding situations, but rather curiously the statues, while erected quite close to them, and even on their sides, are never on the top. Inside the crater, where some twenty statues are still erect, the arrangement is rather more regular; but, on the whole, they are put up in no apparent order. All stood with their backs to the mountain.

They vary very considerably in size; the tallest which could be measured from its base was 32 feet 3 inches, while others are not much above 11 feet. Every statue is buried in greater or less degree, but while some are exposed as far as the elbow, in others only a portion of the top of the head can be seen above the surface (fig. 57), others no doubt are covered entirely. The number visible must vary from time to time, as by the movement of the earth some are buried and others disclosed. An old man, whose testimony was generally reliable, stated, when speaking of the figures on the outside of the mountain, that while those nearer the sea were in the same condition as he always remembered them, those farther from it were now more deeply buried than in his youth.

Various old people were brought out from the village at Hanga Roa to pay visits to the camp, but the information forthcoming was never of great extent ; one elderly gentleman in particular took much more interest in roaming round the mountain, recalling various scenes of his youth, than in anything connected with the statues. A few names are still remembered in connection with the individual figures, and are said to be those of the makers of the images, and some proof is afforded of the reality of the tradition by the fact that the clans of the persons named are consistently given. Another class of names is, however, obviously derived merely from local circumstances ;

one in the quarry, under a drip from above, is known by the equivalent for " Dropping Water," while a series inside the crater are called after the birds which frequent the cliff-side, " Kia-kia, Flying," " Kia-kia, Sitting," and so forth.   A solitary legend relates to an unique figure, resembling rather a block than an image, which lies on the surface on the outside of the mountain (no. 24, fig. 60).   It is the single exception to the rule mentioned above, that no evolution can be traced in the statues on the island.   The usual conception is there, and the hands are shown, but the head seems to melt into the body and the ear and arm to have become confused.   It is said to have been the first image made and is known as Tai-haré-atua, which tradition says was the name of the maker.   He found himself unable to fashion it properly, and went over to the other side of the island to consult with a man who lived near Hanga Roa, named Rauwai-ika.   He stayed the night there, but the expert remained silent, and he was retiring disappointed in the morning, when he was followed by his host, who called him back.   " Make your image," said he, " like me,"—that is, in form of a man.

On our first visit to the mountain, overcome by the wonder of the scéne, we turned to our Fernandez boy and asked him what he thought of the statues.   Like the classical curate, when the bishop inquired as to the character of his egg, he struggled manfully between the desire to please and a sense of truth; like the curate, he took refuge in compromise.   " Some of them," he said doubtfully, he thought " were very nice."   If the figures at first strike even the cultured observer as crude and archaic, it must be remembered that not only are they the work of stone tools, but to be rightly seen should not be scrutinised near at hand.   " Hoa-haka-nanaia," for instance, is wholly and dismally out of place under a smoky portico, but on the slopes of a mountain, gazing in impenetrable calm over sea and land, the simplicity of outline is soon found to be marvellously impressive. The longer the acquaintance the more this feeling strengthens ; there is always the sense of quiet dignity, of suggestion and of mystery.

While the scene on Raraku always arouses a species of awe, it is particularly inspiring at sunset, when, as the light fades, the images gradually become outlined ás stupendous black figures against the gorgeous colouring of the west.   The most

FIG. 58.

STATUES ON RANO
RARAKU, SHOW-
ING DISTENSION
OF EAR.

LOBE
REPRESENTED AS
A ROPE.

[Nos. 27 and 29. Fig. 60.]

FIG. 59.

LOBE CONTAINING A DISC.
[No. 23. Fig. 60.]

KEY TO DIAGRAMMATIC SKETCH.

FIG. 60.

EXTERIOR OF RANO RARAKU.   EASTERN PORTION OF SOUTHERN ASPECT.

Diagrammatic sketch showing position of statues.

184B]

FIG. 61.

DIGGING OUT A STATUE.
For same image after excavation see fig. 69.

striking sight witnessed on the island was a fire on the hill-side ; in order to see our work more clearly we set alight the long dry grass, always a virtuous act on Easter Island that the live-stock may have the benefit of fresh shoots; in a moment the whole was a blaze, the mountain, wreathed in masses of driving smoke, grew to portentous size, the quarries loomed down from above as dark giant masses, and in the whirl of flame below the great statues stood out calmly, with a quiet smile, like stoical souls in Hades.

The questions which arise are obvious: do these buried statues differ in any way from those in the workings above, from those on the ahu or from one another ? were they put up on any foundation ? and, above all, what is the history of the mountain and the *raison d'être* of the figures? In the hope of throwing some light on these problems we started to dig them out. It had originally been thought that the excavation of one or two would give all the information which it was possible to obtain, but each case was found to have unique and instructive features, and we finally unearthed in this way, wholly or in part, some twenty or thirty statues. It was usually easy to trace the stages by which the figures had been gradually covered. On the top was a layer of surface soil, from 3 to 8 inches in depth ; then came debris, which had descended from the quarry above in the form of rubble, it contained large numbers of chisels, some forty of which have been found in digging out one statue ; below this was the substance in which a hole had been dug to erect the image, it sometimes consisted of clay and occasionally in part of rock. Not unfrequently the successive descents of earth could be traced by the thin lines of charcoal which marked the old surfaces, obviously the result of grass or brushwood fires. The few statues which are in a horizontal position are always on the surface (no. 31, fig. 60), and at first give the impression that they have been abandoned in the course of being brought down from the quarries ; as they are frequently found close to standing images, of which only the head is visible, it follows that, if this is the correct solution, the work must still have been proceeding when the earlier statues were already largely submerged. The juxtaposition, however, occurs so often that it seems, on the whole, more probable that the rush of earth which covered some, upset the foundations of others, and either threw them down where they stood or carried them with it on top of the flood. These various landslips allow of no approximate deductions as to the date, in the manner which is possible with successively deposited layers of earth.

To get absolutely below the base of an image was not altogether easy. The first we attempted to dig out was one of the farther ones within the crater (no. 19, fig. 47) ; it was found that, while the back of the hole into which it had been dropped was excavated in the soft volcanic ash, the front and remaining sides were of hard rock. This rock was cut to the curvature of the figure at a distance of some 3 inches from it, and as the chisel marks were horizontal, from right to left, the workmen must have stood in the cup while preparing it : in clearing out the alluvium between the wall of the cup and the figure, six stone implements were found. The hands, which were about 1 foot below the level of the rim, were perfectly formed. The next statue chosen for excavation was also inside the crater (no. 107, fig. 47) ; it was most easily attacked from the side, and this time it was possible to get low enough to see that it stood on no foundation, and that the base instead of expanding, as with those which stood on the ahu, contracted in such a manner as to give a peg-shaped appearance ; this confirmed the impression made by the previous excavation, that the image was intended to remain in its hole and was not, as some have stated, merely awaiting removal to an ahu (fig. 62).

The story was shown not only in the sections of the excavation, but in the degrees of weathering on the figure itself : the lowest part of the image to above the elbow exhibited, by the sharpness of its outlines and frequently of the chisel cuts also, that it had never been exposed, the other portions being worn in relative degrees. Traces of the smoothness of the original surface can still be seen above-ground in the more protected portions of some of the statues, such as in the orbit and under the chin (see frontispiece) ; but a much clearer impression is of course gained of the finish and detail of the image when the unweathered surface is exposed. The polish is often very beautiful, and pieces of pumice, called " punga," are found, with which the figures are said to have been rubbed down. The fingers taper, and the excessive length of the thumb-joint and nail are remarkable (fig. 72). The nipples are in some cases so pronounced that the natives

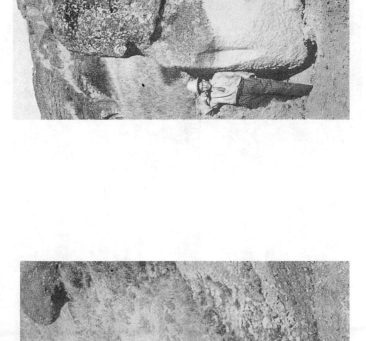

FIG. 62.

FIG. 63.

Showing effect of weathering and peg-shaped base.
[No. 107. Fig. 47.]

EXCAVATED IMAGES.

Showing scamped work in lower part of figure, no right
hand carved, and surface only coarsely chiselled.
[No. 36. Fig. 47.]

FIG. 64.

DESIGNS ON BACKS OF IMAGES.

BACK OF AN EXCA-VATED STATUE.

Showing (*a*) typical raised rings and girdle ; (*b*) exceptional incised carvings.

[No. 109. Fig. 47.]

FIG. 65.

P. Edmunds.

STATUE ON AN AHU AT ANAKENA.
Rings on centre and lower portion of back.

often characterised them as feminine, but in no case which we came across did the statues represent other than the nude male figure[1]; the navel is indicated by a raised disc. On the statue with the contracting base, which is one of the best, the surface modelling of the elbow-joint is clearly shown. The orbital cavity in the figures on Raraku is rather differently modelled from those on the ahu; in the statues on the mountain the position of the eyeball is always indicated by a straight line below the brow, the orbit has no lower border (fig. 72). On the terraces the socket is constantly hollowed out as in the figure at the British Museum (fig. 31).

The eye is the only point in which the two sets vary, with the important exception that some on the mountain have a type of back which never appears on the ahu. This question of back proved to be of special interest: in some images it remained exactly as when the figure left the quarry, the whole was convex, giving it a thick and archaic appearance, particularly as regards the neck; in other instances, the posterior was beautifully modelled after the same fashion as those on the terraces, the stone had been carefully chipped away till the ears stood out from the back of the head, the neck assumed definite form, and the spine, instead of standing out as a sharp ridge, was represented by an incised line. This second type, when excavated, proved, to our surprise, to possess a well-carved design in the form of a girdle shown by three raised bands, this was surmounted by one or sometimes by two rings, and immediately beneath it was another design somewhat in the shape of an M (figs. 64 and 106). The whole was new, not only to us, but to the natives, who greatly admired it. Later, when we knew what to look for, traces of the girdle could be seen also on the figures on the ahu where the arm had protected it from the weather. It was afterwards realised with amusement that the discovery of this design might have been made before leaving England by merely passing the barrier and walking behind the statues in the Bloomsbury portico. One case was found, a statue at Anakena, where a ring was visible, not only on the back but also on each of the buttocks, and in view of subsequent information these lower rings became of special importance. The girdle in this case consisted of one line only; the detail of the

[1] The sole possible exception was probably due to some flaw in the stone.

carving had doubtless been preserved by being buried in the sand (fig. 65). The two forms of back, unmodelled and modelled, stand side by side on the mountain (figs. 66, 67).

The next step was to discover where and when the modelling was done. Certainly not in the original place in the quarry, where it would be impossible from the position in which the image was evolved; generally speaking there was no trace of such work, and it was not until many months later that new light was thrown on the matter. Then it was remarked that in one of the standing statues on the outside of the hill, which was buried up to the neck (fig. 59), while the right ear was most carefully modelled, showing a disc, the left ear was as yet quite plain, and that the back of the head also was not symmetrical. Excavations made clear that the whole back was in course of transformation from the boat-shaped to the modelled type, each workman apparently chipping away where it seemed to him good (fig. 68). Two or three similar cases were then found on which work was proceeding; but on the other hand, some of the simpler backs were excavated to the foot, and others a considerable distance, and there was no indication that any alteration was intended. There are three possible explanations for these erect and partially moulded statues : Firstly, it may have been the regular method for the back to be completed after the statue was set up, in which case some kind of staging must have been used ; one of our guides had made a remark, noted, but not taken very seriously at the moment, that " the statues were set up to be finished " ; some knowledge or tradition of such work, therefore, appeared to linger. Secondly, the convex back may be the older form, and those on which work was being done were being modelled to bring them up to date. Alteration did at times take place ; a certain small image presented a very curious appearance both from the proportion of the body, which was singularly narrow from back to front, and because it was difficult to see how it remained in place as it was apparently exposed to the base ; it turned out that the figure had been carved out of the head of an older statue, of which the body was buried below (no. 14, fig. 60). Thirdly, these particular figures may have been erected and left in an unfinished condition; if so, their deficiencies were high up and would be obvious.

Scamping did not often occur, and when it did so it was in

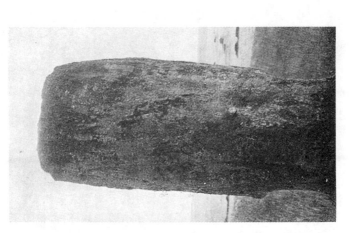

FIG. 67.

FIG. 66.

BACKS OF STANDING STATUES, RANO RARAKU.

Modelled.

Unmodelled.

FIG. 68.

FIG. 69.

EXCAVATED STATUES.

Showing back in process of being modelled.

Showing image wedged by boulders.

[No. 23. Fig. 50.]

the concealed portions. In one case the left hand was correctly modelled, but the right was not even indicated beyond the wrist (fig. 63). The statue shown in the frontispiece, which rejoices in the name of Piro-piro, meaning " bad odour,"[1] stands at the foot of the slope, and appears to remain as it was set up without further burial. It is a well-made figure, probably one of the most recent, and the upper part of the back is carefully moulded, but on digging it out it was found that the bottom had not been finished, but left in the form of a rough excrescence of stone ; there was no ring, but a girdle had been carved on the protruding portion, so that this was not intended to be removed. In another instance a large head had fallen on a slope at such an angle that it was impossible to locate the position of the body; curiosity led to investigation, when it was found that the thing was a fraud, the magnificent head being attached to a little dwarf trunk, which must have been buried originally nearly to the neck to keep the top upright. These instances of " jerry-building " confirm our impression that at any rate a large number of the statues were intended to remain *in situ*.

Indications were found of two different methods of erection, and the mode may have been determined by the nature of the ground. By the first procedure the statue seems to have been placed on its face in the desired spot, and a hole to have been dug beneath the base. The other method was to undermine the base, with the statue lying face uppermost ; in several instances a number of large stones were found behind the back of the figure, evidently having been used to wedge it while it was dragged to the vertical. The upright position had sometimes been only partially attained; one statue was still in a slanting attitude, corresponding exactly to the slope of a hard clay wall behind it ; the interval between the two, varying from three yards to eighteen inches, had been packed with sub-angular boulders which weighed about one hundredweight, or as much as a man could lift (fig. 69).

A few of the figures bear incised markings rudely, and apparently promiscuously, carved. This was first noted in the case of one of two statues which stand together nearest to the entrance of the crater ; here it has been found possible to work the rock at a low level, and in the empty quarry, from which they no

---

[1] The farthest outstanding figure to the left in fig. 46.

doubt have been taken, two images have been set up, one slightly in front of the other; six still unfinished figures lie in close proximity (figs. 70 and 71). The standing figure, nearest to the lake, bore a rough design on the face, and when it was dug out the back was found to be covered with similar incised marks. The natives were much excited, and convinced that we should receive a large sum of money in England when the photograph of these was produced, for nothing ever dispelled the illusion that the expedition was a financial speculation. It was these carvings more especially that we ourselves hastily endeavoured to cover up when, on the arrival of Admiral von Spee's Squadron, we daily expected a visit from the officers on board. The markings have certainly not been made by the same practised hand as the raised girdle and rings, and appear to be comparatively recent (fig. 64). Other statues were excavated, where similar marks were noticed, but, except in this case, digging led practically always to disappointment. It was the part above the surface only which' had been used as a block on which to scrawl design, from the same impulse presumably as impels the school-boy of to-day to make marks with chalk on a hoarding. On one ahu the top of the head of a statue has been decorated with rough faces, the carving evidently having been done after the statue had fallen.

In digging out the image with the tattooed back, we came across the one and only burial which was found in connection with these figures; it was close to it and at the level of the rings. The long bones, the patella, and base of the skull were identified; they lay in wet soil, crushed and intermixed with large stones, so the attitude could not be determined beyond the fact that the head was to the right of the image and the long bones to the left. These bones had become of the consistency of moist clay, and could only be identified by making transverse sections of them with a knife, after first cleaning portions longitudinally by careful scraping.

In several other instances human bones were discovered near the statues, but, like the carvings, they appeared to be of later date than the images. One skull was found beneath a figure which was lying face downwards on the surface; another fragment must have been placed behind the base after the statue had fallen forward. The natives stated that in the epidemics which

FIG. 70.

TWO IMAGES ERECTED IN QUARRY.   FRONT VIEW.
Prior to excavation.

[Nos. 108–109.   Fig. 47.]

FIG. 71.

TWO IMAGES ERECTED IN QUARRY.   BACK VIEW.

After excavation.

[Nos. 109-108.   Fig. 47.   See also Fig. 64.]

191

ravaged the island the statues afforded a natural mark for
depositing remains. In the same way a head near an ahu, which
was at first thought to be that of a standing statue, turned out
to be broken from the trunk and put up pathetically to mark
the grave of a little child. There is a roughly constructed ahu
on the outside of Rano Raraku at the corner nearest to the sea,
of which more will be said hereafter, and a quarried block of
rock on the very top of the westerly peak was also said to be
used for the exposure of the dead (no. 75, fig. 47). Close to
this block there are some very curious circular pits cut in
the rock; one examined was 5 feet 6 inches in depth and
3 feet 6 inches in diameter (no. 74, fig. 47). It is possible
they were used as vaults, but, if so, the shape is quite different
from those of the ahu. The conclusion arrived at was that
the statues themselves were not directly connected with burials.
There seems also no reason to believe that they are put up in
any order or method; they appear to have been erected on any
spot handy to the quarries where there was sufficient earth, or
even, as has been seen, in the quarry itself when circumstances
permitted.

The South-Eastern Side of Rano Raraku is a problem in itself.
The great wall formed by the cliff is like the ramparts of some
giant castle rent by vertical fissures. The greatest height, the
top of the peak, is about five hundred feet, of which the cliff
forms perhaps half, the lower part being a steep but comparatively smooth bank of detritus. Over the grassy surface of this
bank are scattered numerous fragments of rock, weighing from
a few pounds to many tons, which have fallen down from above.
The kitchen tent in our camp at the foot had a narrow escape from
being demolished by one of these stones, which nearly carried it
away in the impetus of its descent. It has never been suggested
that this face of the mountain was being worked, nevertheless, it
was subsequently difficult to understand how we lived so long
below it, gazing at it daily, before we appreciated the fact that
here also, although in much lesser degree, were both finished and
embryo images. At last one stone was definitely seen to be in
the form of a head, and excavation showed it to be an erected
and buried statue. A few other figures were found standing
and prostrate, and some unfinished images ; these last, however,

were in no case being hewn out of solid rock, but wrought into
shape out of detached stones.   On the whole, it is not probable
that this portion was ever a quarry, in the same way as the
western side and the interior of the crater.   It is, of course,
impossible to say what may be hidden beneath the detritus, but
the lower part of the cliff is too soft a rock to be satisfactorily
hewn, and the workmen appear simply to have seized on fragments which have fallen from above.   " Here," they seem to have
said, " is a good stone; let us turn it into a statue."

One day, when making a more thorough examination of the
slope, our attention was excited by a small level plateau, about
half-way up, from which protruded two similar pieces of stone
next to one another.   They were obviously giant noses of which
the nostrils faced the cliff.   Digging was bound to follow, but it
proved a long business, as the figures it revealed were particularly
massive and corpulent.   Their position was horizontal, side by
side, and the effect, more particularly when looking down at
them from the cliff above, was of two great bodies lying in their
graves (fig. 73).   The thing was a mystery; they were certainly
not in a quarry, but if they had once been erect, why had they
faced the mountain, instead of conforming to the rule of having
their back to it ?   Orientation could not account for it, as other
statues on the same slope were differently placed.   Then again,
if they had once stood and then fallen, and in proof of this one
head was broken off from the trunk, how did it come about that
they were lying horizontally on a sloping hill-side ?   The upper
part of the bodies had suffered somewhat from weather, and a
small round basin, such as natives use for domestic purposes,
had been hollowed out in one abdomen, but the hands were quite
sharp and unweathered.   We used to scramble up at off moments,
and stand gazing down at them trying to read their history.

It became at last obvious they had once been set up with the
lower part inserted in the ground to the usual level, and later
been intentionally thrown down.   For this purpose a level
trench must have been cut through the sloping side of the hill
at a depth corresponding to the base of the standing images, and
into this the figures had fallen.   While they lay in the trench
with the upper part of the bodies exposed, one had been found
a nice smooth stone for household use.   A charcoal soil level
showed clearly where the surface had been at this epoch, which

FIG. 72.

EXCAVATED STATUE.

South-east side, Rano Raraku.   Showing form of hands.

FIG. 73.

Face of cliff.   Eastern Headland.   Camp.   Ahu Tongariki.

PROSTRATE STATUES, SOUTH-EAST SIDE, RANO RARAKU, AFTER EXCAVATION

must have been comparatively recent, as an iron nail was found in it. Finally, a descent of earth had covered all but the noses, leaving them in the condition in which we found them.

This, though a satisfactory explanation as far as it went, did not account for the fact that the figures were facing the mountain, and here for once tradition came to our help. These images had, it was said, marked a boundary; the line of demarcation led between them, from the fissure in the cliff above right down to the middle statue in the great Tongariki terrace. To cross it was death; but as to what the boundary connoted no information was forthcoming; there seemed no great tribal division—the same clans ranged over the whole of the district. When, however, the line is followed through the crevice into the crater (fig. 47), it is found to form on both sides the boundary where the image-making ceased (no. 1 is a detached figure being brought down, not in a quarry), and was probably the line of taboo which preserved the rights of the image-makers. I was later given the cheering information that a certain " devil " frequented the site of my house, which was just on the image side of the boundary, who particularly resented the presence of strangers, and was given to strangling them in the night. The spirits, who inhabit the crater, are still so unpleasant, that my Kanaka maid objected to taking clothes there to wash, even in daylight, till assured that our party would be working within call.

Isolated Statues.—The finished statues, as distinct from those in the quarries, have so far been spoken of under two heads, those which once adorned the ahu and those still standing on the slope of Raraku ; there is, however, another class to consider, which, for want of a better name, will be termed the Isolated Statues. It has already been stated that, as Raraku is approached, a number of figures lie by the side of the modern track, others are round the base of the mountain, and yet other isolated specimens are scattered about the island. All these images are prostrate and lie on the surface of the ground, some on their backs and some on their faces. These were the ones which, according to legend, were being moved from the quarries to the ahu by the old lady when she stopped the work in her wrath ; or, according to another account, quoted by a visitor before our day, " They walked, and some fell by the way."

13

There must, we felt, have been roads along which they were taken, but for long we kept a look-out for such without success. At last a lazy Sunday afternoon ride, with no particular object, took one of us to the top of a small hill, some two miles to the west of Raraku. The level rays of the sinking sun showed up the inequalities of the ground, and, looking towards the sea, along the level plain of the south coast, the old track was clearly seen; it was slightly raised over lower ground and depressed somewhat through higher, and along it every few hundred yards lay a statue. Detailed study confirmed this first impression. At times over hard stony ground the trail was lost, but its main drift was indisputable; it was about nine feet or ten feet in width, the embankments were in places two feet above the surrounding ground, and the cuttings three feet deep. The road can be traced from the south-western corner of the mountain, with one or two gaps, nearly to the foot of Rano Kao, but the succession of statues continues only about half the distance. It generally runs some few hundred yards further inland than the present road, but a branch, with a statue, leads down to the ahu of Teatenga on the coast, and, another portion, either a branch or a detour of the main road, also with a statue, goes to the cove of Akahanga with its two large image ahu (fig. 32). There are on this road twenty-seven statues in all, covering a distance of some five miles, but fourteen of them, including two groups of three, are in the first mile. Their heights are from fifteen feet to over thirty feet, but generally over twenty feet.

As a clue had now been obtained, it was comparatively simple to trace two other roads from Raraku. One leads from the crater, and connects it with the western district of the island. It commences at the gap in the mountain wall, in the centre of which an image lies on its face with weird effect, as if descending head foremost into the plain; and runs for a while roughly parallel to the first road but about a mile further inland. It is not quite so regular as the south road, and is marked for a somewhat less distance by a sequence of images, some fourteen in number, which in the same way grow further apart as the distance from the mountain increases. When the succession of statues ceases, the road divides; one track turns to the north-west, and reaches the sea-board through a small

FIG. 74.

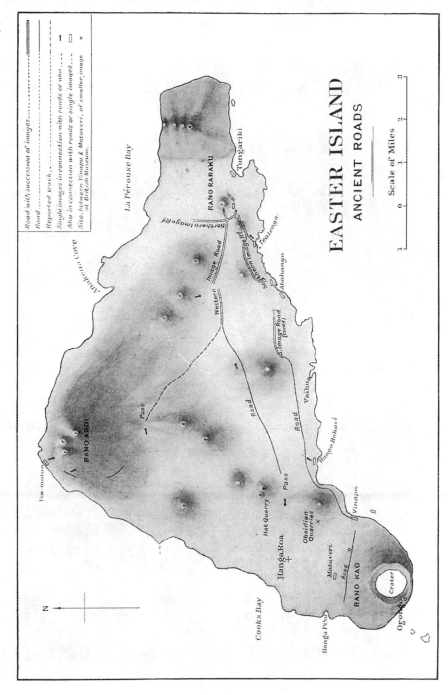

EASTER ISLAND

ANCIENT ROADS

Scale of Miles

Road with succession of images ....
Road ....
Reported track ....
Single images in connection with roads or ahu ....
Ahu in connection with roads or single images ....
Site between Vinapu & Mataveri, of smaller image
at British Museum.

La Pérouse Bay

Anakena Cove

Va matua

RANO AROI

Pass

RANO RARAKU

Northern Image Rd

Western

Image Road

Southern Image Rd

Tongariki

Tealonga

Akahanga

S. Image Road
(coast)

Vaihu

Road

Hanga Itahavé

Road

Pass

Hat Quarry

Obsidian
Quarries

Pass

Hanga Roa

Mataveri

Vinapu

Road

RANO KAO

Crater

Orongo

Hanga Piko

Cooks Bay

N

FIG. 75.

AN IMAGE ON ITS BACK,
Unbroken; if erect, would face westwards.

FIG. 76.

AN IMAGE ON ITS FACE.
Showing by cleavage and only partial fall that 't has been erect and faced westwards.

pass in the western line of cones; the other continues as far as a more southerly pass in the same succession of heights. In each pass there is a statue.

The third road, which runs from Raraku in a northerly direction, is much shorter than those to the south and west. It has only four statues covering a distance of perhaps a mile, and it then disappears; if, however, the figures round the base of the mountain belonged to it, and they lie in the same direction, it started from the southern corner of the mountain, led in front of the standing statues and across the trail from the crater, before taking its northward route up the eastern plain. The furthest of the images is the largest which has been moved; it lies on its back, badly broken, but the total of the fragments gives a height of thirty-six feet four inches. In addition to these three avenues, there are indications that some of the statues on the south-eastern side of Raraku may have been on a fourth road along that side beneath the cliff.

So far the matter was sufficiently clear, but another problem was still unsolved: if the images were really being moved to their respective ahu all round the coast, how was it that, with very few exceptions, they were all found in the neighbourhood of Raraku? If also they were being moved, what was the method pursued, for some lay on their backs and some on their faces? With the hope of elucidating this great question of the means of transport, we dug under and near one or two of the single figures without achieving our end—nothing was found; but the close study which the work necessitated called attention to the fact that on one of them the lines of weathering could not have been made with the figure in its present horizontal attitude. The rain had evidently collected on the head and run down the back; it must therefore have stood for a considerable time in a vertical position. It was again a noticeable fact that, though some single figures are lying unbroken (fig. 75), others, like the large one on the north road, proved to be so shattered that no amount of normal disintegration or shifting of soil could account for their condition— they had obviously fallen. So wedded, however, were we at this time to the theory that they were in course of transport, that it was seriously considered whether they could have been moved in an upright position. The point was settled by finding one day by the side of the track, some two miles from the mountain, a partially buried head. This was excavated, and a statue found that had been originally set up in a hole and, later, undermined, causing it to fall forward. This was the only instance of an isolated figure where the burial had been to any depth, but in various other cases it was then seen that soil had been removed from the base, and one or two more of the figures had not quite fallen (fig. 76).

When the whole number of the statues on the roads were in imagination re-erected, it was found that they had all

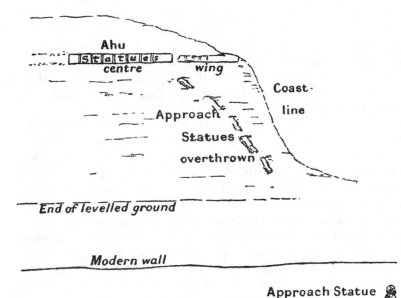

FIG. 77. DIAGRAM SHOWING CEREMONIAL AVENUE OF AHU HANGA PAUKURA.

originally stood with their backs to the hill. Rano Raraku was, therefore, approached by at least three magnificent avenues, on each of which the pilgrim was greeted at intervals by a stone giant guarding the way to the sacred mountain (map of roads). One of the ahu on the south coast, Hanga Paukura, has been approached by a similar avenue of five statues facing the visitor. These five images when first seen were a great puzzle, as some of them are so embedded in the earth that their backs are even with the levelled sward in front of the ahu; later

FIG. 78.

AHU PARO,
With image which was the last to be overthrown.

Foreground.—Hillock, traditionally utilised for placing the crown in position.
Distance.—Eastern Headland, with three cones, from which Spanish sovereignty was proclaimed in 1770.

there seemed little doubt that, like the two giants on the south-east side of Raraku, trenches had been dug into which they had fallen. Subsequently, a sixth statue was discovered, the other side of a modern wall, weathered and worn away, but of Raraku stone and still upright. This is the only instance of an erect figure to be found elsewhere than on the mountain (fig. 77).

In addition to the images which have stood in these processional roads, there are, excluding one or two figures near the mountain whose *raison d'être* is somewhat doubtful, fourteen isolated statues in various parts of the island, for whose position no certain reason could be found. Some of these may have belonged to inland ahu which have disappeared, or they may be solitary memorials to mark some particular spots, but the greater number appear to have stood near tracks of some sort. Some of these last may have been boundary stones, and in this class may perhaps fall the smaller statue now at the British Museum, which is a very inferior specimen. According to local information it stood almost half-way on the track leading from Vinapu to Mataveri along the bottom of Rano Kao ; the hole from which it was dug was pointed out, and our informant declared that he remembered it standing, and that the people used to dance round it. The larger figure at the British Museum was in a unique position, which will be spoken of later.

No statues were, therefore, found of which it could be said that they were in process of being removed, and the mode of transport remains a mystery. An image could be moved down from the quarry by means of banks of earth, and though requiring labour and skill, the process is not inconceivable. Similarly, the figures may have been, and probably were, erected on the terraces in the same way, being hauled up on an embankment of earth made higher than the pedestals and then dropped on them. Near Paro, the ahu where the last statue was overthrown, there is a hillock, and tradition says that a causeway was made from it to the head of the tall figure which stood upon the ahu, and along this the hat was rolled (fig. 78)—a piece of lore which seems hardly likely to have been invented by a race having no connection with the statues. But the problem remains, how was the transport carried out along the level? The weight of some amounted to as much as 40 or 50 tons. It would simplify matters very much if there were any reason to suppose that the images were moved, as was the case with the hats, before being wrought, merely as cylinders of stone, in which case it would be possible to pass a rope under and over it, thus parbuckling the stone or rolling it along, but the evidence is all to the contrary. There is no trace whatever of an unfinished image on or near an ahu, while, as we have seen, they are found at all stages in the quarry. Presumably rollers were employed, but there appears never to have been much wood, or material for cordage, in the island, and it is not easy to see how sufficient men could bring strength to bear on the block. Even if the ceremonial roads were used when possible, these fragile figures have been taken to many distant ahu, up hill and down dale, over rough and stony ground, where there is no trace of any road at all.

The natives are sometimes prepared to state that the statues were thrown down by human means, they never have any doubt that they were moved by supernatural power. We were once inspecting an ahu built on a natural eminence, one side was sheer cliff, the other was a slope of 29 feet, as steep as a house roof, near the top a statue was lying. The most intelligent of our guides turned to me significantly. "Do you mean to tell me," he said, "that that was not done by *mana* ?" The darkness is not rendered less tantalising by the reflection that could centuries roll away and the old scenes be again enacted before us, the workers would doubtless exclaim in bewildered surprise at our ignorance, " But how could you do it any other way ? "

Besides the ceremonial roads and their continuations, there are traces of an altogether different track which is said to run round the whole seaboard of the island. It is considered to be supernatural work, and is known as Ara Mahiva, "ara" meaning road and "Mahiva" being the name of the spirit or deity who made it. On the southern side it has been obliterated in making the present track—it was there termed the " path for carrying fish "; but on the northern and western coasts, where for much of the way it runs on the top of high cliffs, such a use is out of the question. It can be frequently seen there like a long persistent furrow, and where its course has been interrupted by erosion, no fresh track had been made further inland ; it terminates suddenly on the broken edge, and resumes its course on the other side. It is best seen in certain lights running up both the western

FIG. 79.

THE CRATER FROM WHICH THE HATS OF THE IMAGES WERE HEWN, ON
THE SIDE OF THE HILL PUNAPAU.

Rano Kao in the distance.

FIG. 80.

AN UNFINISHED HAT NEAR THE QUARRY.

FIG. 81.

A FINISHED HAT AT AHU HANGA O ORNU; OTHERS IN THE DISTANCE.

[ʃ⌐

and southern edges of Rano Kao. Its extent and regularity appeared to preclude the idea of landslip. There is no reason to suppose that it is due to the imported livestock, and it has no connection with ahu, or the old native centres of population, yet to have been so worn by naked feet it must constantly have been used. This silent witness to a forgotten past is one of the most mysterious and impressive things on the island.

STONE CROWNS OF THE IMAGES

Mention must finally be made of the crowns or hats which adorned the figures on the ahu. Their full designation is said to be " Hau (hats) hiterau moai," but they are always alluded to merely as " hiterau " or " hitirau."

These coverings for the head were cylindrical in form, the bottom being slightly hollowed out into an oval depression in order to fit on to the head of the image; the depression was not in the centre, but left a larger margin in front, so that the brim projected over the eyes of the figure, a fashion common in native head-dresses. They are said by the present inhabitants to have been kept in place by being wedged with white stones. The top was worked into a boss or knot. The material is a red volcanic tuff found in a small crater on the side of a larger volcano, generally known as Punapau, not far from Cook's Bay (fig. 79). In the crater itself are the old quarries. A few half-buried hats may be seen there, and the path up to it, and for some hundreds of yards from the foot of the mountain, is strewn with them. They are at this stage simply large cylinders, from 4 feet to 8 feet high, from 6 feet to 9 feet across (fig. 80), and they were obviously conveyed to the ahu in this form and there carved into shape (fig. 81). An unwrought cylinder is still lying at a hundred yards from the ahu of Anakena. The finished hats are not more than 3 feet 10 inches to 6 feet in height, with addition of 6 inches to 2 feet for the knob ; the measurement across the crown is from about 5 feet 6 inches to 8 feet. The stone is more easily broken and cut than that of the statues, and while many crowns survive, many more have been smashed in falling or used as building materials.

It is a noteworthy fact that the images on Raraku never had hats, nor have any of the isolated statues ; they were confined to those on the ahu.

CHAPTER XV

NATIVE CULTURE IN PRE-CHRISTIAN TIMES

Sources of Information : History, Recent Remains, Living Memory—
Mode of Life : Habitations, Food, Dress and Ornament—*Social
Life :* Divisions, Wars, Marriages, Burial Customs, Social
Functions.

It has been seen that any knowledge which exists on the island
with regard to the origin of the monuments is of the most vague
description, and it is therefore necessary, in the attempt to solve
the problem, to rely principally on indirect evidence. It becomes
in particular essential to collect all possible information about
the present people ; not only for its intrinsic anthropological
interest, but in order to find if any links connect them with the
great builders, or if we must look for an earlier race.

As a first step in the search the scientist naturally turns to
the most ancient accounts which he can find describing the
island, its inhabitants, and remains ; these are not yet two
hundred years old. The first European to see it was a Dutch
Admiral named Roggeveen, who came upon it on Easter Day,
1722, during his search for another and mysterious island known
as Davis or David's Island.[1] He concluded that it was not the
place for which he was looking, christened it Easter Island, and
went further afield. His ship lay off the north side of the
island for a week, but only on one day did landing take place,
and one or two of the party have left us short descriptions.
There were, they say, no big trees, but it had a rich soil and good
climate ; there were sugar-cane, bananas, potatoes and figs, and

[1] An island was reported in lat. 27° by an English buccaneer named
Davis in 1687. It was, he said, five hundred miles from the coast of Chile,
low and sandy, and some twelve leagues to the west of it was seen " a
long tract of pretty high land." The description in no way applies to
Easter, with which it has sometimes been identified. The probability seems
to be that Davis was out of his reckoning, as was by no means unusual
in the case of the early mariners, and it has been suggested that the island
he saw was Crescent Island, the high ground in the distance being the
Gambier group. The latitude of Easter Island is 27° 8′ S., that of Crescent
Island is 23° 20′ S.

the natives brought them a number of fowls, estimated varyingly from sixty to five hundred. One of the voyagers goes so far as to say that "all the country was under cultivation." As for the inhabitants, they were, they tell us, of all shades of colour, yellow, white, and brown, and wore clothes made of a " field product," evidently tapa. They were " painted," which apparently signifies tattooed, and it was the habit to distend the lobes of their ears so that they hung to the shoulders, and large discs were worn in them. " When these Indians," wrote Roggeveen, " go about any job which might set their ear-plugs wagging, and bid fair to do them any hurt, they take them out and hitch the rim of the lobe up over the top of the ear, which gives them a quaint and laughable appearance." [1]

The natives were extraordinarily thievish, stealing the caps from the seamen's heads, while one actually climbed into the port-hole of the cabin and took the cloth off the table. These habits gave rise to an unfortunate incident, as when the visitors came on shore, a scuffle took place over the sanctity of property, and the natives began throwing stones, on which a petty official gave the order to fire, ten or twelve natives being killed. The occurrence, however, was duly explained, and did not terminate amicable relations. We learn that at this time the great statues, of which this is of course the first report, were then, as has already been noted, standing and in place. The Dutchmen describe them as " remarkable, tall, stone figures, a good 30 feet in height," and notice that they have crowns on their heads ; a clear space was, they said, reserved round them by laying stones. They have no doubt that the figures are objects of worship; the natives " kindle fires in front of them, and thereafter squatting on their heels with heads bowed down, they bring the palms of their hands together and alternately raise and lower them." Another observer adds, in connection with this worship, that they " prostrated themselves towards the rising sun." A great step would have been gained towards the solution of the problem if we could feel assured that these last remarks were justified and were not merely the result of imperfect observation.[2]

[1] Precisely the same habit obtains among the Akikuyu.
[2] For Roggeveen's description of the Island see *Voyage of Gonzalez.* Hakluyt Society, Series II., vol. xiii., pp. 3 to 26.
A statement of the evidence *re* Davis Island is given in the introduction to the same volume.

For fifty years darkness once more descends on the history of the island. Then, within a period of sixteen years, it was visited by three expeditions, Spanish, English, and French respectively. The Spanish were under the command of Gonzalez.[1] They too were searching for David's Island when, in 1770, they touched at Easter, and they also came to the conclusion that it was not their goal. They took, however, formal possession of it, and named it San Carlos. Their ships lay at anchor in the same place as had those of Roggeveen, the bay on the north coast now called after La Pérouse. From this anchorage three curious hillocks on the northern slope of the great eastern volcano form striking objects (fig. 78) ; on each of these they planted a cross, and proclaimed the King of Spain with banners flying, beating of drums, and artillery salutes. The natives appear to have thoroughly enjoyed the proceedings, and " confirmed them," according to the solemn statements of the Spaniards, by marking the official document with their own script. This is the first that we hear of a form of native writing. The expedition sent a boat round the island, which made a very creditable map of it.

Four years later Cook cast anchor on the west side in the bay which is known by his name. He was there three days and did not himself explore inland, but his officers did so, including the elder Forster, the botanist of the expedition, and his account of what they saw was published by his son.[2]

In 1780 La Pérouse anchored in the same place, and also sent some of his men inland, who covered partly, but not entirely, the same districts as those of Cook.[3]

As these expeditions were so nearly of the same date, their remarks may fairly be compared and contrasted with those made by Roggeveen half a century earlier. All three give very similar descriptions of the people, their appearance and dwellings, which also resemble the accounts of the Dutch. Cook is very much impressed with the long ears, though La Pérouse does not refer to them. There is the same story of the native powers of ap-

[1] *Voyage of Gonzalez,* p. 27 *seq.*

[2] *A Voyage Towards the South Pole and Round the World,* by James Cook, 1st ed., 4to, 1777, pp. 276–96.
A Voyage Round the World, George Forster, 4to, 1777. Vol. i., pp. 551–602.

[3] *Voyage de La Pérouse autour du Monde.* 4to edn., London, 1799. Vol. i., pp. 319–36.

propriating the goods of the strangers. Cook says that they were " as expert thieves as any we had yet met with," and Pérouse, whose own hat they stole while helping him down one of the image platforms, is particularly aggrieved at such conduct, considering that he has given them sheep, goats, pigs, and other valuable presents ; peace was only kept between the crew and the natives by official compensation being given the seamen for their lost property.

Here, however, the resemblance of these accounts with that of Roggeveen ends. The descriptions which are given by these later expeditions of the state of the country, and its facilities as a port of call, are very different from those of the Dutchmen. The Spaniards speak of it as being uncultivated save for some small plots of ground. The Englishmen are the reverse of enthusiastic. Forster calls it a " poor land," and Cook says that " no nation need contend for the honour of the discovery of this island, as there can be few places which afford less convenience for shipping." " Poultry " now consists of only a " few tame fowls"—later still we find that only one is produced. Pérouse, although he is not so depressed as Cook, tells us that only one-tenth of the land is cultivated. With regard to the population Roggeveen gives no number, and probably was not in a position to do so. The estimates made by the Spanish and English are very similar. Gonzalez puts it at nine hundred to one thousand, Cook at seven hundred ; both of them, however, state that the number of women seen seemed to be disproportionately small. La Pérouse, writing of course some years later, speaks of the number as two thousand and has seen many women and children. Both English and French are interested to find that the language is similar to that spoken elsewhere in the Pacific.

Again, in dealing with the state of the monuments and the way in which they were regarded, the impressions of the later observers differ greatly from those of Roggeveen. The Spaniards do not tell us very much. They saw from the sea what they thought were bushes symmetrically put up on the beach, and dotted about inland ; later they found that they were in reality statues, and they wondered particularly how their crowns, which they observed were of a different material, were raised into place. It was one of the Spanish officers who states, as recorded at the beginning of this book, that the seashore was lined with stone

idols,[1] from which it may be gathered that the great majority
were still erect.   The figures were, they tell us, all set up on
small stones, and burying-places were in front.   It is interesting,
in view of what we know of the prohibition of smoke near the
ahu,[2] to find one of the Spanish writing : " They could not bear
us to smoke cigars ; they begged our sailors to extinguish them,
and they did so.   I asked one of them the reason, and he made
signs that the smoke went upwards ; but I do not know what
this meant."[3]   Cook's people observed that the natives disliked
these burying-places being walked over, but whereas Roggeveen
was convinced, whether rightly or wrongly, that the cult of the
statues was what we should call " a going concern," Cook, fifty
years later, is equally certain that it is a thing of the past ; some
of the figures are still standing, but some are fallen down, and the
inhabitants " do not even trouble to repair the foundations of
those which are going to decay."   " The giant statues," he says,
" are not in my opinion looked upon as idols by the present
inhabitants, whatever they may have been in the days of the
Dutch."   Forster also remarks that " they are so dispropor-
tionate to the strength of the nation, it is most reasonable to
look upon them as the remains of better times."   La Pérouse
does not agree with this last sentiment; he admits that at
present the monuments are not respected, but he sees no reason
why they should not still be made even under existing conditions ;
he thinks that a hundred people would be sufficient to put one
of the statues in place.   The objection he sees is that the people
have no chief great enough to secure such a memorial.   It is
unfortunate that the mountain of Rano Raraku is so far removed
from both the north and west anchorages, that none of the
voyagers discovered it, although Cook's men were very near
that from which the crowns were obtained.

In the nineteenth century we have a few accounts from passing
voyagers.   Lisiansky, in 1804, found no people with long ears,[4]
but in 1825 Beechey in H.M.S. *Blossom* says that there were
still a few to be seen.   With regard to the statues, the process of

---

[1] MS. copy in the British Museum of a letter sent by one of the officers
of the Spanish ship to a Canon or a Prebendary in Buenos Aires.   MSS.
17607 (18).   Our attention was drawn to this document by Dr. Corney.
[2] See above, p. 171.
[3] *Voyage of Gonzalez*, p. 126.
[4] *Voyage Round the World in the Ship " Neva,"* Lisiansky, Lond. 1814, p. 58.

FIG. 82.

[Drawn from Nature by W. Hodges.

MONUMENTS IN EASTER ISLAND.

From *A Voyage Towards the South Pole*, James Cook, 1777, vol. i., part of pl. xlix.

The artist has not observed the features or arms of the images, nor that they stand on stone platforms. The hats, as shown, greatly exceed their true proportion to the figures. The picture has probably been redrawn from memory.

demolition has gone so far that Beechey declares " the existence of any busts is doubtful."[1] It is amusing to find, a hundred years after Roggeveen's similar experience, that the *Blossom* has an affray with natives over the stealing of caps. While attention has been drawn to the importance of these early narratives, it must be remembered that all the visits were of very short duration, and that the old voyagers were not trained observers. The Dutchmen, for instance, deliberately tell us that the statues have no arms. The accounts frequently give the impression of being written up afterwards from somewhat vague recollection, and in most cases the narrators have read those of their predecessors and go prepared to see certain things. One navigator who never landed assures us that the houses are the same as in the days of La Pérouse. On the other hand, with regard to the stores available, they are, so to speak, on their own quarter-deck, and their remarks can be accepted without question.

In the " sixties " of last century the great series of changes took place which brought Easter Island into touch with the modern world. The first of these largely broke those chains with the past which the archæologist now seeks to reconstruct. Labour was needed by the exploiters of the Peruvian guano fields, and an attempt which was made to introduce it from China having failed, slave-raids were organised in the South Sea Islands. As early as 1805 Easter had suffered similarly at the hands of American sealers, and it was amongst the principal islands to be laid under contribution in December 1862.

It is pathetic even now to hear the old men describe the scenes which they witnessed in their youth, illustrating by action how the raiders threw down on the ground gifts which they thought likely to attract the inhabitants, and, when the islanders were on their knees scrambling for them, tied their hands behind their backs and carried them off to the waiting ship. The natives say that one thousand in all were so removed from the island, and, unfortunately, there were amongst them some of the principal men, including many of the most learned, and the last of the ariki, or chiefs. Representations were made by the French Minister at Lima, and a certain number were put on board ship to be returned to their home. Smallpox, however, had been contracted by them, and out of one hundred who were

[1] *Voyage to the Pacific, H.M.S. "Blossom," p. 41.*

to be repatriated, only fifteen survived. These, on their return to the island, brought the disease with them, which spread rapidly with most fatal results to the population.

Meantime, shortly before the raid, the attention of the Roman Catholic " Congregation of the Sacred Heart of Jesus and Mary " in Valparaiso had been drawn to the island by the account received from a passing ship, and they determined to inaugurate a mission. Three of the Community left for Easter Island, their route taking them by way of Tahiti. Finally, only one continued, Eugène Eyraud, who landed on the island in January 1864. Eyraud was a lay brother in the Order, having been a merchant in South America; he devoted his life to the call to take the Gospel to Easter, and the accounts of his work, which are extraordinarily interesting, leave a great impression of his courage and devotion.[1] He was alone on the island for eight or nine months, and was at the mercy of the natives, who stole his belongings, even to the clothes he was wearing, and compelled him to make a boat for them. In March 1866, Eyraud, after a visit to Chile, returned with another missionary, Father Roussel, and the two were for a while blockaded in a house which they had put up, but the tide now turned. Either Roussel was a man of greater determination than Eyraud, or with increased numbers a firmer attitude was possible. Surgeon Palmer of H.M.S. *Topaze* tells us that when one of the natives took up a stone with a menacing gesture, Roussel quietly felled him with his stick and went on his way, after which there' was no further trouble. The missionaries were joined later in the year by two more of their number, and became a power in the land.

Eyraud on his return from Chile was suffering from phthisis, of which he died in August 1868. When he was nearing his end he asked Roussel if there still remained any heathen in the island, to which the Father replied " not one " ; the last seven had been baptized on the Feast of the Assumption. It seems natural to connect with Eyraud's illness the fact that there was at the same time a severe epidemic of phthisis in the island ; so little was the need of precaution understood at this date, that even Surgeon Palmer, writing of the inroads made by consumption, remarks " which they (the natives) believe infectious." [2]

[1] See *Annales de la Propagation de la Foi*, 1866, 1867, 1869.
[2] *Journal Ethnological Society*, Vol. i. p. 373.

The ravages of this disease, following on those of smallpox, reduced the population, which at the time of the arrival of the mission had stood at twelve hundred, by about one-fourth.

The remarks of the missionaries on native customs, particularly those dealing with their ceremonies, reflect credit on the observers at a time when such things were too often thought beneath notice ; they will be referred to later. Their ethnological work was, however, limited by more pressing exigencies, by the difficulties of locomotion on the island, and by the language. Roussel compiled a vocabulary, which is useful to students, though not free from the mode of thought found in a well-known missionary dictionary, which translates hansom cab into the Swahili language. It is a curious fact that so completely were the terraces now ruined that the Fathers never allude to the statues, and seem scarcely to have realised their existence ; but it is through them that we first hear of the wooden tablets carved with figures. The body of professors acquainted with this art of writing perished, either in Peru or by epidemic, and this, in connection with the introduction of Christianity, led to great destruction of the existing specimens of this most interesting script. The natives said that they burnt the tablets in compliance with the orders of the missionaries, though such suggestion would hardly be needed in a country where wood is scarce ; the Fathers, on the contrary, state that it was due to them that any were preserved. Some certainly were saved by their means and through the interest shown in them by Bishop Jaussen of Tahiti, while two or three found their way to museums after the natives became aware of their value ; but some or all of these existing tablets are merely fragments of the original. The natives told us that an expert living on the south coast, whose house had been full of such glyphs, abandoned them at the call of the missionaries, on which a man named Niari, being of a practical mind, got hold of the discarded tablets and made a boat of them wherein he caught much fish. When the " sewing came out," he stowed the wood into a cave at an ahu near Hanga Roa, to be made later into a new vessel there. Pakarati, an islander now living, found a piece, and it was acquired by the U.S.A. ship *Mohican*.

Side by side with the establishment of the religious power the secular had come into being. The master of the ship who had brought the last two missionaries was a certain Captain Dutrou Bornier. He had been attracted by the place, and, having made financial arrangements with the mercantile house of Brander in Tahiti, settled himself on the island and proceeded to exploit it commercially. Title-deeds were obtained from the natives in exchange for gifts of woven material. The remaining population was gathered together into one settlement at Hanga Roa, the native name for the shore of Cook's Bay. This was the state of things when H.M.S. *Topaze* touched in 1868 and carried off the two statues now at the British Museum.

Dutrou Bornier had at first spoken enthusiastically of the work of the missionaries; later, however, the not unknown struggle arose between the religious and secular powers. According to the accounts of the missionaries, they protested against the actions of Bornier in taking over two hundred natives, practically by force, and shipping them to Tahiti to work on the Brander plantations. Bornier retaliated by rendering their position impossible, and the Fathers ultimately received orders to transfer their labours to the Gambier islands. Jaussen tells us that their converts desired to accompany them, and that almost the whole population went on board with them. The captain, however, instigated by Bornier, refused to carry so many, and one hundred and seventy-five were sent back to the shore. This, therefore, " was the whole population " in 1871. We have not Bornier's account of the quarrel, but there seems to have been some justification for the attitude of the missionaries towards him, as five years later he was murdered by the natives, and, if current stories are to be believed, his end was well merited.

Subsequently one of the Branders lived at Mataveri, and Mr. Alexander Salmon, to whom the missionaries sold their interests, at Vaihu on the south coast.[1] The Salmon family had intermarried with the royal family of Tahiti, and the new resident was well aware of the value of antiquities. According to native accounts he organised a band to search the caves and hiding-places for articles of interest. They also state that he employed skilled natives to produce wooden objects connected with their older culture for sale to passing ships. He spoke the

[1] The above statement is made on the authority of Mr. John Brander of Tahiti. According to report of H.M.S. *Sappho*, which visited the island in 1882, Salmon was then an agent of the Maison Brander

language of the island, and when the U.S.S. *Mohican* arrived in 1886, he was the source of much of the information which they subsequently published. It is an important but difficult matter to know how far the material thus gleaned thirty years ago was carefully obtained and reproduced. One or two of the folk-tales are still told very much as retailed by Salmon, but he appears to have taken little interest in the surviving customs and failed to understand them. The report of the *Mohican*, made by Paymaster Thomson, has been the only account of the island in existence with any pretention to scientific value.[1] The *Mohican* was there eleven days, and Thomson went rapidly round the island with a party from the ship. The amount of ground covered and work done is remarkable, although his statements are naturally not free from the errors inseparable from such rapid observation.

In 1888 the Chilean Government formally took possession. In 1897 M. Merlet, of Valparaiso, purchased from the representatives of Brander, Bornier, and Salmon, their interest in Easter Island, with the exception of a tract of land containing the village of Hanga Roa, which the Chilean Government acquired from the missionaries and retained in the interest of the inhabitants ; this land covers a far larger space than the natives are able to utilise. The population is again increasing, as will have been seen from the fact that during our visit they numbered two hundred and fifty. M. Merlet subsequently sold his holding to a company, of which he became chairman.

Easter Island has had many names. That given by the Dutchman has become generally accepted, but the Spaniards christened it San Carlos, and in some maps it is termed " Waihu," a name of a part of the island erroneously understood as applying to the whole. A native name is Te Pito-te-henua, " *henua* " means usually " earth " and " *pito* " " navel."[2] Thomson says it was ascribed to the first comers. Elsewhere in the Pacific " *pito* " also means " end." Churchill holds the name signified simply " Land's End," and was applied to all these angles of the island, which was itself without a name.[3] Rapa-nui (or Great Rapa) is another native name for which various explanations are offered.

---

[1] *Smithsonian Report,* 1889.

[2] In the *Odyssey* Athene speaks of Odysseus as " in a sea-girt isle, where is the navel of the sea." (*Odyssey*, Bk. I., l. 50, Butcher & Lang.)

[3] *Easter Island. The Rapa-nui Speech.* W. Churchill, p 3.

14

The island of Rapa, sometimes known as Rapa-iti, lies some two thousand miles to the westward. Thomson states that the name Rapa-nui only dates from the time when the men kidnapped by the Peruvians were being returned to their homes. The Easter Islanders, finding no one knew the name Te Pito-te-henua, and that some comrades in distress from the other Rapa managed to make their place of origin understood, called their own home Rapa-nui; a story which sounds hardly probable, but was presumably obtained from Salmon.

According to the report of H.M.S. *Topaze*, the Islanders of their day believed that Rapa was their original home. Others state the name was given by a visitor from that island.

The brief accounts which have been referred to are all that is known from external evidence of the original life of the present people, and but little hope was held out to us in England that those fragments could still be supplemented. There were found, however, to be still in existence two possible sources of information, namely, the memories of old inhabitants, and the actual traces which still remain of the life led by the people previous to the Peruvian raid and the coming of Christianity. The great ahu which have so far been described are only a part, although the most imposing portion, of the stone remains of the island. It is fortunate for the student that when civilisation appeared the natives were gathered into one settlement, for they left behind them, sprinkled over the island, various erections connected with their original domestic life. These buildings were certainly being used in recent times, and are treated from this point of view, but for all we know they may have been, and very possibly were, contemporary with the great works.

The study of the remains on the island, from the greatest to the least, is by no means so simple as may hitherto have appeared. Our earliest attempts at descriptions, although conscientious, were almost ludicrous in the light of subsequent knowledge, and Captain Beechey's error on the subject of " the busts " is at least comprehensible. Easter, it must be remembered, is a mass of disintegrating rocks. When in an idle moment the Expedition amused itself by inventing an heraldic design for the island, it was universally agreed that the main emblem must undoubtedly be a " stone," " and as supporters," suggested one frivolous member, " two cockroaches rampant." The most correct representation would be a stone vertical on a stone horizontal. Every individual who has lived, even temporarily, in the place, has collected stones and put them up according to taste ; and every succeeding generation, also needing stones, has, as in the instance of the manager's wall, found them most readily in ruining or converting the work of their predecessors. Even when a building is comparatively intact, the original design and purpose can only be grasped by experience, and matters become distinctly complicated when the walls of an ahu have been made into a garden enclosure and a chicken-house turned into an ossuary. It must be remembered also that rough stone buildings bear in themselves no marks of age. The cairns put up by us to mark the distances for rifle fire from the camp were indistinguishable from those of prehistoric nature made for a very different purpose. The result is that the tumble-down remains of yesterday, and the scenes of unknown antiquity blend together in a confusing whole in which it is not always easy to distinguish even the works of nature from those of man.

The other source of information which was open to us was the memory of the old people. If but little was known of the great works, it was possible that there might still linger knowledge of customs or folk-lore which would throw indirect light on origins. This field proved to be astonishingly large, but it was even more difficult to collect facts from brains than out of stones. On our arrival there were still a few old people who were sufficiently grown up in the sixties to recall something of the old life ; with the great majority of these, about a dozen in number, we gradually got in touch, beginning with those who worked for Mr. Edmunds and hearing from them of others. It was momentous work, for the eleventh hour was striking, day by day they were dropping off ; it was a matter of anxious consideration whose testimony should first be recorded for fear that, meanwhile, others should be gathered to their fathers, and their store of knowledge lost for ever. Against the longer recollection of extreme old age, had to be put the fact that the memories of those a little younger were generally more clear and accurate. The feeling of responsibility from a scientific point of view was very great. Ten years ago more could have been done; ten years hence little or nothing will remain of this source of knowledge.

Most happily, these authorities were in almost every case willing and ready to talk, and our debt to them is great. They came with us, as has been seen, on our explorations of the island, but the greater part of the work was done when we were living near the village. Some of them took pleasure in coming up to Mataveri and talking in the veranda, enjoying still more, no doubt, the practical outcome of their subsequent visits to Bailey's domain—the kitchen. Others were more at ease in their own surroundings, and then we went down to the village and discussed old days in their little banana-plots, while interested neighbours came in to join the fray. Sometimes a man did better by himself, but on other occasions to get two or three together stimulated conversation. Unfortunately, some of the old men who knew most were confined to the leper settlement some three miles north of Hanga Roa, and the infectious power of leprosy was not a subject which we had got up before leaving England. The Captain of the *Kildalton* feared lest even the distance of the settlement from the Manager's house might not suffice to prevent the plague being carried there by insects, and told a gruesome tale, within his knowledge, of two white men who had gone for a visit to a Pacific island, one of whom on their return to an American port had been immediately sent back to a leper colony. But how could one allow the last vestige of knowledge in Easter Island to die out without an effort? So I went, disinfected my clothes on return, studied, must it be confessed, my fingers and toes, and hoped for the best.

It would not be easy for a foreigner to reconstruct English society fifty years ago, even from the descriptions of well-educated old men; it is particularly difficult to arrive at the truth from the untutored mind. Even when the natives knew well what they were talking about, they would forget to mention some part of the story, which to them was self-evident, but at which the humble European could not be expected to guess. The bird story, for example, had for many months been wrestled with before it transpired precisely what was meant by the "first egg." Deliberate invention was rare, but, when memory was a little vague, there was a constant tendency to glide from what was remembered to what was imagined. Scientific work of this nature really ought to qualify for a high position at the bar. The witness had to be heard, and discreetly cross-examined without

FIG. 83.

HÉ.
Clan Marama.

VIRIAMO.
Clan Ureohei.

TE HAHA.
Clan Miru.

JUAN TEPANO.
Clan Tupahotu.

any doubt being thrown on his story, which would at once have given offence; then allowed to forget and again re-examined, his story being compared with that of others who had been heard meanwhile.   Counsel had also to be judge and to act as reporter, and at the same time keep the witness amused and prevent the interpreter from being bored, or the court would promptly have broken up.   Though great care has been exercised, it must be remembered, when a particular account is quoted, as, for example, that of Te Haha regarding the annual inspection of the tablets, while it is believed to rest on fact, its absolute accuracy cannot be guaranteed.

The language question naturally added to the difficulty.   On landing two courses had been open, either to go on with Spanish, of which the younger men had a certain knowledge, and which was used by Mr. Edmunds, or to try to get some hold of the native tongue.   The latter plan was decided on, and though at one time the difficulties seemed so great that this course was almost regretted, in the end it was vindicated.   There is, as stated, a vocabulary in French made by the missionaries, and also one in Spanish, but there is no grammar of any kind. The French carpenter, Varta, was some assistance, particularly at the beginning.   The first steps were the easiest.   The Kanakas were much interested in my endeavours, and rushed round wildly, bringing any object they could lay hands on in order to teach its name ; but even with the nouns an unexpected complication arose.   The natives speak, not only their own language, but, side by side with it, that of Tahiti, which is used in their religious books and services ; there are affinities between the two, but they are quite dissimilar, and to understand conversation it was necessary to learn both.   This very much prolonged the task, and also lessened the results obtained.

The next stage, the putting together of sentences, was still more difficult.   How was it possible to talk in a language which had no verb " to be " ?   I had, it is true, a native maid (fig. 29), but, after the simplest phrases had been learnt, topics for conversation were difficult to find.   We looked through illustrated magazines together, but wild beasts, railway trains, and the greater part of the pictures of all kinds, conveyed nothing to her.   The plan was therefore hit on of a tale, after the manner of the *Arabian Nights*, dealing with imaginary events on the island ; it was very weird, but served its purpose, though there were initial difficulties. The heroine, for instance, was christened " Maria," but " there were," Parapina said, "three Marias on the island. Which was it ? " and it was long before she grasped, if indeed she ever did so entirely, that the lady was imaginary. A certain sequence of events was somehow made intelligible to her. She was then induced to repeat the story, while it was taken down. It was copied out and next day read again to her for further correction. Every word and idea gained was a help in understanding local names and the native point of view. Before the end, in addition to using the language for the ordinary affairs of life, it was found possible to get simple answers direct from the old men, and understand first-hand much of what they said.

Any real success in intercourse was, however, due to the intelligence of one individual who was known as Juan Tepano. He was a younger man about forty years of age, a full-blooded Kanaka, but had served his time in the Chilean army, and thus had seen something of men and manners; he talked a little pidgin English, which was a help in the earlier stages, but before the end he and I were able to understand each other entirely in Kanaka, and he made clear to the old men anything I wished to know, and explained their answers to me. It was interesting to notice how his perception gradually grew of what truth and accuracy meant, and he finally assumed the attitude of watch-dog to prevent my being imposed on. Happily, it was discovered that he was able to draw, and he took great delight in this new-found power, which proved most useful. The tattoo designs were obtained, for example, by giving him a large sheet of paper with an outline of a man or woman, also a pencil and piece of candle ; these he took down to the village, gathered the old men together in their huts in the evening, and brought up in the morning the figure adorned by the direction of the ancients (fig. 88). He took a real interest in the work, learning through the conversations much about the island which was new to him, and at the end of the time triumphantly stated that " Mam-ma now knows everything there is to know about the island."

It is proposed to unite the information gained from locality and memory, referring where necessary to the accounts of the early voyagers, and give as complete descriptions as possible

FIG. 84.

CANOE-SHAPED HOUSES.

STONE FOUNDATIONS.

ENTRANCE AND PAVED AREA.

of the primitive existence which continued on Easter Island till the middle of last century. It will be seen that the condition of the people on the coming of Christianity, as we were able to ascertain it, corresponded almost exactly with that described by the first visitors from Europe, more than a hundred years earlier. Such traditions as linger regarding the megalithic remains have already been alluded to earlier in this book, but attention will be drawn to the point whenever this line of research seems successful in throwing indirect light on the origin of the great works.

Mode of Life.—The present natives, in talking of old times, say that their ancestors were " as thick as grass," and stood up like the fingers of two hands with the palms together ; a statement from which deduction must be made for pictorial representation. The early mariners never, as we have seen, estimate the population at more than two thousand, but the land could carry many more. Mr. Edmunds calculates that about half of the total amount (or some 15,000 acres) could grow bananas and sweet potatoes. Two acres of cultivated ground would be sufficient to supply an ordinary family.

Housing accommodation presented no great problem. Many slept in the open, and even to-day, in the era of Christianity and European clothes, a cave is looked upon as sufficient shelter. When on moving from our " town " to our " country " house we inquired where our attendants were to sleep, we were cheerfully informed " it was all right, there was a very good cave near Tongariki "—and this cave, called Ana Havea, became a permanent annexe to the establishment (fig. 124). Some of these caves had a wall built in front for shelter.

Houses, however, did exist, which were built in the form of a long upturned canoe ; they were made of sticks, the tops of which were tied together, the whole being thatched successively with reeds, grass, and sugar-cane. In the best of these houses, the foundations, which are equivalent to the gunwale of the boat, are made of wrought stones let into the ground ; they resemble the curbstones of a street pavement save that the length is greater. In the top of the stones were holes from which sprang the curved rods, which were equivalent to the ribs of a boat, and formed the walls and roof (figs. 84 and 85). The end stones of the house are carefully worked on the curve, and it is very rare to find them still in place, as they were comparatively light, weighing from one to two hundredweight, and easily carried off. Even the heavier stones were at times seized upon as booty in enemy raids; one measuring 15 feet was pointed out to us near an ahu on the south coast, which had been brought all the way from the north side of the island. In the middle of one side of the house was a doorway, and in the front of it a porch, which had also stone foundations. The whole space in front of the house was neatly paved with water-worn boulders, in the same manner as the ahu. This served as a stoep on which to sit and talk, but its practical utility was obvious to ourselves in the rainy seasons, when the entrance to our tents and houses became deep in mud (fig. 84A). Near the main abode was a thatched house which contained the native oven, the stones of which are often still in place. The cooking was done Polynesian fashion: a hole-about 15 inches deep is lined with flat stones, a fire is made within, and, when the stones are sufficiently heated, the food, wrapped up in parcels, is stacked within and covered with earth, a fire being lighted on the top.

Many of the surviving old people were born and brought up in these houses, which are known as "haré paenga." The old man, for example, before alluded to, who was brought out to Raraku, roved round the mountain telling with excitement who occupied the different houses in the days of his youth. He gave a particularly graphic description of the scene after sundown, when all were gathered within for the evening meal. In addition to the main door, there was, he said, an opening near each end by which the food was passed in and then from hand to hand; as perfect darkness reigned, a sharp watch had to be kept that it all reached its proper owners. He lay down within the old foundations to show how the inhabitants slept. This was parallel to the long axis of the house, the head being towards the door; the old people were in the centre in couples, and the younger ones in the ends. The largest of these houses, which had some unique features, measured 122 feet in length, with an extreme width of 12 feet; but some 50 feet by 5 feet or 6 feet are more usual measurements. They were often shared by related families and held anything from ten to thirty, or even more, persons.

The food consisted of the usual tropical produce, such as

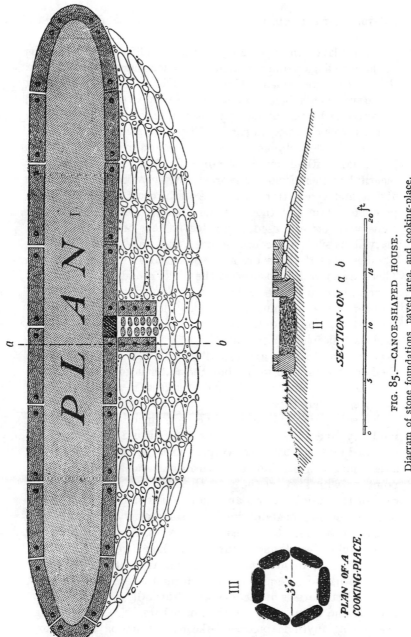

PLANⁱ

II

SECTION·ON·a·b

0   5   10   15   20 ft

III

PLAN·OF·A
COOKING·PLACE.

30'

FIG. 85.—CANOE-SHAPED HOUSE.

Diagram of stone foundations, paved area, and cooking-place.

potatoes, bananas, sugar-cane, and taro.   Animal diet formed a
very small part of it, rats being the only form of mammal; but
chickens played an important rôle in native life, and the remains
of the dwellings made for them are much more imposing than
those for human beings.   They are solid cairns, in the centre of
which was a chamber, running the greater part of their length ;
it was entered from outside by two or more narrow tunnels, down
which the chickens could pass.   They were placed here at night
for the sake of safety, as it was impossible to remove the stones
in the dark without making a noise (fig. 86).   Fish are not very
plentiful, as there is no barrier reef, but they also were an article
of diet, and were bartered by those on the coast for the vegetable
products obtained by those further inland.   Fish hooks made of
stone were formerly used, and a legend tells of a man who had
marvellous success because he used one made of human bone.
The heroes of the tales are also spoken of as fishing with nets.
There are in various places on the coast round towers, built of
stone, which are said to have been look-out towers whence
watchers on land communicated the whereabouts of the fish to
those at sea ; these contained a small chamber below which was
used as a sleeping apartment (fig. 87).   Turtles appear on the
carvings on the rock, and are alluded to in legend, and turtle-
shell ornaments were worn; but the water is too cold for them
ever to have been common, and Anakena is almost the only
sandy bay where they could have come on shore.

The sole form of dress was the cloth made from the paper
mulberry, and known throughout the South Seas as tapa ; it
was used for loin-cloths and wraps, which the Spaniards describe
as fastening over one shoulder.   Head-gear was a very important
point, as witnessed by the way the islanders always stole the
caps of the various European sailors.   The natives had various
forms of crowns made of feathers, some of them reserved for
special occasions.   Cherished feathers, particularly those of
white cocks, were brought out of gourds, where they had been
carefully kept, to manufacture specimens for the Expedition.
The crowns are generally made to form a shade over the eyes,
like the head-dresses of the images.   Naturally, every effort was
made to find the prototype of the image hats.   No one recollected
ever seeing anything precisely like it, but among the pictures
drawn for us of various head-decorations was a cylindrical hat

FIG. 86.

HOUSE FOR CHICKENS.

FIG. 87.

A TOWER USED BY FISHERMEN.

made of grass; the brim projected all the way round as with a European hat, but it had the same form of knot on the top as that of the statues.

Tattooing was a universal practice, and the exactness of the designs excited the admiration of the early voyagers, who wondered how savages managed to achieve such regularity and

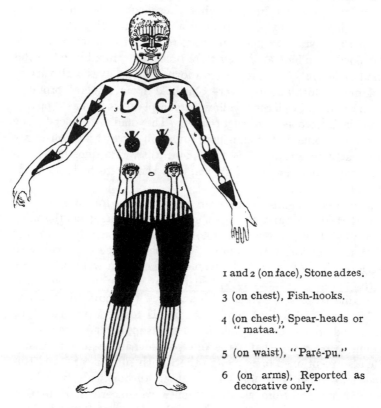

1 and 2 (on face), Stone adzes.

3 (on chest), Fish-hooks.

4 (on chest), Spear-heads or " mataa."

5 (on waist), " Paré-pu."

6 (on arms), Reported as decorative only.

FIG. 88.—DESIGNS USED IN TATTOOING, DRAWN BY NATIVES.

accuracy. The drawings made for us from the descriptions of the old people show the men covered, not only with geometrical designs, but with pictures of every-day objects, such as chisels and fish-hooks; even houses, boats, and chickens were represented in this way according to taste. The most striking objects were drawings of heads, one on each side of the body, known as

" paré-pu," which the old mariners describe as " fearsome monstrosities " [1] (fig. 88).   Various old persons said that they remembered seeing men with a pattern on the back similar to the rings and girdle of the images.   It seems, however, doubtful whether the image design merely represented tattoo, in view of the fact that it was raised, not incised, and in any case this would only put the search for its prototype a stage further back. The fact, however, remains that those particular marks were still being perpetuated, and form a link connecting the present with the past.   Beechey, in 1825, tells us the women were so tattooed as to look as if they wore breeches.   In addition to this kind of decoration, the islanders adorned themselves with various colours: white and red were obtained from mineral products found in certain places ; yellow from a plant known as " pua," [2] and black from ashes of sugar-cane.   They had a distinct feeling for art.   Some of the paintings found in caves and houses are obviously recent, and it is a frequent answer to questions as to the why and wherefore of things, that they were to make some object " look nice."

It will be remembered that not only have the images long ears, but that all the early voyagers speak of them as general among the inhabitants.   It was therefore somewhat surprising to find that no such thing was known as a man whose ears had been perforated, though with the women the custom went on till the introduction of Christianity, and two or three females with the lobe dilated in this manner still survived (fig. 90).   At last one old leper recalled that the father of his foster-father had long ears, and on asking as a child for the reason, he had received the illuminating reply that " the old people had them like that." He also mentioned one or two others with similar ears, and this was subsequently confirmed by other authorities.   It will be seen that the custom, as far as men were concerned, of dilating the lobe of the ear, must have been abandoned at the end of the eighteenth century, or just about the time of the visits of the Spanish, English, and French Expeditions.   That this was cause and effect, and that they imitated the appearance of the foreign sailors, seems more than a guess ; it will appear from other

[1] *Voyage of Gonzalez*, p. 90.
[2] One of the Scitamineæ—further determination awaits the blooming of plants brought back to Kew.

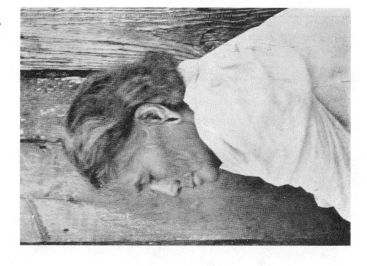

FIG. 90.

AN OLD WOMAN OF EASTER ISLAND WITH
DILATED EAR-LOBE.

FIG. 89.

MAHANGA.
A native of the Paumotu.

sources how great was the impression which was made by the foreigners.

Social Life.—Roggeveen's description of the people as being of all shades of colour is still accurate. They themselves are very conscious of the variations, and when we were collecting genealogies, they were quite ready to give the colour of even remote relations: " Great-aunt Susan," it would be unhesitatingly stated, was " white," and " Great-aunt Jemima black." The last real ariki, or chief, was said to be quite white. " White like me ? " I innocently asked. " You ! " they said, " you are red " ; the colour in European cheeks, as opposed to the sallow white to which they are accustomed, is to the native our most distinguishing mark. It is obvious that we are dealing with a mixed race, but this only takes us part of the way, as the mixture may have taken place either before or after they reached the island.

They were divided into ten groups, or clans (" máta "), which were associated with different parts of the island, though the boundaries blend and overlap; members of one division settled not infrequently among those of another. Each person still knows his own clan.

In remembered times there were no group restrictions on marriage, which took place indiscriminately between members of the same or of different clans. The only prohibition had reference to consanguinity, and forbade all union nearer than the eighth degree or third cousins. These ten clans were again grouped, more especially in legend or speaking of the remote past, into two major divisions known as Kotuu (or Otuu), and Hotu Iti, which correspond roughly with the western and eastern parts of the island. These divisions were also known respectively as Mata-nui, or greater clans, and Mata-iti, or lesser clans. The lower portions of the island were the most densely populated parts, especially those on the coast, and the settlements on the higher ground appear to have been few (fig. 91).

In Kotuu, the Marama and Háumoana inhabited side by side the land running from sea to sea between the high central ground and the western volcano Rano Kao. They had a small neighbour, the Ngatimo, to the south, and jointly with the Miru spread over Rano Kao and formed settlements by the margin of the crater lake. The Miru lived on the high, narrow strip

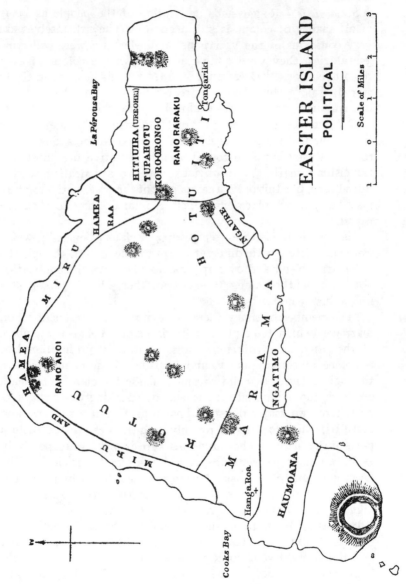

FIG 91.

EASTER ISLAND

POLITICAL

Scale of Miles

Note.—The dividing lines shown are not defined boundaries.

between the mountain in the apex and the cliff, and mixed up with them was a lesser people, the Hamea. To the east was another small clan, the Raa, which is spoken of in conjunction with the Miru and Hamea.

The principal Hotu Iti clans were the Tupahotu, the Koró-orongo, and the Hitiuira. The last were generally known as the "Ureohei"; they inhabited jointly the level piece of ground from the northern bay to the south coast, and had some dwellings on the eastern headland. Next to them on the south coast was a small group, the Ngaure.[1] The particular importance of the clans lies in the fact that, while they may be merely groups of one body, they may, on the other hand, represent different races or waves of immigrants. If there have been two peoples on Easter Island, these divisions are one place where we must at least look for traces for it.

Legend tells of continual wars between Hotu Iti and Kotuu. In recent times general fighting seems to have been constant, and took place even between members of one clan. A wooden sword, or paoa, was used, but the chief weapon was made from obsidian, and took from it the name of "mataa." This volcanic glass is found on the slope of Rano Kao, but the principal quarries are on the neighbouring hill of Orito. Tradition says its use was first discovered by a boy who stepped on it and cut his foot. The obsidian was knapped till it had a cutting edge, and also a tongue, which latter was fitted into a handle or stick (fig. 92). The various shapes assumed were dignified by names, fourteen of which were given, such as "tail of a fish," "backbone of a rat," "leaf of a banana." It was very usual to pick up these mataa, and hoards were occasionally found ; in one instance fifty or sixty were discovered below a stone in a cave, and in another case the hammer-stone was found with them which had been used in the process of squeezing off the flakes. The weapon was

---

[1] Of these clan names, " Raa " means the sun and " Marama " the light. The signification of the others is not equally clear, and the natives could give no assistance ; but Mr. Ray gives the following interesting information from other Polynesian sources. " Haumoana " means the sea-breeze ; " Hitiuira " is probably " hiti-ra " or sunrise ; and " Ure-o-hei " another version of " ura-o-hehe," or red of sundown. " Koro-orongo " is doubtless from " Koro-o-Rongo," or the ring of Rongo (a well-known Polynesian deity), that is the rainbow. " Kotuu " appears to be a contraction of " Ko Otuu," meaning " The Hill " ; the name " Otuu " is used alternatively for the same district. " Hotu " is another form of the word for hill and " Iti " signifies small, it presumably refers to Rano Raraku.

used both as a spear and as a javelin. A site is pointed out near Anakena, where a man throwing down hill killed another at about thirty-five yards. The art of making these mataa is, of course, practically extinct, but one old man, commonly known as " Hé " (fig. 83), brought us some which he had manufactured himself for the Expedition, and which were fairly well wrought.

With the exception of the Miru, of which more will be said, there were no chiefs nor any form of government; any man who was expert in war became a leader. The warfare consisted largely of spasmodic and isolated raids; an aggrieved person gathered together his neighbours and descended on the offenders. It is related incidentally that one man, going along the south coast, " found war going on," one set of men having blocked up another in a cave. Another story is told of six men, called Gwaruti-mata-keva, of the clan Tupahotu, who lived in a cave in a certain hillock on the south coast, known as Toa-toa. They went round in a boat to Hanga Piko, stole fish, and returned rapidly to their cave. A hundred men from Hanga Piko then came overland to punish the robbery, and made a fire of grass before the cave in which the men lay hidden. When the attackers assumed that the enemy were all dead from suffocation, they went into the cave; but those within had buried their faces in holes scraped in the earth, and when the men from Hanga Piko entered, they arose and slew the whole hundred. A more interesting fact came out incidentally in connection with this gang of Toa-toa, connecting them with the secret societies found elsewhere in the Pacific. They were, it was said, in the habit of going about after dark with their faces painted red, white, and black, and visiting houses, where they declared they were gods, and demanded food, which the inhabitants accordingly gave them. The fraud, however, finally came to light when one day a man, who was travelling with his servant, saw them washing paint off their faces, " so they knew that they had deceived the people, and the people gathered together and killed them."

In these internecine fights fire was very generally set to the enemy's dwellings. " He often burnt houses," a young man said, pointing to an older one, and the impeachment was not denied. The ahu, too, were raided and bodies burnt, which seems to be the cause of the burnt bones recorded by certain travellers; there is no reason to suppose there was cremation

FIG. 92.

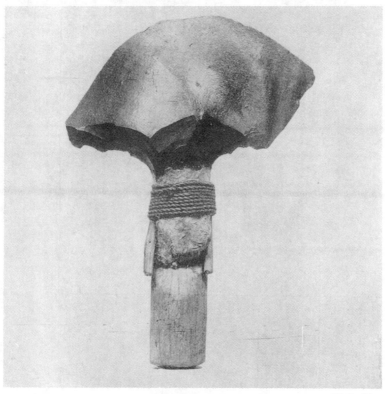

OBSIDIAN SPEAR-HEADS.
(Mataa.)

FIG. 93.

AHU, HANGA MAIHIKO[1]

Old Image Ahu, converted to semi-pyramid form, with paved approach ; also two stones on which were exposed the corpses of slain men.

or sacrifice on Easter Island. It was in this sort of warfare that the last images were overthrown.

While legends record how many people were eaten after each affray, all living persons deny, with rather striking unanimity, not only that they themselves have ever been cannibals, but that their fathers were so. If this is correct, the custom was dying out for some reason before the advent of Christianity; [1] their grand-fathers, the old people admit, ate human flesh, but, if there were any rites connected with it, they "did not tell." The great-grandmother of an old man of the Miru clan was, according to his account, killed on the high central part of the island by the Ureohei and eaten. In revenge for the outrage, one of her sons, Hotu by name, killed sixty of the Ureohei. Another son, who had pacifist leanings, thought the feud ought then to be ended, but Hotu desired yet more victims, and there was a violent quarrel between the two brothers, in which the peace-maker was struck on the head with a club; for, as Hotu remarked, if they had slain his father, it would have been different, but really to eat his mother was "no good."

Our acquaintance with the person said to have been "the last cannibal," or rather with his remains, came about accident-ally during the time when I was alone on the island. A little party of us had ridden to the top of the volcano Rano Kao; and on the southern side of the crater, that opposite Orongo, some of the natives were pointing out the legendary sites con-nected with the death of the first immigrant chief, Hotu-matua. Suddenly one of them vanished into a crevice in the rocks, and reappeared brandishing a thigh-bone to call attention to its large size. I dismounted, scrambled into a little grotto, or natural cave, where a skeleton was extended; the skull was missing, but the jaw-bone was present, and the rest of the bones were in regular order; the individual had either died there or been buried. Bones were in the department of the absent member of the Expedition, but it was of course essential to collect them, from the view of determining race, and the natives never resented our doing so. I therefore passed these out, packed them in grass

---

[1] Since writing the above the following has been seen: "The higher Polynesian races, such as the Tahitians, Hawaiians, Samoans, had one and all outgrown, and some of them had in part forgot, the practice (cannibalism) before Cook or Bougainville had shown a top-sail in their waters."—*In the South Seas*, R. L. Stevenson, p. 94.

15

in the luncheon-basket, and, sitting down on a rock, asked to be told the story of the cave. " That," my attendants replied, " is Ko Tori." He was, they said, the last man on the island who had eaten human flesh. In this hiding-place he had enjoyed his meals, and no one had ever been able to track him. There had formerly been a cooking-place, but it was now hidden by a fall of stones. He had died as a very old man at the other end of the island, apparently in the odour of sanctity ; to judge by the toothless jaw if he had not deserted his sins they must long ago have deserted him. His last desire was to be buried in the place with which he had such pleasant connections, and in dutiful regard to his wishes, or because it was feared that his ghost might otherwise make itself unpleasant, some of the young men bore the corpse on stretchers along the south coast and up to the top of the mountain, depositing it here. The next thing was to get at some sort of date ; chronology is naturally of a vague order, and the most effective method is, if possible, to connect events with the generation in which they happened. " Did your grandfather know him," was asked, " or your father ? " The answer was unexpected. " Porotu," they said, pointing to one of the old men, " helped to carry him," and silence fell on the group. My heart sank; I had then undone this last pious work and committed sacrilege. To my great relief, however, strange sounds soon made it clear that the humorous side had appealed to the escort; they were suffocating with mirth. " And now," they said, gasping between sobs of laughter, " Ko Tori goes in a basket to England." As I write, Ko Tori resides at the Royal College of Surgeons, and has done his bit towards elucidating the mystery of Easter Island.

Sexual morality, as known to us, was not a strong point in life on the island, but marriage was distinctly recognised, and the absolute loose liver was a person apart. Polygamy was usual, but many seem to have had only one wife. The children belonged to the father's clan, and are often distinguished by his name being given after their own. At the same time the clan of the mother was not ignored, and a man would sometimes fight for his maternal side. If a man had sons by more than one wife, after his death each claimed the body of his father to lie on the ahu of his mother's clan, and the corpse might thus be carried to several in turn, finally returning to its own destination. We collected a certain number of genealogical trees, the various dramatis personæ being for this purpose represented by matches or buttons. It was not a very popular line of research, the cry being apt to be raised, " Now let's talk of something interesting "; but some two hundred names were in this way placed in their family groups, with details of clan, place of residence and colour, and some knowledge obtained with regard to many more. It is not of course enough ground on which to found any theory, but it was very useful in checking information gathered in other ways. Only in one case was it possible to get back beyond the great-grandfather of our informant, but the knowledge of family connections was often greater than would be found among Europeans. The number of childless marriages was striking.

The early story of Viriamo (fig. 83), the oldest woman living in our day, gives a picture of this primitive state of things. She belonged to the clan of Ureohei, and her family had lived for some generations, as far back as could be remembered, on the edge of the eastern volcano, not far from Raraku. The great-grandfather, who was dark, had as his only wife a white woman of the Hamea. Their son was white, and had two wives, one of the Tupahotu and one of the Ngaure. By the first, although she also was white, he had a dark son who married a white wife of his own clan, Ureohei, but of a different group. Viriàmo was the second of their eight children, all of whom were white save herself and her eldest brother. Four of the girls died young in the epidemic of smallpox in 1864. Viriamo and two of her sisters were initiated as children into the bird rite.[1] When older she was tattooed with rings round her forehead and with the dark-blue breeches. Somewhat later, but still as a young woman, she went over to Anakena and had her ears pierced, but she never had the lobe extended, preferring to let it remain small. When asked about her marriage, she bridled as coyly as a young girl. Her first union was a matter of arrangement, the husband, who was also of the Ureohei, giving her father much food, and, if she had refused to accept the situation, she would, she said, have been beaten. There was no ceremony of any kind, no new clothes nor feasting; her father simply took her to her new home and handed her over. The house was near the two statues with

[1] See below, pp. 266-68.

the projecting noses, excavated on the south-eastern slope of Raraku (fig. 73), and, when she wanted water, rather than cross the boundary and go round to the lake by the gap, through the hostile dwellers on the western side, she used to clamber with her vessel up the boundary rift in the cliff face. There was one white child, who died young, but her marriage was not a success, and Viriamo left the man and went off to live with one of the Miru clan at Anakena. His house already contained a wife and family, also four brothers, but they all got on quite happily together. She had five children by this man, who, like their father, were all white ; four of them, however, died in infancy. This was the result of the parents having most unfortunately fallen foul of an old man, whose cloak had been taken without his consent, and who had accordingly prophesied disaster. The remaining child, a daughter, was living and unmarried when we were on the island. The last husband was the most satisfactory of the three; he was a Tupahotu living near Tongariki. She was handed over to him as a matter of family arrangement, in discharge of a debt, but she was quite amenable to the exchange, and was very fond of him. He was light in colour, but her only child by this marriage, our friend Juan, was dark, taking, as he said, "after my mam-ma."

The women do not seem, judging by existing remains, to have had always a happy time. Dr. Keith, who examined the skulls collected by the Expedition, concludes his report on one of the female specimens as follows : " The most likely explanation is that the indent of the left temple was the cause of death, produced by the blow of a club, and that the suppuration and repair of the right side has been also produced by a former blow which failed to prove fatal. Two other skulls, also those of women, show indented fractures in the left temporal region."

Any deficiency at marriages, in the way of social festivity, was made up at funerals. These were attended by persons from all over the island, for " when they were not fighting, they were all cousins." In answer to the remark that " considering the population their whole time must have gone in this way," it was cheerfully observed that " they had nothing else to do, so they all went, everybody took food and everybody ate." The parents of one of our friends, Kapiera, lived at Anakena, but he was born on the south side of the island near Vaihu " when his mother went for a funeral." The men who knew the tablets went also and sang, but there seems to have been little or nothing in the way of rites. The missionaries were impressed with the fact that there was no ceremony of any kind at a burial.

Most elaborate spells were, however, performed in connection with a man who had been slain, known as " tangata ika," or fish-man ; the corpse was kept from resting either day or night while his neighbours went in pursuit of vengeance. In front of one ahu, on the north coast, some pieces of the old statues have been formed into a rude chair. On this, it was said, had been seated the naked body of a man belonging to the district, Kotavari-vari by name, who had been killed at Akahanga on the south coast. One man kept the corpse from falling, while two others sat behind and chanted songs to aid the avengers. These watchers were covered with black ashes, wore only feather hats, and carried the small dancing-paddle known as "rapa " (fig. 116) ; the chief man in charge of the ceremony was known as the " timo." It must have been an eerie scene as dusk came on. The story is told of a murder near Tongariki. In this case the victim's corpse was placed on the ahu and turned over at intervals by the watchers. Hanga Maihiko, a converted image ahu on the south coast, is one of those which have a paved approach, and there are on the pavement two stones—pieces of a hat and a statue—specially used for exposing " fish-men " (fig. 93). If these charms failed to act, there was a still more reliable way. The clothes of the victim were buried beneath the cooking-place of the foe, and when he had partaken of food prepared there he would certainly die the night following. Some of the carved tablets were connected with these rites ; one was certainly known as that of the " Ika," while there is said to have been another called " Timo," which was the " list " kept by each ahu of its murdered men.

The custom of exposing the dead was, as has been stated, going on in living memory. The information already given on this head is confirmed by the accounts of the missionaries,[1] but

---

[1] " These bodies, enveloped in mats, are placed on a heap of stones or on a kind of wooden structure, the head being turned towards the sea. Now, as all the population live round the island, dried skeletons are to be met all along this coast, and no one seems to take any notice of them."— Letter from Brother Eyraud—*Annals of the Propagation of the Faith*, Jan. 1866.

burial was also practised, the mode of disposal being a matter of choice. There were two drawbacks to exposure : firstly, if the deceased was for any reason an uncanny person, his ghost might make itself unpleasant—he was safer hidden under stones ; secondly, the body, if left in the open, might be burnt by enemies ; this latter was the reason given for the burial of the last great chief, Ngaara, who was interred in one of the image ahu on the western coast. Not only were the ruins of the greater ahu still being used, but up till 1863 smaller ones were being

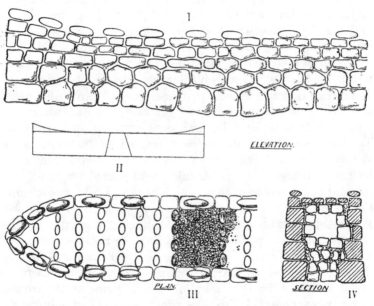

FIG. 94.—DIAGRAM OF AHU POE-POE (CANOE-SHAPE).

built. One was pointed out on the north coast as having been put up for an individual, the maternal aunt of our guide, the lady having had the misfortune to be killed by a devil in the night. It was a small structure, ovoidal in shape, 10 feet in length, with a flat top sloping from a height of 9 feet at the end towards the sea, to 4 feet 6 inches at that towards the land ; there was beneath it a vaulted chamber for bones.

Burial cairns, called " ahu poe-poe," were being made in modern times, and a man skilled in their construction was amongst those who were carried off to Peru. The word " poe-poe " is described as meaning a big canoe, such as their ancestors came in to the island. It is applied to two types of ahu, one of which is obviously built to resemble a boat; of this kind there are about twelve in the island. One large one (fig. 94) measured as much as 178 feet in length, the width being 20 feet, while the ends, which are made like the bow and stern of a canoe, are about 10 feet to 15 feet in height. The flat top is paved with sea-boulders, and is surrounded by a row of the same in imitation of the gunwale of a boat. In one such ahu two vaults were found by us just below the surface with perfect burials. One was the body of an old man, the other of a woman with a child. Both had been wrapped in reeds, and with the body of the woman were some glass beads. On the surface of the ahu were a few bones, possibly of a body which had been exposed there, but the ahu had apparently been built for the two interments. It is less obvious why the same name, " ahu poe-poe," should be applied to a burial-place which was wedge-shaped in form. It follows the lines of the image ahu in so far as having a wall towards the sea flanked on the land sides by a slope of masonry. It might be held to represent the prow of a boat, but resembles rather a pier or jetty. Only some six of these were seen, of which the longest was 70 feet. One in a lonely spot, at the very edge of a high cliff, which overlooked Anakena Bay, formed a most striking abode for the dead (fig. 95).

In a few cases the term ahu is given to a pavement, generally by the roadside, neatly made of rounded boulders and edged with a curb; the form was said to be ancient. One of those on the west road was reported as specially dedicated to mata-toa— which signifies victors or warriors—and the same was said of a differently made ahu on the south coast.[1]

Neither exposure nor interment was necessarily confined to ahu, and corpses were frequently disposed of in caverns, as in the case of Ko Tori. Three instances were mentioned, an uncle and two nephews, where the corpses, after being exposed, were lowered with a rope down the crevasses of the cliff of Raraku

---

[1] When all those ahu which can be placed in categories as Image, Semi-Pyramid, Canoe, Wedge-shaped, or Pavement have been noted, there remain, out of the total of two hundred and sixty burial-places, some fourteen which are unique in design; and between sixty and seventy which cannot be classified, either because they are mere cairns or in too ruined a condition to be identified.

in order to evade the enemy. One of the nephews, who had been of the party when the final statues were overthrown, had met with a tragic end, being drowned by catching his hand in a rock when diving for lobsters under water. With the exception of those near the standing statues, we practically never found an earth burial. This seems to account for the exaggerated estimates of the number of human remains on the island ; it is doubtful if even five hundred skulls could be collected, but, whether in caves or ruined ahu, a large proportion of those which exist are very much in evidence.

Memorials of the dead were erected in various places independently of the actual locality where the corpse rested. Some of these were simply mounds of earth, which can be seen on various hills ; there is a regular succession on the landward rim of the Raraku crater, opposite to the great cliff, but one at least of these was a memorial to a man whose body had been disposed of in the clefts of the cliff. Others of these independent memorials were in the shape of cairns about 6 feet in height, known as " pipi-hereko," and were formerly surmounted by a white stone. Many of them still exist, and they are particularly numerous on the high ground above Anakena Cove. The locality was chosen as one which was but little inhabited, for the taboo for the dead (or pera) extended to them, and no one went near them in the daylight, on penalty of being stoned, till the period of mourning had been terminated with the usual feast. Various voyagers commented on these cairns, which were marked objects, and Cook thinks that they may have been put up instead of statues.

It would seem by the following tale, which imposes a somewhat severe strain on the European imagination, that piles of stones had in the native mind a certain resemblance to the human figure. " There was once an old lady who had an arm so long that it could have reached right across the island. She was a bad old woman, and once a month had a child to eat, so a certain man determined to put an end to her power for doing harm. He took her out in a boat to fish, first telling his small son to collect stones, and after they had gone to put them in piles in front of the house of the woman, and also to make a fire and much smoke. When the canoe had got out to sea, he looked back and found the boy had done as he was told, and glimpses of the cairns could be seen among the clouds of smoke. Then

FIG. 95.

AHU POE-POE (WEDGE SHAPE).

he called to the old woman, ' Look, there are men at your house ! '
So she put out her long arm to seize what she thought were the
people going to rob her hut, whereon the man seized the paddle
and brought it down on her arm and broke it ; then he killed
the old woman and threw her body into the sea.

Life was by no means dull in Easter Island, for if a feast was
not being given to commemorate a departed relation, it was
arranged in honour of one whilst still alive. The " PAINA," which
means simply picture or representation, was given by the family
as a testimonial of esteem to a father, or possibly a brother who
might be either alive or dead ; it was a serious matter, and the
original direction for the celebration came from a supernaturally
gifted individual known as an " ivi-atua." The paina was a large
figure made of woven rods, and the host would clamber up inside
it and look through eyes or mouth; it had a crown made of
the wings of a particular sea-bird, known as " makohe," and long
ears. Occasionally it was put up on a special spot, where, for
example, a man had been killed, but the interesting point in
connection with the paina is that the usual place for erection was
in front of an image ahu on its landward side, and at most, or
all, of the large ahu, there can still be seen, in the grass at the
foot of the paved slope, the holes where the paina have stood.
It was kept in place by four long ropes, one of which passed over
the ahu. The feast was held in the summer, and lasted from
two to four days ; at any given ahu there might be only one
in the season or as many as five. The drawbacks, which would
have seemed obvious to such a locality, do not seem to have
clouded the entertainment; the feasting was great, and consisted
largely of rats which were caught in the hen-houses. The recollection of these entertainments and the crowds who attended
them were very vivid, and Viriamo's eyes brightened as she told
of the singing, dancing, and feasting of her youth.

There are records of another figure which appears to have
been different from the paina ; it was clothed and known as
" KO PEKA." The Spanish Expedition in 1770 says that the
islanders brought down to the beach, on the day when the three
crosses were set up, an idol about 11 feet high like a " Judas,"
stuffed with straw; it was all white, and had a fringe of black
hair hanging down its back. They put it up on stones and sat

cross-legged around it, howling all night by the light of flares. As no information was volunteered to us about such celebrations, the natives were asked if they had ever known a similar figure, and an old man at once replied that there had existed one just like the description, made of reeds, as a memorial of a dead wife or " fine " child ; it stood in front of the house, or was sometimes carried to a hillock where the people assembled to mourn. One of the officers of the La Pérouse Expedition also described a figure seen near a platform; it was 11 feet in height, clothed in white tapa (" *étoffe blanche du pays* ") ; it had hanging round the neck a basket covered with white, and by the side of this bag the figure of a child 2 feet long. This seems to confirm the information that it was intended to represent a woman.

Another great festivity, given for a father either living or dead, was the " KORO." This was a house-party on a very extended scale. A special dwelling made with poles and thatched was put up, and, according to accounts, which surround it no doubt with a halo from the past, measured some hundreds of feet in length and 20 feet in height. An old man stated that at a celebration at which he was present there were " a hundred guests," a number which is probably a guess, but the addition that there were " ten cooking-places " sounds like memory. Invitations to these festivities were much in request, as there was " no work to do " ; presents of food were brought to the hero who distributed them to the party. They seem to have lasted indefinitely, going on for months, and the time was passed with various entertainments. The old people sang, the young people danced, and the host, who lived in a little house near, came and looked on. On the last day there was a great feast, and the house was broken down with the aid of the carved wooden lizards, which are associated with the island (fig. 117). We were puzzled in coming across a rough stone building, near Anakena, which seemed to be neither ahu, dwelling, nor chicken-house; it had been, the men told us, a shelter for the posts of the koro, where they were kept in readiness for the next celebration.

There was yet another entertainment which is said to have been in honour of a mother, as a koro was of a father. In at least four different places on the island are to be seen a dancing-ground known as " KAUNGA." It is a narrow strip paved with pebbles, over 200 feet in length by 2 feet in width, and not unlike the paved approach to some of the ahu. A demonstration was given of the way it was used. The dancers, " fine men, fine women," as was explained with emphasis, proceeding along it single file, holding rapa in both hands. In connection with some or all of the kaunga there was a house where the party remained indoors for a long time previous to the dances, in order to " get their complexions good," a touch which shows that a white skin was admired.

These feasts were held in certain months only, determined by the appearance of the heavens after nightfall. On the extremity of the eastern headland there is an outcrop of boulders, one of which is incised with a spiral design ; the place is known as " Ko Te Papa-ui-hetuu," or, " The Rock-for-seeing-stars," and here the old men came to watch the constellations. About two hundred yards from these boulders there is another engraved stone on which ten cup-shaped depressions are visible; this represented, it is said, "a map of the stars."

The season for the Paina depended on the position of the three central stars of Orion, with regard to which the following story is related. A certain married woman, on going down to bathe, was carried off by a stranger. When her husband discovered this, he slew her in his anger, and she fled up to be a star. The husband then took their two boys, one in each hand, and followed her to the sky, where the three form the belt of Orion. The wife, however, would have nothing to do with them, and remained in a separate part of the heavens. This is the only nature myth which we encountered on the island.

CHAPTER XVI

NATIVE CULTURE IN PRE-CHRISTIAN TIMES (*continued*)

Religion—Position of the Miru Clan—The Script—The Bird Cult—
Wooden Carvings.

RELIGION

THE religion of the Islanders, employing the word in our sense, seems always to have been somewhat hazy,[1] and the difficulty in grasping it now is increased by the fact that since becoming Roman Catholics they dislike giving the name of "atua," or god, to their old deities ; it only drops out occasionally. They term them "aku-aku," which means spirits, or more frequently "tatane," a word of which the derivation is obvious. The confusion of ideas was crystallised by a native, who gravely remarked that they were uncertain whether one of these beings was God or the Devil, so they " wrote to Tahiti, and Tahiti wrote to Rome, and Rome said he was not the Devil, he was God "; a modern view being apparently taken at headquarters of the evolution of religious ideas. Both these words, tatane and aku-aku, will be employed for supernatural beings, without prejudice to their original character, or claims to divinity ; some of them were certainly the spirits of the dead, but had probably become deified ; the ancestors of Hotu-matua were reported to have come with him to the island. They existed in large numbers, being both male and female, and were connected with different parts of the island ; a list of about ninety was given, with their places of residence. No worship was paid, and the only notice taken of these supernatural persons was to mention before meals the names of those to whom a man owed special duty, and

[1] Our impressions on this head are confirmed by a remark of Brother Eyraud. " Though I have lived in the greatest of intimacy and familiarity with them, I have never been able to discover them in any act of actual religious worship."—*Annals of the Propagation of the Faith*, Jan. 1866.

invite them to partake ; it was etiquette to mention with your own the patron of any guest who was present. There was no sacrifice; the invitation to the supernatural power was purely formal, or restricted to the essence of the food only. Nevertheless, the aku-aku, in this at least being human, were amiable or the reverse according to whether or not they were well fed. If they were hungry, they ate women and children, and one was reported as having a proclivity for stealing potatoes ; if, on the contrary, they were well-disposed to a man, they would do work for him, and he would wake in the morning to find his potato-field dug, which, as our informant truly remarked, was " no like Kanaka."

The aku-aku appeared in human form, in which they were indistinguishable from ordinary persons. One known as Uka-o-hoheru looked like a very beautiful woman, and was the wife of a young Tupahotu who had no idea she was really a tatane. She lived with him at Mahatua on the north coast, and bore him a child. One very wet day she was obliged to leave the house to take fresh fire to the cooking-place where it had gone out. When she returned, her husband was angry that she had no red paint on her face, and, not heeding her explanation that the rain had washed it off, took a stick to beat her. She ran away, and he followed, till at last she sat down on the edge of the eastern headland, where there is now an ahu known by her name. When by and by he came up, she told him to go back and look after the child, and fled away like a rushing whirlwind over the sea and was no more seen.

Two other female tatane are reported to have lived together in a cave on the cliff-side of Paréhé,[1] whose names were Kava-ara and Kava-tua. They heard all men tell of the beauty of a certain Uré-a-hohové, a young man who lived near Hanga Roa ; so they went down to see him, put him to sleep, and carried him on his mat up to their cave, where they left him. Before going away they told an old woman, also an aku-aku, that she was not to go and look into the cave. This she naturally proceeded to do, and, finding Uré, warned him to eat nothing the two tatane might give to him, supplying him herself with some

---

[1] The outermost of the three hillocks on the eastern volcano on which the Spaniards set up the crosses in 1770. Half of it has been worn away by coastal erosion (fig. 78).

chicken. When therefore his captors came back and offered him food, he only pretended to take it, and ate the chicken instead. They then went away again. The old woman came back, and said, " If cockroaches come, kill them ; if flies come, kill them ; but if a crab comes, do not kill it." Uré did as he was told, and killed the cockroaches and flies, which were other tatane; but the crab he did not kill, it was the old woman. Meanwhile for many days the father of Uré wept for him, till some men sailing under the cliff while fishing, heard a song, and looking up saw the missing man ; but they would not go and fetch him, though the father gave them much food, for the cliff was steep and the cave difficult to reach. At last a woman volunteered for the task, and was lowered over the cliff in a net, and by this means succeeded in fetching Uré safely to the top. The history ends with his return to his home, and does not mention if, in correct fashion, he married his fair deliverer.

Aku-aku were not immortal. A man called Raraku, after whom the mountain is said to have been named, caught a big " heke," which seems to have been an octopus, in the sea near Tongariki and ate it, with the result that he went mad, and all people gave chase to him. He caught up a wooden lizard (fig. 117), and, using it as a club, ran amok among tatane across the north shore and down the west coast, killing them right and left; the names of twenty-three were given who thus met their fate.

Human beings, on the other hand, were liable to be attacked by tatane, more particularly at night, when there was risk, not only to their bodies, but also to their own spirits,[1] which were at large while they slept. It is still firmly believed that in dreams the soul visits any locality present to the thought. On one of the ahu is a rough erection of slabs, said to be the house of the aku-aku Mata-wara-wara, or "Strong-Rain." He had as a partner another aku-aku called Papai-a-taki-vera, and they arranged between them that Mata should bring on rain, while Papai constructed a house of reeds which was only there at night; then when the spirits of sleeping people, which were wandering abroad, became cold with the rain, they went into the house and the tatane killed them. The unfortunate sleeper waked in the morning feeling distinctly unwell, he lingered on for two or three

---

[1] The same word aku-aku was used for the spirit both of the living and the dead, or else the Tahitian " varua "; they were said to be equivalent.

days, and then died. It was not essential to life to have a soul, but you could not really get on comfortably without it. No knowledge survives of any belief or ideas with regard to a future state. The spirit, it was said, appeared occasionally for five or ten years after a man's death and then vanished.

Pan in the shape of tatane is by no means dead. Not only do such beings haunt the crater of Rano Raraku, but tales are told of weird apparitions at dusk which vanish mysteriously into space.

There were no priests, but certain men, known as " koromaké," practised spells which would secure the death of an enemy, and there was also the class known as " ivi-atua," which included both men and women. The most important of these ivi-atua, of whom it was said there might be perhaps ten in the island, held commune with the aku-aku, others were able to prophesy, and could foresee the whereabouts of fish or turtle, while some had the gift of seeing hidden things, and would demand contributions from a secreted store of bananas or potatoes, in a way which was very disconcerting to the owner.

There was practically only one religious function of a general nature ; it was very popular and had a surprising origin. Attention was attracted on the south coast by a particularly long stoep of rounded pebbles measuring 139 feet, and obviously connected with a thatched house now disappeared. That, our guides said in answer to a question, " is a haré-a-té-atua, where they praised the gods." " What gods ? " " The men who came from far away in ships. They saw they had pink cheeks, and they said they were gods." The early voyagers, for the cult went back at least three generations, were therefore taken for deities in the same way as Coók was at Hawaii. The simplest form of this celebration took place on long mounds of earth known as " miro-o-orne," or earth-ships, of which there are several in the island, one of them with a small mound near it to represent a boat. Here the natives used to gather together and act the part of a European crew, one taking the lead and giving orders to the others. A more formal ceremony was held in a large house. This had three doors on each side by which the singers entered, who were up to a hundred in number, and ranged themselves in lines within ; in one house, of which a diagram was drawn, a deep hole was dug in the middle, at the bottom of which was a gourd covered with a stone to act as a drum. On the top of this a man danced, being hidden out of sight in the hole.

In other cases, two, or perhaps three, boats were constructed inside the house, the masts of which went through the roof; these boats were manned with crews clad in the garments of European sailors, the gifts from passing vessels being kept as stage properties. Fresh music was composed for every occasion, and in one song, which was quoted, much reference is made to the " red face of the captain from over the seas." The position of chief performer was one of great honour, being analogous, on a glorified scale, to the leader of a cotillon of our own day. It was stated by an old man that his great-grandfather had so acted, and even the words sung were still remembered. Te Haha, a Miru (fig. 83), gave us to understand that he had been a great social success in his youth, and counted up three koro, and seven haré-até-atua at which he had been present. As he was a handsome old man, and was connected with the court of the chief Ngaara, his pride of recollection was very probably justified. Juan, mixing up, no doubt, recollections of a later date, gave a vivid representation on one of these spots of the pseudo-captain striding about and using very strong language, while he called upon the engineer to " make more smoke so that the ship should go fast."

THE MIRU CLAN

On the border-line, between religion and magic, wherever, if anywhere, that line exists, was the position of the clan known as the Miru. Members of this group had, in the opinion of the islanders, the supernatural and valuable gift of being able to increase all food supplies, especially that of chickens, and this power was particularly in evidence after death. It has been known that certain skulls from Easter are marked with designs, such as the outline of a fish; these are crania of the Miru, and called " puoko-moa," or fowl-heads, because they had, in particular, the quality of making hens lay eggs (fig. 96). Hotu, the Miru, whose mother, it may be remembered, was the victim of a cannibal feast, made his own skull an heirloom, as " it was so extremely good for chickens," that he did not wish it to go out of the family. His son gave it

FIG. 96.

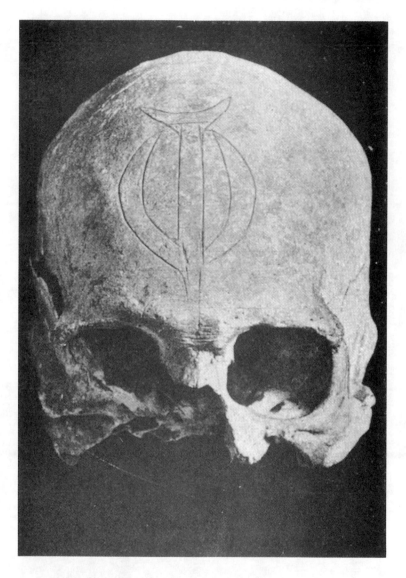

[*Butterworth.*

A MIRU SKULL WITH INCISED DESIGN.

FIG. 97.

ANAKENA COVE.
Hill on left has terraced summit.

to a relative, who was the father of an old man from whom we managed to obtain it.   When the time came to hand it over to us, the late owner began to cling to it affectionately, and say that " he wept much at the thought of its going to England "; as, however, the bargain had already been completed, we remained obdurate, and at the time of writing Hotu resides with Ko Tori at the Royal College of Surgeons.

The Miru were unique in other ways; they were the only group which had a headman or chief, who was known as the "ariki," or sometimes as the "ariki-mau," the great chief, to distinguish him from the "ariki-paka," a term which seems to have been given to all other members of the clan.[1]   The office of ariki-mau was hereditary, and he was the only man who was obliged to marry into his own clan.   It was customary when he was old and feeble that he should resign in favour of his son.   There are various lists of the succession of chiefs, counted from the first immigrant, Hotu-matua.   The oldest lists are those given by Bishop Jaussen[2] and by Admiral Lapelin,[3] which contain some thirty names. Thomson gives one with fifty-seven.   In our day there was admittedly much uncertainty about the sequence, but the number was said to be thirty,[4] and two independent lists were obtained.   All these categories differ, though they contain many of the same names, particularly at the beginning and end.

The last man to fill the post of ariki with its original dignity was Ngaara ; he died shortly before the Peruvian raid, and becomes a very real personage to anyone inquiring into the history of the island.   He was short, and very stout, with white skin, as had all his family, but so heavily tattooed as to look black.   He wore feather hats of various descriptions, and was hung round both back and front with little wooden ornaments, which jingled as he walked.   When our authorities can remember him his wife was dead and he lived with his son Kaimokoi.   It was not permitted to see them eat, and no one but the servants was allowed to enter the house.   His headquarters were at Anakena, the cove on the island where, according to tradition,

---

[1] Evidence on this head was rather contradictory, but no Miru could be found, male or female, to whom the title was not given.

[2] " L'Ile de Paques," M. Tépano Jaussen, *Bulletin Géographique*, 1893, p. 241.

[3] *Revue Maritime et Colonial*, vol. xxxv, p. 109.

[4] Thirty is, however, a very favourite number : cf. the folk-tales.

16

the first canoe landed. It is unique in having a sandy shore, and is surrounded by an amphitheatre of low hills. Behind it to the west rises the high central ground of the island, beyond it, on the other side, is the eastern plain ; it thus approximately terminates the strip of land held by the Miru (fig. 97). There are now at Anakena the remains of six ahu, a few statues, and the foundations of various houses. Ngaara held official position for the whole island, but he was neither a leader in war, nor the fount of justice, nor even a priest ; he can best be described as the custodian of certain customs and traditions. The act most nearly approaching a religious ceremony was conducted under his auspices, though not by him personally. In time of drought he sent up a younger son and other ariki-paka to a hill-top to pray for rain : they were painted on one side red, on the other black with a stripe down the centre. These prayers were addressed to Hiro, said to be the god of the sky, a supernatural being in whom we seem getting nearer the idea of a divinity, as distinct from a spirit of the dead, and of whom we would gladly have learnt more than could be discovered.

The ariki-paka had other duties besides praying for rain; they made " maru," or strings of white feathers tied on to sticks, which they placed among the yams to make them grow. They buried a certain small fish among the sugar-canes to bring up the plants, and when a koro was being held, and it was consequently particularly desirable that the fowls should thrive, an ariki-paka painted a design in red, known as the " rei-miro," below the door of the chicken-house (fig. 115).

Te Haha, the " social success," who was an ariki-paka in the entourage of Ngaara, gave graphic descriptions of life at Anakena when he was a boy. If, he said, people wanted chickens, they applied to the Ariki-mau, who sent him with maru, and his visits were always attended with satisfactory results.

Ngaara never consumed rats, and one day, coming across the boy watching rats being cooked, he was extremely angry, for it transpired that, if Te Haha had eaten them, his power for producing chickens would have diminished ; presumably because he would have imbibed ratty nature, which was disastrous to eggs and young chickens. The Ariki, however, made himself useful to him on occasion. The younger Miru had long hair reaching to his heels, and one day, when he was asleep in a cave, some one cut it off. So he went to Ngaara, who told him to bring ten coconuts, which he broke and put in pieces of the sacred tree, "ngau-ngau"; the spell blasted the offender, who promptly died. Ngaara himself attended the inauguration of any house of importance. The wooden lizards were put formally on each side of the entrance to the porch, and the Ariki and an ivi-atua, who "went with him like a tatane," were the first to eat in the new dwelling : only the houses with stone foundations were thus honoured. The Ariki was visited one month in the year by "all people," who brought him the plant known as pua on the end of sticks, put the pua into his house, and retired backwards.

He also held receptions on other occasions, seated on the broken-off head of an old image, which was pointed out on a grassy declivity among the hills behind Anakena ; these were special occasions for criticising the tattoo. Those who were well tattooed were sent to stand on one hill slope, whilst those who were badly done were sent to another; the Ariki and men behind him laughed contemptuously at the latter, which, as the process was permanent and could not be altered, seems slightly unkind. These receptions were also attended by men who had made boats, and by twins, to whom the Ariki gave a "royal name." Such children were not, as in so many countries, considered unlucky, but it was necessary that at birth they should live in a house apart, otherwise they would not survive. This superstition still exists. Shortly before our arrival a woman in the village had given birth to twins, for whom a little grass house was put up; another woman went in and brought them out to the mother to nurse.

The Script

Closely connected with the subject of the Miru clan is that of the method of writing. While we can only catch glimpses of the image cult through the mists of antiquity, the tablets, known as "koháu-rongo-rongo,"[1] were an integral part of life on the island within the memory of men not much past middle age (fig. 98). The highest authority on them was the ariki Ngaara. It was tantalising to feel how near we were to their translation and yet how far. Te Haha had begun to learn to write, but found that his hand shook too much, besides, as he explained, Ngaara

---

[1] Sometimes called koho-rongo-rongo.

used " to send him to the chickens." Juan had had the offer
of learning one form of such script, but, not unnaturally, had
looked upon it with some contempt, preferring European accom-
plishments. The information which could be gathered was,
therefore, with one exception, which will be noted later, simply
that of the layman, or man in the street, who had been aware
of the existence of the art and seen it going on around him, but
had no personal knowledge.

The tablets were of all sizes up to 6 feet. It was a picturesque
sight to see an old man pick up a piece of banana-stem, larger
than himself, from among the grove in which we were talking,
and stagger along with it to show what it meant to carry a
tablet, though, as he explained, the sides of the tablet were flat,
not round like the stem. It is said that the original symbols
were brought to the island by the first-comers, and that they
were on " paper," that when the paper was done, their ancestors
made them from the banana plant, and when it was found that
withered they resorted to wood. Every clan had professors in
the art who were known as rongo-rongo men (" tangata-rongo-
rongo "). They had houses apart, the sites of which are shown in
various localities. Here they practised their calling, often sitting
and working with their pupils in the shade of the bananas ; their
wives had separate establishments. In writing, the incision was
made with a shark's tooth : the beginners worked on the outer
sheaths of banana-stems, and later were promoted to use the
wood known as " toro-miro." [1]

The glyphs are, as will be seen, so arranged that when the
figures of one row are right way up, those of the one immediately
below it are on their heads ; thus only alternate rows can, at the
same time, be seen in correct position (fig. 98). The method
of reading was, according to Te Haha, to read one row from left
to right, then come back reading the next from right to left, the
method known as boustrophedon, from the manner in which an
ox ploughs a furrow. The finished ones were wrapped in reeds
and hung up in the houses. According to two independent
authorities they could only be touched by the professors or their
servants, and were taboo to the uninitiated, which, however,
does not quite agree with other statements, nor with that of the
missionaries, that they were to be found in " every house." They

[1] Sophora Toromiro.

FIG. 98.

PORTION OF AN INCISED TABLET (*Kohau-rongo-rongo*).

FIG. 99.

TOMENIKA'S SCRIPT

were looked upon as prizes to be carried off in war, but they were often burnt with the houses in tribal conflict.

Ngaara is said to have had " hundreds of kohau " in his house, and instructed in the art, which he had learnt from his grandfather. He is described, with a vivid personal touch, as teaching the words, holding a tablet in one hand and swaying from side to side as he recited. Besides giving instruction, he inspected the candidates prepared by other professors, who were generally their own sons ; he looked at their kohau and made them read, on which he either passed them, clapping if they did well, or turned them back. Their sponsors were made personally responsible. If the pupils acquitted themselves creditably, presents of kohau were made to the teachers; if the youth failed, the tablets of the instructor were taken away.

Every year there was a great gathering of rongo-rongo men at Anakena, according to Te Haha, as many as several hundreds of them came together. The younger and more energetic of the population assembled from all districts in the island to look on. They brought "heu-heu" (feathers on the top of sticks), tied pua on to them, and stuck the sticks in the ground all round the place. The inhabitants of the neighbouring districts brought offerings of food to Ngaara, that he should be able to supply the multitude, and the oven was " five yards along." The gathering was near the principal ahu, midway between t:.e sandy shore and the background of hills. The Ariki and his son Kaimokoi sat on seats made of tablets, and each had a tablet in his hand ; they wore feather hats, as did all the professors. The rongo-rongo men were arranged in rows, with an alley-way down the centre to the Ariki. Some of them had brought with them one tablet only; others as many as four. The old ones read in turn, or sometimes two together, from the places where they stood, but their tablets were not inspected. Te Haha and his comrades stood on the outskirts, and he and one other lad held maru in their hands. If a young man failed, he was called up and his errors pointed out ; but if an old man did not read well, Ngaara would beckon to Te Haha, who would go up to the man and take him out by the ear. Our informant repeated this part of the story identically months later, and added that the Ariki would say to the culprit, " Are you not ashamed to be taken out by a child ? "; the offender's hat was taken away, but the tablet was not inspected.

The entire morning was spent in hearing one half of the men read ; there was an interval at midday for a meal, after which the remainder recited, the whole performance lasting till evening. Fights occasionally ensued from people scoffing at those who failed. Ngaara would then call Te Haha's attention to it, and the boy would go up to the offenders with the maru in his hand and look at them, when they would stop and there would be no more noise. When the function was over, the Ariki stood on a platform borne by eight men and addressed the rongo-rongo men on their duties, and doing well, and gave them each a chicken. Another old man, Jotefa, gave a different account of the great assembly, by which the Ariki sat on his stoep and the old men stood before him and " prayed " ; according to this version they either did not bring their tablets or their doing so was voluntary. In addition to the great day, there were minor assemblies at new moon, or the last quarter of the moon, when the rongo-rongo men came to Anakena. The Ariki walked up and down reading the tablets, while the old men stood in a body and looked on.

Ngaara used also to travel round the island, staying for a week or two in different localities with the resident experts. Another savant on the south coast was said to be " too big a man to have a school," and also went about visiting and inspecting learned establishments in the same manner.

Ngaara, before the end, fell on evil days. The Ngaure clan was in the ascendancy, and carried off the Miru as slaves; the Ariki was taken to Akahanga on the south coast with his son, Káimokoi, and grandson, Maurata. They were there five years in captivity, and the " Miru cried much " ; at the end of that time the clan united with the Tupahotu and rescued the old man. He was then ill, and died not long afterwards at Tahai, on the west coast, near Hanga Roa, while living with his daughter, who had married a Marama. For six days after his death everyone worked at making the sticks with feathers on the top (heu-heu), and they were put all round the place. He was buried in the ruined image ahu at Tahai, his body being carried on three of the tablets, and followed through a lane of spectators by the rongo-rongo men; the tablets were buried with him. His head paid the penalty of its greatness, and was subsequently stolen; its whereabouts was unknown. Ten or fifteen of his tablets were given to old men ; the rest went to a servant, Pito, and on his death to Maurata. When Maurata went to Peru, Také, a relative of Te Haha, obtained them, and Salmon asked Te Haha to get hold of them for him. Také, however, unfortunately owed Te Haha a grudge, because when Te Haha was in Salmon's service, and consequently well off, he did not give him as many presents as his relative thought should have been forthcoming, and he consequently refused to surrender them. They were hidden in a cave whose general locality was surmised, but Také died without making known the exact site, and they could never be found. Kaimokoi's tablets were burnt in war.

The question remains what were the subjects with which the tablets dealt, and in what manner did they record them ? Various attempts have been made to deal with a problem which will probably never be wholly solved. Twice before our own day native assistance has been sought to decipher them. It will be remembered that the existence of these glyphs was first reported by the missionaries; but even at that time, when volunteers were asked for who could translate them, none came forward. Bishop Jaussen, Vicaire Apostolique of Tahiti, managed to find in that island a native of Easter among those brought there to work on the Brander plantations, who was supposed to understand them, and who read them after the boustrophedon method. From the information given by him, the Bishop was satisfied that the signs represented different things, such as sun, stars, the ariki, and so forth, and has given a list of the figures and their equivalent. At the same time he held that each one was only a peg on which to hang much longer matter which was committed to memory. The other attempt to obtain a translation was that of Paymaster Thomson, of U.S.S. *Mohican*, in 1886. There was then living an old man, Ure-vae-iko by name, who was said to be the last to understand the form of writing ; he declined to assist in deciphering them on the ground that his religious teachers had said it would imperil his soul. Photographs, however, were shown, and, by the aid of stimulants, he was induced to give a version of their meaning, the words of which were taken down by Salmon. It was, however, remarked that when the photographs were changed, the words proceeded just the same.

Inquiries were made by the Expedition about this old man, and it was agreed by the islanders that he had never possessed any tablets nor could he make them, but that he had been a servant of Ngaara and had learnt to repeat them. Before leaving the island we went with the old men through the five translations given by Thomson. Of three nothing was known ; one which describes the process of creation was recognised as that of a kohau, but looked at a little askance, as there were Tahitian words in it. The last was laughed out of court as being merely a love-song which everyone knew.

Our own early experiences had resembled those of the Americans. Photographs of tablets, which were produced merely to elicit general information, were to our surprise promptly read, certain words being assigned to each figure ; but after a great deal of trouble had been taken, in drawing the signs and writing down the particular matter, it was found that any figure did equally well. The natives were like children pretending to read and only reciting. It was noted, however, with interest, that in perhaps half a dozen cases different persons recited words approximately the same, beginning, " He timo te ako-ako, he ako-ako tena," and on inquiry it was said that they were derived from one of the earliest tablets and were generally known. It was " like the alphabet learned first "; Ure-vai-iko had stated that they were the " great old words," all others being only " little ones." To get any sort of translation was a difficult matter, to ask for it was much the same as for a stranger solemnly to inquire the meaning of some of our own old nursery rhymes, such as " Hey diddle diddle, the cat and the fiddle "—some words could be explained, others could not, the whole meaning was unknown. It seems safe, however, to assume that at least we have here the contents of one of the old tablets.

With regard to other kohau, a list was obtained of the subjects with which they were believed to deal. These amounted to thirteen in all, most of the names being given by several different persons. We have seen that there was a kohau of the " Ika," the murdered men ; this was known to only one professor, who taught it to a pupil, and the two divided the island between them, the master taking the west and north coast to Anakena and the pupil the remainder. A connected, or possibly the same, tablet was made at the instance of the relatives of the victim and helped to secure vengeance. Certain kohau were said to be lists of wars ; some dealt with ceremonies, and others

formed part of ceremonies themselves. They were in evidence
at koro, where Ngaara and the professors used to come and
" pray for the father," and a woman went on to the roof of the
house holding the "Kohau-o-te-puré" (prayer tablet). In another
case, a woman who wished to honour her father-in-law, and at
the same time secure fertility, set up a pole round which she
walked holding a child and a tablet, given her by Ngaara, while
he and other rongo-rongo men who brought their kohau at his
order stood by and sang.

Perhaps the most interesting tablet was one known as the
" Kohau-o-te-ranga." The story was told to us sitting on the
foundation of a house on the east side of Raraku, the aspect
which is not quarried. This house, it was said, had been the
abode of two men, who were old when the informant was a boy,
and who taught the rongo-rongo ; some days ten students would
come, other days fifteen. The wives and children of the old
men lived in another house lower down the mountain. One of
the experts, Arohio by name, was a Tupahotu, and had as a
friend another member of the same clan called Kaara. Kaara
was servant to the Ariki, and had been taught rongo-rongo by
him, and Ngaara, trusting him entirely, gave into his care this
most valuable kohau known as " ranga." It was the only one
of the kind in existence, and was reported to have been brought
by the first immigrants ; it had the notable property of securing
victory to its holders, in such a manner that they were able to
get hold of the enemy for the " ranga "—that is, as captives or
slaves for manual labour. Kaara, anxious to obtain the talisman
for his own clan, stole the kohau and gave it to Arohio, who kept
it in this house. When Ngaara asked for it, the man said that
it was at Raraku, but before the Ariki could get hold of it, Arohio
sent it back to Kaara, and these two thus sent it backwards and
forwards to one another, lying to Ngaara when needful. The
Ariki seems to have taken a somewhat feeble line, and, instead
of punishing his servant, merely tried to bribe him, with the
result that he never again saw his kohau. The son of Arohio
sold it to one of the missionaries, and it is presumably one of
those which went to Tahiti. The matters with which it would
naturally have been supposed that the rongo-rongo would deal,
such as genealogies, lists of ariki, or the wanderings of the people,
were never mentioned.

We were fortunately just in time to come across a man who had been able to make one species of glyphs, though he was no longer, alas ! in the hey-day of his powers. We were shown one day in the village a piece of paper taken from a Chilean manuscript book, on which were somewhat roughly drawn a number of signs, some of them similar to those already known, others different from any we had seen (fig. 99). They were found to have been derived from an old man known as Tomenika. He was, by report, the last man acquainted with an inferior kind of rongo-rongo known as the " tau," but was now ill and confined to the leper colony. We paid a visit to him armed with a copy of the signs, but found him inside his doorway, which it was obviously undesirable to enter, and disinclined to give help ; he acknowledged the figures as his work, recited " He timo te ako-ako," and explained some of the signs as having to do with " Jesus Christ." The outlook was not promising.

Another visit, however, was paid, this time with Juan's assistance, and though the old man appeared childish, and the natives frankly said that " he had lost his memory," things went better.

He was seated on a blanket outside his grass-hut, bare-legged, wearing a long coat and felt hat ; he had piercing brown eyes, and in younger days must have been both good-looking and intelligent. He asked if we wanted the tau, and requested a paper and pencil. The former he put on the ground in front of him between his legs, and took hold of the pencil with his thumb above and first finger below ; he made three vertical lines, first of noughts then of ticks, gave a name to each line, and proceeded to recite. There was no doubt about the genuineness of the recitation, but he gabbled fast, and when asked to go slowly so that it could be taken down, was put out and had to begin again ; he obviously used the marks simply to keep count of the different phrases. At the end of the visit he offered to write something for next time. We left some paper with him, and on our return two or three days later he had drawn five lines horizontally, of which four were in the form of the glyphs, but the same figure was constantly repeated, and there were not more than a dozen different symbols in all. It was said by the escort to be " lazy writing." Tomenika complained that the paper was not " big enough," so another sheet was given, which was put by the side of the first and the lines continued in turn horizontally. He drew from left to right rapidly and easily. Unfortunately, it did not seem wise to touch the paper, but the writing was copied, by looking over it as he went on, with the sincere hope that his blanket did not contain too many inhabitants of some infectious variety. The recitation was partly the same as on the previous occasion, the signs taking the place of ticks ; anything from three or four to ten words were said to each sign. If he made a variation when asked to repeat, it was in transposing the order of two phrases ; evidently the signs themselves were not to him, now at any rate, connected with particular words.

When we subsequently went with our escort into the meaning of the words, it was found that the latter half of each phrase generally consisted of one of the lower numericals preceded by the word "tau," or year—thus, " the year four," " the year five," etc. ; the numbers, roughly speaking, ran in order of sequence up to ten, recommencing with each line. The first part of the phrase was generally said to be the name of a man, but of this it was difficult to judge, as children were called after any object or place ; thus " flowering grass " might be the name of a thing, or of a place, or of a man called after either the object or the locality.

Happily, one of the most reliable old men, Kapiera by name, had at one time lived with Tomenika, who was said to have been in those days always busy writing ; and he was able to explain the general bearing of the tau. When a koro was made in honour of a father, an expert was called in to commemorate the old man's deeds, " how many men he had killed, how many chickens he had stolen," and a tablet was made accordingly. There was, in addition, a larger tablet containing a list of these lesser ones, and giving merely the name of each hero and the year of his koro. It would read somewhat thus, " James the year four, Charles the year five," and so forth, going up to the year ten, when the numbers began again. If there were two koro in a year, they came under the same numeral. It was this general summary which had been recited by Tomenika, and, though there was a certain amount of confusion, each line seems to have represented a decade. In addition, as will be seen, " James " and " Charles " each had a kohau of their own.

Kapiera was able to give a specimen of the lesser tau ; it illustrates interestingly the general method of condensation in which, even in the recitations, a few words assume or implicate extended knowledge. It ran thus, " Of Kao the year nine," " Ngakurariha the eldest " ; then come five men's names followed by the name of a fish ; then a doubtful word ; then " that side island my place." " I see Ngakurariha at the koro." The story, as explained, was that Kao, a man of Vinapu on the south coast, and Ngakurariha, his eldest son, went to Mahatua on the north side and stayed with the five men whose names are given, who were brothers, and learnt from them the tau. Having done this, they proceeded to murder them, and went and took a fish, then returned to Rano Kao, made a koro and the tau.

The tau was, it was said, originally made by an ancestor of the first immigrant chief, Hotu-matua ; it was not taboo in the same way as the other rongo-rongo, and was not known to Ngaara. There were, about the beginning of last century, only three personages acquainted with it. One was Omatohi, a Tupahotu, whose son, Tea-a-tea, was Tomenika's foster-father and instructor in the art. It was said by Tomenika himself and by others that he " only knew part," and there were other signs with which he was not acquainted, for his foster-father had died before he knew all.

A great effort was subsequently made to get further information from Tomenika, more particularly as to the exact method of writing, but he was back in his hut very ill, and all conversation had once more to be done through the doorway. Every way that could be thought of was tried to elicit information, but without real success. He did draw two fresh symbols, saying first they were " new " and then " old," and stating they represented the man who gave the koro, but " there was no sign meaning a man." " He did not know that for ariki, the old men did," " the words were new, but the letters were old," " each line represented a koro." An attempt to get him to reproduce any tau made by himself was a failure. The answers, on the whole, were so wandering and contradictory, that after a second visit under those conditions, making five in all, the prospect of getting anything further of material value did not seem sufficient to justify the risks to others, however slight. As the last interview drew to a close, I left the hut for a moment, and leant against the wall outside, racking my brains to see if there was any question left unasked, any possible way of getting at the information ; but most of what the old man knew he had forgotten, and what he dimly remembered he was incapable of explaining. I made one more futile effort, then bade him good-bye and turned away. It was late afternoon on a day of unusual calm, everything in the lonely spot was perfectly still, the sea lay below like a sheet of glass, the sun as a globe of fire was nearing the horizon, while close at hand lay the old man gradually sinking, and carrying in his tired brain the last remnants of a once-prized knowledge. In a fortnight he was dead.

No detailed systematic study of the tablets has as yet been possible from the point of view of the Expedition, but it seems at present probable that the system was one of memory, and that the signs were simply aids to recollection, or for keeping count like the beads of a rosary. To what extent the figures were used at will, or how far each was associated with a definite idea it is impossible to say. Possibly there was no unvarying method ; certain ones may conveniently have been kept for an ever-recurrent factor, as the host in the tau, and in well-known documents, such as " he timo te ako-ako," they would doubtless be reproduced in orthodox succession. But in the tablets which we possess the same figures are continually repeated, and the fact that equivalents were always having to be found for new names, as in that of the fish-man, or ika, suggest that they may have been largely selected by the expert haphazard from a known number. As Tomenika said, " the words were new, but the letters were old," or to quote Kapiera to the same effect, they were " the same picture, but other words." It will be noted how few men are reported to have known each variety of rongo-rongo, and that while Ngaara looked at the tablets of the boys, apparently to see if they were properly cut, it was in the recitation only of the older men that accuracy was insisted on. The names which Bishop Jaussen's informant assigned to some five hundred figures may or may not be accurate, but whether the native or anyone else could have stated what the signs conveyed is another matter. It is easy to give the term for a knot in a pocket-handkerchief, but no one save the owner can say whether he wishes to remember to pay his life insurance or the date of a tea-party.

In trying to enter into the state of society and of mind which evolved the tablets there are two points worth noticing.   Firstly, the islanders are distinctly clever with their hands and fond of representing forms. Setting aside the large images, the carving of the small wooden ones is very good, and the accuracy of the tablet designs is wonderful. Then they have real enjoyment in reciting categories of words; for example, in recounting folk-tales, opportunity was always gleefully taken of any mention of feasting to go through the whole of the food products of the island. In the same way, if a hero went from one locality to another, the name of every place *en route* would be rolled out without any further object than the mere pleasure of giving a string of names. This form of recitation appears to affect them æsthetically, and the mere continuation of sound to be a pleasure.   Given, therefore, that it was desired to remember lists of words, whether categories of names or correct forms of prayer, the repetition would be a labour of love, and to draw figures as aids to recollection would be very natural.

Nevertheless, the signs themselves have no doubt a history, which as such, even apart from interpretation, may prove to be signposts in our search for the origin of this mysterious people.

THE BIRD CULT

Knowledge of the tablets was confined to a few, and formed a comparatively small element of life in the island ; the whole of social existence revolved round the bird cult, and it was the last of the old order to pass away. The main object of the cult was to obtain the first egg of a certain migratory sea-bird, and the rites were connected with the western headland, Rano Kao. Little has yet been said of this volcano, but, from the scenic point of view, it is the most striking portion of the island. Its height is 1,300 feet, and it possesses a crater two-thirds of a mile across, at the bottom of which is a lake largely covered with weeds and plant-life. On the eastward, or landward face, the mountain, as already explained, slopes downward with a smooth and grassy incline, and the other three sides have been worn by the waves into cliffs over 1,000 feet in height. On the outer-most side the sea has nearly forced its way into the crater itself; and the ocean is now divided from the lake at this point by only a narrow edge, along which it would be possible but

CRATER LAKE, RANO KAO : ORON

FIG 100.

URED ROCKS ON THE RIGHT.

Cave on right, s

FIG. 101

bird rites.   [254A]

FIG. 102.

PAINTINGS ON ROOF OF ANA KAI-TANGATA.

Top, a bird superimposed on a European ship.

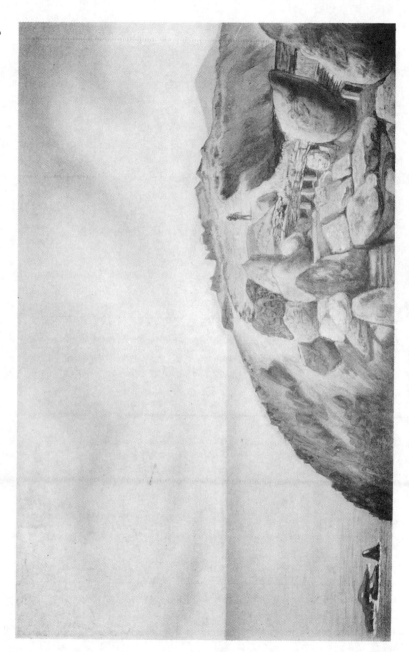

ORONGO, END HOUSES AND CARVED ROCKS.

not easy to walk with safety. At some near date, as geological ages reckon, the island will have a magnificent harbour (figs. 100 and 108). Off this part of the coast are three little islets, outlying portions of the original mountain, which have as yet withstood the unceasing blows of the ocean. Their names are Motu Nui, Motu Iti, and Motu Kao-kao, and on them nest the sea-birds which have for unknown centuries played so important a part in the history of the island. On the mainland, immediately opposite these islets, there is on the top of the cliff a deserted stone village ; it is known as Orongo, and in it the islanders awaited the coming of the birds. It consists of nearly fifty dwellings arranged in two rows, both facing the sea, and partly overlapping ; the lower row terminates just before the narrowest part of the crater wall is reached. The final houses are built among an outcrop of rocks; they are betwixt two groups of stones, and have in front of them a small natural pavement. The stones nearest the cliff look as if at any moment they might join their brethren in headlong descent to the shore below (fig. 103). Both the upstanding rocks and pavement are covered with carvings; some of them are partly obliterated by time, and can only be seen in a good light, but the ever-recurrent theme is a figure with the body of a man and the head of a bird ; portions of the carvings are covered by the houses, and they therefore antedate them.

The whole position is marvellous, surpassing the wildest scenes depicted in romance. Immediately at hand are these strange relics of a mysterious past ; on one side far beneath is the dark crater lake ; on the other, a thousand feet below, swells and breaks the Pacific Ocean, it girdles the islets with a white belt of foam, and extends, in blue unbroken sweep, till it meets the ice-fields of the Antarctic. The all-pervading stillness of the island culminates here in a silence which may be felt, broken only by the cry of the sea-birds as they circle round their lonely habitations.

The stone village formed the scene of some of our earliest work during our first residence at the Manager's house ; for some weeks, weather permitting, we rode daily up the mountain, an ascent which took about fifty minutes, and spent the day on the top studying the remains, and picking the brains of our native companions. Some of the houses have been destroyed in order to obtain the painted slabs within, but most are in fair, and some in perfect, preservation. The form of construction suitable to the low ground has perhaps been tried here and abandoned, for some of the foundation-stones, pierced with the holes to support the superstructure of stick and grass, are built into the existing dwellings. The present buildings (fig. 104) are well adapted to such a wind-swept spot; they are made of stone laminæ, with walls about 6 feet thick; the inside walls are generally lined with vertical slabs, and horizontal slabs form the roof.

The greater number are built at the back into rising ground, and their sides and top are covered with earth; the natives call them not "haré," or houses, but "ana," or caves. Where space permits it, the form is boat-shaped, but some have been adapted to natural contours.[1] The dwellings vary in shape and size, from 52 feet by 6 feet to 8 feet by 4 feet; the height within varies from 4 feet to over 6 feet, but it is the exception to be able to stand upright. In some cases they open out of one another, and not unfrequently there is a hatch between two through which food could be passed. The doorway, with its six foot of passage, is just large enough to admit a man. Into each of them, armed with ends of candles, we either crawled on hands and knees, or wriggled like serpents, according to our respective heights. The slabs lining the wall, which are just opposite the doorway, and thus obtain a little light, are frequently painted; some of them have bird and others native designs, but perhaps the most popular is a European ship, sometimes in full sail, and once with a sailor aloft in a red shirt (fig. 105). Inside the houses we found the flat, sea-worn boulders which are used as pillows and often incised with rough designs; there were also a few obsidian spear heads, or mataa, and once or twice sphagnum from the crater, which was used for caulking boats, and also as a sponge to retain fresh water when at sea. Outside many of the doors are small stone-lined holes, which we cleared out and examined. They measure roughly rather under 2 feet across by some 15 inches in depth. Our guides first told us that they were "ovens," but, as no ash was found, it seems probable that their second thoughts were right, and they were used to contain stores.

[1] An accurate large scale plan of the village was made by Lieutenant R. D. Ritchie, R.N., and every house was measured and described by the Expedition.

FIG. 104.

CENTRAL PORTION OF ORONGO VILLAGE.

Left, house which contained image; centre, three houses opening on small quadrangle; right, canoe-shaped house with double entrance,

FIG. 105.

I.

II.

PAINTED SLABS FROM HOUSES AT ORONGO.

I. Two pictorial representations of ao.
II. A face adorned with paint.   A European ship.
[Height of slabs, 3 ft. to 3 ft. 6 in.]

The groups of dwellings have various names, and are associated with the particular clans, who, it is said, built them. One house, which stands near the centre of the village, Taurarenga by name, is particularly interesting as having been the dwelling of the statue Hoa-haka-nanaia, roughly to be translated as " Breaking wave," now resident under the portico of the British Museum (fig. 31). Lying about near by were two large stones, which had originally served as foundations for the thatched type of dwelling, but had apparently been converted into doorposts for the house of the image ; on one of them a face had been roughly carved (fig. 107). The statue is not of Raraku stone, and it will be realised how entirely exceptional it is to find a statue under cover and in such a position. The back and face were painted white, with the " tracings " in red. The bottom contracts, and was embedded in the earth, though a stone suspiciously like a pedestal is built into a near wall. The house had to be broken down in order to get the figure out. According to the account of the missionaries, three hundred sailors and two hundred Kanakas were required to convey it down the mountain to H.M.S. *Topaze* in Cook's Bay. The memory of the incident is fast fading, but our friend Viriamo repeated in a quavering treble the song of the sailors as they hauled down their load.[1] The figure is some eight feet high and weighs about four tons.

Day by day, as we worked, we gazed down on the islets. The outermost, which, as its name Motu Nui signifies, is also the largest, is more particularly connected with the bird story, which we were gradually beginning to grasp, and at last the call to visit it could no longer be resisted (fig. 109). It was not an easy matter, for *Mana* was away; the boats of the natives left a good deal to be desired in the way of seaworthiness, and it was only possible to make the attempt on a fine day. Finally, on arrival at the island, it required not a little agility to jump on to a ledge of rocks at the second the boat rose on the crest of the waves, before it again sank on a boiling and surging sea till the heads of the crew were many feet below the landing-place. We

[1] Recollection is naturally clearer of the removal of the statue now at Washington, and particularly of the excellent food given to the natives who assisted. The figure is reported to have been taken from Ahu Apépé, an inland terrace not far from Rano Raraku, and been dragged down to the ship as she lay in La Pérouse Bay.

17

managed, however, between us to get there three times in all.
Once, when I was there without S., there was an anxious moment
on re-embarking. No one quite knew what happened. Some
of the crew said that the gunwale of the boat, as she rose on a
wave, caught under an overhanging shelf of rock, others were of
the opinion that the sudden weight of the last man, who at
that moment leapt into the boat, upset her balance ; anyway,
this tale was very nearly never written. Once landed on the
island, the surface is comparatively level and presents no difficulties ; it is about five acres in extent, the greater part is covered
with grass, and in every niche and cranny of the rock are sea-
birds' nests. By a large bribe of tobacco one of the most active
old men was induced to accompany us, and to point out the sites
of interest. Later, we followed up the story at Raraku, and so
little by little at many times, in divers places, and from various
people was gathered the story of the bird cult which follows.

Not many sea-birds frequent this part of the Pacific, but on
Motu Nui some seven species find an abiding-place. Some stay
for the whole year, some come for the winter, and yet others for
the summer. Among the last is a kind known to the natives as
manu-tara [1] ; it arrives in September, the spring of the southern
hemisphere. The great object of life in Easter was to be the
first to obtain one of the newly laid eggs of this bird. It was
too solemn a matter for there to be any general scramble. Only
those who belonged to the clan in the ascendancy for the time
being could enter on the quest. Sometimes one group would
keep it in their hands for years, or they might pass it on to a
friendly clan. This selection gave rise, as might be expected,
to burnings of hearts ; the matter might be, and probably often
was, settled by war. One year the Marama were inspired with
jealousy because the Miru had chosen the Ngaure as their
successors, and burnt down the house of Ngaara. This was,
perhaps, the beginning of the fray when the old Ariki was
carried off captive.

The fortunate clan, or clans, for sometimes several combined,
left nothing to chance ; in fact, as soon as one year's egg had
been found, the incoming party made sure of their right of way
by taking up their abode at the foot of Rano Kao—namely, at

[1] Sooty Tern.

FIG. 106.

BACK OF STATUE FROM ORONGO,

Showing raised ring and girdle, also incised figures of bird-man, ao, and Kos-Mari.
(Front of statue, fig. 31.)

FIG. 107.

CARVED DOOR-POST, ORONGO.

Mataveri. Here there were a number of the large huts with stone foundations ; in these they resided, with their wives and families. One of our old gentlemen friends first saw the light in a Mataveri dwelling, when his people were in residence, or, to use the proper phraseology, when his clan were " the Ao."[1] This name "ao" is also given to a large paddle, as much as 6 feet in length, used principally, if not exclusively, in connection with bird rites and dancing at Mataveri. In some specimens a face is fully depicted on the handle ; in others the features have degenerated to a raised line merely indicating the eyebrows and nose. There are pictures of it on slabs in the Orongo houses, in which the face is adorned with vertical stripes of red and white after the native manner, as described by the early voyagers (figs. 105 and 118).

Naturally the months passed at Mataveri were occupied by the residents in feasting as well as in dancing, and equally naturally the victims were human. It was to grace one of these gatherings, when the Ureohei were the Ao, that the mother of Hotu, the Miru, was slain in a way which he considered outraged the decencies of life, and it was in revenge for another Mataveri victim that the last statues were thrown down. It is told that the destined provender for one meal evaded that fate by hiding in the extreme end of a hut, which was so long and dark that she was never found. Some of these repasts took place in a cave in the sea-cliff near at hand. Here the ocean has made great caverns in a wall of lava, into which the waves surge and break with booming noise and dashing spray. The recess which formed the banqueting-hall is just above high-water mark, and is known as " Ana Kai-tangata," or Eat-man Cave (fig. 102). The roof is adorned with pictures of birds in red and white ; one of these birds is drawn over a sketch of a European ship, showing that they are not of very ancient date (fig. 103).

When July approached, the company, or some of them, wound their way up the western side of the hill, along the ever-narrowing summit to the village of Orongo ; the path can just be traced in certain lights, and is known as the "Road of the Ao." They spent their time while awaiting the birds in dancing each day in front of the houses ; food was brought up by the women,

---

[1] The men of the ascendant clan are also often spoken of as the Mata-tōa, or warriors, the other clans being the Mata-kio, or servants.

of whom Viriamo was one. The group of houses at the end
among the carved rocks was taboo during the festival, for they
were inhabited by the rongo-rongo men, the western half being
apportioned to the experts from Hotu Iti, the eastern to those
from Kotuu. " They chanted all day; they stopped an hour
to eat, that was all." They came at the command of Ngaara,
but it is noteworthy that he himself never appeared at Orongo,
though he sometimes paid a friendly call at Mataveri.

A short way down the cliff immediately below Orongo is a cave
known as " Haka-rongo-manu," or " listening for the birds " ;
here men kept watch day and night for news from the islet below.

The privilege of obtaining the first egg was a matter of competition between members of the Ao, but the right to be one of
the competitors was secured only by supernatural means. An
" ivi-atua," a divinely gifted individual, of the kind who had
the gift of prophecy, dreamed that a certain man was favoured
by the gods, so that if he entered for the race he would be a
winner, or, in technical parlance, become a bird-man, or " tangata-manu." The victor, on being successful, was ordered to
take a new name, which formed part of the revelation, and this
bird-name was given to the year in which victory was achieved,
thus forming an easily remembered system of chronology. The
nomination might be taken up at once or not for many years ;
if not used by the original nominee, it might descend to his son or
grandson. If a man did not win, he might try again, or say that
" the ivi-atua was a liar," and retire from the contest. Women
were never nominated, but the ivi-atua might be male or female,
and, needless to say, was rewarded with presents of food. There
were four " gods " connected with the eggs—Hawa-tuu-také-také,
who was " chief of the eggs," and Maké-maké, both of whom
were males ; there were also two females, Vie Hoa, the wife of
Hawa, and Vie Kenatea. Each of these four had a servant,
whose names were given, and who were also supernatural beings.
Those going to take the eggs recited the names of the gods before
meat, inviting them to partake.

The actual competitors were men of importance, and spent
their time with the remainder of the Ao in the stone houses of
the village of Orongo ; they selected servants to represent
them and await the coming of the birds in less comfortable
quarters in the islet below. These men, who were known as

FIG. 108.

RANO KAO FROM MOTU NUI

FIG. 109.

MOTU NUI AND MOTU ITI.

" hopu," went to the islet when the Ao went up to Orongo, or possibly rather later. Each made up his provisions into a " pora," or securely bound bundle of reeds; he then swam on the top of the packet, holding it with one arm and propelling himself with the remaining arm and both legs. An incantation, which was recited to us, was said by him before starting. In one instance, the ivi-atua, at the same time that he gave the nomination, prophesied that the year that it was taken up a man should be eaten by a large fish. The original recipient never availed himself of it, but on his death-bed told his son of the prophecy. The son, Kilimuti, undeterred by it, entered for the race and sent two men to the islet ; one of them started to swim there with his pora, but was never heard of again, and it was naturally said that the prophecy had been fulfilled. Kilimuti wasted no regret over the misfortune, obtained another servant, and secured the egg ; he died while the Expedition was on the island.

The hopu lived together in a large cave of which the entrance is nearly concealed by grass. The inside, however, is light and airy ; it measures 19 feet by 13, with a height of over 5 feet, and conspicuous among other carvings in the centre of the wall is a large ao more than 7 feet in length. A line dividing the islet between Kotuu and Hotu Iti passed through the centre of the cave, and also through another cave nearer the edge of the islet ; in this latter there was at one time a statue about 2 feet high known as Titahanga-o-te-henua, or The Boundary of the Land.[1] As bad weather might prevent fresh consignments of food during the weeks of waiting, the men carefully dried on the rocks the skins of the bananas and potatoes which they had brought with them, to be consumed in case of necessity. It was added with a touch appreciated by those acquainted with Easter Island, that, if the man who thus practised foresight was not careful, others who had no food would steal it when he was not looking.

The approach of the manu-tara can be heard for miles, for their cry is their marked peculiarity, and the noise during nesting is said to be deafening ; one incised drawing of the bird shows

[1] This statue was removed to the mainland shortly before our arrival, and we were able to procure it in exchange for one of the yacht blankets. It is now at the Pitt Rivers Museum, Oxford (fig. 111).

it with open beak, from which a series of lines spreads out fanwise, obviously representing the volume of sound ; names in imitation of these sounds were given to children, such as " Piruru," " Wero-wero," " Ka-ara-ara." It is worth noting that the coming of the tara inaugurates the deep-sea fishing season ; till their arrival all fish living in twenty or thirty fathoms were considered poisonous. The birds on first alighting tarried only a short time ; immediately on their departure the hopu rushed out to find the egg, or, according to another account, the rushing out of the hopu frightened away the birds. The gods intervened in the hunt, so that the man who was not destined to win went past the egg even when it lay right in his path. The first finder rushed up to the highest point of the islet, calling to his employer by his new name, " Shave your head, you have got the egg." The cry was taken up by the watchers in the cave on the mainland, and the fortunate victor, beside himself with joy, proceeded to shave his head and paint it red, while the losers showed their grief by cutting themselves with mataa.

The defeated hopu started at once to swim from the island to the shore, while the winner, who was obliged to fast while the egg was in his possession, put it in a little basket, and, going down to the landing-rock, dipped it into the sea. One meaning of the word hopu is " wash." He then tied the basket round his forehead and was able to swim quickly, as the gods were with him. At this stage sometimes accidents occurred, for if the sea was rough, an unlucky swimmer might be dashed on the rocks and killed. In one instance, it was said, only one man escaped with his life, owing, as he reported, to his having been warned by Maké-make not to make the attempt. When the hopu arrived on the mainland, he handed over the egg to his employer, and a tangata-rongo-rongo tied round the arm which had taken it a fragment of red tapa and also a piece of the tree known as " ngau-ngau," reciting meanwhile the appropriate words. The finding was announced by a fire being lit on the landward side of the summit of Rano Kao on one of two sites, according to whether the Ao came from the west or east side of the island.

It will be remembered that on the rocks which terminate the settlement of Orongo the most numerous of the carvings is the figure of a man with the head of a bird ; it is in a crouching

FIG. 110.

A ROCK AT ORONGO CARVED WITH FIGURES OF BIRD-MEN

Sculptured surface, 6 ft. by 5 ft.

FIG. III.

[*Pitt Rivers Mus.*

BOUNDARY STATUE FROM MOTU NUI
[Measure shown = 1 ft.]

FIG. 112.

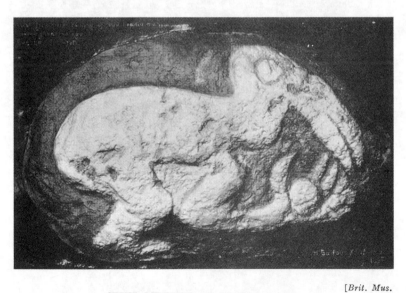

[*Brit. Mus.*

STONE EXHUMED AT ORONGO, 1914.
Bird-man in low relief with egg in hand. Length of carving, 36·5 cm.

attitude with the hands held up, and is carved at every size and angle according to the surface of the rock (fig. 110). It can still be counted one hundred and eleven times, and many specimens must have disappeared : all knowledge of its meaning is lost. The figure may have represented one of the egg gods, but it seems more probable that each one was a memorial to a bird-man ; and this presumption is strengthened by the fact that in at least three of the carvings the hand is holding an egg (fig. 112). The history of another figure, a small design which is also very frequent, still survives and corroborates this by analogy ; within living memory it was the custom for women of the island to come up here and be immortalised by having one of these small figures ("Ko Mari") cut on the rock by a professional expert. We know, therefore, that conventional forms were used as memorials of certain definite persons.[1]

The bird-man, having obtained the egg, took it in his hand palm upwards, resting it on a piece of tapa, and danced with a rejoicing company down the slope of Rano Kao and along the south coast, a procedure which is known as "haka epa," or "make shelf," from the position of the hand with regard to the egg. If, however, the winner belonged to the western clans, he generally went to Anakena for the next stage, very possibly because, as was explained, he was afraid to go to Hotu Iti ; some victors also went to special houses in their own district, otherwise the company went along the southern shore till they reached Rano Raraku.

Amongst the statues standing on its exterior slope, there is shown at the south-west corner the foundations of a house (no. 7, fig. 60). This is the point which would first be approached from the southern coast, and here the bird-man remained for a year, five months of which were spent in strict taboo. The egg, which was still kept on tapa, was hung up inside the house and blown on the third day, a morsel of tapa being put inside. The victor did not wash, and spent his time in "sleeping all day, only coming out to sit in the shade." His correct head-dress was a crown made of human hair ; it was known as "hau oho,"

[1] The figures of the bird-man, also of the ao and Ko Mari, are all roughly carved on the back of the Orongo statue (fig. 106). They appear, like those on the Raraku image, to be later workmanship than the raised ring and girdle. Permission to inspect can be obtained in the hall of the British Museum ; unfortunately the light in the portico is bad.

and if it was not worn the aku-aku would be angry. The house was divided into two, the other half being occupied by a man who was called an ivi-atua, but was of an inferior type to the one gifted with prophecy, and apparently merely a poor relation of the hero ; there were two cooking-places, as even he might not share that of the bird-man. Food was brought as gifts, especially the first sugar-cane, and these offerings seem to have been the sole practical advantage of victory ; those who did not contribute were apt to have their houses burnt. The bird-man's wife came to Raraku, but dwelt apart, as for the first five months she could not enter her husband's house, nor he hers, on pain of death. A few yards below the bird-man's house is the ahu alluded to on p. 191 (fig. 60) ; it consists merely of a low rough wall built into the mountain, the ground above it being levelled and paved. It was reserved for the burial of bird-men ; they were the uncanny persons whose ghosts might do unpleasant things— they were safer hidden under stones. The name Orohié is given to the whole of this corner of the mountain, with its houses, its ahu, and its statues. To this point the figures led which were round the base of the hill. If they were re-erected, they would stand with their backs not to the mountain, but to Orohié.[1] As the bird-man gazed lazily forth from the shade of his house, above him were the quarries with their unfinished work, below him were the bones of his dead predecessors, while on every hand giant images stood for ever in stolid calm. It is difficult to escape from the question, Were the statues on the mountain those of bird-men ?

The hopu also retired into private life ; if he were of the Ao, he could come to Orohié, but he might, if he wished, reside in his own house, which was in that case divided by a partition through which food was passed ; it might not be eaten with his right hand, as that had taken the egg. His wife and children were also kept in seclusion and forbidden to associate with others.

The new Ao had meanwhile taken up their abode at Mataveri. From here a few weeks after their arrival they went formally to Motu Nui to obtain the young manu-tara, known from their cry as " piu." After the brief visit of the birds when the first egg was laid, they absented themselves from the islet for a period varyingly reported as from three days to a month. On their

[1] Nos. 1, 2, and 3, fig. 60, form part of this series. See also fig. 74.

return they laid plentifully, and, as soon as the nestlings were hatched, the men of the celebrating clan carried them to the mainland, swimming with them in baskets bound round the forehead after the manner of the first egg. They were then taken in procession round the island, or, according to another account, only as far as Orohié. It was not until the piu had been obtained that it was permissible to eat the eggs, and they were then consumed by the subservient clans only, not by the Ao. The first two or three eggs, it was explained, were " given to God " ; to eat them would prove fatal. Some of the young manu tara were kept in confinement till they were full grown, when a piece of red tapa was tied round the wing and leg, and they were told, " Kaho ki te hiva," " Go to the world outside." There was no objection to eating the young birds. The tara departed from Motu Nui about March, but a few stragglers remained ; we saw one bird and obtained eggs at the beginning of July, but the natives failed to get any for us in August. When in the following spring the new bird-man had achieved his egg, he brought it to Orohié and was given the old one, which he buried in a gourd in a cranny of Rano Raraku ; sometimes, however, it was thrown into the sea, or kept and buried with its original owner. The new man then took the place of his predecessor, who returned to ordinary life.

The last year that the Ao went to Orongo, which is known as " Rokunga," appears to have been 1866 or 1867. The names of twelve subsequent years are given, during which the competition for the egg continued, and it was still taken to be interred at Raraku. The cult thus survived in a mutilated form the conversion of the island to Christianity, which was completed in 1868 ; it is said that once the missionaries saw the Ao dancing with the egg outside their door in Hanga Roa and " told the people it was the Devil." It must have been celebrated even after the assembly of the remains of the clans into one place, which occurred about the same time, but it was finally crushed by the secular exploiters of the island, whose house at Mataveri, that of the present manager, rests on the foundation-stones of the cannibal habitation (fig. 25). The cult admittedly degenerated in later years. A new practice arose of having more than one bird-man, with other innovations. The request to be given the names of as many bird-years as could be remembered met with an almost embarrassing response, eighty-six being quoted straight away ; some of these may be the official names of bird-men and not represent a year, but they probably do so in most cases ; chronological sequence was achieved with fair certainty for eleven years prior to the final celebration at Orongo. In addition to the bird-name, the names of both winner and hopu were ascertained, with those of their respective clans.

FIG. 113.

Porotu acted as a hopu. He refused to be photographed, and the sketch was surreptiti- ously made whilst obtaining the account of his official ex- periences. He also assisted in carrying the re- mains of Ko Tori (p. 225).

TAKÉ AND MANU

Two other ceremonies were mentioned in connection with Orongo and Motu Nui, but to obtain detailed information was very difficult. It finally transpired that of "také" no first-hand knowledge existed, as the rites had been abandoned thirty years before the coming of the missionaries. All that can be safely said is that those concerned went into retreat on Motu Nui, living, it was stated, in the cave where the hopu awaited the birds; the period was generally given as three months. A vigorous discussion took place on the subject between Viriamo and Jotefa, the oldest man in the village, seated on a log in the garden of the old lady. She was positive, in agreement with other authorities, that také was for children—"the boys and girls went in a canoe to the island "; he firmly adhered to the statement that his father went for také, after he, the son, was born. Tomenika stated that

FIG. 114.

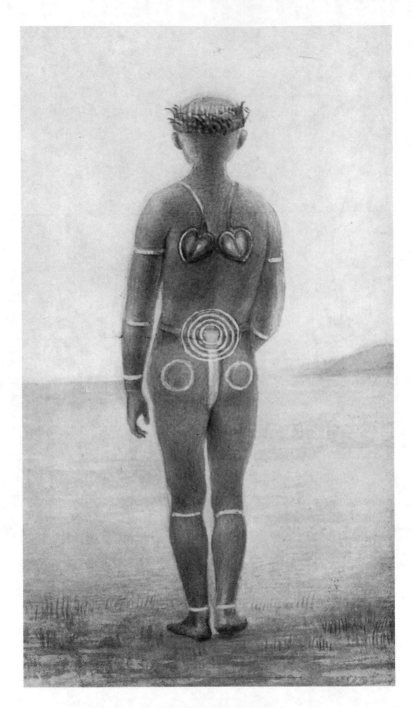

BIRD-CHILD (*POKI-MANU*).

Ceremonial ornamentation, from a drawing made by natives.

také formed the subject of one of the tablets, and drew one of its figures, which bears no resemblance to any other known symbol.

The details of manu were more satisfactory. It was known as " te manu mo te poki," or, " the bird for the child," and the child so initiated became a " poki-manu," or " bird-child." It could not be found that any special benefit resulted from it, but a child whose parents had not performed the ceremony, and whose love affairs, for instance, went wrong, might even kill his father in revenge for the omission. An expert, known as " tangata-tapa-manu," the man who, as Dr. Marett would tell us, " knew the right things to say," was called in and given a hen's egg—on this last point much stress was laid ; he was at the same time told the child's name, which was subsequently inserted in the ritual. The child was shaved, decorated with white bands, and hung round with coconuts, or, as these were not readily obtainable in Easter Island, with pieces of wood carved to represent them called " tahonga." A number of children, each with an expert, then went up to Orongo ; the correct month was December, and the Ao were therefore below at Mataveri. Jotefa, on whose final account I principally rely, stated that he and nine other children, with their parents, and ten tangata-tapa-manu, went to Orongo from his home on the north coast, a distance of some eleven miles ; they took with them ten chickens. The party danced in front of all the houses, went to the carved rocks at the end, and, coming back, stood in a semicircle in front of the door of Taura-renga, the house of the statue, the experts being behind and all singing ; no offering was made to the image. Another authority stated that the parents and children went on the roof of the house, the experts being below, and the parents gave chickens to the men. Jotefa's party returned to their home, had a feast, and gave more food to the professionals. The tangata-tapa-manu subsequently repeated the ritual at any koro which were being held in the island, the object apparently being to make public the child's initiation.

If, by reason of the state of the island, it was not possible to go to Orongo, the ceremony could take place at any of the big ahu with images. Viriamo, whose home, as will be remembered, was near Raraku, said with much pride that she was a " poki-manu " ; she and her three younger sisters had been taken at the same time to the ahu of Orohié. Both parents

went, and " the mother took two chickens, one in each hand,
and the mother and children stood upright and the " maori sang " ;
they did not go to Orongo because there was war. A drawing
was made for us by Juan and the old men of the poki-manu in
ceremonial attire (fig. 114) ; it was particularly interesting to
find, when it was handed in, that circles of white pigment were
made on the child's back, and also on each buttock, in a way
which recalls the adornment of the Anakena image (fig. 65).

Wooden Carvings

The stone sculpture of Easter Island belongs to an era which
is now forgotten ; there are a number of wooden carvings which,
whatever their original age, are connected with a recent past,
and even in a limited sense with the present.

The most important of these works, the tablets, have
already been dealt with, and mention has been made of the
lizard figures, they have the head of that animal on a human
body (fig. 117). The "ao," the large dancing-paddle, and
the smaller one, the "rapa," are of much the same
character, though used on different occasions (figs. 116 (a), 118).
The "ua" is a club, on the handle of which are two
heads back to back ; these clubs were dignified with individual
names. The "paoa" was a wooden sword. There were also
bird ornaments carved in wood which were worn on the last
day of the koro and by Ngaara. The "rei-miro" is a breast
ornament of a crescent shape, with a face at one or both ends;
it is found depicted on the Orongo rocks and frequently on the
tablets. It was especially a woman's decoration, but a number
of small ones were said to have been worn by Ngaara. The
specimen in the British Museum is embellished with glyphs, of
which no account was forthcoming (fig. 115).

Wooden objects which are peculiarly interesting are the
small male and female figures some twenty to thirty inches
in height; the natives term them " moai," adding the word
" miro," or wood (fig. 119). In a certain number of these the
ribs are very prominent, giving the effect of emaciation; they are
called " moai kava-kava," or the statues with ribs. It has been
suggested that this represents the condition in which the first
inhabitants reached the island, but such an explanation is

OBJECTS CARVED IN WOOD.

FIG. 115.

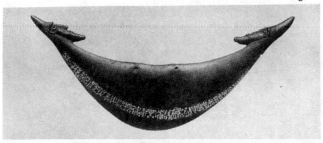

[*Brit. Mus.*]

REI-MIRO, A BREAST ORNAMENT.
16 inch.

FIG. 116.　　　　　FIG. 117.　　　　　FIG. 118.

[*Brit. Mus.*]

[*Univ. of California.*]

(*a*) RAPA.
Dancing-
paddle.
38 in.

(*b*) UA.
Club with
two faces.
60 in.

MOKO-MIRO.
Lizard's head on
human body.
15 in.

AO.
Dancing-paddle.
Usual length
about 6 ft.

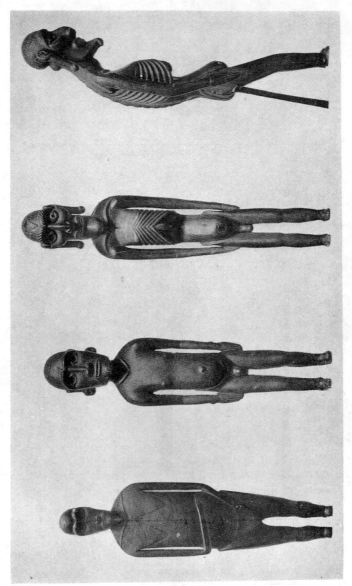

FIG. 119.

WOODEN IMAGES (*MOAI-MIRO*).

Female Image.
(*Moai Papa*.)

Male Image.
(*Moai Tangata*.)

Male Image showing Ribs.
(*Moai Kava-kava*).
Front view.

Profile.

strenuously denied by the present people, who assert that their ancestors arrived with plenty of food. The figures have long ears, like the statues in stone, and a marked feature is their little goatee beards. These beards are found in three or four statues at Raraku, in a head in relief on Motu Nui, and one is indicated in fig. 31. But the most striking link with the stone figures is the back, where there is a ring similar to that found on the larger statues : the girdle and M-like design below it also appear in varying degree (fig. 120). A comparative study of the backs of the wooden images has suggested the idea[1] that this M-like marking in stone may be simply the last stage of an evolution in design, which originally showed the lines of the lower portion of the back and thigh.[2] It would be satisfactory if, in the same way, the triple belt could be connected with the ribs and the ring with the vertebræ, but for this the evidence is less conclusive, although the ribs of the body with the lizard head closely approach the conventional. It must be remembered that the figures are nude, and that therefore these designs can scarcely represent any form of dress. There is a pronounced excrescence on the buttocks in the wooden figures, which is also a mystery, but which recalls the way in which the rings on the image found at Anakena (fig. 65) and those on the poki-manu (fig. 114) emphasise the same part of the anatomy. The heads are embellished with ornaments, some of which are bird designs (fig. 121). These figures were worn by men only, and hung round the neck on important occasions; they were parts of the festival dress at Mataveri and at the koro.

The tradition of the origin of the wooden images is one of the best known and uniformly narrated, but obviously bears the marks of endeavouring to explain facts whose genesis has been forgotten. It runs thus: Tuukoihu, an ariki, and one of the first immigrants, was a clever man or " tangata-maori "; he had two houses, one at Ahu Tepeu on the west side and one at Hanga Hahavé on the south coast—the foundations of both are shown. One night, when he was sleeping at the latter dwelling, two female aku-aku appeared to him, by name Papa Ahiro and Papa

---

[1] We owe this suggestion to Captain T. A. Joyce.

[2] Those unacquainted with the manner in which the drawing of a natural object can, through constant repetition, lose all resemblance to it and become purely conventional are referred to *Evolution in Art*, by Dr. A. C. Haddon.

Akirani.[1] When he awoke he took the wood called toro-miro, and carved two figures with faces, arms, and legs, just as he had seen the aku-aku. When he had finished the work, he went over to Hanga Roa to fish. He slept there, and returned at daybreak, going back by the quarry of the stone hats. Two male aku-aku, by name Ko Hitirau and Ko Nuku-te-mangoa, were sleeping by the way, but were aroused on his approach by two more aku-aku, whose names are given, who told them that there was a man coming who would notice that their ribs were exceedingly " bad." The two sleepers awoke, saw Tuukoihu, and asked him, " Have you seen anything ? " He discreetly replied " nothing," and they disappeared. They again met him on the road and put the same question, to which he gave the same answer. When he got to his house, he made two statues with ribs to represent the apparitions. After dark they prowled round the house, listening, with their hands up to their ears, to hear if he gossiped about what he had seen, intending if he did so to kill him. The Ariki, however, held his tongue. Later he went to his other home ; there he took the wooden moai, both male and female, and made them walk. The house bears the lengthy name of " The House of the Walking Moai of Tuukoihu, the Ariki," and is the large one whose measurements were given on p. 216. Tuukoihu once lent a moai-miro to a man, whose house took fire while it was in his possession. The Ariki, on hearing of the disaster, told the image to fly away, which it promptly did, and was subsequently found in the neighbourhood unharmed.

Wooden figures are said to have been made in a considerable variety of forms, some of them being in a sitting position, others with hands crossed, etc. ; names were bestowed on them—twenty-one such were repeated to us. It was not found possible to ascertain exactly what they are all intended to portray, the information being somewhat confused and contradictory, but on the whole the female figures and those with ribs seem to have been considered to be supernatural beings ; they are generally called aku-aku, and sometimes atua, while the others represent

[1] The term " papa " is also applied to any flat, horizontal surface of fused igneous rock. The double use seems to be explained by connecting it with the facts that in Hawaii, Papa is the name of the female progenitor of the race (or at least of a line of chiefs), while in the Marquesas and Hervey Islands Papa is the earth personified, the Great Mother.—See *A Brief History of the Hawaiian People*, Alexander, p. 20

FIG. 120.

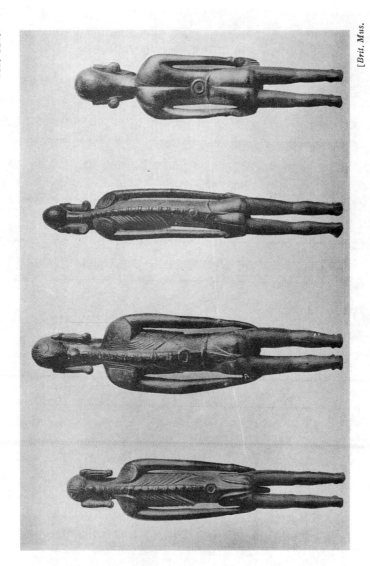

[*Brit. Mus.*

1   2   3   4

BACKS OF WOODEN IMAGES.

Showing resemblance to stone figures and possible evolution of conventional design from natural lines of figure.

men. It appears probable that they are portraits, or memorial figures, of which the older may have attained to deification: this is confirmed by the fact that there is one such figure at the Pitt Rivers Museum at Oxford, with short ears, which is said to have been made to represent Captain Cook.

When our friend Kapiera was a boy, there were about ten experts in the island, who made wooden articles of various descriptions, including the images, of whom three at least were alive in our time. Te Haha, who was one of the old workmen, could still be seen sitting in his garden engaged in carving moai miro. We have, therefore, a craft existing in modern days which can be traced back to pre-Christian culture, and which has strong affinities with the prehistoric stone figures. There is, of course, no sentiment connected with the figures of to-day; they are roughly done, and merely for sale. The trade is extended to copies of stone images which are bought by unsuspecting visitors, with circumstantial tales as to their history or discovery which would deceive the very elect. The statues on the ahu near the village, which are made of stone from Raraku, have had pieces cut off them to manufacture into these articles. One Kanaka had in our day a still more brilliant idea which saved him all trouble, he sold a fragment of this rock at a

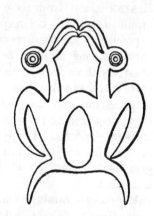

FIG. 121.—BIRD DESIGN FROM HEAD OF WOODEN IMAGE. (*Brit. Mus.*)

high price to a passing vessel as the " last morsel of image stone to be found in the island." Local opinion regarding the intelligence of the visitors is not high. One man brought to us a wooden figure for sale which he said was " very old." " Indeed," remarked my husband, " it has grown up quickly; it was a new-born infant when I saw it being carved in the village a few weeks ago." " Ah," said the proud possessor, slightly disappointed, but nursing his creation like a child and stroking it affectionately, " he very fine, muy antiqua, I keep him for ships ; capitano man-o-wari, all same damn fool."

CHAPTER XVII

CAVES AND CAVE-HUNTING

Residential Caves—Caves as Hiding-Places for Treasure—Burial Caves.

EASTER Island, from its geological formation, is a land of underground cavities ; between the harder volcanic strata lie softer deposits, which have been gradually washed away, either by subterraneous streams or, as in certain localities round the coast, by the action of the waves, leaving above and below the more durable substance. There are thus formed grottoes and crannies innumerable ; they were used, as has been seen, for sleeping-places and for burial, and they also came in handy as treasure deposits. Large caves are comparatively rare, though in one district underground ways filled with water extend to a great length, and the whole surface rings hollow to the tread of a horse.

We daily examined such caves and grottoes as came under our notice; and systematically excavated some half-dozen, which had apparently been used in former days as native habitations. Below the floor of one, Mr. Edmunds had already discovered a small chamber walled and roofed with slabs, which the natives said had been used as a place of hiding in cannibal days ; but generally the earth deposit is very shallow, and the yields were the same only as those of the houses at Orongo, a few spear heads, bone needles, and sea-shells whose contents had been used for food. There were few objects among the natives which lent themselves to preservation for any length of time ; they never made pottery, although there is clay in the island ; wooden articles would generally rot, and they had no form of metal. This reflection reconciled us in some degree to what was otherwise a disappointment, our inability to reach the

most thrilling of the caves, which are half-way up the great
sea-cliffs ; they can be seen from the ocean, and are known to
have been used, but the original track has either been washed
away by the encroaching waves or lies in a tumbled mass on the
beach below. A special voyage was made round the island in
Mana with the object of studying these caves; some of
the Expedition went in the yacht, and signalled their situation
to a second party, who rode along the coast and placed marks
on the cliff as a guide for subsequent exploration. We finally,
however, gave up the idea of attempting to reach them ; it
would have been possible, no doubt, to have done so from the
top, with a rope and experienced climbers, but a certain amount
of danger would have been inevitably involved, and, considering
the smallness of our numbers and the circumstances, we felt it
unwise to take the risk of accident. We do not believe, in view
of our experience elsewhere, that they are likely to contain
anything of material value, but, in any case, they remain unrifled
for our successors.

Articles which were considered of value by the owners were
kept, not in these larger caves, but in little holes and crannies
where they could be easily concealed. This practice still continues, both for legitimate and illegitimate purposes ; it made
it, for example, impossible to trace the stores which were stolen
soon after our arrival. The natives are naturally secretive,
and do not confide the whereabouts of their hiding-places, so
that when a man dies his hoard is lost. One old leper, who was
said to have some five tablets, reported to his friends that
when Mr. Edmunds was making a wall on the estate, the
men went so near his cache that he was in momentary dread of
its discovery, but they passed it by ; he died soon after, and all
knowledge of it was lost. The most tragic story is the authenti-
cated one of a man who disappeared with his secret store. He
had been bargaining with visitors, and went to fetch for sale
some of his hidden possessions ; he was never heard of again.
Presumably some accident happened, and he either fell down a
cliff or was buried alive. Sometimes a man on his death-bed
will give directions to his son as to where things are hidden, but
natural landmarks alter, and this information seems seldom
sufficient to enable the place to be recognised ; treasure-hunting
on Easter Island is therefore a most disappointing pursuit, as

18

we found to our cost. Soon after our arrival a man died in the village who was said to have things hidden among the rocks in a part of the coast not far from the village. His neighbours turned out to dig. We offered high rewards for anything found, which were to be doubled if the objects were left untouched till our arrival on the scene, and we wasted much time ourselves superintending the search, but nothing appeared. A young man volunteered the information that he had a cave on Rano Kao where his father had hidden things, and another half-day was spent in riding to the spot; the whereabouts had only been described generally, and he could not find the place.

Yet another day we rode round the eastern headland to find some stone statues, the locality of which had been confided to Juan by the old man Kilimuti, who was a member of his family. The search was again in vain, and Juan indignantly characterised his ancient relative as " a liar." An interesting, but equally futile, expedition was made to look for a tablet, said to have been hidden by a rongo-rongo man near Anakena ; the cave in this case proved to have an entrance like a well, artificially built up, and to be a long, natural, subterranean chamber. There were certain traces which might have been those of decayed wood, but nothing more. We subsequently discovered that this sort of thing is usual ; the natives possess, not " castles in Spain," but caves in certain localities which they speak of definitely as " theirs," but which are quite as reluctant to materialise as any southern château.

Mr. Edmunds assured us, with amused sympathy, that his initial experiences and disillusionment had been precisely similar to our own. The natives themselves, nevertheless, continue to hunt with undiminished zeal for these hidden articles, whose value is well known ; it is the one form of work which they enjoy. Rumour had come from Tahiti, shortly before we reached the island, that articles were hidden in a recess in the coast not far from the Cannibal Cave ; the whole place was dug over and ransacked by treasure-hunters from the village, without result so far as we ever heard.

Caves were frequently used as places of burial. Generally, as in the case of Ko Tori, an isolated corpse was placed in a grotto, but on Motu Nui we came across two subterranean chambers which had been definitely prepared as vaults. One of these had obviously not been visited for some time, as a considerable amount of clearance had to be effected before it could be reached. The entrance proved to be a small, properly constructed doorway, two feet high and eleven inches in width, from which a short passage descended at a sharp angle. To wriggle down this narrow way felt much like a rabbit going into a burrow. The cave below proved to be a circular vault, under ten feet in diameter. Four corpses lay side by side on the floor, while a fifth had been hurriedly shoved in, head foremost, through the doorway above. The ceiling and walls were artificially made and covered with white pigment. On the walls were three heads, carved in relief, the only ones encountered ; they were adorned with touches of red paint. The one which was best wrought was twenty inches in length, and projected some two to three inches from the surface of the wall ; it had a pronounced " imperial." The sides of the cave were also adorned with incised drawings of birds. In order to copy these carvings by the light of a small candle, it was necessary to encamp among the damp mould of the floor in contact with the remains of the dead. The proceeding felt not a little gruesome, even to a now hardened anthropologist, and the return to daylight was very welcome.

The other cave on the islet was very similar, but smaller in size, and the carvings were not so good. The corpses which it contained had evidently been buried in tapa. No information of special interest was forthcoming to account for these burials on Motu Nui ; if they were associated with any particular family or class the fact has been forgotten.

The custom is said to have existed of enclosing such articles as chisels and fish-hooks in the wrappings of a corpse, and it is recorded that the bird-man's egg sometimes accompanied him to his last home; the idea also of placing her *prie-Dieu* in Angata's grave seemed to be a survival of such a practice. With the one exception, however, of the beads in the canoe-shaped ahu, we never found any objects with the dead. The natives who were generally most anxious to reach the inaccessible caves in the hope of treasure, felt no interest in one which can be seen from below to have a wall across the mouth, and which was said to be a place of burial ; they considered that it would contain nothing of value. It seems therefore probable that belongings buried with the deceased were speedily stolen, and have not been available in the memory of this generation. It is difficult to suppose that any fear of punishment here or hereafter would deter an Easter Islander from appropriating any such article for which he had a fancy.

There may still be accidental discoveries in grottoes of forgotten hoards, or a few things treasured in this way by old men may be disclosed, but personally we are persuaded that the secret of this land must be sought elsewhere than in its caves.

FIG. 122.

AHU OROI.

An out-crop of rock utilised as an image ahu.

CHAPTER XVIII

LEGENDS

First Arrival on the Island—The Long Ears exterminated by the
Short Ears—The Struggle between Kotuu and Hotu Iti.

IT remains to be seen what accounts the islanders give of their
origin and history in addition to the vague fragments already
quoted. These legends fall into three groups, which, though
they touch at some points, are in reality separate, and their
relation to one another in point of time cannot be certainly
ascertained. It need hardly be said that, like all such legends,
they cannot be regarded as more than suggestive ; when the
mysteries have been solved, it will no doubt be easy to see where
they have been founded on fact, and where error has crept in,
and essential points distorted or forgotten ; meanwhile, the clues
they afford can only be partial. These groups deal respectively,
firstly with the arrival of the islanders under Hotu-matua ;
secondly with the destruction of the Long Ears ; and thirdly
with the war between the two sides of the island, Kotuu and
Hotu Iti. The stories have necessarily been somewhat abbreviated.

FIRST ARRIVAL ON THE ISLAND

The ancestors of the present inhabitants came, it is said, from
two neighbouring islands known as Marae Renga and Marae
Tohio. Here, on the death of the chief, Ko Riri-ka-atea, a
struggle for supremacy arose between his two sons, Ko Te Ira-ka-
atea and Hotu-matua, in which Hotu was defeated. Now there
was on one of the islands a certain Haumaka, who had tattooed
Hotu, and received from him in return a present of mother-of-
pearl which had been given to Hotu's father by an individual
called Tuhu-patoea. Tuhu had seen that the men who went
down to get pearls were eaten by a big fish, so he invented a net

by which the precious shell could be obtained without risk, and
the pearl so procured he had presented to his chief, Ko Riri.
This man, Haumaka, had a dream, and during it his spirit went
to a far country, and when he awoke he told six men, whose
names are given, to go and seek for it ; they were to look for a
land where there were three islets and a big hole, also a long
and beautiful road.   So the six men went, each on a piece of
wood, and they found the three islets, Motu Nui, Motu Iti,
Motu Kao-kao, and the big hole, which was the crater of Rano
Kao.   They landed on that part of the island and planted yams,
and then walked round the island, beginning by the south
coast.

When they were near Anakena, one of them, Ira, saw a turtle
and tried to take it, but it was too heavy for him to lift, so the
other five went to help, but it was still too heavy for them, and it
struck out and injured one named Kuku ; he was taken to a
neighbouring cave and begged the others not to leave him, but
his companions made five cairns outside the cave [1] and departed,
and Kuku died in the cave.   The men went to Hanga Roa and
on to Orongo.   A sixth man then appeared on the scene, but
whence he came is not known, and the other five told him
that " this was a bad land," for when they had planted yams,
grass had grown up.   Then the men went to Motu Nui and slept
there, and in the morning, when they woke, two boats were seen
approaching.   The vessels were bound together, but as they
came near the land the cord which united them was cut.   The
name of the one boat was " Oteka," and in it were Hotu-matua
and his wife, Vakai-a-hiva ; and the name of the other boat was
" Oua," and in it were a certain Hinelilu and his wife, Avarepua.
Ira called to them, and told them also that " this was a bad
land " ; to which Hotu-matua replied that they too came from
a bad land, " when the sea is low we die few, when the sea is
high we die many."

Then the boats divided, and Hotu-matua went round the
south and east coasts, and Hinelilu by the west and north.
Hotu wished to be the first to reach Anakena, which the previous
arrivals had told him was a good place to land, so when he saw
the other vessel approaching, he " said to himself a word," which
made his own boat go fast and Hinelilu's go slow; so he got

[1] cf. p. 232.

first to the cove. A son was born there to Vakai and named Ko Tuumaheke. Hinelilu was a man of intelligence, and wrote rongo-rongo on paper he brought with him. Amongst those who came in the boats was the ariki Tuukoihu, the maker of the wooden images; two of his sons and two grandsons have given their names to four subdivisions of the Miru clan.

Among Hotu-matua's company there was a concealed passenger whose name was Oroi; he was an enemy of Hotu's, who had killed his children in the place whence they came, and had hidden himself on board. He got on shore at Anakena, without anyone having guessed at his presence, and killed everyone. One day the five children of a man named Aorka went to bathe at Owaihi, a small cove east of Anakena, and as they lay on a rock in the sea, Oroi came from behind and killed them and took out their insides. When they did not return, the father said to the mother, " Where are the children ? " The mother said, " On the rock "; but when Aorka went to look, the rock was covered with water, for it was high tide ; when by and by the water went down, he saw the five children and that they were dead. Aorka then told Hotu-matua : " Oroi, that bad man, is here, for he has killed my children." Now Hotu-matua went to see his daughter who was married, and as he went Oroi put a noose in his path and tried to catch his foot in it, but Hotu stepped on one side. When he had finished his visit to his daughter, he said to her and her husband, " Follow me as I go home." And as he returned he saw that the cord was still there, and his enemy hidden behind the rock. This time Hotu-matua intentionally stepped on to the rope and fell, and when Oroi came up, he got hold of him and killed him, and then called to his daughter and son-in-law to see that he was dead. When, however, they put the corpse in the oven to cook him he came to life again, so they had to take him over to the other side of the island to where the ahu is called Oroi (fig. 122), and there he cooked quite satisfactorily, and they ate him.

Hotu-matua had many sons from whom the different clans are descended, and whose names they bear. He quarrelled with the eldest, Tuumaheki, and with his own wife, Vakai; the two having behaved badly to him, he finally gave up his position to Tuumaheki and retired to the top of Rano Kao, where he lived on the south side of the crater, that opposite to Orongo.

He was old and blind and became also very ill; his elder sons came to see him, but he kept asking for Hotu-iti, the youngest, who was his favourite. When Marama appeared, the old man felt the calf of his leg, and said, " You are not Hotu-iti, you are Marama; where is Hotu-iti? " Koro-orongo answered as if he were Hotu-iti, and said, " I am here," but he lied, and his father took hold of his leg, and said again, " You are not Hotu-iti "; and the same thing happened with Ngaure, and Raa, and Hamea, and the others; and at last came Hotu-iti, and Hotu-matua knew him, for he was small, and his leg was slight, and said to him, " You are Hotu-iti, of Mata-iti, and your descendants shall prosper and survive all others." And he said to Kotuu, " You are Kotuu, of Mata-nui, and your descendants shall multiply like the shells of the sea, and the reeds of the crater, and the pebbles of the beach, but they shall die and shall not remain." And when he had said this he left his house, and went along to the cliff where the edge of the crater is narrowest, and stood on it by two stones, and he looked over the islet of Motu Nui towards Marae Renga, and called to four aku-aku in his old home across the sea, " Kuihi, Kuaha, Tongau, Opakako, make the cock crow for me," and the cock crew in Marae Renga, and he heard it across the sea; that was his death signal, so he said to his sons, " Take me away." So they took him back to his house, and he died. Thus Hotu-matua came to his end and was buried at Akahanga.

Many of the gods of Marae Renga, who were the ancestors of Hotu-matua, came with him in his boat, and he knew they were there though the others did not see them. The names of eleven of them were given, four of which were independently quoted as amongst the aku-aku associated with Akahanga.

The Story of the Long Ears

Now the Long Ears (" Hanau Epé ") and Short Ears (" Hanau Momoku ") lived together mixed up all over the land, but one of the Long Ears, Ko Ita by name, who lived at Orongo, had in his house the bodies of thirty boys, whom he had killed to eat. Among his victims were the seven sons of one man, Ko Pepi. Ko Pepi went mad, and ran round and round till he fell down, and his brothers took their mataa and killed the Long Ears at Vinapu and at Orongo. They were joined by the other Short Ears, till the Long Ears took refuge in the eastern headland, across which they then dug a ditch and filled it with brushwood in order to make a fire in self-defence. Now a body of the Short Ears were drawn up in array in front of the ditch, but another party were shown the way round at night by an old woman, and thus turned their flank; so when morning dawned the Long Ears found themselves attacked both from behind and before, and then were swept into the ditch of their own making.[1] There they were all burnt except two, who made their way to a cave, near Anakena, where they hid, but they were dug out of it and killed, calling aloud "Oroini," the meaning of which is not known.

Such is the outline of these stories; the most definite and agreed points are the most incomprehensible—namely, the landing of the six men prior to that of the main wave, and the concealed arrival of Oroi. The sons of Hotu-matua are not known exactly. Kotuu is sometimes identified with Ko Tuu-maheki, and is sometimes a separate person. Miru occasionally figures as one of them, which is inconsistent with the statement that four of Tuukoihu's descendants are the ancestors of four subdivisions of that clan. Miru is also the name given in all the lists to Tuumaheki's son, the third ariki. Hotu Iti was always a district, never the name of a clan. On the most interesting point—namely, the origin of the Long Ears—there is the most vagueness. According to Kilimuti, who was a recognised authority, and whose account of the landing has been followed, Hotu-matua and those in his boat were the Short Ears, Hinelilu and the crew of the second boat the Long Ears. When asked how it was that the two came together, he merely replied that it was in the same way as we ourselves had various nationalities on the yacht. According to this authority, the destruction in the ditch took place in the time of Hotu-matua's children. Another version, given by three old men in conclave, was that the Long Ears came into existence on the island through

---

[1] The ditch is still shown; there is a marked depression running across the island dividing the eastern volcano from the mainland, but after much consideration we came to the conclusion that it was a natural phenomenon due to geological faulting. A mound of earth is, however, to be seen in places on its higher or eastern side, and it is possible that persons holding the mountain may have utilised it for defensive purposes by erecting a rampart in this manner.

the " mana " of the third ariki. Discussion one day waxed quite fierce on the point till Te Haha's wife, who was a shrewd middle-aged woman, turned and said, " Never mind them, Mama, they don't know anything about it," which probably summed up the situation. The story of the ditch and the final extinction is well-established legend. The term Long Ears seemed to convey to the natives not the custom of distending the ears, but having them long by nature.

It is interesting to compare the versions of these stories given to the Expedition with those taken down from Salmon by Paymaster Thomson of the *Mohican*. The statement made by him, and repeated by various travellers, probably from the same source, that Hotu-matua came from the east, was never met with by us. Kilimuti did not know whence he came ; the direction in which Hotu-matua looked when dying would be west, or more accurately, south-west. Juan put the home of the first immigrants in the Paumotu ; as a young man his knowledge of legend was a step further from the original, but it was often useful as summing up the general impression he had received. According to the *Mohican* story the six early arrivals included the brother of Hotu-matua and his wife ; Oroi had been the rejected suitor of this lady, and it was the competition for her favour which had caused the quarrel with the family. The same authority states that Hotu was in the boat which went by the south and east and his wife Vakai in the other ; Hinelilu does not appear. Hotu is depicted as dividing the land between his sons, but there is no mention of the ultimate triumph of the descendants of Hotu-iti over those of Kotuu, which, as told to us on more than one occasion, was the chief point in the story. The finale, in which the old man looked towards his old home, is omitted. The Long Ears suddenly appear on the island at a much later time.[1] The story of the ditch is much the same.

WARS BETWEEN KOTUU AND HOTU ITI

Kainga was a great man, and he lived near Tongariki. He had three young sons ; two of them lived with him, one of whom was named Huriavai, and the other was called Rau-hiva-aringa-

[1] " The tradition continues by a sudden jump into the following extraordinary condition of affairs. Many years after the death of Hotumatua the island was about equally divided between his descendants and the long-eared race."—*Smithsonian Report*, 1889, p. 528.

erua (literally, " Twin two faces "), for he had been born with
two faces, one of which looked before and the other behind.
Kainga's third son was named Mahanga-raké-raké-a-Kainga ;
he was not treated well at home, and had been adopted by a
woman who lived not far away, and there he had much fish to
eat. Now one day two men came to Kainga's house and slept
there ; they were Marama from Hanga Roa, and their names
were Makita and Roké-ava. Kainga killed two chickens, and
cooked the food and took it to his guests. Roké was asleep, and
Makita said, "What is this ? " and Kainga replied, " Chicken,"
and Makita said, " I do not like it ; I want man." Kainga did
not like to refuse, and went outside and said to his two boys,
" Go and tell Mahanga to come here." So the children went and
gave the message. When Mahanga heard it, he cried, but when
he had done weeping he went back with his brothers. Kainga
said to him, " Lie down and go to sleep," and Kainga took a
club and hit the child on the head and killed him. Then he
cooked part of the body and gave it to Makita, saying, " Here is
food," and went back to the cooking-place. Makita saw that it
was human flesh, and wakened Roké and told him, and Roké
was alarmed, and said, " I do not like it." He broke the house
of Kainga, and hurried away. Makita also departed quickly.
Kainga was very angry, and said to the two men, " Why do you
throw away my food ? " And he took the body of the child
and wrapped it in reeds and put it on the ahu.

Kainga then said, " Bring me much wood to make a boat " ;
and all men worked at the boat of Kainga, and he gave them
much food—chickens and potatoes and bananas, sugar-cane,
hens and fish and eels—but they did not make it well. Then
Kainga sent for Tuukoihu, the chief who lived at Ahu Tepeu,
on the western side, and said, " Come to me to make the boat " ;
and Tuukoihu came, and he made a good boat twenty fathoms
long, and when it was finished it was launched, and thirty men
went in it to row. Now Makita and Roké and the people from
Hanga Roa and that part of the island had taken refuge on
Motu Nui and other islets of the coast off Rano Kao. Kainga
went in the boat to Motu Nui and rowed all round it, and Kainga
called to the people on the island, " Come out that I may see
you " ; and they were all very frightened of Kainga because he
was a big man, so one after another all the men on the island

came out that he might see them, and he said, " Are there no more ? " and they looked and saw that there were two more hidden; so they brought them out, and they were Makita and Roké, and Makita he slew, but Roké he let go.

．　　　．　　　．　　　．　　　．　　　．

Now there was war between one side of the island and the other side. The Koro-orongo, the Tupahotu, the Ureohei and Ngaure fought the Haumoana, Miru, Marama, Hamea, and the Raa. Kainga fought with his spear against one of the Miru named Toari, and was angry because he could not kill him. He went to his house and killed a white cock and gave it to the child Huriavai to eat, and then he took five mataa and bound them on wood. That evening Huriavai went to, sleep; he dreamed that the white cock was coming towards him, and that he threw a stone at the bird and killed it, and he waked up afraid. Kainga said, " What is it, child ? " and the boy answered, " It is the white cock; he is dead "; and Kainga was glad of the dream, and said joyfully, " He is dead ! To-morrow morning early, at five o'clock, we will go and fight." So on the morrow he took the five mataa in his hand and Huriavai on his back. The men of Hotu Iti fought the men of Anakena and Hanga Roa. Kainga did not go into the battle, but he stood a little way off with the child, and he saw that Toari no one could kill, and he said to the child, " Go, boy, and take two spears." Huriavai was frightened, but he took two spears and went into the battle. The men of Anakena came to kill the boy, but he did not run away. They threw their spears, but they glanced off the child. Then all Kainga's men came forward, and they threw their spears at Toari; but Huriavai threw one spear, and he killed him and he lay dead. Kainga saw his enemy was slain, and took the boy on his back and went away quickly. When Kainga was gone, all the people of Hotu Iti fled, and the people of Anakena pursued, and they killed all the people of Hotu Iti, thousands and thousands and thousands, women and children and little children, big children and young men, and old men who could not walk away quickly. Some of those who escaped took refuge in the cave known as Ana Te Ava-nui, and others fled to the island of Marotiri (fig. 284). Kainga went to Marotiri, but Huriavai hid in a hole on the mainland opposite ; his brother, who had two

FIG. 123.

EASTERN HEADLAND AND ISLAND OF MAROTIRI.

FIG. 124.

ANA HAVEA.

The figure in the sea stands at a spring of fresh water.

285]

faces, was killed by a man named Pau-a-ure-vera. The face behind said, " I see Pau-a-ure-vera; he comes to me with a spear in his hand. You look too." But the face in front said, "I do not like to look; you look." The face behind was angry, and said, " You look too." And while the two faces talked, Pau struck the boy with his spear in the neck, and he fell dead, and Kainga saw from the island the fall of his son.

The day after the battle, when Hotu Iti had been vanquished, Poié, who was one of the Haumoana and a big man, came to live at Ana Havea, the cave near Tongariki (fig. 124), and took a large boat with thirty men and went to the island of Marotiri. On the island were many thousands of the people of Hotu Iti, but among them there was one man, Vaha ; his father was of Hotu Iti, but his mother was of Anakena. He was the father of Toari, who was killed by Huriavai, so he hated the men of Hotu Iti, but no man dared kill him. When Poié came in his boat, he said to Vaha, " Give me men to cook." Vaha gave him one thousand in the boat, and Poié went back to the shore and gave each of the men of Anakena a man to eat ; he took thousands of children by the leg and dashed them against the stone. Every day he did the same again, and brought a thousand men from Marotiri. One day, when the boat came back, a man called Oho-taka-tori, a Miru, was at Ana Havea and saw Poié throwing the men on shore, and among them a man named Hanga-mai-ihi-te-kerau; and Oho-taka-tori said to Poié, " Give me for my fish that man with a fine name." Poié said, " I give no fish with a fine name to you who begin work at nine o'clock in the morning." Oho was angry with Poié ; he was wearing a hat with cocks' feathers sticking out in front, and he turned it round back side front, and went to the house of his daughter, who had married a man of Hotu Iti called Moa, and lived near Tongariki. He said to her, " Do not let your husband mourn for the men of Hotu Iti "; the girl replied, " He does not tell me, but I think he mourns much." She gave her father food to eat, and he went to his own home, the other side of the island. When Moa came in from digging potatoes, his wife said, " Your father-in-law has been here, and he said that you were not to cry for the men of Hotu Iti "; and Moa replied, " I must mourn, but you are of Hanga Roa," and he did not eat any potatoes, but wept.

The men who had not taken refuge on Marotiri were, as has

been told, in Ana Te Ava-nui,[1] and the men of Anakena had made twenty holes in a row in the cliff above, and they stood in the holes one behind the other, and lowered a net over the edge of the cliff with two men in it with spears, and the men in the holes held the rope and let down the net, and the men in the net shouted to them " Pull up," or " Give way," till they were opposite the cave, and then they killed the men in the cave with their spears, and three brothers of Oho worked with these men.

At five o'clock in the evening, when his wife did not know, Moa took all sorts of food, and buried them so that no man should see, and at seven o'clock he said to his wife, " Give me the big net," and she said, " Are you going to take fish ? " and he said, " Yes," but he lied; he was going to Te Ava-nui. He took the net and the food. By and by he left the net behind, but he kept the food and went to Maunga Tea-tea.[2] There were many of Poié's men there, and all over Poike, but they were asleep. He gathered there eight branches of palm, put them on his back, and went to the cave, and all the men on the top of the cliff were asleep, and Moa went down the cliff by the track and entered the cave. The men inside did not sleep. They said, " Who are you ? " and he said, " Hush, I am Moa." There were only thirty men alive. For two and a half months they had had nothing to eat in the cave, and only the strongest were left. Moa gave the men the juice of the sugar-cane like water, and little bits of potato, and then he asked, " Where are the bones of the warrior Peri-roki-roki ? " They replied, " He is down there." So Moa said, " Bring them to me " ; and Moa made fish-hooks of bone, and bound a hook to a palm branch ; then he said to the men, " I have made one for you; make seven," and he went back. When the net came down in the morning, the men in the cave caught it with the hooks on the branches of palm, and the men in the net called to those above to " drag up," but the men gave more line, and the men in the cave killed the men in the net, and then they climbed up the rope and killed all the men at the top except the brothers of Oho, those they did not kill.

[1] *I.e.* " Cave of the great descent." It is in the cliff of the eastern volcano beyond Marotiri, and is one of those which can be seen from the sea, but to which the path has disappeared.

[2] The centre hillock of the three on which Spaniards erected the crosses. The name means White Mountain, from the colour of the ash which composes it (see fig. 78).

Three days before this the men on Marotiri had rid themselves
of Vaha; it was in this way. The boy Huriavai, who was in
a hole on the mainland, was very hungry, for he was not
old enough to catch fish, and he ate seaweed. Vaha on the
island opposite took the stem of a banana and cut it into pieces,
so that it looked like yams, and put it where the boy could see
it, and Huriavai said, " My father has plenty of food." So he
swam across, and Vaha killed him. Then Vaha took the corpse and
swam with it to the mainland. It was dark, but Kainga listened,
and heard the swish of the water, and he too went into the sea
and followed him, and when he got to shore he hid behind a big
stone, and when he saw Vaha coming, carrying on his back the
body of the child, he wept, and Kainga said, " Who are you ? "
and he replied, " I am Vaha " ; and Kainga said, " I am Kainga,
the slayer of Vaha." And he slew him, and took the corpse of
Huriavai to the ahu, and then came and took the body of Vaha
as fish-man for food, brought it to Marotiri, and gave pieces to
all the people on the island. There were thirty men then left
there, but they had no fire, so they cooked the flesh in their
armpits.

Three days after this the men from Te Ava-nui came along,
and they shouted across from the mainland, " We have killed
the men in the net " ; and Marotiri shouted back, " We too
have killed a man," and they were all full of joy. The island
men swam ashore, and they killed all the men at Ana Havea.
The men from Marotiri went in one direction and the men from
Te Ava-nui in another, killing and slaying every one ; but
Kainga went with neither, for he wished to find Poié. He went to
Ana Havea, but his enemy had fled, and he followed him all along
the south coast, till they were not far from Vaihu. Poié was a
very big man, but Kainga was a little one, and he had nothing
to eat. He called to Poié, " You have food, I have none ; I shall
not kill you, I will go back ; but another day I will kill you."
The two parties of Hotu Iti men had now joined one another,
and Kainga went with them. Men and old men, old women and
children they killed all, but the fine women they took ; the
sixty men divided the women between them. A man would
say to a woman, " Do you like me ? " and if she said " No," then
he killed her. Kainga told the men from Te Ava-nui to go to
one place, and the men from Marotiri to go to another, and

live with their wives and beget children, and so they did ; but Poié went to Hanga Roa.

. . . . . .

Kainga told a Tupahotu called Maikuku to give his daughter to Poié, so she went to him and bore him many children, and one day, when years had gone by, Kainga called together his men and went over at night to the other side of the island to fight. Maikuku was staying in the house of his daughter, and Kainga had told him, " If Poié is not in the house, sleep with your head outside the door " ; and Kainga came and looked and saw that the head of Maikuku was outside, and he said to him, " Then Poié is not here ? " and he said, " No, he has gone to the sea." The grand-daughter of Maikuku heard, and was angry for her father, and she went a little way up the hill outside, and cried aloud, " The enemy are coming to fight, and your father-in-law is very bad, although he has had bananas and fish and much to eat." Poié heard the child speak, and he and his five brothers hid their net and the fish, and they ran along the coast towards Rano Kao, and Kainga went too, and then they swam to Motu Nui. Kainga followed, and they went on to Motu Iti and then swam to the land again, and came ashore at the foot of the cliff below Orongo, and Poié's brothers tried to run up the hill, but Kainga's men caught them and killed four. As Poié came up, the blood of his brothers flowed down, and he wept ; but Poié they did not kill, because he had married the daughter of Maikuku, and because they were all afraid. Now Kirireva, a child of Hotu Iti, whose father had been killed by Poié, stayed at Orongo, and the child asked if they were not going to kill Poié, and the old men said, " No, we have already killed four." Kirireva shaved all his hair and his eyebrows, and put on red paint and told Poié to stand up, and he ran three times between his legs, and the third time Poié fell, and the boy killed him with a club because he had slain his father. Now, when Poié was dead, Kotuu was finished and Hotu Iti victorious according to the words of Hotu-matua.

The middle part of this story is briefly told by Thomson, but his account differs in important points from the foregoing. Moa is represented as the son of Oho-taka-toré, instead of his son-in-law, and his action is designed to avenge his father ; this is a more comprehensible version. Kainga is dead. Huriavai is on Marotiri, and on swimming ashore is killed by one of the enemy. Vaha is Huriavai's friend, who kills the slayer, and swims back to Marotiri with the enemy's body.

Our informant, Kapiera, was quite positive that the events took place during the time of Ngaara's grandfather, and refused to be dislodged from his position because Juan pertinently pointed out that this was inconsistent with the boat being made by Tuukoihu, who landed with Hotu-matua.

CHAPTER XIX

THE PRESENT POSITION OF THE PROBLEM

" Do not be afraid of making generalisations because knowledge is as yet imperfect or incomplete, and they are therefore liable to alteration. It is only through such generalisations that progress can be made."—Dr. A. C. Haddon as President of the Folk Lore Society, 1919.

As we leave Easter Island, we pause to review our evidence and find how far we have progressed towards the solution of its problems.

We may dismiss the vague suggestion that the archæological remains in the island survive from the time when it was part of a larger mass of land. Whatever may be the geological story of the Pacific, no scientific authorities are prepared to prove that such stupendous changes have taken place during the time which it has been inhabited by man.[1]

[1] Theosophists, indeed, contend that it has been revealed by occult means that Easter Island is the remaining portion of an old continent named "Lemuria," which occupied the Pacific and Indian Oceans, and the writer has been informed by correspondents that she " may be interested to learn " that such is the case. Representations even of the world at this remote epoch have been, it is said, received by clairvoyance and are reproduced in theosophical literature : in the case of a later continent of Atlantis, which has also disappeared, it was permitted to see its proportions on a globe and by other means ; but, unfortunately, in the case of Lemuria, "there was only a broken terra-cotta model and crumpled map, so that the difficulty of carrying back the remembrance of all the details, and consequently of reproducing exact copies, has been far greater " (*The Lost Lemuria*, Scott Elliot, p. 13). The world at the Lemurian epoch was, we are informed, inhabited by beings who were travelling for the fourth time through their round of the planets, and undergoing for the third time their necessary seven incarnations on the earth during this round. At the beginning of this third race of the fourth round, man first evolved into a sexual being, and at the end was highly civilised. The makers of the Easter Island statues were of gigantic size. To prove this last point, Madame Blavatsky quotes a statement to the effect that " there is no reason to believe that any of the statues have been built up bit by bit," and proceeds to argue that they must consequently have been made by men of the same size as themselves. She states that "the images at Ronororaka—the only ones now found erect—are four in number " ; and gives the following account of the head-dress of the statues, " a kind of flat cap with a back piece attached to it to cover the back portion of the head " (*Secret Doctrine*, vol. ii. p. 337). The readers of this book can judge of the correctness of these descriptions. Theosophists must forgive us, if, in the face of error as to what exists to-day, we decline to accept without further proof information as to what occurred " nearer four million than two million years ago.".

Instead of indulging in surmises as to the state of the world in a remote past, it is safer to begin with existing conditions and try to retrace the steps of development. It has already been seen that various links connect the people now living on Easter Island with the great images. Tradition is not altogether extinct; in a few cases the names of the men are actually remembered who made the individual statues, and also those of their clans, which are still in existence. But the two strongest bonds are the wooden figures and the bird-cult. The wooden figures were being made in recent times, and they have a design on the back resembling that on the stone images, while they also possess the same long ears. There is no reason why a defunct type should have been copied, and it is probable that they date at least as far back as the same epoch. The bird-cult also was alive in living memory. It is allied to that of the statues by the residence of the bird-man among the images, by the fact that the bird rite for the child was connected with them, and above all by the presence of a statue of typical form in the centre of the village at Orongo.

Assuming then, at any rate for the sake of argument, that the stone figures were the work of the ancestors of the people of to-day, the next step is to inquire who these people are. Here for a certain distance we are on firm ground. They are undoubtedly connected with those found elsewhere in the Pacific ; much of their culture is similar ; and even the earliest voyagers noted that their language resembled that found on the other islands. The suggestion that Easter Island has been populated from South America may therefore, for practical purposes, be ruled out of the question. If there is any connection between the two, it is more likely that the influence spread from the islands to the continent.

Having reached this point, however, we are faced by the larger problem. Who were the race or races who populated the Pacific ? Here our firm ground ends, for this is a very complicated subject, with regard to which much work still remains to be done. It is impossible as yet to make any broad statement, which is not subject to qualification, or which can be implicitly relied on.

The Solomon group and other islands off the coast of Australia are inhabited by a people known as Melanesians, who have dark skins, fuzzy hair, and thick lips, resembling to some extent the natives of Africa ; this area is called Melanesia. Certain outlying islets are, however, populated by a different race, who possess straight or wavy hair and fairer skins. Eastward of a line which is drawn at Fiji this whiter race, called Polynesian, predominates, and the eastern part of the Pacific is known as Polynesia.

Broadly speaking, the theory generally accepted has been that negroid people are the earliest denizens, and that the lighter race came down into Melanesia through the Malay peninsula, and thence passed on through Melanesia in a succession of waves. A large proportion of the invaders were probably of the male sex, and took wives from amongst the original inhabitants. They absorbed in many ways the culture of the older people, but did not wholly abandon their own. It is suggested, for instance, that while as a whole the conquerors adopted existing religions, the secret societies, so often found in the Pacific, are connected with their own rites and beliefs, which were guarded as something sacred and apart.

It will easily be seen that the task of tracing these migrations is by no means simple. Canoes, carrying fighting men or immigrants, bent on victory or colonisation, passed continually from one island to another, and each island has probably its own very complicated history. The Maoris of New Zealand, for example, are a Polynesian race, but there are also traces there of a darker people. Absolutely negroid elements are found as far east as the Marquesas. Our servant Mahanga, whose features are of that type, came from the Paumotu Islands (fig. 89).

The marvellous feats of seamanship performed in these wanderings, often against the prevailing trade wind, would be incredible if it were not obvious that they have been actually accomplished. The loss of life was doubtless very great, and many boats must have started forth and never been heard of more. The fact remains, however, that native canoes have worked their way over unknown seas as far north as the Hawaiian or Sandwich Islands, and that somehow or other they reached that little spot in the waste of waters now known as Easter Island. The nearest land to Easter now inhabited, with the exception of Pitcairn Island, is in the Gambier Islands, about

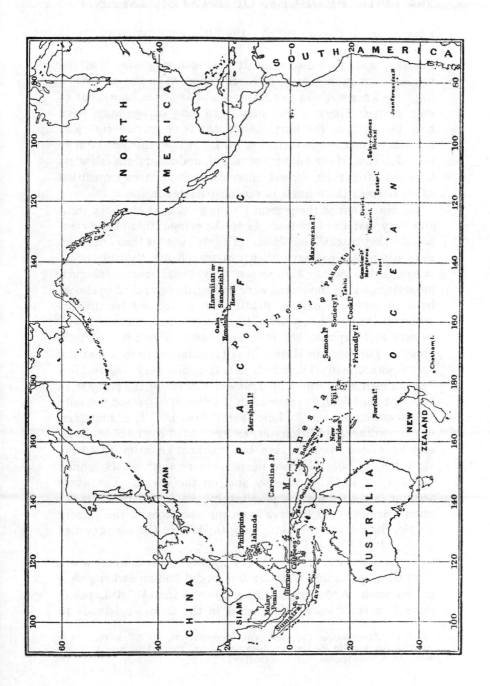

1,200 miles to the westward ; the little coral patch of Ducie Island, which lies between the two, is nearly 900 miles from Easter, and has no dwellers. It has been suggested that the original immigrants may have intended to make a voyage from one known island to another and have been blown out of their course. However this may be, a long voyage must have been foreseen, or the boats would not have carried sufficient provisions to reach so distant a goal. It is even more strange to realise that, if the mixture of races found among the islanders occurred after their arrival, more than one native expedition has performed the miracle of reaching Easter Island.

The traditions of the present people do not, as has been seen, give very material assistance as to the composition of the crew nor how they reached the island. They tell us that their ancestors were compelled to leave their original home through being vanquished in war. This was a very usual reason for such migrations, as the conquered were frequently compelled to choose between voluntary exile or death ; but to account for the discovery of the island they are obliged to take refuge in the supernatural and explain that its whereabouts were revealed in a dream. The story of Hotu-matua gives no suggestion that the island was already inhabited, save for one very vague hint. The six men who formed the first detachment of the party were told that the island as revealed in the dream possessed not only a great crater, but also "a long beautiful road." The Long Ears, who according to tradition were exterminated by the Short Ears, may have been an earlier race, but it cannot be claimed that the story tells us so. The two peoples are represented as coming together, or as living side by side on the island. The whole account is rendered more puzzling by the fact that, while the Short Ears are said to have been the ancestors of the present people, the fashion of making long the lobe of the ear prevailed on the island till quite recently.

It is noteworthy, however, that a legend exists elsewhere which definitely reports that the later comers did find an earlier people in possession. According to the account of Admiral T. de Lapelin,[1] there is a tradition at Mangareva in the Gambier Islands to

---

[1] *Revue Maritime et Coloniale*, vol. xxxv. (1872), p. 108, note. It is unfortunate that M. de Lapelin does not give us more details as to when and from whom the account was received.

the effect that the adherents of a certain chief, being vanquished, sought safety in flight ; they departed with a west wind in two big canoes, taking with them women, children, and all sorts of provisions. The party were never seen again, save for one man who subsequently returned to Mangareva. From him it was learned that the fugitives had found an island in the middle of the seas, and disembarked in a little bay surrounded by mountains ; where, finding traces of inhabitants, they had made fortifications of stone on one of the heights. A few days later they were attacked by a horde of natives armed with spears, but succeeded in defeating them. The victors then pitilessly massacred their opponents throughout the island, sparing only the women and children. There are now no stone fortifications visible at Anakena, but one of the hill-tops to the east of the cove has, for some reason or other, been entrenched (fig. 96).

Turning to more scientific evidence, we find that the islanders have always been judged to be of Polynesian race, as indeed would naturally be expected from the easterly position of the island in the Pacific Ocean. They have certainly traces of that culture, and the great authority on the subject, Mr. Sydney Ray, has pronounced the language to be Polynesian. The surprise, therefore, which the results of the expedition have brought to the anthropological world, is the discovery of the extent to which the negroid element is found to prevail there both from the physical and cultural points of view.

Melanesian skulls are mainly of the long-headed type, while Polynesian are frequently broad-headed. A collection of fifty-eight skulls was brought back from Easter and examined by Dr. Keith. He says in his report : " The Polynesian type is fairly purely represented in some of the Easter Islanders, . . . but they are absolutely and relatively a remarkably long-headed people, and in this feature they approach the Melanesian more than the Polynesian type." A similar statement was quite independently made to the Royal Geographical Society on this head. In the discussion which followed the reading of a paper on behalf of the Expedition, Capt. T. A. Joyce of the British Museum, remarked that a few years ago he had examined the skulls brought back from Easter Island by the late Lord Crawford. " I then," he continued, " wrote a paper which I never published. It remained both literally and metaphorically a skeleton in my cupboard, because I could not get away from the conclusion that in their measurements and general appearance these skulls were far more Melanesian than Polynesian." [1] In speaking of skulls, Dr. Keith makes the interesting remark that the islanders are the largest-brained people yet discovered in the islands or shores of the Pacific, and shows that their cranial capacity exceeds that of the inhabitants of Whitechapel.

In the culture of the island also, the Melanesian influence is very strong. The custom of distending the lobe of the ear is much more Melanesian than Polynesian. Dr. Haddon has pointed out that an early illustration of an Easter Island canoe depicts it with a double outrigger, after a type found in the Nissan group in Melanesia. [2] An obsidian blade has been found in the area of New Guinea influenced by Melanesian culture, which has been described and figured by Dr. Seligman [3]; he draws attention to its striking likeness to the mataa of Easter Island. Weapons of the same type, and wooden figures in which the ribs are a prominent feature, have been found in the Chatham Islands, [4] but the respective amount of Polynesian and Melanesian culture in these islands is as yet under discussion.

The most striking evidence is, however, found in connection with the bird-cult. It has been shown by Mr. Henry Balfour that a cult with strong resemblance to that of Easter existed in the Solomon Islands of Melanesia. It is there connected with the Frigate bird, a sea-bird which usually nests in trees and is characterised by a hooked beak and gular pouch. In treeless Easter Island the sacred bird is the Sooty Tern, which is without the gular pouch and has a straight beak. In many of the carvings on the island, however, the sacred bird is represented with a hooked beak and a pouch (fig. 112). "This seems to point to a recollection retained by the immigrants into Easter Island of a former cult of the frigate-bird which was practised in a region where this bird was a familiar feature, and which was gradually given up in the new environment when this bird,

[1] *Royal Geographical Journal*, May 1917. It has been pointed out that Dr. Hamy, examining skulls from Easter Island some thirty years ago, and W. Volz (*Arch. f. Anth.* xxiii. 1895, p. 97 ff.) attained the same result. Mr. Pycraft also came independently to the same conclusion.
[2] *Folk Lore*, June 1918, p. 161.
[3] *Man*, 1918, No. 91, pl. M. Also in *Anthropological Essays*, presented to E. B. Tylor, 1907, pl. iii. fig. 2, and p. 327.
[4] H. Balfour, *Man*, Oct. 1918, No. 80. *Folk Lore*, Dec. 1917, pp. 356–60.

FIG 125.

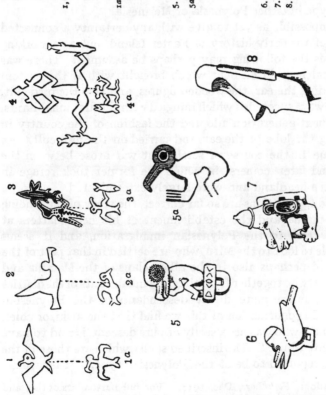

BIRD AND HUMAN DESIGNS.

1, 2, 3, 4, from the Solomon Islands.

1a, 2a, 3a, 4a, from the script, Easter Island.

BIRD HEADS ON HUMAN BODIES.

5. Wooden float for fishing-net, Solomon Islands.

5a. Painting from an Orongo house, Easter Island.

HUMAN HEADS WITH BIRD CHARACTERISTICS.

6. On a bird body. Float for net, Solomon Islands.

7. On a human body. Canoe-prow god, Solomon Islands.

8. Profile of a stone statue, Easter Island.

BIRD-HUMAN FIGURES IN THE SOLOMON ISLANDS AND EASTER ISLAND.

Selected from the figures illustrating an article by H. Balfour, Curator of the Pitt-Rivers Museum, Oxford. *Folk Lore*, December 1917.

though probably not unknown, was certainly not abundant " ; [1] the cult being transferred to the locally numerous Tern.

Figures were also made in the Solomon Islands composed partly of bird and partly of human form. Bird heads appear on human bodies, as in Easter Island, and also human heads on bird bodies (fig. 125). It is noteworthy that, even when the head which is drawn on the bird body is human, it is depicted with bird-like characteristics, the lower part of the face being given a beak-like protrusion, till sometimes it is almost impossible to distinguish whether the head is that of a man or a bird (no. 6). This prognathous type, with the protrusion of the lower facial region, appears to have become a convention, and it is found in figures where the body as well as the head are human (no. 7). This is the kind found in a modified form in the Easter Island stone figures; they differ from any normal human type in either Polynesia or Melanesia.

It is impossible as yet to give with any certainty a connected account of the early history of Easter Island, but as a working hypothesis the following may perhaps be assumed. There was an original negroid element which brought with it the custom of distending the ear, the wooden figures, and also the bird-cult. A whiter wave succeeded which mingled with the first inhabitants, and the next generation adopted the fashion of the country in stretching the lobe of the ear, and carried on the bird-cult. At some time in the course of settlement war arose between the earlier and later comers, in which the former took refuge in the eastern headland and were largely exterminated.

If these suppositions are so far correct, the story of the landing of Hotu-matua and the establishment of his headquarters at Anakena refer to the Polynesian immigration, and it seems reasonable to look to the Miru, who are settled in that part of the island, and perhaps also to the allied clans of the Marama and Haumoana, who together form the chief inhabitants of the district of Kotuu, as the more direct descendants of the Polynesian settlers. In confirmation of this we find that the ariki, or chief, the only man who was necessarily of pure descent, is said to have been " quite white." The inscribed skulls, which are those of the Miru, are reported to be of the Polynesian type. It is a some-

---

[1] H. Balfour, *Folk Lore*, Dec. 1917. For full particulars of this and the following points readers are referred to the paper itself.

what striking fact also that the ariki, in spite of his prominent position in the island, took no part in the bird-cult ceremonies.

In endeavouring to arrive at even an approximate date for these immigrations to the island, evidence outside its borders is likely to prove our best guide. In the present state of our knowledge we cannot even guess how long the negroid element has been in the Pacific, but the lighter races are believed to have entered it not earlier than the Christian era. The colonisation of the Paumotus is placed at A.D. 1000,[1] and it has been suggested by Volz that the Polynesian wave reached Easter Island about A.D. 1400.

There is at present no evidence to show whether the great works were initiated by the earlier or the later arrivals. There are other megalithic remains in the Pacific, notably great walls of stone in the Caroline Islands. The Expedition found a stone statue in Pitcairn,[2] but we have as yet no complete information with regard to these works or the circumstances of their construction. The Polynesians are accredited with having carried with them the fashion of erecting such monuments, but, if they brought it to Easter Island, the form which it took was apparently governed by conventions already existing in the island.

On the other hand, it seems possible that the makers of the images may have come from a country where they were accustomed to model statues in wood, and finding no such material in the island, substituted for it the stone of Raraku. Sir Basil Thomson has pointed out that there were in the Marquesas wooden statues standing on erections of stone and also wooden dolls. Further knowledge of what exists elsewhere will probably throw light on the matter, but it is, in any case, owing to the fact that there is to be found at Easter a volcanic ash which can be easily wrought that we have the hundreds of images in the island.

With regard to the duration of the image era, it has been shown that the number of statues, impressive as it is, does not necessarily imply that their manufacture covered a vast space of time. It must, however, in all probability have extended over several centuries. As to its termination, the worship is reported as having been in existence in 1722 ; at any rate the ahu and statues were then in good repair. By 1774 some of the statues

---

[1] *Hawaiki*, S. Percy Smith, p. 294.   [2] See below, pp. 313–4.

had fallen, and by about 1840 none remained in place.   It seems, therefore, on the whole, most likely that the cult, and probably also the manufacture of the images, existed till the beginning of the eighteenth century.   The alternative explanation can only be that though the cult had long been dead the statues remained in place, not materially injured either by man or weather, until Europeans first visited the island, and that then an era of devastation set in which in a hundred years demolished them all. This, though not actually impossible, does not seem equally probable.

We know that a large number, probably the majority, of the statues came to their end through being deliberately thrown down by invading enemies.   The legendary struggles between Kotuu and Hotu Iti, in which Kainga played so prominent a part, are always spoken of as comparatively recent history, and one old man definitely asserted that they took place in the time of the grandfather of the last ariki, which may be as far back as the eighteenth century. If these wars occurred between the visit of the Dutchmen in 1722 and that of the Spaniards in 1770, it is at least possible that it was during their course that the manufacture of the images ended and their overthrow began.   It will be remembered that, while Roggeveen speaks of the island as cultivated and fertile, the navigators fifty years later are greatly disappointed with the barren condition in which they find it. In the curious absence, however, of any reference in these legends to the conditions of the images, this must remain, for the present at any rate, as surmise only.

It would be interesting to know more clearly the part played by the advent of the white men in the evolution of the culture of the island.   While it cannot be definitely stated that it was their arrival which, by detracting from the reverence paid to the statues, hastened their downfall, we know that it largely affected native conceptions.   Not only was it the probable cause of the abandonment at the end of the eighteenth century of the practice of distending the lobe of the ear,[1] but it inspired a new form of worship.   It is interesting to see in the drawings of foreign ships,

---

[1] If it were not that the strife between the Long and Short Ears is always placed in very remote ages, we might be tempted to see in it a struggle between the adherents of the older and newer fashion.   In the Hawaiian Islands such a combat took place before the advent of Christianity, see p. 322.

which appear side by side with older designs, a new cult actually in course of intermingling with the old forms. Did we not possess the key to them, these pictures would add one more to the mysteries of the island.

Such evidence as can be obtained from the condition of the images points to the fact that it cannot be indefinite ages since they were completed. For example, in certain statues, those which are generally considered the most recent, the surface polish still remains in its place in the cavity representing the eye, and on parts of the neck and breast where it has been somewhat sheltered by the chin, notwithstanding the fact that the soft stone is one that easily weathers (*Frontispiece*).

The question as to what the statues represent is not yet fully solved. It seems probable that the form was a conventional one and was used to denote various things. Some of the statues may have been gods; the name of a single image on an inland ahu, one of the very few which were remembered, was reported to be " Moai Te Atua." It is, however, probably safe to regard ahu statues as being in general representations of ancestors, either nearer or more distant, this does not necessarily exclude the idea of divinity. The hat may have been a badge of rank; warriors in Tahiti wore a certain type of hat as a special mark of distinction.[1] Reasons have been given for suggesting that the images on Raraku may have been memorials of bird men ; and we know that some of the statues, as those on the southern slope of Raraku and in Motu Nui, denoted boundaries. Lastly, it is not impossible that some of the figures, such as those approaching the ahu of Paukura, were simply ornamental, " to make it look nice." The nearest approach which we ourselves have to such divers employment of the same design is in our use of the Latin cross. Fundamentally a sacred sign, it is used not only to adorn churches and for personal ornament, but also to mark graves and denote common and central grounds, such as the site of markets and other public places. It is also used to preserve the memory of certain spots, as for instance, Charing Cross, where the body of Queen Eleanor rested.

The last problem to be considered is that dealing with the tablets. An account has been given elsewhere of what is known

[1] *Quest and Occupation of Tahiti*, Hakluyt Society, vol. ii. p. 270.

of their general meaning.   The figures themselves may be classed as ideograms—that is, signs representing ideas—but it is doubtful, as has been shown, if a given sign always represented the same idea.   Each sign was in any case a peg on which to hang a large amount of matter which was committed to memory, and is therefore, alas ! gone for ever.

No light has yet been thrown on the origin of the script.   No other writing has been found in the Pacific, if we except a form from the Caroline Islands, and a few rock carvings in the Chatham Islands, whose connection with the glyphs of Easter Island is as yet very doubtful.

It would be satisfactory, in view of the relation of the Miru ariki to the tablets, and the tradition that they came with Hotumatua, if internal evidence could show that it was of Polynesian origin.   Unfortunately for this theory, the Melanesian bird figures largely among the signs.   It is, of course, conceivable that they may have undergone local adaptation.   While it is not probable that we shall ever be able to read the tablets, it is not impossible that further discovery may throw light on the history of the signs, and show to what extent the script has been imported from elsewhere, or how far it is, with much of its other culture, a product of the isolation of Easter Island.

PART III

THE HOMEWARD VOYAGE
EASTER ISLAND TO SAN FRANCISCO

CHAPTER XX

Lieutenant Bligh went to the Pacific in 1788, in command of H.M.S. *Bounty*, with orders to obtain plants of the bread-fruit, and introduce it into the English possessions in the West Indies.

He spent six months at Tahiti, collecting the fruit, and there the crew fell victims to the charms of its lotus-eating life, its sunshine, its flowers, and its women. Soon after the ship sailed the majority of the men mutinied, being led by Christian, the Master's mate. They set Bligh and eighteen others adrift in an open boat, and returned in the ship to Tahiti. Subsequently, fearing that retribution might follow, Christian and eight fellow mutineers left Tahiti on the *Bounty*, taking with them nine native women, and also some native men to act as servants. For years their fate remained a mystery.

The refuge found by the party was the lonely island of Pitcairn. They took out of the ship everything that they required, and then sank the vessel, fearing that her presence might betray them. The new habitation proved anything but an amicable Eden. The native servants were ill-treated by their masters, and in 1793 rose against them, murdering Christian and four other white men ; but were finally themselves all killed by the Europeans. The women also were discontented with their lot, and in the following year they made a raft in order to quit the island, an attempt which was of course foredoomed to failure.

Of the four mutineers left, one, McCoy, committed suicide through an intoxicating drink made from the ti plant. Another, Quintal, having threatened the lives of his two comrades, Adams and Young, was killed by them with an axe, in self defence. A woman who witnessed the scene as a child, survived till 1883, and we were told by her grandchildren that her clearest recollection was the blood-spattered walls and the screaming women and children. Young, who had been a midshipman on the *Bounty*, died shortly after, and in 1800 John Adams (*alias* Alexander Smith) was left the sole man on the island, with the native women and twenty-five children.

Later ensued not the least strange part of the story. Adams was converted by a dream, and awoke to his responsibility towards the younger generation. He taught them to read from a Bible and Prayer-book saved from the *Bounty*, and the offspring of the mutineers became a civilised and God-fearing community.

The small colony were first found by an American ship, the *Topaz*, in 1808, but little seems to have been heard of the discovery, and six years later H.M. ships *Briton* and *Tagus*, sailing near the island were much astonished at being hailed by a boat-load of men who spoke English.

By 1856 the population of Pitcairn numbered about one hundred and ninety, and they were removed, by their own request, to the larger Norfolk Island. Six homesick families, however, against the strong advice of Bishop Selwyn, subsequently returned to Pitcairn.

In the afternoon of Wednesday, August 18th, 1915, the last vestige of the long coast of Easter Island dipped below the horizon. We realised that we were homeward bound. Owing to the war, and our prolonged residence on the island, it was no longer possible to keep to the plan made before leaving England and follow up Easter trails elsewhere in the Pacific. We decided, however, to adhere to the original arrangement of going first to Tahiti, and then to make the return voyage by the Panama Canal, which was now open. One of our principal objects in visiting Tahiti was to collect all the letters, newspapers, and money which had been forwarded to us there during the last twelve months. With the exception of one stray letter, written the previous November, we had had no mail since *Mana's* first return to the island a year before. It seemed desirable to visit Pitcairn Island on the way thither; it was but little out of our route, and was said to have prehistoric remains.

We had a very good voyage for the 1,100 miles from Easter to Pitcairn, staggering along with a following wind. The wind was indeed so strong that we became anxious for the safety of the dinghy in her davits, and swung her inboard for, I believe, the only time on the voyage. We arrived at Pitcairn on August 27th. The island, as seen from the sea, rises as a solitary mass from the water. It is apparently the remaining half of an old crater, and is some two miles in width. An amphitheatre of luxuriant verdure faces northwards; its lowest portion, or arena, is perhaps 400 feet above sea level, and rests on the top of a wall of grey rock. The other three sides of the amphitheatre are encircled by high precipitous cliffs. The green gem, in its rocky setting, was a refreshing change after treeless Easter Island.

Mana was welcomed by a boat-load of sturdy men, who were definitely European in appearance and manner; they were mostly of a sallow white complexion, though a few had a darker tinge. They spoke English, though with an intonation different

FIG. 126.

PITCAIRN ISLAND FROM THE SEA.

FIG. 127.

PITCAIRN ISLAND: CHURCH AND RESIDENCE OF MISSIONARIES,

FIG. 128.

PITCAIRN ISLAND : BOUNTY BAY.

from that of the Dominions, America, or the Homeland. A local patois is sometimes used on the island which is a mixture of English and Tahitian, but pure Tahitian is not understood. A graceful invitation was given by the Chief Magistrate, Mr. Gerard Christian, to come and stay on shore, and was accepted for the following day, which, the Islanders said, "will be the Sabbath." This was a somewhat surprising statement, as the day was Friday, and caused a momentary wonder whether something had gone wrong with the log of *Mana*. "We will explain all that later," added our hosts.

The next morning therefore the big ten-oared boat turned up again, Mr. Christian bringing us the following kind letter from the missionaries, who we now learned were on the island. It was addressed "To the Gentlemen concerned."

PITCAIRN ISLAND.
27. 8. 1915.

"DEAR SIR AND MADAM,
"It is with pleasure that we extend this invitation to you to share with us the few comforts of our little Island home. We cannot offer luxury, we live simply yet wholesomely. Should you be planning to sleep ashore, it will be well to bring your pillows, towels and toilet soap. We trust that your stay will be attended with success.
"Yours very cordially,
"MR. and MRS. M. R. ADAMS."

We suggested bringing food, but that was declined as unnecessary. The trip to the shore, even in so big a boat, is somewhat adventurous. The landing-place is in Bounty Bay, below the precipitous cliffs off the north-east corner of the island, beneath whose waters were sunk the remains of His Majesty's ship. The shore is reached, even under propitious circumstances, through a white fringe of drenching surf ; happily the Islanders are excellent oarsmen, for the boat is apt to assume the vertical position usually associated with pictures of Grace Darling. A lifeboat sent as a gift from England in 1880 has proved too short for the character of the waves. The village is gained by a steep path, cut at times in the rock, and at the summit we found standing under the trees a group in white Sunday attire waiting to welcome us.

We were now beginning to understand the meaning of the difference in days. Service used to be held at Pitcairn after the manner of the Church of England, but in 1886 the island was visited by one of the American sect calling themselves "Seventh Day Adventists." The Society is Christian, but the members regard as binding many of the Old Testament rules. Saturday is observed as the divinely appointed day of rest, pork is considered unclean, and a tenth part of goods is set aside for religious purposes. Special attention is paid to Biblical prophecy, and the end of the world is thought to be near. It was not difficult to convert the reverent little community on Pitcairn to views for which it was claimed that they were the plain teaching of the Bible, and various persons were shortly baptised in the sea.

The group who awaited us were headed by our most kind hosts, the missionary and his wife, Mr. and Mrs. Adams, who were of Australian birth.[1] Sunday school was just over and service about to begin. It was held in an airy building filled with a large congregation. The sermon was on prophecy as found in the books of Daniel and Revelation, and fulfilled in the division of the Empire of Alexander the Great. It was depressing to be told that the late war is only the beginning of trouble.

We went back with Mr. and Mrs. Adams to luncheon, which was served at 2.30, and composed principally of oranges and bananas. It was a very dainty if, to some of us who had breakfasted at 7 o'clock, a rather unsubstantial repast. Our hosts were vegetarians and had only two meals a day, but subsequently kind allowance was made for our less moderate appetites. I was glad of a rest in the afternoon, but S., who attended a second service, said it had been the most interesting part of the Sunday observances; it was a less formal gathering, when personal religious testimonies were given by both young and old. Later we were shown a little settlement of huts in the higher part of the island, where once a year the community retire for ten days and have a series of camp meetings.

The teachings of the new religion are practically observed. The tithe barn, at the time of our visit, held £100 worth of dedicated produce which was awaiting shipment. It was the prettiest sight to see the fruits of the earth, being brought into it, in the form of loads of various tropical produce. The whole

---

[1] They had, of course, no connection with Adams the mutineer.

community abstains from alcohol and, nominally at any rate, from tobacco, though one old gentleman was not above making an arrangement for a private supply from the yacht. Tea and coffee are thought to be undesirable stimulants, and even the export of coffee was beginning to be discouraged. The place suffers admittedly from the social laxity characteristic of Polynesia ; but the evil is being combated by its spiritual leaders, and is cognisable by law. The whole atmosphere is extraordinary ; the visitor feels as if suddenly transported, amid the surroundings of a Pacific Island, to Puritan England, or bygone Scotland. It is a Puritanism which is nevertheless light-hearted and sunny, without hypocrisy or intolerance.

The general influence of the missionaries seemed very helpful to the little community, and they also conducted a school for its younger members. Most of the inhabitants can read, but the subject matter of books is too far away for them to be of much interest, and the only application, it was noticed, which was made to the yacht for literature, was for picture papers of the war. We gave by request an hour's talk on the travels of the *Mana*, and it was listened to with apparent understanding, or at any rate with politeness ; the chief interest shown was in the manner of life of the Easter Islanders, about which many questions were asked.

The houses are substantially built of wood with good furniture. A well-made chest of drawers was a birthday present to the missionary's wife from the young men of the island. There is a separate bedroom or cubicle for nearly every inhabitant, and some houses have a room set apart for meals. Hospitality was shown without stint, and we were entertained during our stay to a series of attractive repasts in various homes ; our hosts bore such names as Christian, Young, and McCoy. Meat is limited to goat or chicken, but there is a profusion of tropical produce, and oranges are too numerous to gather. The coconut trees are unfortunately dying. Each household has a share of the ground rising behind the village, and the hillside is traversed by shady avenues of palms and bananas, which afford at every turn glimpses of outstanding cliffs and the brilliant blue of the ocean. The standard of life compares very favourably with that of an English village, and is immeasurably superior to that achieved on Easter Island under similar circumstances.

Pitcairn has the dignity of being a democratic self-governing community, with a Magistrate and two houses of legislature. The present Constitution was suggested by the Captain of H.M.S. *Champion* in 1892, and superseded an earlier one. The Lower House, known as " the Committee," comprises a Chairman and two members, also an official Secretary ; it makes regulations which are submitted to the Upper House or " Council." The Council consists of the Chief Magistrate, with two assessors and the Secretary, and it acts also as a court of justice. The two committee members and a constable are nominated by the magistrate, but the other officials are elected annually by all inhabitants over eighteen years ; Pitcairn was therefore the first portion of the British Empire to possess female suffrage.

It was interesting to see the Government Records, though the present book does not go back beyond above fifty years, earlier ones having apparently disappeared. This contained the Laws of 1884 revised in 1904; regulations for school attendance ; a category of the chief magistrates ; a chronicle of visits from men-of-war and mention of Queen Victoria's presents, consisting of an organ in 1879 and newly minted Jubilee coins received in 1889. There were also recorded the births, marriages, and deaths of the island since 1864 ; and a description of the various brands adopted by respective owners for their goats, chickens, and trees.

Among the legislative enactments was more than one concerned with the preservation of cats, the object being to keep down rats. Thus the laws of 1884 direct that :

" Any person or persons after this date, September 24th, 1884, maliciously wounding or causing the death of a cat, without permission, will be liable to such punishment as the Court will inflict. . . . Should any dog, going out with his master, fall in with a cat, and chase him, and no effort be made to save the cat, the dog must be killed ; for the first offence—fine 10s. Cats in any part of the island doing anyone damage must be killed in the presence of a member of Parliament."

Illicit medical practice is forbidden, and the regulation on this head runs as follows :

" It may be lawful for parents to treat their own children in case of sickness. But no one will understand that he is at liberty to treat, or give any dose of medicine, unless it be one of his own family, without first getting licence from the President. Drugs may not be landed without permission."

More recent laws enact, that each family may keep only six breeding nannies ; and that coconuts may only be gathered under supervision of the Committee or in company with their owners of the same patch, in case of want, however, they may be plucked for drinking. Persons killing fowls must present the legs (*i.e.* the lower portion which bears the brand) to a member of the Government.

With the entries of deaths are recorded their known, or presumed, cause ; those occasioned by accident are somewhat numerous, and include fatal results from climbing cliffs after birds, chasing goats, and falling from trees. Wills can be made by simply writing them in the official book, but entries under this head were not numerous.

The island is in the jurisdiction of the British Consul at Tahiti, but the Magistrate explained sadly that it was then two years since it had been possible for his superior to send any instructions. In very serious matters, such as murder or divorce, reference is necessary to the High Commissioner at Fiji, and five years may elapse before an answer is received.

It is indeed comparatively simple to communicate from Pitcairn with the outside world, particularly now that it lies near the route from Panama to New Zealand. Warning of the approach of a vessel is given by the church bell, and all hands rush forthwith to launch the boat and pull out to the ship. It is reported that once the bell sounded whilst a marriage was being celebrated, the crowded church emptied at once, and the bride, bridegroom, and officiator were left alone. Sooner or later a letter can thus be handed on board, but to obtain a reply is another matter ; no steamer will undertake to deliver passengers, goods, or mails to the island. It does not pay to spend time over so small a matter, the liner may pass in the night, or the weather at the time may render communication with the shore impossible. During our visit notice was given that a ship was approaching ; the men, who were at the time engaged in digging for the Expedition, threw down their tools and the boat started for the vessel, only to founder among the breakers of Bounty Bay. The place is too remote to be visited by the trading vessels which visit the Gambier Islands, and as there is no anchorage, it is by no means easy for the Islanders to keep any form of ship on their own account. In normal times a British warship calls every alternate year, but its visits were suspended during the war. Of the two islands, Easter, which has at least definite bonds with a firm on the mainland, is on the whole the easier of access.

The economic problem of Pitcairn lies in the difficulty of making it self-supporting. Food and housing materials abound, but clothes, tools, and similar articles must be obtained from elsewhere ; while to secure in return a market for its small exports is almost impossible. It is sometimes said that as the result, the inhabitants have grown so accustomed to be objects of interest and charity, that they have become pauperised and expect everything to be given them freely by passing ships. This was certainly not our experience. They made us a large number of generous gifts, such as bundles of dried bananas and specimens of their handiwork—hats, baskets, and dried leaves, cleverly embroidered and painted. On the other hand they took with gratitude any articles which were given by us, either as presents or in return for the things we purchased. One request has been received since we left the island ; it was made with many apologies by the Chief Magistrate, and was for a Bible of the Oxford Teachers' Edition.

The position, however, is unsatisfactory, and it seems very desirable that if possible more frequent communication should be established. In any case it is to be hoped that now peace reigns, a warship may visit the place at least once a year.

It is frequently suggested that the Pitcairners must have deteriorated in physique by intermarriage; as far, however, as we were able to observe, such is not the case. It has been re-marked, indeed, that a large number have lost their front teeth, but in this they are not unique. Dr. Keith observes, in the report previously alluded to, that many Pacific Islanders are extremely liable to disease and loss of teeth. The effect of such disease is, he states, to be seen in every one of the skulls from Easter regarded as belonging to a person of over twenty-five years ; " tooth trouble is even more prevalent in Easter Island than in the slums of our great towns."

We were asked to collect pedigrees on Pitcairn and make observations from the point of view of the Mendelian theory ;

this would, however, have been a very long and troublesome business, and we did not feel assured that the results would be sufficiently exact to justify it. While there has probably been no fresh infusion of South Sea blood, the Islanders have constantly been in contact with white men. Between 1808 and 1856, three hundred and fifty vessels touched at Pitcairn, and on various occasions shipwrecked mariners and others have taken up their abode on the island, and intermixed with the population.

The Pitcairn Islanders have been described as the " Beggars of the Pacific," and, on the contrary, have also been depicted as saints in a modern Eden. Needless to say they are neither the one nor the other, but inheritors of some of the weaknesses and a surprising amount of the strength of their mixed ancestry.

From the point of view of its main and scientific object, our visit had satisfactory results. The island was uninhabited when the mutineers arrived, but there were traces of past residents. The sites of three " marae," or native structures, among the undergrowth were pointed out. They are said to have been preserved by the first Englishmen, but were unfortunately destroyed comparatively recently and very little of them is still preserved. The old people could remember when bones could be seen lying about in their vicinity. The Islanders most kindly offered to dig out what still existed of these remains, and two days running the whole population turned out for excavation. The most interesting of the erections proved to be one situated on the cliff looking down on to Bounty Bay ; we were only able roughly to examine it on the morning of our departure. It appeared to have been made of earth, not built of stone, and by clearing away some of the scrub we were able to arrive at the conclusion that it had been an embankment some 12 feet high, built on the immediate edge of the vertical cliff, and had had two faces. The face that was directed seawards was almost vertical, whilst the one towards the land formed an inclined plane, that measured 37 feet between its highest and its lowest points. It seemed clear that both sides had been paved with marine boulders. In general character it resembled to some extent one of the semi-pyramid ahu of Easter, but dense vegetation and tree growth rendered it impossible to speak definitely, and the form may have been determined by the shape of the cliff. It was remembered that three statues had stood on it, and that one in particular had been thrown down on to the beach beneath. The headless trunk of this image is preserved ; it is 31 inches in height, and the form has a certain resemblance to that of Easter Island, but the workmanship is much cruder. There is said to have been also a statue on a marae on the other side of the island.

There are interesting rock carvings in two places, both of which are somewhat difficult to reach. S. managed however to photograph one set, and a dear old man undertook the scramble to the other site, which was practically inaccessible to booted feet, and made drawings of them for the Expedition.

Then we had a great whip-up for any stone implements which might have been found ; Miss Beatrice Young most kindly assisted and induced the owners to bring out their possessions. Over eighty were produced. The Islanders were much pleased to think that their contribution would be numbered among the treasures of the British Museum, but the argument that " a hundred years hence they would still be there " left them cold ; for, as they explained, " the end of the world would have come before then."

We spent in all four nights on the island, which forms, we believe, a record sojourn for visitors ; it is a very happy memory. A large portion of the population asked for passages to Tahiti, but the hearts of most failed before the end, and we on our part drew the line at taking more than two men, who would work their passage. Those who finally came with us were brothers, Charles and Edwin Young, descendants of Midshipman Young. They arrived on board with their hats wreathed with flowers— true Polynesian fashion—accompanied by many friends and relatives. Charles had been on one of the island trading vessels, but Edwin had never before left his home (fig. 132).

From Pitcairn we made for Rapa, known as Rapa-iti or Little Rapa, to distinguish it from Rapa-nui or Great Rapa ; which, as has been seen, is one of the names for Easter. It is a French possession and only visited by a vessel occasionally. It is seven hundred miles from Pitcairn, and was somewhat out of our route for Tahiti, but the Sailing Directions reported a number of pre-historic buildings, which they termed " forts." We were anxious to inspect them and see what relation, if any, they bore to build-ings on Easter Island ; but disappointment, alas ! awaited us.

The side of the island on which is the settlement was at the time of our visit the windward aspect ; there was a strong breeze and quite a heavy sea. We remained abreast the village for some hours awaiting the pilot, who is said to come off to visiting vessels, but no one appeared, nor was any signal made on the shore. Either they were afraid of us, or did not like the look of the weather. It was not one of the islands we had originally intended visiting, and we had no chart.

We had to sail the ship the whole time in order to keep our station, and eventually our forestay gave out ; this meant putting her instantly before the wind, or we should have been dismasted. We therefore ran under the lee of the land and made good our damage. It would have taken a long time to thrash back to our original station, so we reluctantly gave up the attempt to make a landing. The coast is extremely fine, bold, and precipitous, but that, and the illustration given, is all that we can tell of Rapa.

FIG. 129.—THE ISLAND OF RAPA.

CHAPTER XXI

TAHITI, HAWAIIAN ISLANDS, SAN FRANCISCO

Tahiti—Voyage to Hawaiian Islands—Oahu, with its capital Honolulu—Visit to Island of Hawaii—San Francisco—The Author returns to England.

TAHITI

Wallis is the first European known certainly to have seen Tahiti. He visited it in 1767, and was followed two years later by Cook. The predominant chiefs on the island at this time were Amo and his wife Purea, of the district of Paparo on the south coast. They are chiefly notorious as the founders of the great marae—or "temple"—of Mahaiatea, which they built in honour of their infant son, Teriiere. This work must have been in progress when Wallis anchored on the other side of the island. The demands which they made on their fellow natives in order to secure its erection were so extortionate that a rising took place against them ; and by the time Cook made his first appearance they were shorn of much of their glory. Subsequently various other navigators visited the island. Cook anchored there a second time, and H.M.S. *Bounty* made a prolonged sojourn. In 1797 thirty missionaries arrived, sent from England by the London Missionary Society.

By this time another native family was in the ascendant, whose territory was on the north coast. They have become known as the Pomare, a name crystallised by the missionaries, but which was in reality only one of the minor appellations which had been adopted, native fashion, by the chief of the day. Pomare II. was baptised in 1819.

About forty years later Roman Catholic missionaries arrived, and a struggle for ascendancy took place between them and the London Society. The Home Government refused to support the Protestants. Queen Pomare IV., therefore, though she much preferred the English, was compelled to apply for a French protectorate, which was established in 1843. On the death of the old Queen in 1877, the French recognised her son, Pomare V., who had married his cousin Marau. The new Queen was the daughter of a chiefess known as Arii Taimai, who had married an English Jew named Salmon.[1] Miss Gordon Cumming, who visited the island at the time, gives an interesting account of the procession round the island to proclaim the new sovereigns, in which she herself took part. In 1880 Pomare handed over his claims to the French Government, by whom the island was then formally annexed.

[1] Another daughter was the wife of Mr. Brander, the connection of whose firm with Easter Island has already been seen.

WE sighted Tahiti on the 16th of September, 1915, sailed along its coast with interest, and anchored in the afternoon at Papeete on the north shore. It was wonderful to return once more to the great world, even in its modified form at Tahiti, and the Rip van Winkle sensation was most curious. The Consul, Mr. H. A. Richards, was early on board with a kind welcome, and sent us round the longed-for sacks containing a year's accumulation of letters and newspapers. The mail, however, brought bad personal news, and though life had to go on as usual, recollections of the island have suffered from every point of view.[1]

Tahiti, as seen from the sea, with its mass of broken mountains covered with verdure, is undoubtedly very beautiful; and the sunset effects over the neighbouring island of Moorea are particularly striking. The lagoon too is fascinating, and refreshing expeditions were made in the motor launch to study the wonders of its protecting coral reef. When on land, however, the charm of the island is somewhat dissipated. The inhabited strip round the coast, which varies from nothing up to some two miles in width, is covered with bungalows and little native properties, and is so full of coconuts and palms that all effect of the mountains is lost. Though it was only the month of September at the time of our visit it was very hot and airless, making all mental and physical exertion an effort. I went one morning for a walk at 6.30 in the hope of better things, but even then it felt as if Nature had forgotten to open her windows. The wild charm of romance which greeted the early voyagers and which must have assuaged the struggle of the first missionaries is now no more. Papeete is civilised: it is a port for the mail steamers between America and New Zealand. It is under French rule, but a large proportion of business is in the hands of the British and also of the Chinese.

We lived at the hotel, as *Mana* had to go on the slip, and had an interesting fellow guest in an American geologist. He was travelling in the Pacific with the object of proving that it had

---

[1] My budget contained, with over twenty letters from my Mother, the news that she had died suddenly the preceding April; and that the old home no longer existed. The tidings were no surprise. I had had the strongest conviction, dating from about one month after her death, that she was no longer here. The realisation came at first with a sense of shock, which was noted in my journal and written to friends in England; afterwards it continued with a quiet persistence which amounted to practical certainty.

never been a continent, but that the islands were sporadic volcanic upheavals from the ocean bed. He had found himself involved in the everlasting quarrel between geologists and biologists, who each want the world constructed to prove their own theories. In this case a biologist wished for continuity of land to account for the presence of the same snail in islands far removed. Our friend had contended that the molluscs might have travelled on drift-wood, but was told in reply that salt water did not "suit their constitution." He had then argued that they could easily have gone with the food in native canoes. "Anyhow," he concluded, with a delightful Yankee drawl, " to have the floor of the ocean raised up fifteen thousand feet, for his snails to crawl over, is just too much."

S. was presented by the Consul to the French Governor, and I called, according to instructions, to pay my respects to his wife, who proved to be both young and charming. She was good enough subsequently to send an invitation to a tea-party, which differed interestingly from similar functions at home. It took place in a large room where twenty chairs, covered with brocade, were arranged in a circle which was broken only by a settee. On this sat the hostess, and by her side, either as the greatest stranger, or as having taken the precaution to be an early arrival, the Stewardess of the *Mana*. One by one the chairs filled up, and each fresh arrival, after greeting her entertainer, went round and shook hands with every one already there. The hostess retained her seat, from which she conversed across to various points of the circle. No one moved except that when a delightful tea came in, it was handed round by the young girls ; no servant appeared—they are almost impossible to get. The Governor earned our particular gratitude by his kindness in sending daily a copy of the war bulletin, which arrived by wireless from Honolulu and New Zealand ; though the installation was not at the time sufficiently advanced to be capable of sending out messages.

The Germans were interned in the bay on what was known as Quarantine Island, and were employed to do a certain amount of leisurely work on the roads, at a comparatively high rate of pay ; at the same time the French subjects, native and half-caste, had been called up for much harder military service and received the standard remuneration, which was much lower.

FIG. 130.

OCÉANIE FRANÇAISE   ANCIEN TAHITI

Vues de Papeete et Famille Royale

A TAHITIAN PICTURE POST-CARD,
Used as menu card at a luncheon given by the ex-Queen Marau.

1. Papeete, capital of Tahiti, with the Island of Moorea in the distance.   From a sketch by Miss Gordon Cumming.   2. Queen Pomare IV.   3. King Pomare V.   4. Titaua, sister of Queen Marau.   5. The harbour of Papeete.   6. Himène (or chorus) singers: performance in honour of Accession of Pomare V and Marau.   From a sketch by Miss Gordon Cumming, 1877.   7. Queen Marau, with autograph.

It was commonly reported that the latter had sent in a petition humbly begging that they might be considered as German prisoners.

During our time on the island the anniversary occurred of the visit of Von Spee's fleet on their way to Easter Island, and the trees were adorned with official notices proclaiming a public holiday in memory of the French victory. What happened on that occasion is not precisely clear, and each person gives a different account. It seems, however, that as the cruisers *Scharnhorst* and *Gneisenau* appeared without any proper announcement, the shore batteries fired across their bows to stop them. The Germans replied, and some houses in the town were set on fire. The French gun-boat *Zelée* was sunk in the harbour, also a German ship which had been taken as a prize. The custodian of the coal supply set it on fire to prevent it from falling into the enemy's hands ; this action was subsequently justified, as it transpired that the Germans had given out that they were going to Papeete in order to obtain coal. After a certain number of shots had passed in both directions, the enemy went on their way.

We had particular pleasure in making the acquaintance of the late Queen, widow of Pomare V., an able and cultured lady, who lives in a villa in Papeete, and calls herself simply " Madame Marau Taaroa." She was kind enough to lend us a valuable book written by her mother, Arii Taimai, which tells the history of the island as related by family traditions and combines with this account the information given by the early voyagers. Her charming daughter, Princess Takau Pomare, who had been educated in Paris, placed us under a great obligation by constituting herself our cicerone. She took us to see the monument on Venus Point, erected to mark the spot where Cook observed the transit of Venus ; and also the Pomare mausoleum. Miss Gordon Cumming records that it was the ancient habit at Tahiti for the dead to be placed in a house, watched till only dust and ashes remained, and then buried securely in the mountain to guard against possible desecration ; this custom, she states, still survived in her day in the case of departed royalty.

We had also a delightful motor drive with the Princess to some family property on the south side of the island, lunching at a small hotel which was nothing if not up-to-date, being dignified with the name of the Tipperary Hotel. The proprietor, a Frenchman, advertised it by stating that while it was a " long, long way to Tipperary," it was only a short way to his establishment. He had adorned the walls of the dining-room with large frescoes of the flags of the Allies, leaving, as he explained, " plenty of room for Holland, Greece, and America."

The marae of Tahiti have vanished, but on the way back we stopped to see all that remains of a once famous pile. Nothing now exists but a mass of overgrown coral stones, converted into a lime kiln. Fortunately Cook and his companion Banks both visited Mahaiatea in its glory and have left us descriptions, and we have also a drawing of it. It is obvious that these structures in no way resembled the ahu of Easter Island. Mahaiatea was a pyramid of oblong form with a base 267 ft. by 71 ft. ; it was composed of squared coral stones and blue pebbles, and consisted of eleven steps each some 4 ft. in height. It impressed Banks as " a most enormous pile, its size and workmanship almost surpassing belief." [1] The pyramid formed one side of a court or square, the whole being walled in and paved with flat stones.

Marae, as Arii Taimai explains, were sacred to some god ; but the god was only a secondary affair ; a man's whole social position depended on his having a stone to sit on within his marae enclosure. Cook was asked for the name of his marae, as it was not supposed possible that a chief could be without one, and took refuge in giving the name of his London Parish, Stepney.

Princess Takau kindly acted as interpreter when we went to look up the Easter Islanders who came here to work on the Brander plantation and who still form a little colony. One of our main objects in visiting Tahiti had been to inspect the tablets and Easter Island collection of Bishop Jaussen who died in 1892. In this we met with disappointment ; the present authorities, whom we saw more than once, took no interest at all in the subject, and said that on Bishop Jaussen's death, the Brothers had sent the articles home as curios to their friends in Europe. They gave us an address in Louvain, which it has not of course up to the present been possible to follow up.

Our crew underwent some alterations at Tahiti. The post of engineer had been filled by a Chilean, and one deck hand had

[1] Journal of Sir Joseph Banks, p. 102.

FIG. 131.

MARAE MAHAIATEA, TAHITI.

(From *A Missionary Voyage in the Ship Duff*, 1796–98.)

FIG. 132.

CHARLES AND EDWIN YOUNG.

The great-great-grandsons of Midshipman Young, the only commissioned officer among the mutineers of the *Bounty* who took refuge on Pitcairn Island, 1790.

already gone home as a reservist; two more now desired to
return direct to "serve their country," one of these was
my friend Bailey, the cook. As he had had no opportunity of
spending his wages, he was, on being paid off, quite a millionaire.
He invested in a number of white washing suits and took up his
residence at our hotel. I was presented with his photograph
clad in the new raiment. An officer travelling to England from
New Zealand was kind enough to undertake to give him some
care on the journey, and managed to get him safely home,
though most of his fortune had disappeared *en route*. He took
service as a ship's cook, and we saw his name subsequently, with
most sincere regret, in a list of " missing."

Bailey's place was taken by an American, who had formed
part of the crew which had been discharged from a ship which
they had brought to Tahiti from California. He declined to
come on board till just before we sailed, as he was engaged for a
prize-fight with a noted coloured champion; the prospective
fight excited a good deal of local interest, but ended lamentably
in the white man being knocked out at the first blow. As we
were still short-handed, we arranged with our two Pitcairn
Islanders to come on with us to England; Charles Young was
signed on as deck-hand, and Edwin, who was of less strong
physique, as steward. They both gave every satisfaction, and
Edwin, though he had of course to be taught his duties, was the
best steward we ever had.

We had considerable conversation with our Consul, Mr. Richards, on the subject of Pitcairn, in which he has always taken
great interest, doing all that he could for the Islanders. He had
been anxious if possible to make a stay there of some duration,
feeling, no doubt rightly, that the only way to solve its difficulties
was for someone to dwell there long enough to see the situation,
not as a visitor, but as a resident. Circumstances had not, so
far, rendered this feasible, but it is to be hoped it may still be
accomplished.

It was impossible to make a direct passage from Tahiti to Panama, as the Trade Wind would have been dead against us, we
had, therefore, to turn its flank by going as far north as the
Sandwich Group, or, to give them their American name, the
Hawaiian Islands. We passed within sight of one or two of the

21

Paumotu group, which was our first introduction to coral atolls ; but I do not think we saw a ship during the whole voyage.

It was a long run, as we met with calms in the Doldrums, and were without the use of the motor, which stood in need of some simple repairs, that could not be done in Tahiti. Being becalmed is certainly unpleasant, there is no air, everything hangs loose, rattles and bangs, and cheerful calculations are made as to how much damage per hour is being done to the gear ; but on the whole the patience of seamen is marvellous. Occupation happily was provided in the stupendous quantity of arrears of newspapers. We read them most diligently, but it is hardly fair to journalists to deal with their output a year after it is written, the mistakes and false prophecies of even the most sober papers become painfully obvious. We became acquainted, for example, at one and the same time with the birth and death of the " Russian steam-roller " theory, and other similar figments. My diary is diversified by such items of domestic interest as " showed Edwin how to look after the brass." " S. taught Edwin to clean silver."

HAWAIIAN ISLANDS

The group is composed of eight inhabited islands which stretch in a line from north-west to south-east. Hawaii, the most southerly, is the largest, and now gives its name to the whole, but the principal modern town, Honolulu, is on the more northerly island of Oahu. The islands were known to the early Spanish voyagers, but their connection with the civilised world really dates from their rediscovery by Cook. He called them after Lord Sandwich, who was at that time First Lord of the Admiralty. The great navigator was murdered on Hawaii in 1779. Vancouver touched there more than once, and obtained the consent of the natives to a British Protectorate, which he proclaimed on Hawaii in 1794 ; the action was however ignored by the Home Government.

At this time a powerful chief of Hawaii, Kamehameha I, rose to pre-eminence. He captured the island of Oahu in 1795, and consolidated the group under one government. Contact with the outside world gradually undermined the native beliefs and the old ceremonial taboos became wearisome. After the death of Kamehameha they were overthrown by his son, in 1819, though not without armed resistance from the more orthodox section. The islands were for a short time " a nation without a religion " ; but Christianity was introduced almost immediately by American missionaries.

The group was nominally independent till the time of Queen Liliuokalani, who succeeded in 1891. Her rule roused much resentment among the foreign residents, and during a period of unsettlement she was imprisoned in her palace for nine months. An

FIG. 133.

HEIAU PUUKOHOLA, HAWAII.

appeal was made to the United States, and the islands were formally annexed by that power in 1898.

Oahu.—After a five-weeks' voyage, which included an abortive attempt to call at the island of Hawaii, we reached Honolulu, in the island of Oahu, on November 11th, 1915.

From the isolation of Easter we had come to the comparatively busy life of Tahiti, and now at Honolulu we felt once more in touch with the great world. It is a cheerful and up-to-date city in beautiful surroundings. Seen from the harbour it is not unlike Papeete, but the town is bigger, and the mountains more distant. The roads of the suburbs are frequently bordered by large areas of mown grass, which form part of the gardens of the adjacent villas. It is considered a duty to erect no wall or paling, and the custom, while it deprives the residences of privacy, greatly enhances the charm of the highway. The practice is encouraged by a public-spirited society, interested in the beauty of the place. The aquarium contains fish of most gorgeous colouring, and it is well worth while to explore a coral reef on the eastern shore in a glass-bottomed boat.

In addition to the original population, the place swarms with Japanese, and the Americans seem little more than a ruling caste. The natives are reported to be entirely sophisticated, and quite competent to invent folk-tales or anything else to order. The Bishop Museum has an interesting collection of relics and models of the old civilisation, and we are much indebted to the Director, Dr. Brigham, for his kindness in exhibiting them to us. The principal treasures are the wonderful feather cloaks and helmets of the old chiefs. Fifty men were employed for a hundred years in collecting the yellow feathers from which one cloak is made. The birds, which produce only a few feathers each of the desired colour, were caught on branches smeared with gum.

There is also in the museum an excellent model of one " heiau," or temple; it is shown as a rectangular enclosure containing various sacred erections. This form of heiau has no resemblance either to the marae of Tahiti or the ahu of Easter Island; and the art of building never seems to have approached the excellence reached in the latter. Mr. Gordon, the British Consul, gave us much pleasure by taking us in his motor, accompanied by Dr. Brigham, to see the remains of one of these temples on the eastern side of the island.   Little now exists save a rough enclosing wall.   It is a matter of surprise that, under so enlightened a government as the American, more pains are not taken to preserve the archæological monuments throughout the islands, which are fast disappearing.   Much care is bestowed on attracting visitors, and it would have seemed, even from the financial point of view, that the protection of these objects of interest would have been eminently worth while.

We also visited the famous Pali, the site of a great battle at the time of the conquest of the island by Kamehameha, chief of Hawaii.   A range of mountains runs along the eastern side of the island.   The visitor, approaching from the west, rises gradually till he reaches the summit, and is then confronted by a sheer drop of many hundreds of feet down to the coast below.

The cliff extends for many miles, and the views over land and sea are most striking.   During the invasion, the Hawaiian army pursued the natives up the slope, and drove them headlong over the Pali, or precipice.   Kamehameha is the national hero ; when a statue was erected in Honolulu, to commemorate the centenary of the discovery of the island by Cook, it was dedicated, not to the navigator, but to the Hawaiian chief.

We were accorded an interview with the ex-queen Liliuokalani. It was a distinctly formal occasion.   We were shown into a waiting-room till some previous arrivals had finished their audience, and were then ceremoniously introduced to royalty. The room was furnished after European fashion, but was adorned with feather ornaments.   The old lady, who had a tattoo mark on her cheek, sat with quiet dignity in an arm-chair.   She was obviously frail, and though she spoke occasionally in good English, her secretary did most of the conversation.   She told us that her brother had caused certain native legends and songs to be written down, and she herself, during her imprisonment in 1895, had translated into English an Hawaiian account of the creation of the world.   The secretary presented us with a copy of this book.   We did not gather that either of them had ever heard of Easter Island.   After a short time we took our leave, curtseying again and backing out as we had seen done by our predecessors.   It may be remembered that Liliuokalani visited England at the time of Queen Victoria's Jubilee.   Since our return we have seen the announcement of her death ; so closes the list of the Hawaiian sovereigns.

Being in harbour brought the not unknown domestic excitements. The pugilistic American cook, who had been quite satisfactory on the voyage, proved to be one of those who cannot be in port without going " on the bust." He was rescued once, but he shortly afterwards asked for shore leave at 10 o'clock in the morning. This was naturally declined ; he then said he wanted to have a tooth out. S. assured him he was quite capable of officiating. Finding he could get neither leave, money, nor a boat, he sprang overboard, and swam ashore in his clothes. His place was taken by a Japanese cook from Honolulu.

Hawaii.—When the repairs to the engine had been accomplished, we sent the yacht ahead to San Francisco, and ourselves made a trip by steamer from the island of Oahu to that of Hawaii. Between the two lies the island of Molokai, on which is the leper settlement, connected with Father Damien's heroic work and death. We did not see the settlement itself, but from its photographs it seems an attractive collection of small houses, in the midst of wonderfully beautiful scenery.

The principal sight on Hawaii is the active crater of Kilauea. Instead of the long ride described by Lady Brassey, visitors, landing at the port of Hilo, are now conveyed in motors to a comfortable hotel, on the edge of the crater. We made a detour on the way to see a genuine native settlement, where the standard of living proved to be much the same as on Easter. The crater itself is a subsidiary one on the side of the great mountain, Mauna Loa ; it is 4,000 feet above sea-level, and has a circuit of nearly eight miles. The greater part of the crater is extinct, and its hardened lava can easily be walked over, but one portion is still active, and forms a boiling lake about a thousand feet across. No photograph gives any idea of the impressiveness of the scene, particularly after dark. The floor of the pit is paved with dark but iridescent lava, across which run irregular and ever-varying cracks of glowing gold. First one of these cracks, and then another, bubbles out into a roaring fire, the heat melts the adjacent lava, causing great dark masses to break off and slip into the furnace, where they are devoured by the flames. It is a fascinating spectacle which could be watched for hours. The floor of the pit rises and sinks; when we were there it was some hundreds of feet below the spectator.

Kilauea was considered in olden times to be the special abode of Pele, the goddess of fire; but after the advent of the missionaries, her power was formally defied by Kapiolani, the daughter of a chief who ate the berries consecrated to the deity on the brink of the pit. More than fifty years later, however, in 1880, there was so great an eruption of lava on the other side of Mauna Loa that native royalty had to beseech Pele to stifle her anger and save the people; a prayer which was, it is said, immediately effective.

We decided not to return to Hilo, but to see something more of the island, and catch the steamer at Kawaihae on the western side. We left the hotel at 8 a.m. and motored over a hundred miles, first passing through grass lands and cattle ranches, and then through sugar plantations. The way was diversified by extraordinary flows of lava, through which the road had been cleared : they extended for miles like a great sea ; one of the streams was as recent as 1907. The last stage of the drive was through forest growth and coffee plantations. We spent the night at a small hotel, kept by a lady. An interesting fellow-guest was a government entymologist, who was combating a parasite which was injuring the coffee ; to this end he had introduced an enemy beast of the same nature brought from Nigeria, which was successfully devouring its natural foe.

Below the hotel was the Bay of Kealekakua, which was the scene of the last great drama in the life of Cook. On its shore are the remains of the building where he was treated as the incarnation of the god Loro. It is now only a mass of stones, but is said to have been a truncated pyramid, which is an old form of heiau. On the top of this temple Cook was robed in red tapa, offered a hog, and otherwise worshipped. The conduct of the white men, however, was such that they soon lost the respect of the natives. An affray occurred over the stealing of one of the ship's boats, and Cook was stabbed in the back by one of the iron daggers which he had himself given in barter. An obelisk has been erected to his memory.

On the opposite side of the bay is a " puuhonua," or place of refuge, by name Honaunau. It corresponded with the cities of refuge in the Old Testament. " Hither," says Ellis, " the manslayer, the man who had broken a tabu, . . . the thief and even the murderer, fled from his incensed pursuer and was secure." [1] It covered seven acres, and was enclosed on the landward side by a massive wall 12 ft. high and 15 ft. thick.

In the afternoon we motored on to Waimea by a *cornice* road, which was bumpy beyond description. The hotel consisted of a few rooms behind the principal store. The next morning, on the way to the steamer, we inspected two heiau, a small one at the foot of a hill, and a large and striking one on its summit known as Puukohola. Tradition says that the hero Kamehameha set out to rebuild the former in order to secure success in war, but was told that, if he wished to be victorious, he must erect a temple instead on the higher altitude.

The temple, which adapts itself to the ground, rises on the seaward side by a series of great terraces and culminates on the summit in a levelled area paved with stones. On the landward side the building is enclosed by a great wall, on which stood innumerable wooden idols. It was entered by a narrow passage between high walls. On the area at the top were various sacred buildings, including a wicker tower, out of which the priest spoke, an altar, and certain houses, in one of which the king resided during periods of taboo. Whilst the temple was being built, even the great chiefs assisted in carrying stones, and the day it was completed (1791 *c.*) eleven men were sacrificed on the altar.[2] It is one of the latest, as it is one of the finest of the heiau. From the walls are magnificent views of the two great mountains of Hawaii, Mauna Kea and Mauna Loa, both over 13,000 ft.

It was interesting to recognise in the Hawaiian language not a few words similar to those which we had learnt on Easter Island. In Polynesian the letters K and T are practically interchangeable. Thus Mauna Kea, meaning Mount White, from its usual covering of snow, is equivalent to Maunga Tea-tea, the hill of white ash in Easter. The same is true of the letters L and R. Mauna Loa is Mount Long just as Hanga Roa is Bay Long. The identification of these last letters is not confined to Polynesia. We made one of the Akikuyu in East Africa repeat the same word over and over again, to see if it had the sound of L or R; he used first one and then the other

[1] *Polynesian Researches*, vol. iv. p. 167.　[2] *Thrum. Hawaiian Annual*, 1908.

without any discrimination. The names in Hawaii are said to exist in their present form simply according to the manner in which they have been crystallised in writing.

We duly caught our steamer to Honolulu, and changed there into the boat for San Francisco.

CALIFORNIA

Cortez, Governor of Mexico, was under the impression that America was in close proximity to Asia. Hearing of the success of Magellan in discovering a southern route to the westward, he sent an expedition to the north, with the object of finding a road to India in that direction. The members of this party, which was commanded by Cabrillo, were the first Europeans to discover California (1542). The native Indian population at that time is supposed to have been about seven hundred thousand in number.

For over two hundred years Spain took but little interest in the new country ; but in 1769 she began to be alarmed lest the Russians should descend on it from the north, and its occupation was ordered from Mexico. In this movement, not only was the secular power represented, but Catholic missions played an important part. The Franciscan order was first in the field ; and the mission station, which gave its name to the Bay of San Francisco, was dedicated in 1776. Later the Dominican order also founded religious establishments. These institutions were finally secularised in 1836, but Californians justly regard the remains as the most romantic as well as historic objects in the country.

A wave of immigrants from the United States began to arrive about 1841 ; war broke out with the parent country of Mexico in 1846 ; and in 1848 California was formally transferred to the States. The same year, 1848, the first discovery of gold caused an enormous inrush of population. The journey was no easy one ; for twenty years the would-be immigrant from the east had to choose between the dangerous expedition overland, the unhealthy condition of the Panama route, or a voyage round the Horn. The Pacific railway was at last completed in 1869.

The most dramatic event of recent years has been the earthquake of 1906, which was followed by a great fire, when for three days the city was a mass of flames.

We arrived at San Francisco on December 14th, 1915. The bay recalls in some degree that of Rio de Janeiro, the ocean has in the same way penetrated through a narrow channel into a low district surrounded by mountains and formed it into an inland sea. There, however, the resemblance stops. The Bay of San Francisco runs, for its major portion, parallel to the sea, and thus forms a peninsula on either side of the entrance, the well-known

Golden Gate. The tract on the southern side is sufficiently level to allow of the site of a town. The main frontage of the city is on the bay, but it extends to the seaward side. The population has also spread across the bay, and the suburbs have attained to the magnitude of towns. The large ferry boats which ply across the water are marked features of San Francisco life.

There was nothing in the present fine city to recall the fact that ten years before it had been laid low by the great fire, but any building dating back more than a score of years is treated with respectful interest. A professional guide, who escorts tourists in a motor char-à-bancs, solemnly stated that such and such houses were " in the style of thirty-five years ago," or that a church was " one hundred years old, but still used for service."

It is not, however, in such matters that the youth of California most strikes a visitor from an older country. Its inhabitants appear to him to resemble children who have discovered a new playground, and who are busily occupied in seeing what each can find there. They seem, with notable exceptions, to have little time to spare for those deeper studies and questionings which form part of life in lands where the earlier stage has long been passed. There are, no doubt, in the gay crowd many profound thinkers, numbers with unsatisfied longings and broken hearts, but they are not obvious in the general cheerful absorption as to how much everything costs and everybody is worth. The stranger also, however much theoretically prepared, experiences a shock in finding how little a population formed from manifold races has as yet amalgamated ; the owner of a shop, for instance, may not be able to speak even intelligibly the language of the country of his adoption. Depressing accounts were given of the type of man who thought it worth while to take up political life, and the consequent short-sightedness of some of the legislative measures. We were frankly told that we were much better off with our British monarchy, and once an American-born citizen was even heard to regret the War of Independence.

With regard to the Great War we were told that at that time ninety-five per cent. of the population of San Francisco were pro-Ally, though a few professors still looked to Germany as the home of culture. Conversation on the subject was definitely discouraged, and one man, who spoke to us for a few minutes concerning the struggle, ended by saying, " I have not talked so much about the war for months." It was naturally impossible to appreciate at so great a distance the feeling which pervaded Europe. A high authority, whom we consulted as to where we could see some Indian life, recommended us to go to a certain German mission and " ask for hospitality from the Fathers "; that we should prefer not to do so he obviously thought most narrow-minded. Affairs in Mexico where some Americans had just been killed by the insurgents were much more interesting. Even Japan and Australia appeared more closely connected with everyday life, and not only seemed nearer than Europe, but than the Eastern States themselves. So was brought home the truth of the saying that " oceans unite, not divide "; also that the Pacific and its seaboard are really an entity, however much the atlas may prefer to give a contrary impression. Later it was impossible to think without deep sympathy of this young community plunged whole-heartedly with all its fresh ardour and keen intelligence into the solemn crucible of war.

We received welcome help and hospitality from Mr. Ross, our Consul-General, Mr. Barneson, the Commodore of the leading yacht club, and other kind friends. Mr. Adamson, of Messrs. Balfour & Guthrie, a firm allied to our Chilean friends Williamson & Balfour, came opportunely to our assistance when the censor felt that a cabled draft from England was too dangerous a document to pass without many days of consideration.

We were naturally much interested in making the acquaintance of our anthropological confrères of the University of California, Dr. Waterman and Mr. Gifford, and in hearing of their important work among the surviving Indians. A luncheon party at the University buildings at Berkeley, one of the suburbs on the other side of the bay, was both pleasant and enlarging to the mind. It is a mixed university, with some five or six thousand students ; situated in beautiful surroundings and with an enviable library. One of the guests at luncheon was a German professor, who was at work in New Guinea when the war broke out ; the account runs that the British troops, hearing there was an expedition in the mountains, went there expecting to encounter an armed force. He was detained in California, unable to get home.

Christmas, the third since we left England, we spent in an hotel on the top of Mount Tamalpais, which is on the other side of the Golden Gate, and directly opposite to San Francisco. It is reached by a mountain railway, and gives most beautiful panoramic views of ocean, city, and bay. The management have hit on the ingenious plan of pointing out special sights, by placing tubes on the walks round the mountain, at the level of the eye, oriented on particular places and labelled accordingly. At night the scene is marvellous; the city appears as a blaze of illumination, and lights in every direction are reflected in the still water of the Bay. While on Mount Tamalpais we received a telephone message to say that *Mana* was coming through the Gate. She had taken two days less to do the distance from Honolulu than a four-masted barque which left about the same time. We could not get down before her arrival, so left Mr. Gillam to grapple with the usual officials; and not least with the reporters, seventeen of whom, he declared, came on board.

We had had our share of the representatives of the press, but any temptation to self-complacency would have been quenched by the knowledge that real success in newspaper paragraphs had already been achieved by the American cook who left in so summary a fashion at Honolulu. He had turned up from Hawaii and given out that he had been obliged to quit the yacht because he " could not stand a spook ship with skulls on board." Except by one Christian Science reporter, scientific research was considered dull, but this aspect of our work gave a hope of copy ; and we received a request, from more than one agency, that we would pose for moving pictures on the deck of the yacht exhibiting the said skulls to one another.

The Pitcairn Islanders almost rivalled the cook as objects of popular interest ; as the men had nothing to gain from notoriety, we fixed a modest sum to be given them by each reporter whom they saw ; as might perhaps have been foreseen, an interview then appeared without any such unnecessary preliminary as a previous conversation. Charles and Edwin told us that the life of a great city surpassed even their expectations, but it must be confessed that their most enthusiastic admiration was aroused by Charlie Chaplin as he appeared at the picture palaces.

The Exhibition was just over, and *Mana* was moored alongside the now deserted buildings, which even in their then condition were well worth seeing. We had understood that there would be no difficulty about our new cook, as he was not Chinese, and came from an American dependency, but he was forbidden by the authorities to go on shore. This ruling we had, of course, no means of enforcing ; and we found also that we were liable to a fine of over £100 if we could not produce him when we sailed. It was not encouraging to be told that there were plenty of people who would entice him away for a share in the fine, and it was a relief when *Mana* at length sailed having all her crew safely on board.

It had been arranged that I was to return home overland, in order to avoid the long hot voyage on the yacht, and to put in hand preliminary arrangements there. I left on January 16th, taking the more southerly route across the continent. A night was spent at Santa Barbara, to see the mission buildings which are in the hands of one of the two remaining San Franciscan communities. The Brother who acted as guide, and who was of Hungarian Polish descent, said that it had been instrumental in converting between 4,000 and 5,000 Indians. From Santa Barbara the route runs to Los Angeles, which forms a winter resort for various Central American millionaires. A detour was made to the Grand Canyon, which is perhaps more impressive than beautiful, and so to Washington. A happy time was spent in seeing the city, and being shown over the National Museum by Dr. Walter Hough. The objects brought from Easter by the *Mohican* naturally proved of the greatest interest. At New York the beautiful Natural History Museum excited admiration, and gratitude is owed for the kindness of Dr. Lowie. At that time we were considering the question whether, owing to war conditions, to lay up or sell *Mana* in New York. Nothing could have been kinder than the assistance given in my search for information by more friends than I can mention. It was finally, as will be seen, decided to bring her home. The crossing of the Atlantic in an American vessel was uneventful, and on Sunday, February 6th, 1916, I found myself, with an indescribable thrill, at home once more in the strange new England of time of war ; which was yet the dear familiar England for which her sons have found it worth while to fight and if need be to die.

PART IV

THE HOMEWARD VOYAGE —Continued

SAN FRANCISCO TO SOUTHAMPTON

By S. R.

CHAPTER XXII

SAN FRANCISCO TO PANAMA

Catching Turtle—The Island of Socorro and what we found there—
The tale of a Russian Finn—Quibo Island—Suffering of the
Natives from Elephantiasis—A Haul with the Seine.

ON the 20th of January, 1916, we left the harbour of San Francisco, and proceeded to get well clear of the land, as the glass
told us to expect a blow : and in due course it came—and plenty
of it. We hove-to for twenty-four hours, with oil bags to wind-
'ard, for the seas were high and untrue. The weather then
moderated, so we let draw, and put her on her course, and were
soon in a more pleasant climate.

The Panama Canal had been closed to all traffic for many
months past, in consequence of land-slides. Of course *Mana*,
drawing but 11 feet, and only 72 feet on the waterline, would
experience no difficulty in passing, if the Administration would
permit her to do so. But would it ? We had been unable to
discover, through any source in San Francisco, whether we
should, or should not, be allowed to traverse the Canal. The
only course left open to us was to go to the Isthmus and see
what could be done on the spot : if we could not get through we
must continue onwards to the S'uth'ard, and go round the Horn.
Mr. Gillam and the Owner were quite keen on doing so. Mr.
Gillam thought it was only fair to the vessel "to give her a
chance of showing what a good little ship she was." The crew,
however, said they were quite satisfied on that point, and after
three years of it, sighed only for Britain, Beer, and Beauty. So
firmly were they convinced that our plucky Sailing-master would
take her round the Horn, just for the sake of doing so, should he
chance to come back alone without the Owner, that, when they
signed on again at Tahiti for the voyage home, it was subject
to the proviso that the outside passage round Cape Horn should
not be taken without their consent.

335

So, from the so-called Golden Gate of San Francisco town, to the real Balboa gate of the Panama Canal, sailed we in the pious hope that something would turn up in our favour, and believing that it would do so, for *Mana* is a " lucky ship." And of course that " something " did : but other events, not devoid of interest, intervene and demand recital.

At this point political conditions must be referred to for the due understanding of our story. Absurd though it be, the fact remains that, just as England meekly allows herself to be bamboozled, robbed, insulted, and defied by one petty *san-culotte* province, so do the United States submit to like treatment from Mexico : the same small δ that represents mathematically the consideration in which an Irishman holds the British Government, may be said equally to symbolise the degree of respect in which the American Eagle is held by the patriots of Mexico. Therefore, argued we, as the noble Mexican does not hesitate to pluck the Eagle, whenever that fowl comes hopping on his ground, still less will he refrain from depilating the Lion, should he want some fur for fly-tying. No, we will give the coast of Mexico a good berth. A vessel like the *Mana* would, at the moment, have been an invaluable capture for the " patriots," whose acquaintance we had no wish to cultivate. We thought of the many-oared row-boats of the Riff coast, and how they could come at speed over the smooth windless sea and board us on either quarter. Of course our motor would have been in our favour, but, all the same, discretion was perhaps better than valour, as we were unarmed. So we decided to keep 200 miles off the land in working down the coast of Lower California and Mexico, though it would have been better navigation, and more interesting, to have come close in.

The climate was now delightful : smooth water : gentle fair breezes. These conditions enabled us to capture all the turtle, and more than all, we wanted. They were asleep at the surface : the sea like glass, and heaving rhythmically. The undulations of a sea like this are so long, and wide, and gentle, that one somehow ceases to regard them as waves, and thinks of the movement of the water immediately around the craft as being only a local pulsation.

We had noticed, from time to time, isolated seagulls heaving into sight on the top of the swell. Sometimes there would be as many as three or four within calling distance from one another. Each seemed to stand on a separate piece of drift-wood, never two on the same piece. Some seemed occupied with affairs, swearing all the time, as seagulls always do ; some stood silently on one leg, " a-staring into wacancy " and thinking on their past. Some preened and oiled their feathers. We could not understand why there should be drift-wood, all small, and all over the place like this, so bore down on a sleeping bird, when, to our great surprise, we found that his resting-place was the back of one of Nature's U-boats—a turtle. Some may think then that all we had to do, if we wanted a turtle, was to approach a resting bird, but not a bit of it. If the bird, for reasons of his own, flew away from the back of the turtle, the turtle remained as before, nor did he ever seem to draw the line at the profanity with which his visitor argued some point with the nearest neighbours, but let a boat approach, however gently and innocently, and the gull decide to clear, because he did not like the look of it—even as the bird did so, did Master Turtle down with his head and up with his heels, and where he had been, he was not ; without a splash, or a swirl, or a bubble. If any fail to understand this description, he should betake himself to Africa and stalk rhino in high grass whilst they have their red-billed birds in attendance scrambling all over the huge bodies hunting for ticks. Let but one bird spring up suddenly in alarm from a rhino's back, forthwith will occur proceedings that shall not fail to leave a lasting impression on the observer.

When we wanted a turtle, however, we went to work in this way. The little 12 ft. dinghy, having two thwarts and a stern-seat, was lowered from the starboard quarter and towed astern. A sharp look-out was kept ahead, and to leu'ard, for a turtle asleep on the surface. On one being sighted, the vessel was run off towards it. Simultaneously the dinghy was hauled up alongside, and two of us, barefooted, dropped into her : she was then passed astern again and towed. One man sat in the stern sheets and steered with a paddle, having handy a strong gaff hook lashed on the end of the staff of a six-foot boat-hook : the oarsman occupied the for'ard thwart with his paddles shipped in the rowlocks. The leather of the oars had been well greased previously, so as to make no sound. The dinghy silently sped after the ship. On the vessel arriving within some 50 yards of

22

the turtle, an arm on the quarter deck was waved : the dinghy
slipped her tow line, the ship's helm was put up, and she edged-off
to leu'ard away from the fish, whilst the dinghy continued,
under the way she carried, on the line of the vessel's former
course, and therefore straight towards the turtle.   On the sitter
catching sight of the fish, if the boat was carrying sufficient way
to bring him up to it, he laid`aside the steering oar, and at the
right moment made a sign to his mate, who then gently dipped
one of his paddles in the water.   The boat in consequence made
half a rotation, coming stern-on to the turtle, instead of bows-on
as previously.   The oarsman then saw the fish for the first time
and commenced to back her down with gentle touches of his
two paddles right on to the top of the fish.   Meanwhile the sitter
slid off the after seat, turned himself round so as to face the
stern and knelt on the bottom of the boat with his knees placed
well under the after seat, his chest resting on the transom, his
arm outstretched over the water, rigidly holding the gaff extended like a bumpkin, with the point of the hook directed
downwards towards the water, and about two inches above its
surface.

Now the old turtle is roosting on the water with the edges of
his shell just awash, his dome-shaped back rising just clear of
it, and his head hanging downwards in order that he may keep
his brains cool.   At the opposite end to his head is his tail.
This detail may seem unnecessary.   But it is not so.   It is an
essential point.   When a turtle is surprised he does not express
it by throwing himself backward head uppermost on to his tail,
and show his white waistcoat, and wave his arms in depreciation
of the interview, but he downs with his head and ups with his
heels and the tip of his tail, if you are able to recognise it, is the
last you see of Master Turtle.   And when he acts thus he shows
much decision of character : there is no hesitation : in a moment
of time he is absent.   Hence, when you approach a turtle, you
must first decide where away lies his tail, and so place your craft
that her keel, and the turtle's spine, shall lie in the same straight
line.   Then, as she is backed stern foremost towards him, the
staff of the gaff is brought, by the movement of the boat, immediately above the length of his back.   Now for it !   the fisherman suddenly thrusts the gaff from him till the point of the
hook is beyond the rim of the shell : raises his hand the least

trifle, so as to depress the hook slightly, then savagely snatches the gaff backward, at the same time shortening his grasp on the shaft. The turtle awakes from his dreams to find that he is in a position in which he is helpless—standing on his tail, with his back against the boat's transome, and his fore flippers out of water. But he is not given time to think. As his back touches the flat end of the boat, the fisherman springs from his knees to his feet and, with one lusty heave, hoicks Uncle up on to the edge of the transome and balances him there for the moment. Down goes the stern of the little boat, well towards water level under the combined weight of man and fish. Then the slightest further pull, and into the bottom of the dinghy the turtle slides with a crash, whilst the fisherman, whose only thought now is for the safety of his toes, gracefully sinks down upon the middle thwart, takes hold of the gunnel with either hand, and hangs one bare leg overboard to starboard, and the other to port, until the turtle has decided in which part of the boat he proposes permanently to place his head. Slowly he opens and closes his bill, shaped like the forceps of a dentist, and slowly he blinks his eyne, as much as to say, "Just put a foot in my neighbourhood or even one big toe." Turtles have no charity.

The turtle and the fisherman have engrossed one another's attention so far, but there are three other elements in the equation; they are (a) the boat, (b) the boatman, and (c) the shark. Each of these requires a word in passing. Now a 12 ft. dinghy, like any other of God's creatures, has feelings : these it expresses amongst other ways, when treated unreasonably, by capsizing, and turtle catching it puts in the neighbourhood of the limit. Not infrequently it happens that the long black fin of a San Francisco pilot comes mouching around at a turtle hunt, as if to incite the long-suffering dinghy to show temper. Hence it is sometimes quite interesting to view, from the ship, the sympathetic way in which the oarsman exerts himself to humour every whim of the little boat, in order to induce it to maintain its centre of gravity during the scrimmage. He quite seems to have the idea in his head that, with the shark assisting at the ceremony, a capsize would be anything but a joke for him. Anyhow, it is all right this time, so we make for the vessel, now gently rising high on the top of the swell, anon slowly sinking until only her vane is visible.

" Lee-Oh ! " Round she comes. " Let the staysail bide ! "

As she loses her way the dinghy shoots up towards her, a line comes flying in straightening coils from the bows of the ship and falls, with a whack, across the dinghy's nose. The oarsman claps a turn with it around the for'ard thwart, and quickly gets his weight out of her bows, by shifting to the middle thwart, before the strain comes. At the same time the fisherman nips aft, whilst keeping an eye on Master Turtle's jaws, squats on the after seat, picks up an oar and sheers her in towards the ship. Then a strop falls into the sternsheets : the oarsman slips it over a hind flipper, one of the dinghy's falls is swayed to him, he hooks it into the strop, and up runs Baba Turtle, to be swung inboard the next moment into the arms of the Japanese cook, who receives him with a Japanese smile as he bares his sniggery-snee.

We had now been more than a fortnight at sea. After a run of this length we generally found it well to touch somewhere to refresh. The chart showed ahead of us the Island of Socorro which we could fetch by edging off a little. The Sailing Directions told us it was uninhabited, and rarely visited : that there was no fresh water on it, but nevertheless that sheep and goats were to be found, and that landing was possible. The early morning of February the 5th showed its single lofty peak standing out clearly above the lower mist, and in a line with our bowsprit, whilst a light breeze on our quarter made us raise it fairly fast. In the chart room we pored over the only chart we had, a small-scale one, using it for what it was worth to elucidate the Sailing Directions. These indicated an anchorage and landing-place on its south-western side : poor, but possible : and no outlying dangers. We therefore decided to examine that coast, and see what we could find in the way of anchorage and landing facilities. At the same time the conversation turned on the apparent excellence of the place as a gun-running depot for the Mexican Revolutionaries, and the exceeding awkwardness of our position if we suddenly shoved our nose into any such hornets' nest. The pow-wow finished, up the ladder we tumbled on to the quarter-deck, and turned to the island, and lo ! round a point was emerging a something—first appearing as a boat with bare masts—then as a boat with sails—she has presumably come out under oars and is now getting the canvas on her. She has seen us making for the island and is clearing out ! They are at the game, then, after all! Now she grows into a vessel under canvas: now she fades away. No ship had we seen since getting well clear of San Francisco. We could make nothing of her in the haze and the mirage, for the air was all a-quiver with the heat. The general opinion seemed to be that she was a small schooner sailing with her arms akimbo, which, with the wind as we had it, was impossible. Anyhow she was approaching us rapidly in the teeth of the wind—goose-winged; but anything seems to our mariners possible " in these 'ere fur'rin parts." But alas for Romance! Gradually she revealed herself through the haze as a tramp steamer with a high deck cargo. Her black hull and black-painted mast tops, as she opened the land and partly showed her length, had made her the small boat with bare pole masts: afterwards, when she shifted her helm and came towards us bows on, she became the small schooner running before a fair wind off the land—her light-coloured deck cargo, high built up, and white-painted bridge formed the goose's wings extended on either side of the black masts, that rose above them, and stood out distinctly against the sky. We kept our course. She passed us close to starboard. We ran up our ensign and number and asked her to report us, but she took no notice. Only one man was seen aboard her. We thought at the time she was from the Canal, but afterwards learnt that nothing had come through it for some months, also that a somewhat similar vessel had, in May last, lain for a month off Socorro to . . . . . . admire the Scenery.

We closed with the land, at its western extremity, about 3 p.m., and then slowly ranged along the south-western shore, examining it carefully with the glasses for indications of a landing-place. The water was smooth and crystal-clear, and the sun behind us, so that, comfortably ensconced in the fore-top, we could see well ahead in the line of the ship's progress, and to a great depth. We were able therefore, without risk, to hug the shore, and to examine it with precision. Everywhere was the same low cliff: on its top, scrubby vegetation with a sheen like the foliage of the olive—(sage bush). Immediately below this a broad scarlet band—(disintegrated lava)—then a greyish red, or black, cliff wall of igneous rock—at its foot a snow white girdle of foam from the ocean swell dashing against it.

So we progressed, until we reached what we decided must be

Braithwaite Bay, at the S.W. corner of the island.   The Sailing
Directions gave this as the only anchorage.   Mr. Gillam jumped
into the dinghy and pulled in to examine it, whilst we followed
her in very slowly with the ship.   A couple of whales seemed to
find the floor of the bay quite to their taste as a dressing-room.
The huge fellows quietly spouted and wallowed, " a-cleaning of
themselves," and took no notice of us.   The dinghy did not like
the look of things for either landing or anchorage, so held up an
oar.   Thereupon we put the ship round, and went out on the
same track as that on which we had entered.   Nightfall was now
approaching.   We picked up the dinghy and stood off a bit,
and then hove-to.

Now, immediately before reaching Braithwaite Bay, we had
noticed in the coast-line, from the mast-head, an indentation or
small inlet, across which there was no line of breakers.   Also we
had observed a remarkable white patch set deeply into the land
apparently at the head of this indentation.   Of these points
presently.   During the night, whilst hove to some distance off,
the watch picked up a beautifully modelled painted and weighted
decoy duck, with the initials " H. T." cut into it.   This wooden
fowl, we concluded, had drifted down from San Francisco, for
there they are largely used in duck shooting.   It had broken
its anchoring line, been swept through the Golden Gate, and
then by the prevailing winds and currents carried to the point
where we had picked it up.   The find was interesting as showing
that our navigation was correctly based for current.

With the daylight we again stood in, this time towards the
inlet, and after an early breakfast, the cutter was swung out.
A breaker of water, a cooking-pot or two, a watertight box of
food, another containing ammunition, the photographic and
botanical outfits, and a Mauser rifle in its water-tight bag, were
put into her and, with five hands, we started off.

As we approached the break in the cliffs we again met our
two friends of yesterday—the whales.   They had shifted their
ground and were now right in the entrance to the cove, so we
had to lay on our oars for quite a while, until they gradually
moved away.   It was most interesting to watch the great brutes
comparatively close alongside, yet absolutely indifferent to, or
unaware of, the boat's presence.   Certainly we kept quiet, and
did not allow objects in the boat to rattle or roll.   Sound waves

are transmitted through the water just as they are through the air. Each of these fish would have been worth £1,000 at least at pre-war prices. " Life is full of vain regrets."

Our break in the cliff proved the entrance to a fissure in the land-mass comparatively far extending. On either hand it had nearly vertical cliff walls, and these again had steep ground above and behind them. It had a regular, gradually rising bottom, deep water at the entrance, and at the head a shelving beach of sand and small stones, yet steep-to enough to allow the cutter to float with only her nose aground. Not a trace of swell : an ideal boat harbour. As it had no name, and is to-day undefined in the Admiralty plan of Braithwaite Bay (cf. inset on Chart No. 1936), we christened it Cruising Club Cove—dropping the " Royal " for the gain of alliteration.

As we lay off the entrance, waiting for the whales to shift, many, and varied, were our speculations as to what the white object, previously referred to as situated at the head of the cove, could possibly be. Not till we were close up did we make it out. It then proved to be a red-painted boat, covered with a white sail. Now a dry torrent bed forms the head of our little fiord. The detritus brought down by the torrent is spread out as a small, flat, channel-cut plain, that meets the sea with a fan-shaped border. On to this flat the mystery boat was hauled up, but only to just above high-water mark. Close to her side was a grave with wooden cross. From her bows hung a bottle closed with a wooden plug and sealed with red paint. Keenly interested in it all we disturbed nothing, so that we might the better be able to piece together the evidence, after gathering all we could. She was evidently laid up : practically new : amateur built : her material new deal house-flooring boards : flat-bottomed : sharp at both ends (dory type). Left as she was, the surf of the first gale from the South would lift her. They must have been either weak handed to leave her close to the water's edge like that, or else they had been in a great hurry to get away. No painter and anchor was laid out to prevent her floating off : no seaman would leave a boat thus unsecured. (For there was cordage in her.) Her sail was cut out of an old sail of heavy canvas belonging to some big ship. They had ship's stores to draw upon.

Casting around, we soon found a track running through the

sage-bush scrub. Following this trail for a few yards, we came to a large flat-topped rock beside which it ran. On this rock stood conspicuously another bottle—sealed. The path now began to rise sharply, wending betwixt large rock masses : then it suddenly terminated in a rift in the cliff face, which formed a high, but shallow, cave or grotto. Rough plank seats and bunks were rigged up around, fitted under or betwixt the great rocks, some berths being made more snug by having screens of worn canvas. In the middle of the floor was a table, and in the middle of the table stood a sealed bottle and a box. The box was a small, square, round-cornered, highly ornamented biscuit-tin of American make : it was three parts full of loose salt, bone dry, and on the top of the salt was a wooden box of matches, bone dry and striking immediately. We emptied the salt on to the table—nothing amidst it : we broke the bottle and we found in it a scrap of paper. On this was written in ink, a surname, the day of the month and year, the full initials of the writer and these words, " Look at our Post Office here." [1] We then returned to the flat rock and broke that bottle—the message was the same; then to the boat, to find the message in its bottle was identical in terms, but written in pencil.

" *Look at our Post Office* "—But where was the Post Office ? or what was the Post Office ? The fragments of the broken bottle lay glittering on the grave at our feet. Was the grave the Post Office ?

We had most carefully examined and sounded the cave, and, after our long experience of this class of work on Easter Island, felt fairly satisfied that the Post Office was not there. Every fire site we had suspected and inspected : every sinkage of the surface. Now we had to decide about the grave. The character of the vegetation showed that it was old, and had not been disturbed within the date stated on the letters. A Spanish inscription in customary form, cut very neatly into the arms of the wooden cross, gave simply the name of the dead man, and the date. At one time the cross had been painted black. The point however that determined us to accept the burial as *bona fide*, and not to exhume it as a possible cache, was the fact that the sharp edges of the carving of the inscription were smoothly

---

[1] We had intended to reproduce this note in facsimile, but subsequent events have led us to think that to do so might cause danger to its writer.

rasped away by the driving sand of the shore, in the direction of the prevailing wind, and to a degree commensurate with the date incised. And we were right in our surmises. Sufficient now to say that he whom the writing told to go to the Post Office, was already lying in his own grave elsewhere, with his boots on, and no cross at his head. Life is held cheap in Mexico.

The island is said to possess no fresh water. We found no provision made in the cave for conserving a supply. Scrambling through the sage-bush we made for the dry torrent. Here we found one of the channels had been diverted, and in it sunk a well or shaft, some ten feet deep, with fine soil at its bottom. The end of a rope just showed for about one foot above the surface of the silt at the bottom of the shaft. Near by was a rough cradle and makeshift gear for gold washing. They had been here during the rains, and the torrent had supplied the washing water. Thinking of a possible sealed bottle placed in the shaft bucket at the end of the rope, we left two hands there with orders to follow the rope carefully down to its termination and see what was on the end of it. The cutter with two hands we sent back to the ship.

We and one hand—a Russian Finn who had been for some years on the Alaska Coast—then set off inland to see what the world was like, and to get a sheep if possible. By this time the heat had become very great. The soil—yellow volcanic ash— soaked up the sun's rays and then threw the heat back as would a hot brick. Everything was so dry that we marvelled that vegetation could hold its own. We saw no form of grass, but the surface was generally covered with sage-bush extending from the level of the knee in general to above one's head in the bottoms. We had scrambled up the ravine from our pirates' cave and up the steep ground around it. We now found ourselves on a well-defined ridge that ran parallel to the sea, with a breeze, though a hot one, in our faces, and a glorious view of sea, coast-line, and mountain. Our whales were clearly visible far away in the bight to the west'ard, whilst to the nor'ard lay the great mass of an unnamed volcano, with its top lost in mists, its sides sweeping downwards, with typical curvature, till they reach the sea. We gave the mountain the name of Mount Mana. It is 3,707 ft. high. Much information about it will appear some day.

Between the ridge on which we now stood, and the well-defined foot of Mount Mana opposite to us, was a valley some half a mile wide. We made our way across this valley as far as the mountain's foot, in order to cut across any tracks, human or ovine, that might pass down it, because they would tell us the news, like a file of newspapers—for all movement on the island would pass along this bottom. Here the sage-bush was very strong and high, and we found it difficult to get through. It frequently was tunnelled where it was thick, reminding one of hippo paths leading to the water. In the present case, however, bits of the fleeces of the makers were clinging to the sides of the tunnel. The only signs of man were the brass shell of an exploded military cartridge, and a few heads and horns of sheep lying where the beasts had been shot. Here and there along the course of the valley, masses of black volcanic rock, bare of vegetation, rose above the bright yellow soil and its sage-bush covering. The surface of the plain and of the mountain's base were also punctuated by isolated specimens of a species of fig (*ficus cotinifolia*) having a dark green fleshy leaf somewhat like that of the magnolia, and a number of separate trunks or stems. These trees, like all else, were dwarf and stunted, and about 15 feet high. Every tree formed a flattish roof, as it were, supported on many pillars and impervious to the sun. It was delightful to rest for a short while under each as we came to it for a brief respite from the shimmering heat. Beneath them the ground was bare and smooth. The sheep tracks and tunnels led from tree to tree, and it was evident that the sheep made it their practice to rest on these shady spots, during the heat of the day. Whilst so resting ourselves, we were amused and interested by several little birds of different sorts. They chummed up en route, and kept close to us wherever we went, flitting from bush to bush, and when we sat down in the shade, sidled along the branches till they got as close to us as they could, short of absolutely alighting upon us. They acted just as native children do towards the white man when they have got over their first shyness. Working up wind, we soon found sheep; they were in small bunches varying from three to perhaps a dozen. We got a couple, though both getting up to the game and the shooting was difficult in such cover, and resolved itself into snap-shots as they followed their tracks across the occasional isolated masses of dark basalt that rose above the yellow soil and which supported no vegetation.

Having gralloched our victims and slung the carcases well up on to our shoulders, with both breast strap and brow strap, Micmac fashion, we started back for Cruising Club Cove. It was now about noon, and as a direct line seemed feasible, we decided to take that line. The better road along the sheep tracks, and therefore through their tunnels, along the bottom of the valley, was impossible for a laden man. We did it! Across the valley, often brought to a standstill by scrub that would not yield when leant against. Up the hill side to its delusive gap, often on hands and knees. Down the steep pitch on the other side, with bump and crash, regardless of scratches, thinking only of how to avoid a broken leg or twisted ankle. Then a final wrestle with scrub in the ravine bottom and we were on the shore. What a relief to throw up that brow strap for the last time and to let the mutton fall, with a thump, on the stones! Then off with what remained of our clothes, with which we draped the bushes to dry, and into the tepid shallow water, shallow for fear of sharks. Orders were given that whilst bathing a good fire of scrub wood should be made on a spot sheltered from the sun by the side of a lofty rock. On that fire's glowing cinders when nearly burnt out we presently grilled kidneys of peculiar excellence, and boiled the billy, and thanked the Immortal Gods.

The examination of the dry shaft, which was the job of the two hands left behind, was never made. They reported that soon after beginning work the side of the shaft fell in. On looking at it, it was clear that we could not now do anything there. So we hunted around again, collecting seeds, and plants, and rock samples. Presently, amongst the drift material at storm high-water mark, we came across a cube of wood 12 or 15 inches square: (the end of a baulk of timber sawn off): through it was bored an auger hole, and a rope rove. The end of the rope passed through the block was finished with a " Stopper " knot, a knot known only to seamen. Its other end had one long single strand that had been *broken*: the other two strands were shorter than the first by some two feet. They had been *cut through*. The story was clear. We only wanted a name, and—*mirabile dictu*—we have it. Turning over the block, on one face is deeply cut in letters some three inches long the words ANNIE LARSEN.   Pussy is out of the bag !

For the benefit of those who are not shippy yachty devils, we will now explain.   When you drop your anchor at any spot where the nature of the bottom is such that you may, perhaps, not be able to lift it again by heaving on the chain in the ordinary way, because the anchor has fallen amongst rocks, or into some mermaid's coral cave, under such circumstances it is customary to fasten one end of a rope to the end of the anchor opposite to that to which the chain is attached (*i.e.* to the crown), and to the other end of the rope you make fast a buoy—you " buoy your anchor."   Then, " when the sour moment comes " to take a heave, and you have heaved in vain, you pick up your anchor buoy, and haul on its rope, and up comes your anchor without a struggle, like Cleopatra's red herring.

Our find told us that it belonged to a ship of moderate size, for her anchor was of moderate weight, because the anchor rope was of moderate strength ; and that that ship was probably a sailing ship, because she had no steam winch : for steamers don't usually buoy, having immense steam heaving power.   She had not intentionally left it ; the rope had had two strands cut through by the sharp rocks of the bottom, then the third strand had torn apart from strain, and the buoy, with its short length of rope, drifted away, to be ultimately thrown up above ordinary high-water mark during a gale.   Like the duck, it might have come down from San Francisco !   Not so.   The two cut strands had not been long in the water after they had been cut before they were thrown up high and dry.

It was very compromising for Annie.   Of course we immediately asked, "Anyone know the *Annie Larsen*?"   The Russian Finn, naturally *au courant* with all the coast scandal after a month in San Francisco, was immediately able to inform us that the *Annie Larsen* was an American schooner of about 300 tons, and was in the Mexican gun-running line till captured so laden by a U.S.A. ship of war only a month ago whilst we were at San Francisco.

So we had got to the bottom of things after all, though we had failed to find the Post Office !   Socorro Island was the depot for the late Yankee gun runner *Annie Larsen*: the special, little-used boat was for shipping, not for landing, the stuff: the

Mexicans had come and fetched it away in their own craft as they got the chance. Some of the *Annie Larsen* crowd, being old Alaska hands, had prospected the ravine for gold, Alaska fashion. It was not a case of ship-wrecked men on a waterless island.

The afternoon was now getting late : *Mana* stood boldly in close to the entrance of the cove. She lowered her cutter, the shore party were soon on board again, and at 5.35 p.m. (6.2.16) we bore away for Hicaron Island at the entrance to the Gulf of Panama, S. 69° E., distant 1,834 miles. As we watched the island fade in the dusk, we thought we had done with Socorro for ever ; but it was not thus written. Some six months after our visit a man was arrested at Singapore as a spy, and there detained in prison. That man was the writer of the message in the bottle. In prison he chanced to get hold of a piece of a local newspaper, and that particular number happened to have in it an account of the voyage of *Mana* taken from the London papers. It incidentally mentioned that she had touched at Socorro. A ship then had been to his island ! What had we found ? How much did we know ? *Had we found the Post Office ?* On release he made his way to England to find out. But now is not the time to tell the story : we are bound for Panama, or for Cape Horn—for better or for worse—for heat or for cold. Chance, however, at this time, all unknown to us, had decided our fate.

The rainy season was now approaching, and we even got an occasional warning shower, which made us all the more anxious to reach the Isthmus, and get clear of it, before its unhealthy season set in. But our progress was slow : we could not run the main engine continuously, as we only had a small supply of lubricating oil adapted to the great heat. That with which we had been supplied at San Francisco proved useless. Also we had long before unwisely sent back to England the light canvas and all its gear, in order to get more stowage room. In doing so we thought we would be able to run the ship under power in light airs, and therefore would not want it : 'twas an error. However, we always made something, for if she did not do her 50 miles in the 24 hours, we unmuzzled the motor.

Our engineer, Eduardo Silva of Talcahuano, a Chilean, was a most excellent young fellow : always keen and willing : always grooming his three charges, the engines of the yacht, the life boat, and the electric light, and ever ready to run them, despite the terrible heat in the engine-room. Sometimes when the big 38 h.p. motor had a fit of the tantrums, because it could not get cold water from the sea quickly enough to assuage its body's heat, and he durst not leave it, he would eventually appear on deck, as pale as a sheet, and completely done. On one such occasion he reflectively remarked, as the two of us looked down into the engine-room from the deck, "All same casa del diablo." [1] He did not exaggerate.

Day followed day. We gradually gnawed into our 1,834 miles. The Russian Finn came to the fore as a keen sportsman: from tea-time to dusk he was generally to be found somewhere outside the vessel's bows: sometimes on the bowsprit end, sometimes standing on the bob-stay, regardless of the fact that a shark was very frequently in attendance on us in the eddy water under our counter. Looking over the taffrail you could see the brute weaving from side to side as does a plum-pudding carriage dog at his horses' heels. One experienced a sort of fascination in watching these great fish at night, their every movement displayed by the luminosity of the water, until they themselves, on occasion, seemed to glow with the phosphoric light. *Mana* in these waters generally had shoals or companies of small fish in attendance on her, amongst which were always a few larger ones. We got to know individuals by sight. We thought they kept to her for protection. It certainly was not for what they could get off her copper. With that we never had any trouble: it kept as bright as gold.

One night we were asleep on the locker in the deckhouse companion, and were awakened by an unholy struggle and crash. Nipping out, we found the Russian on lookout for'ard, regardless of the sleepers below him, had leant over her bows and had actually hoiked out with a gaff-hook a large porpoise. It seemed impossible to believe that a man could have had the physical strength to hoist such a mass bodily out of the water, up her high bow, and over the rail. He seems to have fairly lifted it out, by the scruff of its neck, as it rushed alongside after the fish.

He only fell overboard once: that was on the voyage from the Sandwich Islands, when we were not aboard. On reaching

[1] Casa = Sp. house.

San Francisco he brought a note from Mr. Gillam to us at our hotel to report arrival. We of course inquired as to their voyage. The Russian said it had been quite the usual thing : nothing had happened out of the common. Long afterwards he casually informed us that on that run, when he went forward one night from the quarter-deck to the galley to make the coffee for the change of watch at midnight, he went first to do some job on the top-gallant-fo'c's'le head, and got knocked overboard. En route to the land of never-never he found the weather jib-sheet in his hand, and by it was able to haul himself aboard again. As he was supposed to be in the galley, he would never have been expected to show for half an hour, and therefore would not have been missed until the watch mustered. It did not seem to occur to him that he had had a bit of a squeak. He did not get wet, so nobody knew, for he told no one. As an angel, perhaps there was a certain amount of black down underneath his white plumage, but as an A.B. one wished for no better. He was the second of *Mana's* company to be killed by the Huns after our return.

After heaving-to like this, to let the reader into some of the little humours of our domestic life, we must get under way again. Well, everybody seemed quite happy and contented " on this 'ere run " : fish, birds, weird ocean currents and their slack water areas with accumulated drift, sailmending, turning out and painting the fo'c's'le, with life on deck, instead of below, for a few days, a threatened blow that never reached us, but only sent along its swell to justify the actions of the glass, and the ever-varying incidents associated with life on a small craft in unfrequented tropical seas, for we never saw another sail, made us so forgetful of the flight of time, that it seemed that we had but left Socorro, before we found ourselves off Hicaron Island, our prearranged landfall. Thirty-one days had faded away like a dream (map, facing p. 359).

Now, close to the Island of Hicaron lies another one much larger. We had a plan of it, Coiba or Quibo Island. The Sailing Directions said " turtles abound, but they are hard to catch." (We didn't want any more turtle !) " Crabs, cockles, and oysters are plentiful. In the woods monkeys and parrots abound, and in Anson's time, 1741, there were deer, but the interior is nearly inaccessible, from the steepness of the cliffs and the tangled vegetation : explorers should beware of alligators and snakes." The chart showed an excellent anchorage and indicated fresh water. It seemed promising : we would see what it was like. We were particularly desirous of now making good our expenditure of water, as we did not know what were the conditions we might find prevailing at Panama both as regards its quality and the facilities for getting it.

We had sighted Hicaron Island at daylight on Monday, the 6th of March, 1916, but calms, baffling airs, and currents prevented our making our proposed anchorage by daylight. At dusk, therefore, we hove to for the night. *Festina lentiter* was ever our motto. We had the most recent chart certainly, but its last correction was in 1865 and coral patches grow quickly. Not until noon next day did we get abreast of Negada Point, the S.E. extremity of Quibo Island. As the coast was charted free from dangers, we came fairly close in, and starting the motor about one o'clock, ran along the shore under power, with a look-out in the fore-top.

It was very interesting and pleasant, after a month at sea, thus to coast along the fringe of a tropical island : sweeping round rocky points of the land, and peeping into lovely little coves fringed with white coral sand that merged into a dense tropical vegetation, with hills in the background. It soon becomes instinctive to keep the sharpest of look-outs ahead, *i.e.* into the clear water, for a change of colour indicating danger, and yet to see everything around. The most memorable feature of this particular afternoon was the large number of devil-fish that were seen springing into the air : as many as three or four might be observed within as many minutes. Suddenly, near or far, a large object, like a white-painted notice-board, shot vertically into the air to considerable height, to fall back again on its flat with resounding spank and high-flying spray, leaving a patch of milky foam on the smooth blue surface of the water. In British seas this family of fishes is represented by the skate. Here they attain the dimensions of a fair-sized room : a specimen in the British Museum from Jamaica measures 15 ft. by 15 ft. and is between three and four feet thick, hence the statement that " their capture is uncertain and sometimes attended with danger " [1] is probably not far from correct. Perched aloft,

[1] Cf. *Ency. Brit. Edn.* 1911, Vol. xxiii., p. 930, Article RAY.

and thus having a large and unobstructed horizon, we saw one jump probably every ten minutes throughout the afternoon. The motor brought us to our anchorage, and at 5 o'clock we let go in 9 fathoms, sand and mud, the shore distant about 1½ miles.

We had seen hitherto no sign of the island being occupied, nor did we now. After dark, however, at two widely separated points, a fire blazed up and lights showed for a short while. Smoking on deck, when dinner was finished, we speculated as to the meaning of the different mysterious grunts and gurgles, sighs and plunges, that stole over the tepid oily water: the tropical sea after dark seemed to have voices as many and varied as the tropical forest has when the sun is gone. From 6 p.m. onward the thermometer read 87° F.: at 6 a.m. it had fallen to 83°—the cool of the morning!

With the daylight a single pirogue, with two men in her, came alongside. She was a small and roughly made dug-out, very leaky. In the wet of her bottom lay a bunch of bananas, perched on which were a couple of large macaws. Each of these had a strip of bark some two feet long tied to its leg. The bunch of bananas lay like an island above the water in her: on to it as a refuge the parrots crawled. Their jesses entangled amongst the bananas—the boat rolled—so did the banana bunch—each bird would climb upwards, but he could not, the accursed thong held him down: he was being crushed, he was being drowned—he and his mate. And each said so. An American mining captain taking up his parable was not in it with those birds for language.

The two men were negroid in feature. One of them had only one leg, and seemed sad and ill. The other was more cheerful. We could get along together in Spanish. They invited us to come ashore. Hoisting out the cutter, we followed them in. Their lead was useful, as the water is so shoal. Though the rise and fall is but small feet, yet a large area of coral rock flats is dry at low water on either side of a boat channel. At the entrance to this channel an open sailing boat, some 25 feet long, their property, lay at anchor. As the tide was falling, we thought it best to leave our cutter at anchor in sufficiently deep water for her not to take the ground, and got our friends to ferry us from her, one by one, into shoal water in their canoe. It was most comic to see some of our big chaps kneeling on the bottom of

23

the crazy little craft with a hand on either gunnel, whilst they bent forward, like devout Mussulmans on their carpets, endeavouring to get their centre of gravity as low as possible. We were the last of the passengers. When the water got to be only knee deep the native anchored his canoe, and we stepped overboard. So did our one-legged ferryman. His right hand controlled a crutch, in his left he held various treasures obtained from *Mana* ; he also desired to take his two big parrots ashore, so, as the last item of all, he hooked his finger under the cord that tied them together, thus carrying them swinging heads downwards. But apparently he had not taken the cord fairly in the middle. One parrot was suspended by a short length of line : the other by a long : he of the short cord was able to twist himself round and get a hold with his beak on some package in his owner's hand, and was thus reasonably happy. But parrots, like ourselves, can't have it all ways in this world of woe. If his head be up, his tail must be down : hence this tale. He of the long string found himself draggling in the water with every stride of his one-legged owner. In his struggles to avoid drowning by a succession of dips, he managed at last to grasp, with beak and claw, the long dependent tail of his fellow prisoner, and quickly hauling himself up it, he at once proceeded to consolidate his position, by seizing in his beak the softest part of his colleague's hinder anatomy with the vice-like grip of despair, and therefrom he continued to depend in placid comfort, regardless of the other's piercing shrieks and protestations.

It is not always those at the top of the ladder that have the best time of it.

A wide shore line of white sand met us. On it at high-water mark were large quantities of white bleached driftwood trees. On the flat ground behind, beneath a dense tree growth, were some small pools of stagnant rain water, a few coconut palms were dotted about—all else was jungle. On a patch cleared of undergrowth stood a light frame structure open on all sides. The roof was high pitched and had wide eaves : there was no attempt at a floor. It might be 30 ft. by 20 ft. Smaller similar structures adjoined for cooking and stores. A box or two, baskets, hammocks, and a little boat-gear, were suspended from the beams above : a few wooden blocks for stools were on the earthen floor, which was neatly swept. On one such sat a terribly afflicted specimen of humanity—the mother, yet never-theless dignified and courteous. The father, a spare little man with an intelligent face, lay in his hammock and extended his hand feebly over the side simply saying that he was " infirma." He seemed to avoid making any movement. Four or five children of various ages moved listlessly about ; only one of them, a girl of ten or twelve years of age, seemed quite healthy. Then there was the one sound man from the pirogue and the cripple. The whole family were being slowly destroyed by fever and elephantiasis, and apparently must, before long, perish from lack of ability to gather food. No resources were visible—though no doubt they had a little cultivated ground somewhere handy, and of course there was always fish. The whole story of gradually encroaching disease and suffering was so easy to read, and the patient and hopeless resignation with which the little group awaited its predestined extinction was very pathetic. They uttered no complaint nor asked for anything. We made the best of things, and got them quite cheerful and interested, pro-ducing from time to time various trifles from our pockets which we generally carried with us as presents when going ashore. Anxious to please, they gave us various quaint shells and a little fruit, and again pressed on our acceptance the hapless macaws, now secured to a handy branch, whose bedraggled plumage and sorry mien seemed quite in keeping with the surroundings. Altogether our visit seemed to give our hosts pleasure. The man appeared to have some Spanish blood in him and to have known better days. We then returned to the ship, and had breakfast, sending back by the pirogue, which had returned with us, a little present of ship's biscuit, tinned meat, cigarettes, and quinine. It was obvious that no watering was feasible at this landing-place. They told us we should be able to get water at the other spot where we had seen a light the evening before.

Pulling in the heat and sun any considerable distance was out of the question, so we hoisted out the motor lifeboat launch, taking the cutter in tow for landing. We found another wide sandy beach, but with fairly deep water right up to it. There was sufficient breaking swell on it to require the cutter to be hauled up smartly, directly her nose touched, or the next sea would have knocked her broadside on and filled her. The shore was bordered by what appeared to us, from its state of neglect, to be a deserted coconut plantation. We however told the men not to swarm up for nuts for the present—there are generally some low easily climbed trees—until we found out how the land lay. The white man never seems to be able to understand that petty plundering of native plantations is a bad introduction. Needless to say that it was not many minutes before the irrepressible Finn had " found on the ground " a bunch of green nuts and was devouring them with the avidity of a land crab. Foot-prints on the shore, and trails through the scrub, soon brought us to a group of shanties under the palm trees, and therefore close to the shore line. The coconut palm seems to thrive best just beyond high-water mark, and on any flat at about that level behind the furthest point reached by the water. Trees are often to be seen with the soil round their roots partially washed away on one side of the trunk.

A white man came walking along the shore to meet us. Of course the first thing we did was to apologise for the unseemly sight of the men all feeding on his nuts. He was fairly cordial, but evidently greatly perplexed as to who, and what, we were. We told him as well as we could about the ship and the reason of our visit, but it was obvious he thought we lied. All the same he gave us the information we wanted as to supplies and water. Practically nothing was to be had. As it would be shortly our men's dinner hour, we persuaded him to come with us aboard, and he thawed considerably under the influence of luncheon. He told us the coco palms had been planted by his father, and that his name was Guadia. The Sailing Directions, as to this place, are quite wrong. Moreover, they seldom quote their authority, or the date of the information they give, which renders them very untrustworthy.

About twenty fever-stricken natives, many of them cripples from elephantiasis, live here permanently on the plantation under the flimsy shelters. Sr. Guadia said he lived usually in the city of Panama, but came over for some months during the healthy season, occupying a somewhat superior hut in the midst of the native shacks. There are comparatively high hills close to hand, that would be infinitely more healthy as a residential site. He will probably get infected from the natives. The mosquitoes pass the disease along.

As the watering scheme had broken down, we thought we

would devote the afternoon to fishing. Sr. Guadia said that, if we really wanted fish, we ought to go to the mouth of a river some distance away, but that the bottom was all clean opposite his camp, so we thought we would take a few drags of the seine along his front. We faked it down into the cutter and the launch towed her in. All along the beach the water was almost soup-like from the mud in suspension, also in it floated, in immense quantity, tiny fragments of fine marine grasses, the whole being kept constantly churned by the swell. In this opaque water fish could not see the net. Casting off from the launch the cutter backed into the beach : one hand jumped ashore with the head and foot ropes. She then described a semicircle as she shot her net : our seine was 50 fathoms long and 2 fathoms deep : as she completed the semicircle by touching the beach the spare hands jumped ashore with the other head and foot ropes and the boat pulled away to the launch to land that party, for without them it was impossible to haul the net : the resistance was far too great. The natives—the whole population of the huts—grouped themselves together at a little distance, but never offered to lend a hand. At last we got a move on the net, but the resistance was excessive, and we were afraid that she had picked up something. Gradually however the line of buoying corks rose to the surface as the leaded foot rope took the ground, defining the semicircle with a row of dots, whilst over them jumped, at various points of the most distant part of the curve, a multitude of small fry, like a stream of silver darts, and with rainlike patter as they struck the water. Gradually the escaping captives became larger and larger, springing high into the air, and we thought that we should find but little left when we got the net ashore, for the weight in it was such that we could move it but slowly. " Keep her up !—Keep her up !"—was now the cry, to counteract the tendency to haul on either head rope or foot rope unduly in the excitement of the finish—for a seine is simply a moving vertical wall of net, and must be maintained as such in use. At last the contained area began to simmer : then to boil : and then, still hauling evenly, we brought the mass more or less upon and against the sandy beach. Practically it was solid fish : fish of every size, shape and colour. There was comparatively little weed. By their very number they had been rendered helpless. This was great good luck, for amongst them was a large shark some ten or perhaps twelve feet long, and another brute of about the same size and weight, but he chiefly consisted of head, and his head chiefly consisted of mouth. When this mouth, with two little eyes at the sides, looked at you, the shark seemed of benevolent appearance.

Of course our first thought was for the safety of the net; that it was not burst or torn already seemed a miracle. The struggles of the two great brutes would tear it to pieces if we tried to haul them right ashore, so we just held them jammed against the sloping beach. The natives then cautiously ventured to attack them with their machettes—a powerful slashing knife, like a small sabre, used for clearing the forest growth. They directed all their efforts to slashing them along the spine: gingerly approaching the fish by the head, they inflicted the wounds nearer and nearer towards the tail. Having paralysed that, they then blinded them. They did not desire to kill: they wanted the fish to have enough life left in it to be able to struggle away.

Having thus paralysed our two largest captures, we slipped a bowline round their tails, and dragged them clear of the net, and started them off, when they were at once torn to pieces by their fellows. We then proceeded to collect the useful part of the catch. We took what we wanted: the natives appropriated the rest. These natives were not an attractive lot—neither the men, the women, nor the children—they would not lend a hand to haul, got three quarters of the catch for picking it up, and then tried to steal the balance that we had reserved. Sr. Guadia gave us some coconuts, and the antlers of a deer that he had shot: according to him they are plentiful on the island.

As we didn't want anybody to get bitten by mosquitoes, and sunset was approaching, the order was now " All aboard the lugger !" and we reached the ship as her riding-light ran up.

FIG. 134.

SAN FRANCISCO,

From Mount Tamalpais, looking across the Golden Gate.

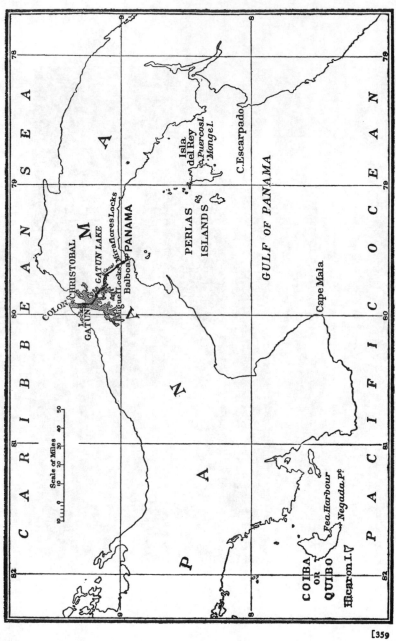

CHAPTER XXIII

PANAMA TO JAMAICA

Navigation of the Gulf of Panama—Balboa and the City of Panama—
Through the Canal—Cristobal—An Incapable Pilot—The
Education of a Cook—A Waterspout—A Further Exciting
Experience.

OUR job was now to get to the entrance of the Canal, which is
situated at the bottom of the bight of the Gulf of Panama. It
is a most difficult one for a sailing vessel. Roughly speaking,
currents from the south-east may be said to sweep round its
coasts, and to form of the Gulf one vast eddy. Here, throughout
the year, persist calms and catspaws from all directions, rain,
lightning, and squalls : the whole caboodleum of the Doldrums,
plus a complex tangle of irregular currents. In addition to the
foregoing joys, there is, towards the head of the Gulf, a large
area studded with islands, rocks, and coral patches. From this
archipelago have been obtained, from the earliest times, at the
price of infamous cruelty, a large supply of the finest pearls—
the group is called the Pearl Islands.

" A vessel unaided by steam power will experience considerable
difficulty and delay in getting out of Panama Bay," say the
Sailing Directions. She will : and so she does in getting into
it. There is a well-known yarn of a ship being here carried
round and round for a year or so, in the olden days, until her
people had nearly all perished from scurvy. Some of the
American newspapers got hold of this story and said we had
found and relieved her, giving pathetic details. In our case,
though we had a motor that gave us $5\frac{1}{2}$ knots through the water,
we found that our only course was to allow ourselves to be
carried right across the mouth of the Gulf to the Colombian coast,
and then to work up along the coast of the Isthmus of Darien,
i.e. along the eastern shore of the Gulf of Panama.

The following summary of our log will show what things are
like. We left Fea Harbour, Quibo Island, at 8.10 a.m. on

Thursday, March the 9th, and motored until noon. Then got the canvas on her. Light airs : E. ; N.N.E.; N.; S.S.E.; S.E.b.E. between noon and midnight. Made good 17½ miles. Much lightning all around in the first watch.

The middle watch of Friday the 10th had easterly airs that gave her an average of three knots, and much lightning. At 9.50 a.m. started motor and ran it until 0.50 p.m. ; and again from 3.24 p.m. to 5.45 p.m. Notwithstanding our using power, it was 10 p.m. before the light on Cape Mala could be entered in the log as just dipping. The motor was only called upon when the current was setting her into what would be a dangerous position. This day we make good 38½ miles.

On Saturday, the 11th of March, we found there was a strong s'utherly set at 11 a.m., and a N.N.W. breeze, so, instead of steering to Panama, we altered course to take full advantage of the breeze to cross the Gulf. We passed from time to time well-defined current-ripples, with much rubbish floating in the dead water. During the afternoon the water became very dark and discoloured, but we got no bottom at 225 fms. At 10 p.m. however we got 55 fms., so we hove-to and waited for the daylight. Our day's run was 79 miles.

At earliest daylight on Sunday the 12th we bore away and at 7.15 a.m. made Cape Escarpado bearing N.42° E. The morning was very hazy with much mirage, and the land very difficult to recognise at any distance. We were now working to wind'ard to the entrance of the Pearl Islands. At 1.35 p.m. we started the motor, and at 4.50 p.m. brought up for the night in 13 fms. between Monge and Puercos islets, which lie off the east coast of the large Isla del Rey. We have done 60 miles to-day.

On Monday, the 13th of March, we made a start at 5 a.m., under sail, working against light airs from N.N.W. westerly. We were now being swept up into the Bight of Panama by the current, so all we had to do was to keep her nicely placed. At noon, when we were distant from Canal entrance 48 miles, we were obliged to start the motor, and did 16 miles under power, stopping it at 3.26 p.m. We then got a gentle N.W. breeze, which we kept till 11.40 p.m., when we brought up off the entrance of the Canal.

Early the next morning a harbour launch, with the Port Officials, came out to us. They told us that the Canal had been closed to all traffic for five months. According to them, our chance of being allowed to pass through was small indeed.

As soon as we had got pratique, we started in our launch for the shore, to learn our fate. From the Port of Balboa on the Pacific, to the Port of Colon on the Atlantic, is 44 miles by canal : by sea the distance is 10,500. If the Powers that Were would not let us through, we must practically again circumnavigate the whole continent of South America. We had already done it once to a very large extent : Pernambuco to Valparaiso. Was it to be our fate to do it a second time ?

Though *Mana* was anchored close to the entrance of the fairway, yet she was hull-down on our looking back when we were abreast of the Balboa frontage, so great is the length of the dredged channel through the smooth shoal water of the Bay, before the Canal begins to have visible land on either side of it.

Messrs. Balfour, Guthrie & Co., of San Francisco, had most kindly advised their agents of our being *en route*, and consequently, when we landed at Balboa, there was a motor-car in waiting. We whisked off, got fresh meat and vegetables for the ship, put it aboard the launch, and despatched her with orders to return to take us off an hour before dark. Then we drove straight to the City of Panama to call on the British Minister, Sir Claud Mallet. He was most kind. He sent us under convoy of the Consul to see Colonel Harding, the acting chief of the Canal in the absence of Colonel Goethals. Colonel Harding was pleased to grant *Mana* the exceptional privilege of at once passing through the Canal, on the ground that she was a scientific research ship,—a favour for which we owe much gratitude both to him and to the Government which he represented. We have sometimes however regretted this stroke of luck, as, had we been compelled to take the s'utherly route, we should have been at Punta Arenas just at the time Sir Ernest Shackleton was there seeking a vessel to rescue his men from Elephant Island, a job for which *Mana* was eminently fitted.

In accordance with arrangements made, next morning a pilot came off and took us, under our own power, from the outer anchorage, up the dredged channel, to the mooring dolphins opposite Balboa, a distance of about 5 miles. Balboa is the name of a new town built by the Americans on the Eastern bank of the Pacific entrance of the Panama Canal. The ground on

which it is situated is not flat, also there are a couple of isolated
volcanic cones, that rise to a height of 363 feet and 650 feet
respectively, in its midst. A fine sanitary city has been designed,
and largely brought into being, and as the work of construction
of the Canal proceeds towards completion, for there is still much
work to be done, so everything connected with the Canal will be
concentrated there. To this new town of Balboa adjoins the
old city of Panama, the capital of the Republic of Panama, but
now isolated from the rest of the republic, being entirely surrounded by U.S.A. territory.

Before we go through the Canal, it will be well to have a
general idea of its character. Let us first consider that of the
Suez. The Isthmus of Suez is a level neck of sand, only slightly
raised above sea level. Across it a gutter has been dug : the
Mediterranean Sea, unobstructed, flows along that gutter, until
it blends its waters with those of the Red Sea.

The Panama is an entirely different proposition. The Isthmus
of Panama is a neck of land formed of volcanic debris and rock.
It is only partially level ; it is humped in the middle, but that
hump is hollowed like a saucer. So we have this sequence :—
A level. A hump. A level.

The Canal therefore is made in this way. Firstly the middle,
or humped part, is changed, by means of embankments, from a
semi-dry saucer into a deep high-level pond, *i.e.* into a pond
whose surface is 85 feet above the level of the sea. That pond
is filled, and kept filled, with sweet water by the rainfall on high
country around it—the inner slope of the edge of the saucer.
As we are only concerned with two embankments which go to
form the pond, we will refer to one as the Eastern and to the
other as the Western.

Next, the Pacific Ocean is brought up a distance of about
4 miles, to the foot of the Western Embankment, by digging a
simple gutter through level country, just as has been done in
the case of Suez : similarly the Atlantic is brought a distance
of about 5 miles to the foot of the Eastern Embankment.

Finally, each embankment is equipped with a series of water
steps, or locks, whereby a vessel is lifted up from the ditch into
the pond, or lowered from the pond into the ditch. Water of
the pond, in measured doses of a lockful at a time, and on
which dose float one or more ships, is first shut off from the

pond, and is then permitted gently to escape into the Pacific Ocean ditch, or into the Atlantic Ocean ditch, as the case may be.

No drop of Atlantic sea water ever mingles with the sweet water of the Central Pond. No drop of Pacific sea water ever mingles with the sweet water of the Central Pond. The Atlantic with the Pacific do not commingle directly or indirectly.

Punctually at 7 a.m. the Canal pilot boarded us, and we left Balboa 7.35 a.m. under our own power, and proceeded up the Canal. It was a real pleasure trip. Engines running to perfection. Pilot most complimentary to them. No navigating to be done. The men highly content at the information that, once through the lock gates, the ship would be in fresh water, and they could wash clothes all day long. Largesse of soap distributed. We reached the Miraflores Locks at 8.15 a.m. Distance from Balboa about 2 miles. The shores of the Canal between Balboa and Miraflores present little of interest—the Canal is here simply a ditch cut through a swamp. We enter the lower lock : the water of the pond above our heads is let in, and we rise about 54 feet. The doors in front of us open, and we pass out into a pool. From this pool we enter a second lock : we again rise about 31 feet : the gates in front of us open, and we are floating in an arm of the artificially formed Gatun Lake.

This lake or pond or saucer is of considerable extent : about ⅓ the size of the Isle of Wight. Here it is deep : there it is shallow. What were marshes, when it was still unflooded, have now become its deeps : what were hillock or hill-tops now appear as isolated islands. It is between such islands that the ship channel threads.

A remarkable feature is that the islands, each of which was lately a hill-top, have as yet no horizontally cut shore or strand : the slope of the hill-side is the same below the surface of the water as above it : the waves have not yet cut a shore bench or shelf. The trees therefore stand immersed in varying degree, some with the foot of the trunk only just awash : others with their topmost boughs only just showing. Where the bottom of the pond is level, large areas of now dead, but still standing, forest trees, partially submerged to an even depth, present a remarkable, because a transient, feature. Presently these will decay and disappear, then the water surface of the pond will appear to be greater than it does to-day.

At 10.10 a.m. we passed out of the Western (Miraflores and Miguel) locks, and proceeded across the pond, and reached the other side—the entrance to the Eastern Locks (the Gatun Locks)—at 4.51 p.m. Here we moored ship, as the Canal people would not drop us from the pond into the Atlantic ditch that night. We observed that the U.S.A. were not taking any risks that they could avoid of German agents causing trouble : sentries were posted everywhere, and no one from the ship was allowed to wander about ashore. So *Mana's* crowd sat in a row on the edge of the lock, like migrating martins on a telegraph wire, and swung their legs, in high good humour. Saturday, March the 18th, at 8.7 a.m. we entered the Gatun Locks : at 8.53 p.m. passed out : and at 10 a.m. came to anchor in Colon Harbour.

That afternoon we moored alongside a pier, and took aboard coal, petroleum, and lubricating oil. The British Consul, Mr. Murray, was most kind and hospitable, and though the flat mud island on which Cristobal stands, and of which it occupies the greater part, is unusually uninteresting, as is also the town, yet, owing to Mr. Murray, we quite enjoyed a week's detention there that Fate had in store for us.

As a vessel steams down the gutter (Gatun Approach) that runs in a straight line from the Eastern Embankment (Gatun Dam) into the Atlantic (Caribbean Sea), she has on her starboard hand, as she approaches the termination of the gutter, a small flat island of alluvium. The Canal water front of that island is occupied now by wharves and jetties, behind which runs a good road bordered with fairly respectable shops, and stores, and drinking-dens. At one end is a large and good hotel : at the other the stores, workshops, and residences of the Canal Officials. To all this is given the name of CristObal—long O. Immediately against Cristobal, and forming part of it, abuts the town of COlon—another long O—a town that practically sprang into being at the first making of the Canal : a twin sister to the town of Suez of the olden days for vice and villainy. If Colon be what it is now, with the U.S.A. in control, what must it have been of yore ? We believe that the Canal Administration allows

the citizens of the Republic of Panama some sort of self government as regards their town of Colon, hence its character. The
redeeming point about it is that it is so frequently and largely
burnt to the ground that it will eventually become quite reasonably sanitary.

At present, Cristobal is the executive centre on the Canal.
Here are all the workshops. Balboa, at the other end, is to-day
the administrative centre only, but gradually all interests connected with the Canal will there be concentrated. To Cristobal
is brought, and from Cristobal is drawn, all labour and supplies.
All food consumed throughout the Canal zone—meat, fresh fish,
vegetables, fruit, is sent frozen from the U.S.A. and there kept
in cold storage—no supplies practically are derived from the
surrounding country. It is only by the courtesy of the Canal
Administration, that anyone, not in its employ, is allowed to
purchase food at its depots. Any foreigner therefore, whose
work requires him to live in the Canal zone, finds housekeeping
a very difficult matter. In our case, however, by the Regulations,
we were entitled to purchase what we wanted, but the same
Regulations specially state that any yacht, U.S.A. or foreign,
shall be charged 20 per cent. more than any other vessel for any
food supplied, or services rendered to her, and we were charged
accordingly. And this though the Administration had only
allowed us to pass through on the ground that we were not a
yacht. In no sense were we one. To an Englishman it seems
strange to find that another people considers it to the interest of
the State to differentiate against yachts : we know, in our case,
what our nation has gained by the widespread and intelligent
interest in maritime affairs, that is the outcome of the British
sport of yachting.

Having got all our essential stores aboard on the day of our
arrival (Saturday), we hoped to be able to get fresh provisions,
pay dues, and clear on the Monday. But now our troubles
began. There were at this time certain repairs that it was
desirable should be done to portions of our machinery. They
were not essential, as we had substituted new spares for each
defective part, but we thought it wise, as we were now at the
only port where we could get the work done, to get the damaged
parts renovated, so as to become spares in their turn. The
original idea was to send down the parts by boat, but eventually

the machine shop desired the vessel to be laid alongside its
wharf.   No vessel by the Regulations is allowed to be moved
without a Canal Pilot aboard her.   He takes absolute command and control.   A pilot accordingly took her alongside all
right.   Then arose delays—but everybody was most obliging,
and the work was well done, though of course prices were
very high.

Meantime our kindly Consul was doing all he could to arrange
for us to have a day's tarpon fishing from the Gatun Weir—from
hearsay it is most thrilling work : you stand on the great weir
with the water boiling in foam 85 feet beneath you and play
a real fighting fish of 100 to 200 lbs. weight. The gentleman who was to have run us up to Gatun in his launch,
and to have helped us to get a fish, was, however, unavoidably
detained.

Day followed day with the vessel alongside the wharf and the
repair work in the workshops.

At this time we were much amused by an old Jamaican coloured
man, who spent most of the day sitting on the quay beside the
vessel close to her stern, where of course the ensign was flying
on the flagstaff.   He, like all the British West Indian coloured
people, of whom there is a very large number at Cristobal-Colon,
was enthusiastically loyal, and told us, " I love to sit under de
ole flag : while you here, I do no more work—all de day I sit
under de ole flag."   The men took a fancy to him, and " de ole
flag " found something to spare for him at every meal, and a
pipe of baccy afterwards.

At last the repairs were completed—shore accounts all settled
up and the Canal Pilot took charge to take us out. We had to
go out of the pool stern foremost.   It turned out subsequently
that the Gatun Locks were at this time passing a vessel through.
This caused a current to flow past the pier head of the dock.
The pilot did not know of it, with the result that *Mana's* stern
crashed into the pier head.   Luckily the piling was very old and
rotten, and *Mana* extraordinarily strong, so that, though the
pier head structure was pretty considerably smashed, our own
damage was confined to broken taffrail stancheons and the iron-
work of the main gallows. We had therefore to return to our
berth and have this new lot of damage made good.   The Pilot,
a Greek, of course tried to make out that the reversing gear had

refused duty when he wanted to handle her, but, before we could find the Captain of the Port, that official had already been aboard and tried the engine, and told us that he found it worked to perfection, and gave us the true cause of the accident. We then asked him to give orders that our damage should be made good by the Canal Administration free of charge, but this he assured us was impossible under the Regulations—we must pay, but the job should be expedited. He also, out of sympathy with our misfortunes, gave us permission, when our job was done, this time to take our ship out ourselves without having another Canal pilot aboard, lest something worse should happen. And this we eventually did, to our own great satisfaction. Before however we could get our clearance, we had to deposit a sum equal to double the estimated cost of our repairs.

The Canal Administration, like the British Post Office, always plays pitch and toss on the terms of "heads I win, tails you lose." It, very properly, compels you to take a pilot. It gives him absolute power, and requires that he himself shall take command and handle the vessel. But such a man's experience is confined to big steamers: with them he is probably quite skilful, but give him a small craft or a yacht, and he knows as much about handling her as he does of piloting an aeroplane. Hence those tears.

The foregoing is equally true of the Suez Canal pilots. The risks to a small craft in the passage of the ship canals are great, and are solely due to the pilots being permitted to attempt to handle them.

As the Regulations of the Panama Canal stand, the Pilot may be mad, or drunk, or incompetent, and elect to ram another vessel, or to butt at a lock gate, nevertheless all damage done to the ship, or by the ship, must be paid by the Owners of the ship, before she is allowed to leave the Canal. Under no circumstances will the Administration accept responsibility for the conduct of their pilots. And there you have it.

At 9.15 a.m. Sunday, March the 26th, 1916, we passed through the breakwater into the Caribbean Sea. We had cleared from Cristobal-Colon for Trinidad, one of our West Indian Islands, but when doing so we never had any intention of going there. We informed the British Consul of our reasons and had his sanction. German sympathisers seemed to take a most kindly interest in us. We were really bound for Bermuda, via the Windward Passage, which is the pass between the two great islands of Cuba and St. Domingo. A strong wind and current sweep at this time of year from East to West the length of the Caribbean Sea, consequently we had to get well to the east'ard so as to make sure of carrying a fair wind and current for rounding Cape Tiburon, the western extremity of the Island of St. Domingo. We therefore at once set to work to beat steadily to wind'ard along the Venezuelan coast, keeping close in with the land, in order to cheat the current and to have as little sea as possible. As this coast is only roughly surveyed, and the lighting cannot be depended on, we exercised special care when standing-in to the land. We saw no craft along this coast except that, one night, what looked like a small tramp steamer of about 800 tons entirely changed her course, and bore down on us until she was close alongside. She did not attempt to communicate. We kept our course and took no notice of her. After a good look at us she took herself off.

We had unfortunately lost, at Cristobal, our excellent and popular Japanese cook, and the coloured Panama man who replaced him proved, after being given some days of grace, such a miserable impostor that even the strenuous and varied educational efforts of the fo'c's'le failed to bring about his regeneration. We heard, indirectly, that the Russian Finn decided that it was a case of demoniacal possession and had attempted to cure it by means of a course of massage of the windpipe. Others of the crew suddenly became afflicted with a variety of complaints for which they drew various drastic drugs from the ship's medicine chest and then, with great self-sacrifice, refraining from taking these themselves, administered them instead to the chef. We aft got along quite comfortably, as the cabin steward, Edwin Young, belonging to Pitcairn Island, had become, since joining, quite a good cook, and was most willing and hard working. But the fo'c's'le very naturally complained, so, in its interest, we decided to alter our course and make for Port Royal, Jamaica, to seek that pearl of price—a good sea cook.

Nothing calling for remark occurred on this run until the 6th of April. At 6.15 a.m. on that day Mr. Gillam, whose watch it was, came below and said, " I wish you would come on deck, Sir ; there's a water-spout bearing down on us." In half a shake of a lamb's tail we were on deck, and a truly wonderful and impressive sight presented itself. Away on our starboard bow was a vast, dark purple cloud mass shaped like an open umbrella, or rather like a vaulted roof with central pendant. The upper surface of the dome blended with the normal clouds. The edge of the dome was sharply defined, and from it small fragments of cloud, all ragged, and looking like pearl-grey silk muslin torn off and crumpled, kept breaking away to be left behind. The dome-shaped mass, on its lower aspect, gradually became columnar, the column extended downward until it almost, but not quite, reached the sea. The lower part of its length was much attenuated, and convoluted, and terminated in ragged mist, and could be seen to be rotating rapidly.

The surface of the sea beneath it, over an area of perhaps a mile in diameter, presented the appearance of a fiercely boiling cauldron. The water rose up as waves of pyramidal form, from which the wind tore off the apices, and whipped the same into spume. The waves had no fixed direction : they simply dashed into one another. Immediately beneath the ragged termination of the central column the surface of the sea seemed to be bodily lifted up, amidst a welter of mist, and froth, and spray, into a cone-shaped form, but, between the apex of this cone, and the rapidly rotating extremity of the column of cloud above it, there always remained a distinct interval of considerable extent, that had the appearance of dense mist : the appearance of a hard rain-squall, seen from afar, as it sweeps over the sea. The cloud came down towards the sea, and the sea rose up towards the cloud, and there was an interval betwixt the two. The column was not quite vertical : though it maintained perfect continuity with the cloud mass above, of which it formed a part, nevertheless its lower extremity tended somewhat to trail or lag behind. It moved along its path towards us, quite slowly and steadily, cutting our wake, at an acute angle, some miles astern. It is difficult to conjecture what would happen to a small craft, or to any craft, that found itself well within the area of disturbance. Apart from anything else, the seas, tumbling down on to the top of her from all quarters, even if they did not break in her decks, could hardly fail to strip her hatch openings. As we watched, we agreed that even *Mana* could scarcely be expected to live amidst such seas, and therefore, obviously,

24

nothing could.   As it was, the surface of the sea, where we were, was little affected, nor was there any weight in the shifts of wind as they occurred.

We then had breakfast and a pipe and settled down to routine work when, at 10 a.m., a small cloud on the horizon, on our lee bow, was observed to be behaving in a way opposed to the ordinary laws of nature.   Though a nice steady breeze was blowing and no other clouds were to be seen anywhere else in this direction on the horizon, yet this one particular patch, like a large sail, remained constant in form and in the same position.   As we drew nearer, it was observed to increase and diminish in volume from time to time.   The only explanation we could think of was that we had fallen in with a ship on fire, so we bore away towards it.   As we reduced the distance betwixt us and it, we gradually made out that it was not one cloud of white smoke, but two separate clouds, that arose, more or less alternately, at two spots situated some two miles or so apart.   Another point too gradually developed.   Each patch of cloud or smoke suddenly burst forth to its maximum size and then gradually blew to leeward, and dissipated.   This led us to think that it must be either gun practice or a naval action.   The wind had now fallen light, so we started our engines, and made up our canvas, and, like rats, headed for the scrimmage.   It was suggested that, following the classical example of Mr. Midshipman Easy, a ladies' wardrobe aboard should be overhauled to find if possible a green silk petticoat under which we might go into action.   As in Easy's case, being unarmed, our approach was likely to be of greater effect than our presence ; but still we all decided to make a claim for prize money.   As we cut down the distance it became evident that it could only be a matter of small craft, for no hull could be made out.   The fighting was taking place on the northern side of Morant's Cays, a group of low lying coral islets that lay between us and the combatants.

The situation gradually developed.   Morant's Cays are coral islets perched on the top of a volcanic area : there had been a seismic disturbance of considerable extent : we had the large-scale Admiralty plan of them.   Great changes had taken place : the sea was now breaking in various directions where deep water was shown on the chart.   At two points, from vents in the sea bottom, steam was being ejected into the air in puffs, each puff forming a dense white cloud perhaps 200 or more feet high. These puffs occurred some $1\frac{1}{2}$ miles apart and one was much larger than the other. The steam was ejected from each vent alternately. We came in pretty close, but breaking water in various directions warned us that we were looking for trouble, so we headed away for Port Royal, Jamaica.

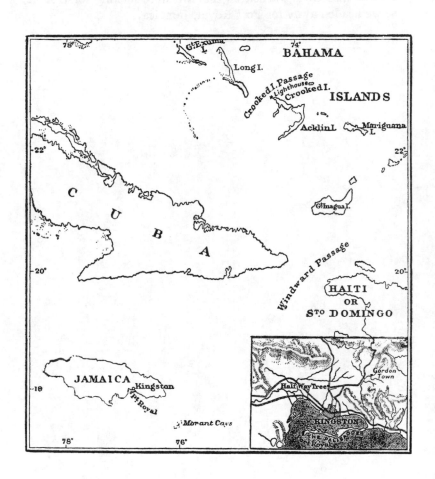

CHAPTER XXIV

JAMAICA TO SOUTHAMPTON

Jamaica, and the Bahamas—Bermudas—Azores—Preparing for
Submarines—Southampton once more

JAMAICA

Jamaica was discovered by Columbus, and belonged to Spain till
1655, when it was captured by an expedition sent out by Oliver
Cromwell.

The Island, from its proximity to the Spanish Possessions, was a
godsend to the Buccaneers. Port Royal, which, as its name shows,
was founded after the Restoration, was full of riches, often ill-gotten:
"always like a Continental mart or fair." In 1692 it was over-
whelmed by an earthquake, and again laid low by fire in 1703.

Kingston, originally begun as a settlement of refugees from Port
Royal after the earthquake, gradually grew in importance, and
finally became the capital of the island.

During the wars which followed the French Revolution, Jamaica
was of importance as the great centre of British interests in the
Western Caribbean.

WE now headed for Jamaica ; Kingston, its capital, lies towards
the eastern extremity of its southern coast. The town is placed
on flat land which gradually rises into dwarf hills. It is built
parallel to, and abutting on to its water-front. Right and left
of the city, when viewed from the sea, extends low country,
whilst behind it, and to the east, rises in the distance a lofty
range of mountains. From the open sea, the town and flat
country is divided by a natural breakwater that maintains the
general trend of the coast. By this breakwater is formed a
lagoon that runs East and West, parallel to the coast, for a
distance of some six miles, with an average breadth of about one
mile, and has practically no arms or branches. This lagoon is
the harbour of Kingston and a fine one, but it lacks the element
of picturesqueness, nor is it a comfortable one for small craft.
The strong easterly wind, known as "The Undertaker," that
daily arises and increases in strength with the sun, sweeps down
its length and knocks up a nasty sea. It is difficult to obtain
shelter, even for a dinghy, when landing at Kingston.

But we are anticipating. We ran down the coast, close in, and at 9.30 a.m., Friday, April the 7th, 1916, we reached the western end of the natural breakwater between which and the mainland is the passage into the lagoon. Here the Port Doctor came on board, and as he went through our bills of health we mutually discovered that we were old hospital friends, though we had never heard of each other for twenty years.

We entered the harbour, and brought up in 15 fms., abreast of the wharf of the old naval dockyard of Port Royal, and distant from it about a cable's length. Port Royal is situated on the inner aspect of the bulbous-headed western extremity of the natural breakwater. The land surface is very limited in extent and is entirely taken up with the old fort, the old dockyard, and old naval and military quarters. All but a few poor closely packed houses is in the occupation of Government. The width of the breakwater to the eastward soon becomes small ; open beach on seaward side, mangroves extending into the lagoon on the other ; and between the two sand and scrub. This part is the well-known Palisadoes, the home of land-crabs and dead men, and the scene of many a duel. Port Royal is now deserted ; no shipping or living workshops ; everything is hushed, but the place is not neglected. Nelson might have left it but yesterday ; the dockyard, with its fittings, stores, and quays, reminded one of that other quaint little marine gem, the old naval dockyard of English Harbour in the island of Antigua. When the place hummed with life, *The Young Sea Officer's Sheet Anchor*, by Falconer, was the text book to work by, and its social life is vividly and accurately given us by Marryat in one of his novels.

As in the dusk, all alone, we passed down the silent corridors, and approached the old mess-room, we somehow listened for, and expected at any moment to hear, through some opening door, the reckless toast of " A bloody war, and a sickly season," the chink of glasses, and the crash of the chorus " Yellow Jack ! Yellow Jack ! " And Jack, thus bidden, used to come, and link his arm in that of some fine young fellow, and together the two would saunter away " to the home of a friend of his in the Palisadoes." Little time for packing up allowed ! Many and many a man, in the prime of life and feeling quite well, has dined at mess one night in snowy uniform : the next night in a white uniform of a different cut as the guest of Jack and Death. These two kept open house in those days.

The R.E. Officer in charge was most kind and hospitable; he took us over the old fort, pointing out, amongst much else, Nelson's former quarters and the adjoining length of parapet overlooking the harbour entrance, now known as Nelson's Walk. Our host informed us that, fishing from the wharves, he got splendid sport.

From Port Royal to Kingston is about four miles by the boat channel. Passes through the coral banks have been blasted where requisite and the channel beaconed. A least depth of $4\frac{1}{2}$ ft. is thus obtained, and a direct course. Our little motor lifeboat carried us backwards and forwards most excellently on various voyages made to attend to our business at Kingston. The way in which she bucked at speed over the short steep seas reminded one of larking over hurdles on a pony.

The work in hand was to get our clearance inwards, to get rid of our food-destroyer from Panama, and to find in his place a live ship's cook, to report particulars of the Morant's Cays upheaval, and finally the usual catering, and bill of health, and clearance outwards. The Chief of the Customs was good enough to interest himself in *Mana's* welfare, so that all these matters were dealt with in due sequence, and with the least possible trouble to us. A coloured cook was procured from an hotel at £16 a month, with, as it proved, but little justification on the ground of ability for drawing such a rate of pay; still, his professional enormities were associated with so many humorous incidents, and as he appeared at least to mean well, we resigned ourselves to the inevitable, and prayed that we might survive his ministrations.

About noon on Sunday, April 9, 1916, we weighed and motored out from Port Royal, unplagued by pilots, and dipping our ensign to the Port Doctor and his wife, in acknowledgment of adieux waved from their garden. Clear of everything, the engines were stopped and *Mana*, bound to " the stormy Bermuthies," proceeded to argue the point with a head wind as to whether she should, or should not, go to windward. By steady hammering she gradually got under the western end of the Island of San Domingo, and then through the celebrated Windward Passage. We had now to threadle our way betwixt the numerous islets that constitute the Bahama group, and it was quite delightful and interesting ; brilliant sunshine, cool moderate breezes, land every few hours, but reliable charts. This was yachting ; we had met a good deal of what bore little semblance to it, so we appreciated our present luck all the more.

The morning of the 19th of April 1916 saw us beating up under the lee of Acklin Island and of Crooked Island ; a fresh N.E. breeze swept in puffs across the long, narrow, flat land. An open native boat, with jib-headed mainsail as usual, was seen heading across our course when we were close in, so we gave her a wave, and, as we came into the wind, she rounded-to under our stern, dousing her sail, unshipping her mast and shooting up alongside our quarter. We dropped into her ; a couple of empty sacks were pitched in, and she was clear of the ship before she had lost her way. The mast is stepped, the sail hoisted, and she is off again with her gunnel steadily kept awash. We now for the first time spoke. The two coloured men, her crew, were most obliging ; they would make for the most convenient landing and then they would accompany us catering.

Everything went off excellently ; we made a tour to different cottages and gardens, collecting whatever was available, particularly grape-fruit, oranges, and tamarinds. We also got exceptionally fine specimens of the shell of the King conch and of the Queen conch. Hundreds of the King conch were piled up at one spot on the shore ready to be burnt into lime.

The natives appeared to be pure-blooded negroes of west-coast type, and in some respects their culture remains unchanged. For instance, the pestle and mortar and winnowing tray for treating maize were exactly similar in pattern to those we had seen used by the Akikuyu of Eastern Central Africa.

When catering, the price of each article is settled by negotiation, and it is definitely bought, as it is met with from time to time in our perambulation, on condition that it shall be paid for as it is passed into the boat on departure—cash on delivery. Much other stuff, though unbought, is also brought down to the boat in the hope of sale at the last moment. This too is generally taken as well, because going cheaply, and also to avoid causing disappointment.

Everybody having been paid, and the already laden boat now

pretty well cluttered-up with an unexpected additional cargo of chickens, eggs, fruit, shells, and sundry ethnological acquisitions, up goes the shoulder-of-mutton, the helmsman ships his twiddling-stick, and, in a few moments, the water is purring beneath our lee gunnel as the little craft slithers through the closely set wavelets of land-sheltered water. Long, narrow, and ballasted, these boats are very fast and are given the last ounce of wind pressure they can stand up to. It seemed to us, however, that her crew wished to show what they could do with her as, halliard and sheet in hand, they lifted the lee gunnel from moment to moment, just sufficiently to prevent her filling, but they did so with an easy nonchalance that told that they were finished boat sailors.

A very few minutes saw us " once more aboard the lugger." We had left *Mana* at noon, and eight bells were striking as the staysail-sheet-tackle scraped to leu'ard along the hairless belly of its horse ; we had explored an island, seen a good deal of its people and their culture, and had revictualled ship, all within four hours, yet without hurry !

Towards sundown we passed out into the Atlantic, through the Crooked Island Passage ; at 8.45 p.m. the Light that marks the Passage dipped over our taffrail, and we turned in with that peace of mind which is the portion of those whose ship is clear of all land.

This day, April the 19th, Gibb's Hill Lighthouse, Bermuda, bore N.42° E., distant 767 miles ; it took us eleven days to do it.

April the 20th.—The sargasso weed formed floating islands sometimes many acres in extent ; when one considers the marine fauna that centres round a piece of floating wreckage in tropical seas, some idea can be formed of the wealth of life associated with this vast sudd. Our patent log could no longer be towed.

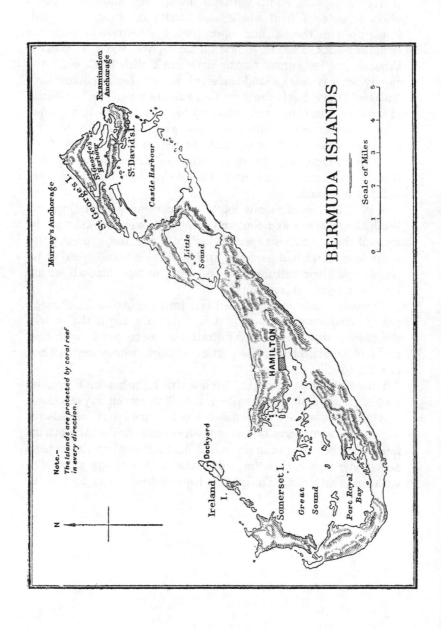

BERMUDA ISLANDS

Scale of Miles

0 1 2 3 4 5

N

Note.—
The Islands are protected by coral reef in every direction.

Murray's Anchorage

Examination Anchorage

St. George's I.

St. George's Harbour

St. David's I.

Castle Harbour

Little Sound

HAMILTON

Ireland I.

Dockyard

Somerset I.

Great Sound

Port Royal Bay

BERMUDAS

The Bermudas are a group of a hundred islands, most of which are, however, bare rocks. They were discovered in the beginning of the 16th century by Juan Bermudez, a Spaniard.

In 1609 attention was drawn to them by Sir George Somers, who was shipwrecked there on his way to Virginia, and found them "the most plentiful place that ever I came to for fish, hogs and fowl." Fifty emigrants were sent out in 1612. Moore, a ship's carpenter, was the first governor. He established his headquarters at St. George's. Later a more central position was needed, and the town of Hamilton was laid out, and became the capital in 1815. The American War brought the islands into notice from a naval point of view, and in 1810 a dockyard was begun on Ireland Island, thousands of convicts being sent out from England for its construction.

The Colony possesses representative institutions, but not responsible government.

We made Bermuda for the sake of gaining our northing. We had new canvas awaiting us there, that we ought to have received at Tahiti, and we had to decide, on cable advices, whether we would lay up *Mana* here in Bermuda, in the United States of North America, or bring her back to England.

The Sailing Directions offered us two harbours, St. George's and Hamilton. They do not point out that all shipping business, practically all business, is done at Hamilton. We selected St. George's. The harbour master came aboard with the pilot, and proved an interesting man, kindly and obliging—an old soldier, a keen conchologist, and a bit of a geologist. The harbour itself is excellent and charming; it extends away *ad infinitum* amongst the islets and coral patches, but there is little indication of its being made much use of by mercantile shipping.

St. George's Island is linked to its big neighbour by causeways and bridges, which are carried across the shallow coral sea. Its quaint, clean, sleepy little townlet, or village, exists by letting lodgings to American visitors, and growing early vegetables for exportation to the States.

The American Tourist is the winter migrant whose nature and idiosyncrasies are by the islanders most deeply studied. He, to the Bermudian, is Heaven's choicest gift—his coconut—the all-sufficing. Nine-tenths of the brain power of the islanders is devoted to inducing the creature to visit the islands and to keeping it contented whilst it is there, the other tenth to supplying it with early vegetables in its continental habitat. Of course

Bermuda is an important naval station, and a certain amount
of business is done in purveying to the naval and military establishments, but that is a thing apart. The Dockyard is situated
on islands well removed from both St. George's and Hamilton.
In this we may see the finger of Providence; placed elsewhere
it would have incommoded the American Tourist.

This cult of the foreigner is the explanation of many things
which at first sight appear strange in Bermuda. It is about
eleven miles by road from St. George's to Hamilton, and there
is no means of public conveyance beyond a covered pair-horse
wagonette, that acts as a carrier's cart for goods and passengers.
We marvelled exceedingly why this should be, whereupon it
was thus explained to us by our butcher, who was also the
proprietor of the shandy-ran express aforesaid, and of a hired-
carriage business, and by his son and partner, the M.P. for the
St. George's Harbour Division. The Americans find the climate
of Bermuda delightful as a winter resort. At Hamilton monster
hotels are built for them, but there is nothing whatever for them
to do. The islands do not possess any features of natural or
historical interest that appeal to tourists. Now the islanders
had observed that the dominant note in the American character
was its restlessness; unless an American could violently rush
around and spend money he was wretched and pined. But the
island had excellent roads and lovely views, so they provided
carriages, and objectives to drive to associated with romance
and story, the evolution of which, from a basis of nothing, is a
standing testimony to their intellectual creative powers, and
of the truth of the axiom that a demand creates a supply.

But the island, for we may ignore the numerous islets, is very
small. With care and good management, and by severely
rationing him in the extent of his daily shay excursions, it was
found that the American could be kept alive, and healthy, and
cheerful for 14 days: from one steamer to the next: all this
time he exuded dollars. "All is well," as the ant said to the
aphis. Then suddenly the heavens fell. A lewd spirit had
prompted our friend the butcher of St. George's to import two
motor-buses and with them run an hourly service between Port
St. George and Hamilton, to the great convenience of the public,
and to his own exceeding profit. As if this were not enough, he
and others were known to have even placed orders in the States

for motor-cars ! Bitter was the cry of the carriage purveyors
of Hamilton, of the hotels, of the furnished apartments. The
American visitor would " do the darned island," every inch of
its roads, twice over, in a single day, and get away by the same
boat he had arrived by—(the boats stay two days loading
vegetables).

But where shall salvation be found if not in " government of
the people, by the people, for the people " ? Many members of
both Houses indirectly, and in some cases directly, were interested in the hired carriage, or apartment, or hotel lines. Trained
in such schools for statesmen, the Legislature was able to visualise
the national danger, and deal with it broadly, regardless of the
vested interests of the day. Without delay both Houses met,
an Act was passed, and the Royal Assent given through the
Governor, whereby the butcher was given the cost price of his
two buses, and a solatium ; the buses were immediately to be
sent back to the States, and, for the future, no form of auto-
mobile was to be landed, owned, or used on the island. Heavy
penalties for infraction. So there is still one spot on earth,
anyhow, where one can escape the scourge of the motor-horn.

For a few days we stayed at St. George's, getting a little
smith's work done and watering ship. There is no surface
water on the island ; the rain water is collected and stored in
great underground cisterns hewn in the solid coral rock of which
the island is formed. The water supply thus conserved has
never been known to fail. In *Mana's* case the Military Authorities kindly sent their large tank-boat alongside. At odd times
we explored in the launch some of the labyrinth of waterways
and islets forming part of St. George's Harbour, or connected
with it. When doing so one afternoon, we made the acquaintance, at nightfall, of a coloured fisherman, by offering him the
courtesy of a pluck home. This man (Bartram of St. George's)
proved an extraordinarily good fellow. He said he never worked
on Sundays, therefore he was free to offer to take us on that
day, as his guest, to try for monsters in a certain wonderful hole,
far out on the edge of the reef, a spot we could reach with the
aid of our launch. He was most keen about it, so we accepted.
The monster-capturing was a failure, but he and his two sons
worked hard all day, and seemed much concerned that they
had failed to show sport, nor would they consider any suggestion

of payment for their long day's work, on our return to the ship. They accepted, however, a clasp-knife each, as a souvenir of our excursion.

Bartram had told us that he had at home a wonderfully fine and rare "marine specimen." (The collection of "marine specimens" is one of the refuges of despair of the American Tourist, and their supply has gradually become a minor industry of Bermuda.) He had found it some years ago. Many millionaires from the hotels or on yachts had offered him big prices for it, but the very fact that they were so keen to get it had made him all the more determined to keep it. Some day he had intended to sell it. Now would we accept it as a gift ? On inspection it proved to be no coral, but a very fine example of a colony of sociable sea snails (Vermetus). We therefore suggested to Bartram that we should take it to England on *Mana* and offer it in his name as a gift to the British Museum (Natural History). This we did, and Dr. Harmer, the Keeper of the Zoological Department, was much pleased with it, and wrote to Bartram accordingly.

The interest of this little story lies in the fact of its being a typical example of the way in which one often finds, in our remote dependencies, the people exhibiting unexpected keenness and pride in associating themselves with England, and her interests, on an opportunity of doing so being pointed out to them. We had found it so at Pitcairn Island.

A more delightful place than Bermuda at which to spend a winter would be hard to find by those who care for pleasure sailing in smooth waters, fishing, sunshine, and the customary amenities of civilised life. Unhappily we could not spare the time to avail ourselves of the possibilities of St. George's. We had constantly to be at Hamilton on ship's business, so after several journeys to and fro in the dreadful covered wagonette, wherein physical discomfort almost rendered us indifferent to a kaleidoscopic succession of humorous persons, situations, and incidents, we got a pilot and went round under power into Hamilton Harbour. Pilotage is compulsory, but free. Once at Hamilton things went much more easily. The Colonial Authorities and the Admiral in Command and his Staff were most kind and hospitable. Admiralty House is a charming eighteenth-century English country residence, of moderate size, and romantically situated. In its garden, peeps of the sea are seen, through graceful subtropical foliage, at every turn, and miniature land-locked coves, reached from above by winding steps down the face of the falaise, afford the most perfect of boat harbours and bathing-pools.

Another delightful official residence is allotted to the officer in command of the Dockyard. In his case he is given a miniature archipelago. His tiny islands rise from 20 to 100 feet above the water. On one is his house; another is his garden; chickens and pigs occupy a third, whilst his milch goats live on various small skerries. As the extent of water between the different islets is proportional to their size, and is deep, the whole makes a very charming and compact picture. Yet he is only ten minutes by bicycle from his office in the Dockyard, although, from his little kingdom, no sign of the Dockyard is to be seen, it being shut off by a wooded promontory.

The Admiral was good enough to offer us every facility for laying up *Mana* in the Dockyard, but on various grounds we eventually decided to take war-time risks and bring her back to England, so receiving from him a signal-rocket outfit, and some kindly advice on the unwisdom of trying to run-down periscopes that showed no wake behind them, the vessel being now refreshed, at 0.55 p.m. on Friday, May the 12th, 1916, we weighed, and proceeded under power from Hamilton to the Examination Anchorage, with pilot aboard. Arriving there at 4.15 p.m. the Examining Officer came alongside and handed us the now usual special Admiralty clearance card, together with a courteous radiogram wishing us luck, from the Officer in Command of the Dockyard. The new trysail was hoisted, the engines stopped, and we commenced our voyage to Ponta Delgada in the Island of St. Miguel, one of the Azores, distant miles 1,869.

BERMUDA TO AZORES

This run was of "yachting" character. Gentle breezes, smooth seas, an occasional sail on the horizon. On the eighth day out, at the beginning of the first watch, the lights of St. Elmo were seen burning on both fore and main trucks. It is rather remarkable that this was the first, and only occasion, on which this phenomenon occurred throughout the entire voyage. Occasionally we got a turtle. Ten o'clock in the morning of the

30th of May showed us the Peak of Pico Island, 65 miles away, and at 10 p.m. next day, Thurs., May the 31st, we hove-to off Ponta Delgada in the island of St. Miguel to await daylight. The 1,869 miles had taken us 18 days.

Having been the victims of the organised dishonesty of the pilots of San Francisco in California, we had long before decided to run no risks of having the vessel again detained for ransom by foreign officials. *Mana* therefore next day, June the 1st, simply stood in and dropped a boat outside the breakwater, and again stood off, whilst we pulled in. Being Good Friday, it was, of course, a *fiesta*, all shops shut, and everybody away in the country. Our consul, too, was away for the day, but his wife kindly gave us our letters. We had been instructed to obtain from him the necessary information regarding war conditions, and the regulations governing shipping bound for British ports. At Bermuda nothing was known.

When pulling up the harbour, we had noticed one British vessel—an armed Government transport, evidently formerly a small German passenger-carrying tramp—so having bought some pineapples, vegetables and cigarettes, nothing else being procurable, we got into our boat and paid her a visit. Her commander was ashore for the day with the Consul fiestaing, but his Chief Officer was good enough to put us *au courant* with things, so we bade adieu to Ponta Delgada without any wish to see more of it, and pulled out to sea. The ship was far away to leeward, set down by wind and current. Not expecting us to get through our work so quickly, she had not troubled to keep her station, but went off to argufy by flag with a Lloyd's Signal-Station which would not admit that she was in its book.

After she had picked us up one of the men left aboard asked whether any of the craft in the harbour were " a-hanging Judas." Though there were several small square-rigged vessels alongside the Mole, none had, however, cock-billed their yards.[1] It was interesting thus to find that the memory and meaning of the old sea custom still survived. Old superstitions and fancies still exist : an ancient shellback who was with us down to the s'uth-'ard reprobated the capture of an albatross—" They is the

---

[1] *Cock-bill.* To put the yards " a-cock-bill " is to top them up by one lift to an angle with the deck. A symbol of mourning.—*The Sailor's Word-Book* (Admiral Smyth, 1867).

spurrits of drownded seamen." Someone objected on doctrinal grounds, but was met with the crushing rejoinder : " I said *spurrits :* their *souls* ar' in 'ell."

AZORES TO SOUTHAMPTON

And now we come to the last lap. On June the 1st, by 1 p.m. we were again aboard *Mana*, the boat hoisted in, and she bore away to round Ferraira Point which forms the extremity of St. Michael's Island. From Ferraira's Point to the haven where we would be was 1101.5 miles, and the direction N.49¼° E. true, or, shall we say, North East.

After making the customary routine entries in the Log Book associated with taking departure—the latitude, the longitude, the reading of the patent log, the canvas set, etc.—our Sailing-master makes the following entry, " And now we are fairly on our way to Dear Old Britain. All the talk now is of the sub-marine risks. I put our chances of getting through unmolested at 85 per cent. But is the *Mana* doomed ? Time will tell, but I don't think."

Nevertheless every preparation was now made, in case we had to leave the ship in a hurry, at the orders of some German sub-marine. The engine was taken out of the lifeboat to save weight. Every detail both for her and the cutter was suitably packed or made up, and placed in the deck house, ready to be passed into her at the last moment before she was lowered. We could only afford room for the photographic negatives and papers of the Expedition. If the ship be sunk, the whole of the priceless, because irreplaceable, archæological and ethnological collections must go with her.

The men, however, proceeded to pack, in their great seamen's bags, all the clutter and old rubbish they had accumulated during a voyage of over three years. Its bulk and weight would have rendered the boats unmanageable. Moreover, each man, when the time came, would be attending to shipping his property instead of giving all thought to getting his boat with her essential equipment safely away from the vessel. But we had taken them this long voyage without accident, and we were not going to let them make fools of themselves at the finish. Moreover, *Mana* carried a pretty mixed crowd : English, Spanish, Portuguese, and West Indian negroes, a Russian Finn, and descendants of the

25

mutineers of the *Bounty*. At a pinch, amongst such a lot, long
knives are apt to appear from nowhere, and self-control and
discipline be at an end, with lamentable result. We therefore
drew up a set of orders in triplicate ; one copy for the fo'c's'le,
one for aft, and one for entry in the official log, in which was
clearly set out a routine that was to be followed to the letter
in the event of our having to take to the boats. The details need
not here be given, suffice to say that they stated that explicit
orders for the common good were now set out in writing, and
that THESE ORDERS WOULD NOT, WHEN THE OCCASION
AROSE, BE REPEATED VERBALLY ; that there was ample
boat accommodation for all, if the lifeboat were got away safely
from the ship before the cutter, but not otherwise, because all
hands were needed to swing out the larger boat. Therefore,
when the ship's bell rang, the Sailing-master would take up his
position by the lifeboat in the waist, to superintend her launching
and stowage, and to give orders, and eventually to take command
of her, and the Master would pick up his loaded repeating rifle
and spare cartridges in clips and go to the taffrail. (It was
obvious from that position he could see and hear everything,
and yet could not be approached or rushed by any, or many.)

Any man failing immediately to appear on deck when the bell
rang would be shot dead without any warning when he did
appear. Any man endeavouring to place his private gear in a
boat would be shot dead in the act, without any warning. The
like if he attempted to enter other than his own boat, or his own
boat out of his turn. The like on a long knife, or other weapon,
being seen in his hand or possession. The like on his failing to
obey the verbal orders as issued.

By the routine laid down the lifeboat would get away safely
with her crew and equipment. The cutter's own crew were
strong enough to load and lower their own boat, after having
assisted the heavy lifeboat, provided they obeyed the orders of
the Mate who had charge of her. He was a good seaman, but
it was essential that he should have the moral support that
comes from a loaded rifle. Once boats all clear and safe, the
lifeboat would pull in to the ship, as close as she thought wise,
whereupon the "Old Man," in a nice cork jacket, would drop
off his taffrail into the water, and she would pick him up.

These orders and the penalties, extreme as they were, met

with general approval as far as we could gather indirectly. Two days after their being posted, when Thomas, the coloured cook, came for orders, we thought we would put him through his catechism. "Have you learnt up the orders in the fo'c's'le that concern you, Thomas?" "Yes, sar!" "When the bell rings, what will *you* do?" "Jump deck quick, damn quick, sar!" "Good! And then?" "I go starn big boat." "And when she is in the water you'll jump into her?" "No, sar! You shoot Thomas. Cutter's my boat." Thomas had got up his orders thoroughly and intelligently, and departed quite pleased with his viva voce exam., and the bundle of cigarettes his reward.

Some of the men, finding that their kit-bags must be left behind, hit out the following ingenious plan for saving their clothes. They first put on their Sunday best suit, over that their weekday go-ashore rig, then their working clothes. To the foregoing must be added a knitted guernsey or two, and any superior underclothing. The result was most grotesque; they could hardly waddle, or get through the fo'c's'le hatch. Had the fine weather continued, their sufferings would have been severe. A gale, however, in which no submarine could show her nose, came to their rescue.

At the time we are writing of—June 1916—the submarines were not operating far out into the Atlantic. Our idea was to keep *Mana* well away until we got on to about the same parallel of latitude as the Scilly Isles, and then wait thereabouts until it blew hard from the S.W. Blow it did, sure enough, with high confused seas: dangerous. Gradually they became bigger, but less wicked. We rode it out dry and comfortably as usual, with oil-bags to wind'ard. Unhappily it was an Easterly gale, instead of the Westerly we had hoped for. It moderated. The wind drew to the Nor'ard. We let her go, and sped up the Channel at a great pace, and arrived in St. Helen's Roads, Isle of Wight, at noon on June the 23rd. Twenty-two days from St. Miguel. We had entered and passed up the English Channel, unchallenged by friend or foe.

In St. Helen's Roads we took aboard the now obligatory Government pilot, who brought us through the different defences to the Hamble Spit Buoy, from which we had started three years and four months earlier.

We had traversed, almost entirely under canvas, without accident of consequence to ship or man, a distance of over One Hundred Thousand miles.

Such is the mana of MANA.

[The Royal Cruising Club Challenge Cup, last held by *Sunbeam* (Lord Brassey), was, in 1917, awarded to *Mana* on her return, by special resolution of the Annual General Meeting of the Club, " for a remarkable cruise in the Pacific."]

EPILOGUE

MANA was once more back in England, and her crew went each on his way. The Brixham and Lowestoft men returned to their homes, having at least enlarged their knowledge of the world. Rosa, the Chilean engineer, and the Jamaican cook disappeared to get engagements back to their respective lands; Rosa, we trust, to realise his dreams of a shop and a wife at St. Vincent. Mr. Gillam applied for service in the Royal Navy, and subsequently became a sub-lieutenant in the R.N.R.

The two Pitcairners were the last left on board; they had proved themselves very intelligent, as well as good workers. Charles could, it is believed, have passed an examination on every port he had visited, and how long he had stayed in each. We endeavoured to make some amends for our lack of Mendelian research on their island, by sending them up to the Royal College of Surgeons, where they were thoroughly measured and examined by Professor Keith.[1]

A still more signal honour awaited them; they were commanded to Buckingham Palace as representatives of England's smallest colony. Mr. Gillam took charge of them in London. He was not intimately acquainted with the great city, and used the map as he would a chart, disdaining the main thoroughfares, unless they lay on the direct route, and steering a straight course by weird and mysterious alleys. Any way, his charges were produced in good time at the Palace.

During the arrangements for the interview, S. had stated that the men spoke " the pure Elizabethan English of the Bible and Prayer Book "; their vocabulary, however, had been enlarged on *Mana*, and I was not without trepidation lest such expressions might crop out as " I don't mind if I do "; which is considered at Brixham the most courteous form of polite accep-

[1] See *Man*, vol. xvii. 1917, No. 88.

tance. All, however, went well. Charles, who acted as spokesman, after a first embarrassment answered readily the questions asked by the King. The Queen graciously accepted some specimens of Pitcairn handiwork, and the men · were much impressed with the kindness and condescension of their Majesties.

Incidentally, during the interview with which we were previously honoured, they made great friends with the royal footman who was on duty outside. He was of course a very imposing person in scarlet and gold, and they shook hands affectionately with him on leaving. Cuttings from the newspapers of official and other paragraphs, announcing the reception of the two inhabitants of Pitcairn by King George and Queen Mary, were taken back by them to be inserted in the State records of the island. Posts were obtained for both men on a New Zealand liner, and we have since heard that they have safely returned to their home, having made the voyage from Tahiti on a little schooner which the plucky Pitcairners have built since we were there. It is to be hoped that this boat may continue a success and solve many of the problems of the island.

This narrative cannot close without that note of pride and sadness which, alas, characterises so many records at this time in the history of the world. Since the first chapter was written two more of our company have laid down their lives. The words of appreciation which it was hoped would have given pleasure can only be wreaths to their memory. Charles Jeffery, of Lowestoft, who joined at Whitstable and was with us to the last, who grew from boyhood to manhood on *Mana*, has met with a hero's death on a minesweeper.

Henry James Gillam rests in a Sicilian grave. Volunteers were called for, for specially dangerous work in capturing submarines; Gillam responded—it is impossible to picture his doing otherwise—and he fell in action in April 1918. The loss to his country is great; to us it is very real and personal. The whole voyage of the *Mana* is a tribute to his skill. His high intelligence and character secured him universal confidence, while his unvarying good temper—in bad times as well as in good—made him a delightful companion. One can only think of him in that other life as still keen for some new work or enterprise, and carrying it out with perfect loyalty and success.

Thus from land and sea, in defence of a Great Cause, have our comrades of the Expedition made their last voyage " westward."

> I know not where His islands lift
> Their fronded palms in air;
> I only know I cannot drift
> Beyond His love and care.
>
> WHITTIER.

* * * * * *

And now the story is told. The Expedition has, we hope, brought some new pieces to fit into the puzzle which it went out to study, but the help is needed of every reader who has more to bring, from whatever part of the world; so alone can be finally solved the Mystery of Easter Island.

ITINERARY OF THE EXPEDITION

OUTWARD VOYAGE

Left Southampton	Feb. 28	1913
Dartmouth	March 1–5	,,
Falmouth	March 6–25	,,
Madeira	April 13–16	,,
Grand Canary	April 18—May 10	,,
Cape Verde Islands	May 17–29	,,
Pernambuco	June 15–21	,,
Bahia de Todos os Santos	June 25–26	,,
Cabral Bay	July 2–4	,,
Cape Frio	July 10–12	,,
Rio de Janeiro	July 14–23	,,
Porto Bello Bay	July 27—Aug. 2	,,
Buenos Aires	Aug. 17—Sept. 19	,,
Port Desire	Oct. 3–6	,,
Entered Magellan Straits	Oct. 16	,,
Punta Arenas	Oct. 20—Nov. 29	,,
Entered Patagonian Channels	Dec. 11	,,
Left Patagonian Channels	Jan. 6	1914
Talcahuano	Jan. 14—Feb. 13	,,
Juan Fernandez	Feb. 16—Feb. 19	,,
Valparaiso	Feb. 22—Feb. 28	,,
Juan Fernandez	March 4—March 9	,,

EASTER ISLAND

Arrival at the Island	March 29	1914
Mana leaves	May 23	,,
Native rising begins	July 1	,,
Arrival of Chilean warship	Aug. 4	,,
Mana returns	Aug. 23	,,
Mana leaves (second time)	Sept. 4	,,
Visit from Von Spee's squadron	Oct. 12–18	,,
S. R. goes to Chile	Dec. 5	,,
Visit of *Prinz Eitel Friedrich*	Dec. 23–31	,,

Return of *Mana* with S. R. . .	March 15 .	. 1915
Mana leaves (third time) . .	March 17 .	. ,,
Mana returns	May 28 .	. ,,
Expedition leaves the Island .	Aug. 18 .	. ,,

HOMEWARD VOYAGE

Pitcairn Island . . .	Aug. 27—Sept. 1, 1915
Tahiti	Sept. 16—Oct 8 . ,,
Honolulu	Nov. 11—Dec. 1 . ,,
Mana leaves Honolulu Nov. 28, arr. San Francisco Dec. 25 . ,,
Hawaii	Dec. 2–6 . . ,,
San Francisco . . arr. Dec. 14, 1915—Jan. 20, 1916
[K.R. leaves Jan. 16—reaches England Feb. 6, 1916]
San Francisco . . .	left Jan. 20 . . ,,
Socorro	Feb. 5–6 . . ,,
Quibo	March 7–9 . . ,,
Panama	March 13–16 . ,,
Through the Canal . .	March 17–18 ,,
Cristobal	March 18–26 . ,,
Jamaica	April 7–9 . . ,,
Bermuda	May 2–12 . . ,,
Azores	May 31—June 1 . ,,
Southampton . . .	June 25 . . ,,

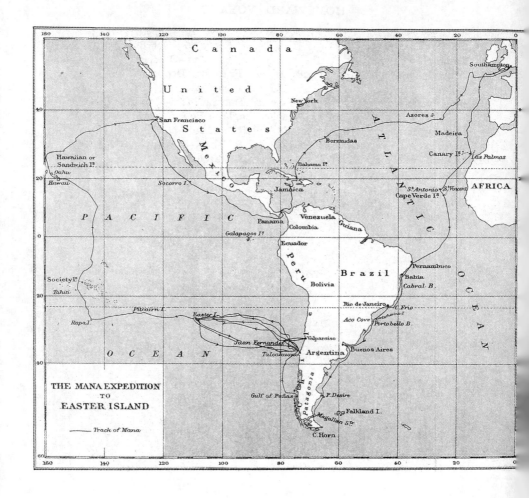

THE MANA EXPEDITION
TO
EASTER ISLAND

——— Track of Mana

INDEX

Note.—Entries other than proper names refer to Easter Island, unless otherwise stated. References to illustrations are given in text.

Jaussen, Bishop, of Tahiti :
— account of departure of missionaries, 208
— list of chiefs by, 241
— translation of tablets attempted by, 207, 247, 253
Jean, French ship :
— crew at Easter Island as prisoners, 160
— destruction by Germans, 157–8, 160
Jeffery, Charles C., boy on *Mana*, 9, 78, 390
Jeneral Baquedano, ship, 144, 147–8
Jotefa, native, 266
Joyce, Captain T. A., views on Easter Island, 269, 295–6
Juan Fernandez :
— animals, 112
— *Dresden* at, 113
— history, 111
— lobster trade, 113
— Selkirk's look-out and cave, 112–3
Juan Tepano, native, 158, 214, 228, 240, 289

Kamehameha, chief of Hawaii, 322, 324, 327
Kaimokoi, son of Ngaara, 241, 246–7
Kainga, legend of, 282–8
Kealekakua, Bay of, Hawaii, 326
Kanakas : *see* Easter Islanders
Kapiera, native :
— knowledge *re* wooden carvings, 271
— tau explained by, 251
— wars of Kotuu and Hotu Iti, date of, 289
Kaunga, ceremony, 234–5
Keith, Dr. : report *re* native skulls, 228, 295
Kelp-geese, 96–7
Kildalton, ship captured by Germans, 157–60
Kilauea, Hawaii, 325–6
Kilimuti, native, 261, 274, 281
King George, 390
Kingston, Jamaica, 373, 375
Ko Mari, carved design, 263
Ko Peka, ceremony, 233–4
Ko Tori, last cannibal, 225–6, 266
Kohau : *see* Tablets
Koro, ceremony, 234–42, 251–2, 267
Koro-orongo clan, 223, 280, 284
Koromaké : *see under* Religion
Kotuu, son of Hotu-matua, 280, 281, 282
Kotuu, territorial division : *see* Hotu Iti

Language, 203, 207, 213–4, 295, 327
Lapelin, Admiral T. de, on origin of Easter Islanders, 294–5
La Pérouse, accounts of Easter Island, 202–4, 234
Las Palmas, 22
Legends :
— of arrival of inhabitants on Easter Island (Hotu-matua), 277–80, 282, 294, 298
— from Mangareva, 294–5
— from Rapa-nui, 300
— of cairns and old woman, 232–3
— of first statue, 184
— of Gwaruti-mata-keva (Secret Society), 224
— of Hotu-matua : *see* Arrival of Inhabitants
— of Long Ears and Short Ears, 280–1
— of Oroi and Hotu-matua, 279–80
— of overthrow of statues, 173, 182
— of supernatural beings, 193, 237–9, 269–70
— of Tuukoihu, 269–70, 283
— of Uré-a-hohové carried off to Paréhé, 237
— of war between Kotuu and Hotu-iti, 282–8
— of wooden figures, 269–70
Lemuria, theories *re*, 290
Leprosy, 212, 250
Light, seaman on *Mana*, 9, 30
Liliuokalani, Queen of Hawaii, 322, 324
Lisiansky, early account of Easter Island, 204
Lizards, wooden, 238, 243, 268
Llay-Llay, Chile, 104
"Long-Ears" : *see under* Ears
Los Andes, Chile, 104, 106
Lowry-Corry, Frederick :
— death, 110
— joins expedition, 8, 72, 92
— typhoid fever, attack of, 108–9
"Luke," under-steward on *Mana*, 14, 73–4

Madeira, history and descriptions, 18
Magellan, discovery of Patagonia, 65
Magellan, Straits of, 69–85
Mahaiatea : *see* Tahiti : Marae
Mahanga, servant, 138–9, 292
Mana, vessel of Expedition :
— accident to, at Cristobal, 366–7
— books on board, 11
— building, 4, 6

Script (*cont.*):
— yearly festival connected with, 245–6
Secret societies, 224, 292
Selkirk, Alexander, 111, 112–3
Seligman, Dr., 296
Sharks, 117–8, 350
Sharp, Captain, of *Kidalton*, 159–60
" Short Ears ": *see under* Ears
Silva, Eduardo, engineer on *Mana*, 320, 349-50, 389
Skulls, race affinity, 295–6
  see also Miru
Slave raids, Peruvian, in South Seas, 124, 205, 208
Socorro Island, 340–9
Soloman Islands, bird cult in, 296–8
Spee, Admiral von :
— at Easter Island, 152, 153
— at Papeete, 319
Sphagnum, 256
Statues :
— on ahu, 166, 168, 170
— at Anakena, 173, 187
— as avenue to ahu, 196
— backs, two types, 187–8
  — design on, 187–8, 220, 269
— bed-plates, dimensions, 168
— as boundary marks, 193, 197, 261, 301
— in British Museum, larger : *see* Orongo statue
  — smaller, 197, 208
— burials in connection with, 190
— carvings incised on, 189, 263 note
— counterfeited by natives, 271
— date of construction, 299–300, 301
— description, general, 166
— details of, 186–9
— dimensions, 166, 170, 173, 182, 183, 195
— early accounts: *see* Easter Island: early accounts
— ears, 166
— erection, 189, 197
— excavation, 151–2, 163–4, 185–91
— hands, 186
— isolated, 193, 197
— legends, 173, 182, 184 : *see also* makers, names, transport
— makers (legendary), 181–2
— material, 175–6
— on Motu Nui, 261
— names, 183–4, 257, 301
— numbers, 168, 179, 183
— orbits, 187
— at Orongo : *see* Orongo
— overthrow, 172–3, 182, 299, 300

Statues (*cont.*) :
— at Paro, 173
— on Pitcairn Island, 313–4
— at Pitt Rivers Museum, 261 footnote
— in quarries : *see* Rano Raraku
— quarrying, method of, 179–80
— at Rano Raraku : *see under* this head
— representation and purpose, 301 : *see also above*, boundary
— on roads, 194–5
— sources of information, 200–5
— tools used in making, 180–1
— transport, problem of, 193, 195–8
— at Washington, 257 footnote
Submarines, preparations for meeting, 385–6
Sunbeam, yacht, 31, 76, 387 footnote

Tablets : *see* Script
Tahai, 246
Tahiti :
— description, 317
— German attack on, 153, 319
— history, 316
— Marae Mahaiatea, 316, 320
Tahonga, 267
Takau, Princess: *see* Pomare family, 247
Také, 266
Talcahuano, Chile, 100, 101–2, 154, 162–3
Tangata-ika : *see* Fish-men
Tangata-manu : *see* Bird Cult—bird-men
Tangata-rongo-rongo : *see* Script—professors
Tapa, 170, 201, 218–9
Tatane : *see* Religion — supernatural beings
Tattooing :
— inspection by Ariki, 243
— practice of, 219–20
Tau : *see under* Script
Taura-renga : *see* Orongo statue
Te Haha, Miru :
— part in socal functions, 240
— service with Chief Ngaara, 242, 243, 245–6
— wooden images made by, 271
Te Pito-te—henua : *see* Easter Island—names.
Tea-tenga, ahu, 194
Telde, Grand Canary, 25–7
Teneriffe : *see as for* Grand Canary
Tepano, Juan : *see* Juan Tepano
Tepeu, ahu, 170, 269

Printed by Hazell, Watson & Viney, Ld., London and Aylesbury.

THE ADVENTURES
UNLIMITED CATALOG

Order from the following pages or
write for our free 56 page catalog of
unusual books & videos!

THE MYSTERY OF EASTER ISLAND
by Katherine Routledge
The reprint of Katherine Routledge's classic archaeology book which was first published in London in 1919. The book details her journey by yacht from England to South America, around Patagonia to Chile and on to Easter Island. Routledge explored the amazing island and produced one of the first-ever accounts of the life, history and legends of this strange and remote place. Routledge discusses the statues, pyramid-platforms, Rongo Rongo script, the Bird Cult, the war between the Short Ears and the Long Ears, the secret caves, ancient roads on the island, and more. This rare book serves as a sourcebook on the early discoveries and theories on Easter Island.
432 PAGES. 6x9 PAPERBACK. ILLUSTRATED. $16.95. CODE: MEI

MYSTERY CITIES OF THE MAYA
Exploration and Adventure in Lubaantun & Belize
by Thomas Gann
First published in 1925, *Mystery Cities of the Maya* is a classic in Central American archaeology-adventure. Gann was close friends with Mike Mitchell-Hedges, the British adventurer who discovered the famous crystal skull with his adopted daughter Sammy and Lady Richmond Brown, their benefactress. Gann battles pirates along Belize's coast and goes upriver with Mitchell-Hedges to the site of Lubaantun where they excavate a strange lost city where the crystal skull was discovered. Lubaantun is a unique city in the Mayan world as it is built out of precisely carved blocks of stone without the usual plaster-cement facing. Lubaantun contained several large pyramids partially destroyed by earthquakes and a large amount of artifacts. Gann shared Mitchell-Hedges belief in Atlantis and lo civilizations (pre-Mayan) in Central America and the Caribbean. Lots of good photos, maps and diagrams.
252 PAGES. 6x9 PAPERBACK. ILLUSTRATED. $16.95. CODE: MCOM

IN SECRET TIBET
by Theodore Illion
Reprint of a rare 30s adventure travel book. Illion was a German wayfarer who not only spoke fluent Tibetan, but travelled disguise as a native through forbidden Tibet when it was off-limits to all outsiders. His incredible adventures make this one of t most exciting travel books ever published. Includes illustrations of Tibetan monks levitating stones by acoustics.
210 PAGES. 6x9 PAPERBACK. ILLUSTRATED. $15.95. CODE: IST

DARKNESS OVER TIBET
by Theodore Illion
In this second reprint of Illion's rare books, the German traveller continues his journey through Tibet and is given directions to a strange underground city. As the original publisher's remarks said, "this is a rare account of an underground city in Tibet by the only Westerner ever to enter it and escape alive! "
210 PAGES. 6x9 PAPERBACK. ILLUSTRATED. $15.95. CODE: DOT

DANGER MY ALLY
The Amazing Life Story of the Discoverer of the Crystal Skull
by "Mike" Mitchell-Hedges
The incredible life story of "Mike" Mitchell-Hedges, the British adventurer who discovered the Crystal Skull in the lost Mayan city of Lubaantun in Belize. Mitchell-Hedges has lived an exciting life: gambling everything on a trip to the Americas as a young man, riding with Pancho Villa, questing for Atlantis, fighting bandits in the Caribbean and discovering the famous Crystal Skull.
374 PAGES. 6x9 PAPERBACK. ILLUSTRATED. BIBLIOGRAPHY & INDEX. $16.95. CODE: DMA

IN SECRET MONGOLIA
by Henning Haslund
First published by Kegan Paul of London in 1934, Haslund takes us into the barely known world of Mongolia of 1921, a lan god-kings, bandits, vast mountain wilderness and a Russian army running amok. Starting in Peking, Haslund journeys to Mong as part of the Krebs Expedition—a mission to establish a Danish butter farm in a remote corner of northern Mongolia. Along way, he smuggles guns and nitroglycerin, is thrown into a prison by the new Communist regime, battles the Robber Princess more. With Haslund we meet the "Mad Baron" Ungern-Sternberg and his renegade Russian army, the many characters of Ur, fledgling foreign community, and the last god-king of Mongolia, Seng Chen Gegen, the fifth reincarnation of the Tiger god and "ruler of all Torguts." Aside from the esoteric and mystical material, there is plenty of just plain adventure: Haslund encounte Mongolian werewolf; is ambushed along the trail; escapes from prison and fights terrifying blizzards; more.
374 PAGES. 6x9 PAPERBACK. ILLUSTRATED. BIBLIOGRAPHY & INDEX. $16.95. CODE: ISM

MEN & GODS IN MONGOLIA
by Henning Haslund
First published in 1935 by Kegan Paul of London, Haslund takes us to the lost city of Karakota in the Gobi desert. We mee Bodgo Gegen, a god-king in Mongolia similar to the Dalai Lama of Tibet. We meet Dambin Jansang, the dreaded warlord o "Black Gobi." There is even material in this incredible book on the Hi-mori, an "airhorse" that flies through the sky (simil a Vimana) and carries with it the sacred stone of Chintamani. Aside from the esoteric and mystical material, there is plenty o plain adventure: Haslund and companions journey across the Gobi desert by camel caravan; are kidnapped and held for rans witness initiation into Shamanic societies; meet reincarnated warlords; and experience the violent birth of "modern" Mong
358 PAGES. 6X9 PAPERBACK. ILLUSTRATED. INDEX. $15.95. CODE: MGM

ATLANTIS REPRINT SERIES

ATLANTIS: MOTHER OF EMPIRES
Atlantis Reprint Series
by Robert Stacy-Judd
Robert Stacy-Judd's classic 1939 book on Atlantis is back in print in this large-format paperback edition. Stacy-Judd was a California architect and an expert on the Mayas and their relationship to Atlantis. He was an excellent artist and his work is lavishly illustrated. The eighteen comprehensive chapters in the book are: The Mayas and the Lost Atlantis; Conjectures and Opinions; The Atlantean Theory; Cro-Magnon Man; East is West; And West is East; The Mormons and the Mayas; Astrology in Two Hemispheres; The Language of Architecture; The American Indian; Pre-Panamanians and Pre-Incas; Columns and City Planning; Comparisons and Mayan Art; The Iberian Link; The Maya Tongue; Quetzalcoatl; Summing Up the Evidence; The Mayas in Yucatan.
340 PAGES. 8x11 PAPERBACK. ILLUSTRATED. INDEX. $19.95. CODE: AMOE

MYSTERIES OF ANCIENT SOUTH AMERICA
Atlantis Reprint Series
by Harold T. Wilkins

The reprint of Wilkins' classic book on the megaliths and mysteries of South America. This book predates Wilkin's book *Secret Cities of Old South America* published in 1952. *Mysteries of Ancient South America* was first published in 1947 and is considered a classic book of its kind. With diagrams, photos and maps, Wilkins digs into old manuscripts and books to bring us some truly amazing stories of South America: a bizarre subterranean tunnel system; lost cities in the remote border jungles of Brazil; legends of Atlantis in South America; cataclysmic changes that shaped South America; and other strange stories from one of the world's great researchers. Chapters include: Our Earth's Greatest Disaster, Dead Cities of Ancient Brazil, The Jungle Light that Shines by Itself, The Missionary Men in Black: Forerunners of the Great Catastrophe, The Sign of the Sun: The World's Oldest Alphabet, Sign-Posts to the Shadow of Atlantis, The Atlanean "Subterraneans" of the Incas, Tiahuanacu and the Giants, more.
236 PAGES. 6x9 PAPERBACK. ILLUSTRATED. INDEX. $14.95. CODE: MASA

SECRET CITIES OF OLD SOUTH AMERICA
Atlantis Reprint Series
by Harold T. Wilkins
The reprint of Wilkins' classic book, first published in 1952, claiming that South America was Atlantis. Chapters include Mysteries of a Lost World; Atlantis Unveiled; Red Riddles on the Rocks; South America's Amazons Existed!; The Mystery of El Dorado and Gran Payatiti—the Final Refuge of the Incas; Monstrous Beasts of the Unexplored Swamps & Wilds; Weird Denizens of Antediluvian Forests; New Light on Atlantis from the World's Oldest Book; The Mystery of Old Man Noah and the Arks; and more.
438 PAGES. 6x9 PAPERBACK. ILLUSTRATED. BIBLIOGRAPHY & INDEX. $16.95. CODE: SCOS

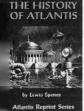

THE SHADOW OF ATLANTIS
The Echoes of Atlantean Civilization Tracked through Space & Time
by Colonel Alexander Braghine
First published in 1940, *The Shadow of Atlantis* is one of the great classics of Atlantis research. The book amasses a great deal of archaeological, anthropological, historical and scientific evidence in support of a lost continent in the Atlantic Ocean. Braghine covers such diverse topics as Egyptians in Central America, the myth of Quetzalcoatl, the Basque language and its connection with Atlantis, the connections with the ancient pyramids of Mexico, Egypt and Atlantis, the sudden demise of mammoths, legends of giants and much more. Braghine was a linguist and spends part of the book tracing ancient languages to Atlantis and studying little-known inscriptions in Brazil, deluge myths and the connections between ancient languages. Braghine takes us on a fascinating journey through space and time in search of the lost continent.
288 PAGES. 6x9 PAPERBACK. ILLUSTRATED. $16.95. CODE: SOA

RIDDLE OF THE PACIFIC
by John Macmillan Brown
Oxford scholar Brown's classic work on lost civilizations of the Pacific is now back in print! John Macmillan Brown was an historian and New Zealand's premier scientist when he wrote about the origins of the Maoris. After many years of travel thoughout the Pacific studying the people and customs of the south seas islands, he wrote *Riddle of the Pacific* in 1924. The book is packed with rare turn-of-the-century illustrations. Don't miss Brown's classic study of Easter Island, ancient scripts, megalithic roads and cities, more. Brown was an early believer in a lost continent in the Pacific.
460 PAGES. 6x9 PAPERBACK. ILLUSTRATED. $16.95. CODE: ROP

THE HISTORY OF ATLANTIS
by Lewis Spence
Lewis Spence's classic book on Atlantis is now back in print! Spence was a Scottish historian (1874-1955) who is best known for his volumes on world mythology and his five Atlantis books. *The History of Atlantis* (1926) is considered his finest. Spence does his scholarly best in chapters on the Sources of Atlantean History, the Geography of Atlantis, the Races of Atlantis, the Kings of Atlantis, the Religion of Atlantis, the Colonies of Atlantis, more. Sixteen chapters in all.
240 PAGES. 6x9 PAPERBACK. ILLUSTRATED WITH MAPS, PHOTOS & DIAGRAMS. $16.95. CODE: HOA

ATLANTIS IN SPAIN
A Study of the Ancient Sun Kingdoms of Spain
by E.M. Whishaw
First published by Rider & Co. of London in 1928, this classic book is a study of the megaliths of Spain, ancient writing, cyclopean walls, sun worshipping empires, hydraulic engineering, and sunken cities. An extremely rare book, it was out of print for 60 years. Learn about the Biblical Tartessus; an Atlantean city at Niebla; the Temple of Hercules and the Sun Temple of Seville; Libyans and the Copper Age; more. Profusely illustrated with photos, maps and drawings.
284 PAGES. 6x9 PAPERBACK. ILLUSTRATED. TABLES OF ANCIENT SCRIPTS. $15.95. CODE: AIS

24 hour credit card orders—call: 815-253-6390 fax: 815-253-6300

email: auphq@frontiernet.net   www.adventuresunlimitedpress.com   www.wexclub.com

ATLANTIS STUDIES

MAPS OF THE ANCIENT SEA KINGS
Evidence of Advanced Civilization in the Ice Age
by Charles H. Hapgood

Charles Hapgood's classic 1966 book on ancient maps produces concrete evidence of an advanced world-wide civilization existing many thousands of years before ancient Egypt. He has found the evidence in the Piri Reis Map that shows Antarctica, the Hadji Ahmed map, the Oronteus Finaeus and other amazing maps. Hapgood concluded that these maps were made from more ancient maps from the various ancient archives around the world, now lost. Not only were these unknown people more advanced in mapmaking than any people prior to the 18th century, it appears they mapped all the continents. The Americas were mapped thousands of years before Columbus. Antarctica was mapped when its coasts were free of ice.
316 PAGES. 7X10 PAPERBACK. ILLUSTRATED. BIBLIOGRAPHY & INDEX. $19.95. CODE: MASK

PATH OF THE POLE
Cataclysmic Pole Shift Geology
by Charles Hapgood

Maps of the Ancient Sea Kings author Hapgood's classic book *Path of the Pole* is back in print! Hapgood researched Antarctica, ancient maps and the geological record to conclude that the Earth's crust has slipped in the inner core many times in the past, changing the position of the pole. *Path of the Pole* discusses the various "pole shifts" in Earth's past, giving evidence for each one, and moves on to possible future pole shifts. Packed with illustrations, this is the sourcebook for many other books on cataclysms and pole shifts.
356 PAGES. 6X9 PAPERBACK. ILLUSTRATED. $16.95. CODE: POP.

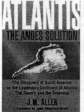

ATLANTIS: THE ANDES SOLUTION
The Theory and the Evidence
by J.M. Allen, forward by John Blashford-Snell

Imported from Britain, this deluxe hardback is J.M. Allen's fascinating research into the lost world that exists on the Bolivian Plateau and his theory that it is Atlantis. Allen looks into Lake Titicaca, the ruins of Tiahuanaco and the mysterious Lake PooPoo. The high plateau of Bolivia must contain the remains of Atlantis, claims Allen. Lots of fascinating stuff here with Allen discovering the remains of huge ancient canals that once crisscrossed the vast plain southwest of Tiahuanaco. A must-read for all researchers into South America, Atlantis and mysteries of the past. With lots of illustrations, some in color.
196 PAGES. 6X9 HARDBACK. ILLUSTRATED. BIBLIOGRAPHY. $25.99. CODE: ATAS

ATLANTIS IN AMERICA
Navigators of the Ancient World
by Ivar Zapp and George Erikson

This book is an intensive examination of the archeological sites of the Americas, an examination that reveals civilization has existed here for tens of thousands of years. Zapp is an expert on the enigmatic giant stone spheres of Costa Rica, and maintains that they were sighting stones similar to those found throughout the Pacific as well as in Egypt and the Middle East. They were used to teach star-paths and sea navigation of the world-wide navigators of the ancient world. While the Mediterranean and European regions "forgot" world-wide navigation and fought wars, the Mesoamericans of diverse races were building vast interconnected cities without walls. This Golden Age of ancient America was merely a myth of suppressed history—until now. Profusely illustrated, chapters are on Navigators of the Ancient World; Pyramids & Megaliths: Older Than You Think; Ancient Ports and Colonies; Cataclysms of the Past; Atlantis: From Myth to Reality; The Serpent and the Cross: The Loss of the City States; Calendars and Star Temples; and more.
360 PAGES. 6X9 PAPERBACK. ILLUSTRATED. BIBLIOGRAPHY & INDEX. $17.95. CODE: AIA

FAR-OUT ADVENTURES   *REVISED EDITION*
The Best of World Explorer Magazine

This is a compilation of the first nine issues of *World Explorer* in a large-format paperback. Authors include: David Hatcher Childress, Joseph Jochmans, John Major Jenkins, Deanna Emerson, Katherine Routledge, Alexander Horvat, Greg Deyermenjian, Dr. Marc Miller, and others. Articles in this book include Smithsonian Gate, Dinosaur Hunting in the Congo, Secret Writings of the Incas, On the Trail of the Yeti, Secrets of the Sphinx, Living Pterodactyls, Quest for Atlantis, What Happened to the Great Library of Alexandria?, In Search of Seamonsters, Egyptians in the Pacific, Lost Megaliths of Guatemala, the Mystery of Easter Island, Comacalco: Mayan City of Mystery, Professor Wexler and plenty more.
580 PAGES. 8X11 PAPERBACK. ILLUSTRATED. REVISED EDITION. $25.00. CODE: FOA

RETURN OF THE SERPENTS OF WISDOM
by Mark Amaru Pinkham

According to ancient records, the patriarchs and founders of the early civilizations in Egypt, India, China, Peru, Mesopotamia, Britain, and the Americas were the Serpents of Wisdom—spiritual masters associated with the serpent—who arrived in these lands after abandoning their beloved homelands and crossing great seas. While bearing names denoting snake or dragon (such as Naga, Lung, Djedhi, Amaru, Quetzalcoatl, Adder, etc.), these Serpents of Wisdom oversaw the construction of magnificent civilizations within which they and their descendants served as the priest kings and as the enlightened heads of mystery school traditions. *Return of the Serpents of Wisdom* recounts the history of these "Serpents"—where they came from, why they came, the secret wisdom they disseminated, and why they are returning now.
400 PAGES. 6X9 PAPERBACK. ILLUSTRATED. REFERENCES. $16.95. CODE: RSW

LOST CITIES OF ATLANTIS, ANCIENT EUROPE & THE MEDITERRANEAN
by David Hatcher Childress

Atlantis! The legendary lost continent comes under the close scrutiny of maverick archaeologist David Hatcher Childress in this sixth book in the internationally popular *Lost Cities* series. Childress takes the reader in search of sunken cities in the Mediterranean; across the Atlas Mountains in search of Atlantean ruins; to remote islands in search of megalithic ruins; to meet living legends and secret societies. From Ireland to Turkey, Morocco to Eastern Europe, and around the remote islands of the Mediterranean and Atlantic, Childress takes the reader on an astonishing quest for mankind's past. Ancient technology, cataclysms, megalithic construction, lost civilizations and devastating wars of the past are all explored in this book. Childress challenges the skeptics and proves that great civilizations not only existed in the past, but the modern world and its problems are reflections of the ancient world of Atlantis.
524 PAGES. 6x9 PAPERBACK. ILLUSTRATED WITH 100s OF MAPS, PHOTOS AND DIAGRAMS. BIBLIOGRAPHY & INDEX. $16.95. CODE: MED

LOST CITIES OF CHINA, CENTRAL INDIA & ASIA
by David Hatcher Childress

Like a real life "Indiana Jones," maverick archaeologist David Childress takes the reader on an incredible adventure across some of the world's oldest and most remote countries in search of lost cities and ancient mysteries. Discover ancient cities in the Gobi Desert; hear fantastic tales of lost continents, vanished civilizations and secret societies bent on ruling the world; visit forgotten monasteries in forbidding snow-capped mountains with strange tunnels to mysterious subterranean cities!
A unique combination of far-out exploration and practical travel advice, it will astound and delight the experienced traveler or the armchair voyager.
429 PAGES. 6x9 PAPERBACK. ILLUSTRATED. FOOTNOTES & BIBLIOGRAPHY. $14.95. CODE: CHI

LOST CITIES OF ANCIENT LEMURIA & THE PACIFIC
by David Hatcher Childress

Was there once a continent in the Pacific? Called Lemuria or Pacifica by geologists, Mu or Pan by the mystics, there is now ample mythological, geological and archaeological evidence to "prove" that an advanced and ancient civilization once lived in the central Pacific. Maverick archaeologist and explorer David Hatcher Childress combs the Indian Ocean, Australia and the Pacific in search of the surprising truth about mankind's past. Contains photos of the underwater city on Pohnpei; explanations on how the statues were levitated around Easter Island in a clockwise vortex movement; tales of disappearing islands; Egyptians in Australia; and more.
379 PAGES. 6x9 PAPERBACK. ILLUSTRATED. FOOTNOTES & BIBLIOGRAPHY. $14.95. CODE: LEM

ANCIENT TONGA
& the Lost City of Mu'a
by David Hatcher Childress

Lost Cities series author Childress takes us to the south sea islands of Tonga, Rarotonga, Samoa and Fiji to investigate the megalithic ruins on these beautiful islands. The great empire of the Polynesians, centered on Tonga and the ancient city of Mu'a, is revealed with old photos, drawings and maps. Chapters in this book are on the Lost City of Mu'a and its many megalithic pyramids, the Ha'amonga Trilithon and ancient Polynesian astronomy, Samoa and the search for the lost land of Havai'iki, Fiji and its wars with Tonga, Rarotonga's megalithic road, and Polynesian cosmology. Material on Egyptians in the Pacific, earth changes, the fortified moat around Mu'a, lost roads, more.
218 PAGES. 6x9 PAPERBACK. ILLUSTRATED. COLOR PHOTOS. BIBLIOGRAPHY. $15.95. CODE: TONG

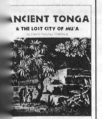

ANCIENT MICRONESIA
& the Lost City of Nan Madol
by David Hatcher Childress

Micronesia, a vast archipelago of islands west of Hawaii and south of Japan, contains some of the most amazing megalithic ruins in the world. Part of our *Lost Cities* series, this volume explores the incredible conformations on various Micronesian islands, especially the fantastic and little-known ruins of Nan Madol on Pohnpei Island. The huge canal city of Nan Madol contains over 250 million tons of basalt columns over an 11 square-mile area of artificial islands. Much of the huge city is submerged, and underwater structures can be found to an estimated 80 feet. Islanders' legends claim that the basalt rocks, weighing up to 50 tons, were magically levitated into place by the powerful forefathers. Other ruins in Micronesia that are profiled include the Latte Stones of the Marianas, the menhirs of Palau, the megalithic canal city on Kosrae Island, megaliths on Guam, and more.
256 PAGES. 6x9 PAPERBACK. ILLUSTRATED. INCLUDES A COLOR PHOTO SECTION. BIBLIOGRAPHY. $16.95. CODE: AMIC

TECHNOLOGY OF THE GODS
The Incredible Sciences of the Ancients
by David Hatcher Childress
Popular *Lost Cities* author David Hatcher Childress takes us into the amazing world of ancient technology, from computers in antiquity to the "flying machines of the gods." Childress looks at the technology that was allegedly used in Atlantis and the theory that the Great Pyramid of Egypt was originally a gigantic power station. He examines tales of ancient flight and the technology that it involved; how the ancients used electricity; megalithic building techniques; the use of crystal lenses and the fire from the gods; evidence of various high tech weapons in the past, including atomic weapons; ancient metallurgy and heavy machinery; the role of modern inventors such as Nikola Tesla in bringing ancient technology back into modern use; impossible artifacts; and more.
356 PAGES. 6x9 PAPERBACK. ILLUSTRATED. BIBLIOGRAPHY. $16.95. CODE: TGOD

VIMANA AIRCRAFT OF ANCIENT INDIA & ATLANTIS
by David Hatcher Childress, introduction by Ivan T. Sanderson
Did the ancients have the technology of flight? In this incredible volume on ancient India, authentic Indian texts such as the *Ramayana* and the *Mahabharata* are used to prove that ancient aircraft were in use more than four thousand years ago. Included in this book is the entire Fourth Century BC manuscript *Vimaanika Shastra* by the ancient author Maharishi Bharadwaaja, translated into English by the Mysore Sanskrit professor G.R. Josyer. Also included are chapters on Atlantean technology, the incredible Rama Empire of India and the devastating wars that destroyed it. Also an entire chapter on mercury vortex propulsion and mercury gyros, the power source described in the ancient Indian texts. Not to be missed by those interested in ancient civilizations or the UFO enigma.
334 PAGES. 6x9 PAPERBACK. RARE PHOTOGRAPHS, MAPS AND DRAWINGS.
$15.95. CODE: VAA

LOST CONTINENTS & THE HOLLOW EARTH
I Remember Lemuria and the Shaver Mystery
by David Hatcher Childress & Richard Shaver
Lost Continents & the Hollow Earth is Childress' thorough examination of the early hollow earth stories of Richard Shaver and the fascination that fringe fantasy subjects such as lost continents and the hollow earth have had for the American public. Shaver's rare 1948 book *I Remember Lemuria* is reprinted in its entirety, and the book is packed with illustrations from Ray Palmer's *Amazing Stories* magazine of the 1940s. Palmer and Shaver told of tunnels running through the earth—tunnels inhabited by the Deros and Teros, humanoids from an ancient spacefaring race that had inhabited the earth, eventually going underground, hundreds of thousands of years ago. Childress discusses famous hollow earth books and delves deep into whatever reality may be behind the stories of tunnels in the earth. Operation High Jump to Antarctica in 1947 and Admiral Byrd's bizarre statements, tunnel systems in South America and Tibet, the underground world of Agartha, the belief of UFOs coming from the South Pole, more.
344 PAGES. 6x9 PAPERBACK. ILLUSTRATED. $16.95. CODE: LCHE

LOST CITIES OF NORTH & CENTRAL AMERICA
by David Hatcher Childress
Down the back roads from coast to coast, maverick archaeologist and adventurer David Hatcher Childress goes deep into unknown America. With this incredible book, you will search for lost Mayan cities and books of gold, discover an ancient canal system in Arizona, climb gigantic pyramids in the Midwest, explore megalithic monuments in New England, and join the astonishing quest for lost cities throughout North America. From the war-torn jungles of Guatemala, Nicaragua and Honduras to the deserts, mountains and fields of Mexico, Canada, and the U.S.A., Childress takes the reader in search of sunken ruins, Viking forts, strange tunnel systems, living dinosaurs, early Chinese explorers, and fantastic lost treasure. Packed with both early and current maps, photos and illustrations.
590 PAGES. 6x9 PAPERBACK. ILLUSTRATED. FOOTNOTES & BIBLIOGRAPHY. $14.95. CODE: NC

LOST CITIES & ANCIENT MYSTERIES OF SOUTH AMERICA
by David Hatcher Childress
Rogue adventurer and maverick archaeologist David Hatcher Childress takes the reader on unforgettable journeys deep into deadly jungles, high up on windswept mountains and across scorching deserts in search of lost civilizations and ancient mysteries. Travel with David and explore stone cities high in mountain forests and hear fantastic tales of Inca treasure, living dinosaurs, and a mysterious tunnel system. Whether he is hopping freight trains, searching for secret cities, or just dealing with the daily problems of food, money, and romance, the author keeps the reader spellbound. Includes both early and current maps, photos, and illustrations, and plenty of advice for the explorer planning his or her own journey of discovery.
381 PAGES. 6x9 PAPERBACK. ILLUSTRATED. FOOTNOTES & BIBLIOGRAPHY. $14.95. CODE: SAM

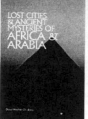

LOST CITIES & ANCIENT MYSTERIES OF AFRICA & ARABIA
by David Hatcher Childress
Across ancient deserts, dusty plains and steaming jungles, maverick archaeologist David Childress continues his worldwide quest for lost cities and ancient mysteries. Join him as he discovers forbidden cities in the Empty Quarter of Arabia; "Atlantean" ruins in Egypt and the Kalahari desert; a mysterious, ancient empire in the Sahara; and more. This is the tale of an extraordinary life on the road: across war-torn countries, Childress searches for King Solomon's Mines, living dinosaurs, the Ark of the Covenant and the solutions to some of the fantastic mysteries of the past.
423 PAGES. 6x9 PAPERBACK. ILLUSTRATED. FOOTNOTES & BIBLIOGRAPHY. $14.95. CODE: AFA

24 hour credit card orders—call: 815-253-6390 fax: 815-253-6300
email: auphq@frontiernet.net   www.adventuresunlimitedpress.com   www.wexclub.com

ANTI-GRAVITY

THE FREE-ENERGY DEVICE HANDBOOK
A Compilation of Patents and Reports
by David Hatcher Childress

THE FREE-ENERGY DEVICE HANDBOOK
A Compilation of Patents & Reports

A large-format compilation of various patents, papers, descriptions and diagrams concerning free-energy devices and systems. *The Free-Energy Device Handbook* is a visual tool for experimenters and researchers into magnetic motors and other "over-unity" devices. With chapters on the Adams Motor, the Hans Coler Generator, cold fusion, superconductors, "N" machines, space-energy generators, Nikola Tesla, T. Townsend Brown, and the latest in free-energy devices. Packed with photos, technical diagrams, patents and fascinating information, this book belongs on every science shelf. With energy and profit being a major political reason for fighting various wars, free-energy devices, if ever allowed to be mass distributed to consumers, could change the world! Get your copy now before the Department of Energy bans this book!
292 PAGES. 8x10 PAPERBACK. ILLUSTRATED. BIBLIOGRAPHY. $16.95. CODE: FEH

THE ANTI-GRAVITY HANDBOOK
edited by David Hatcher Childress, with Nikola Tesla, T.B. Paulicki,
Bruce Cathie, Albert Einstein and others

The new expanded compilation of material on Anti-Gravity, Free Energy, Flying Saucer Propulsion, UFOs, Suppressed Technology, NASA Cover-ups and more. Highly illustrated with patents, technical illustrations and photos. This revised and expanded edition has more material, including photos of Area 51, Nevada, the government's secret testing facility. This classic on weird science is back in a 90s format!

THE ANTI-GRAVITY HANDBOOK
Nikola Tesla
Albert Einstein
NASA
UFOs
and much, much more!

- **How to build a flying saucer.**
- **Arthur C. Clarke on Anti-Gravity.**
- **Crystals and their role in levitation.**
- **Secret government research and development.**
- **Nikola Tesla on how anti-gravity airships could draw power from the atmosphere.**
- **Bruce Cathie's Anti-Gravity Equation.**
- **NASA, the Moon and Anti-Gravity.**

230 PAGES. 7x10 PAPERBACK. BIBLIOGRAPHY/INDEX/APPENDIX. HIGHLY ILLUSTRATED. $14.95. CODE: AGH

ANTI-GRAVITY & THE WORLD GRID

Is the earth surrounded by an intricate electromagnetic grid network offering free energy? This compilation of material on ley lines and world power points contains chapters on the geography, mathematics, and light harmonics of the earth grid. Learn the purpose of ley lines and ancient megalithic structures located on the grid. Discover how the grid made the Philadelphia Experiment possible. Explore the Coral Castle and many other mysteries, including acoustic levitation, Tesla Shields and scalar wave weaponry. Browse through the section on anti-gravity patents, and research resources.
274 PAGES. 7x10 PAPERBACK. ILLUSTRATED. $14.95. CODE: AGW

ANTI-GRAVITY & THE UNIFIED FIELD
edited by David Hatcher Childress

ETHER-TECHNOLGY
A RATIONAL APPROACH TO GRAVITY CONTROL

Is Einstein's Unified Field Theory the answer to all of our energy problems? Explored in this compilation of material is how gravity, electricity and magnetism manifest from a unified field around us. Why artificial gravity is possible; secrets of UFO propulsion; free energy; Nikola Tesla and anti-gravity airships of the 20s and 30s; flying saucers as superconducting whirls of plasma; anti-mass generators; vortex propulsion; suppressed technology; government cover-ups; gravitational pulse drive; spacecraft & more.
240 PAGES. 7x10 PAPERBACK. ILLUSTRATED. $14.95. CODE: AGU

THE UNDERGROUND CLASSIC IS BACK IN PRINT

ETHER TECHNOLOGY
A Rational Approach to Gravity Control
by Rho Sigma

This classic book on anti-gravity and free energy is back in print and back in stock. Written by a well-known American scientist under the pseudonym of "Rho Sigma," this book delves into international efforts at gravity control and discoid craft propulsion. Before the Quantum Field, there was "Ether." This small, but informative book has chapters on John Searle and "Searle discs;" T. Townsend Brown and his work on anti-gravity and ether-vortex turbines. Includes a forward by former NASA astronaut Edgar Mitchell.
108 PAGES. 6x9 PAPERBACK. ILLUSTRATED. $12.95. CODE: ETT

Tapping The Zero-Point Energy
Moray B. King

TAPPING THE ZERO POINT ENERGY
Free Energy & Anti-Gravity in Today's Physics
by Moray B. King

King explains how free energy and anti-gravity are possible. The theories of the zero point energy maintain there are tremendous fluctuations of electrical field energy imbedded within the fabric of space. This book tells how, in the 1930s, inventor T. Henry Moray could produce a fifty kilowatt "free energy" machine; how an electrified plasma vortex creates anti-gravity; how the Pons/Fleischmann "cold fusion" experiment could produce tremendous heat without fusion; and how certain experiments might produce a gravitational anomaly.
170 PAGES. 5x8 PAPERBACK. ILLUSTRATED. $9.95. CODE: TAP

FREE ENERGY SYSTEMS

LOST SCIENCE
by Gerry Vassilatos
Rediscover the legendary names of suppressed scientific revolution—remarkable lives, astounding discoveries, and incredible inventions which would have produced a world of wonder. How did the aura research of Baron Karl von Reichenbach prove the vitalistic theory and frighten the greatest minds of Germany? How did the physiophone and wireless of Antonio Meucci predate both Bell and Marconi by decades? How does the earth battery technology of Nathan Stubblefield portend an unsuspected energy revolution? How did the geoaetheric engines of Nikola Tesla threaten the establishment of a fuel-dependent America? The microscopes and virus-destroying ray machines of Dr. Royal Rife provided the solution for every world-threatening disease. Why did the FDA and AMA together condemn this great man to Federal Prison? The static crashes on telephone lines enabled Dr. T. Henry Moray to discover the reality of radiant space energy. Was the mysterious "Swedish stone," the powerful mineral which Dr. Moray discovered, the very first historical instance in which stellar power was recognized and secured on earth? Why did the Air Force initially fund the gravitational warp research and warp-cloaking devices of T. Townsend Brown and then reject it? When the controlled fusion devices of Philo Farnsworth achieved the "break-even" point in 1967 the FUSOR project was abruptly cancelled by ITT.
304 PAGES. 6x9 PAPERBACK. ILLUSTRATED. BIBLIOGRAPHY. $16.95. CODE: LOS

SECRETS OF COLD WAR TECHNOLOGY
Project HAARP and Beyond
by Gerry Vassilatos
Vassilatos reveals that "Death Ray" technology has been secretly researched and developed since the turn of the century. Included are chapters on such inventors and their devices as H.C. Vion, the developer of auroral energy receivers; Dr. Selim Lemstrom's pre-Tesla experiments; the early beam weapons of Grindell-Mathews, Ulivi, Turpain and others; John Hettenger and his early beam power systems. Learn about Project Argus, Project Teak and Project Orange; EMP experiments in the 60s; why the Air Force directed the construction of a huge Ionospheric "backscatter" telemetry system across the Pacific just after WWII; why Raytheon has collected every patent relevant to HAARP over the past few years; more.
250 PAGES. 6x9 PAPERBACK. ILLUSTRATED. $15.95. CODE: SCWT

THE A.T. FACTOR
A Scientists Encounter with UFOs: Piece For A Jigsaw Part 3
by Leonard Cramp
British aerospace engineer Cramp began much of the scientific anti-gravity and UFO propulsion analysis back in 1955 with his landmark book *Space, Gravity & the Flying Saucer* (out-of-print and rare). His next books (available from Adventures Unlimited) *UFOs & Anti-Gravity: Piece for a Jig-Saw* and *The Cosmic Matrix: Piece for a Jig-Saw Part 2* began Cramp's in depth look into gravity control, free-energy, and the interlocking web of energy that pervades the universe. In this final book, Cramp brings to a close his detailed and controversial study of UFOs and Anti-Gravity.
324 PAGES. 6x9 PAPERBACK. ILLUSTRATED. BIBLIOGRAPHY. INDEX. $16.95. CODE: ATF

THE TIME TRAVEL HANDBOOK
A Manual of Practical Teleportation & Time Travel
edited by David Hatcher Childress
In the tradition of *The Anti-Gravity Handbook* and *The Free-Energy Device Handbook*, science and UFO author David Hatcher Childress takes us into the weird world of time travel and teleportation. Not just a whacked-out look at science fiction, this book is an authoritative chronicling of real-life time travel experiments, teleportation devices and more. *The Time Travel Handbook* takes the reader beyond the government experiments and deep into the uncharted territory of early time travellers such as Nikola Tesla and Guglielmo Marconi and their alleged time travel experiments, as well as the Wilson Brothers of EMI and their connection to the Philadelphia Experiment—the U.S. Navy's forays into invisibility, time travel, and teleportation. Childress looks into the claims of time travelling individuals, and investigates the unusual claim that the pyramids on Mars were built in the future and sent back in time. A highly visual, large format book, with patents, photos and schematics. Be the first on your block to build your own time travel device!
316 PAGES. 7x10 PAPERBACK. ILLUSTRATED. $16.95. CODE: TTH

THE TESLA PAPERS
Nikola Tesla on Free Energy & Wireless Transmission of Power
by Nikola Tesla, edited by David Hatcher Childress
David Hatcher Childress takes us into the incredible world of Nikola Tesla and his amazing inventions. Tesla's rare article "The Problem of Increasing Human Energy with Special Reference to the Harnessing of the Sun's Energy" is included. This lengthy article was originally published in the June 1900 issue of *The Century Illustrated Monthly Magazine* and it was the outline for Tesla's master blueprint for the world. Tesla's fantastic vision of the future, including wireless power, anti-gravity, free energy and highly advanced solar power. Also included are some of the papers, patents and material collected on Tesla at the Colorado Springs Tesla Symposiums, including papers on: •The Secret History of Wireless Transmission •Tesla and the Magnifying Transmitter •Design and Construction of a Half-Wave Tesla Coil •Electrostatics: A Key to Free Energy •Progress in Zero-Point Energy Research •Electromagnetic Energy from Antennas to Atoms •Tesla's Particle Beam Technology •Fundamental Excitatory Modes of the Earth-Ionosphere Cavity
325 PAGES. 8x10 PAPERBACK. ILLUSTRATED. $16.95. CODE: TTP

THE FANTASTIC INVENTIONS OF NIKOLA TESLA
by Nikola Tesla with additional material by David Hatcher Childress
This book is a readable compendium of patents, diagrams, photos and explanations of the many incredible inventions of the originator of the modern era of electrification. In Tesla's own words are such topics as wireless transmission of power, death rays, and radio-controlled airships. In addition, rare material on German bases in Antarctica and South America, and a secret city built at a remote jungle site in South America by one of Tesla's students, Guglielmo Marconi. Marconi's secret group claims to have built flying saucers in the 1940s and to have gone to Mars in the early 1950s! Incredible photos of these Tesla craft are included. The Ancient Atlantean system of broadcasting energy through a grid system of obelisks and pyramids is discussed, and a fascinating concept comes out of one chapter: that Egyptian engineers had to wear protective metal head-shields while in these power plants, hence the Egyptian Pharoah's head covering as well as the Face on Mars! •His plan to transmit free electricity into the atmosphere. •How electrical devices would work using only small antennas. •Why unlimited power could be utilized anywhere on earth. •How radio and radar technology can be used as death-ray weapons in Star Wars.
342 PAGES. 6x9 PAPERBACK. ILLUSTRATED. $16.95. CODE: FINT

24 hour credit card orders—call: 815-253-6390 fax: 815-253-6300

email: auphq@frontiernet.net   www.adventuresunlimitedpress.com   www.wexclub.com

TESLA TECHNOLOGY

THE FANTASTIC INVENTIONS OF NIKOLA TESLA
Nikola Tesla with additional material by David Hatcher Childress
This book is a readable compendium of patents, diagrams, photos and explanations of the many incredible inventions of the originator of the modern era of electrification. In Tesla's own words are such topics as wireless transmission of power, death rays, and radio-controlled airships. In addition, rare material on German bases in Antarctica and South America, and a secret city built at a remote jungle site in South America by one of Tesla's students, Guglielmo Marconi. Marconi's secret group claims to have built flying saucers in the 1940s and to have gone to Mars in the early 1950s! Incredible photos of these Tesla craft are included. The Ancient Atlantean system of broadcasting energy through a grid system of obelisks and pyramids is discussed, and a fascinating concept comes out of one chapter: that Egyptian engineers had to wear protective metal head-shields while in these power plants, hence the Egyptian Pharoah's head covering as well as the Face on Mars!
•His plan to transmit free electricity into the atmosphere. •How electrical devices would work using only small antennas mounted on them. •Why unlimited power could be utilized anywhere on earth. •How radio and radar technology can be used as death-ray weapons in Star Wars. •Includes an appendix of Supreme Court documents on dismantling his free energy towers. •Tesla's Death Rays, Ozone generators, and more...
342 PAGES. 6x9 PAPERBACK. ILLUSTRATED. BIBLIOGRAPHY AND APPENDIX. $16.95. CODE: FINT

SECRETS OF COLD WAR TECHNOLOGY
Project HAARP and Beyond
by Gerry Vassilatos
Vassilatos reveals that "Death Ray" technology has been secretly researched and developed since the turn of the century. Included are chapters on such inventors and their devices as H.C. Vion, the developer of auroral energy receivers; Dr. Selim Lemstrom's pre-Tesla experiments; the early beam weapons of Grindell-Mathews, Ulivi, Turpain and others; John Hettenger and his early beam power systems. Learn about Project Argus, Project Teak and Project Orange; EMP experiments in the 60s; why the Air Force directed the construction of a huge Ionospheric "backscatter" telemetry system across the Pacific just after WWII; why Raytheon has collected every patent relevant to HAARP over the past few years; more.
250 PAGES. 6x9 PAPERBACK. ILLUSTRATED. $15.95. CODE: SCWT

HAARP
The Ultimate Weapon of the Conspiracy
by Jerry Smith
The HAARP project in Alaska is one of the most controversial projects ever undertaken by the U.S. Government. Jerry Smith gives us the history of the HAARP project and explains how works, in technically correct yet easy to understand language. At best, HAARP is science out-of-control; at worst, HAARP could be the most dangerous device ever created, a futuristic technology that is everything from super-beam weapon to world-wide mind control device. Topics include Over-the-Horizon Radar and HAARP, Mind Control, ELF and HAARP, The Telsa Connection, The Russian Woodpecker, GWEN & HAARP, Earth Penetrating Tomography, Weather Modification, Secret Science of the Conspiracy, more. Includes the complete 1987 Eastlund patent for his pulsed super-weapon that he claims was stolen by the HAARP Project.
256 PAGES. 6x9 PAPERBACK. ILLUSTRATED. $14.95. CODE: HARP

ANGELS DON'T PLAY THIS HAARP
Advances in Tesla Technology
by Jeane Manning and Dr. Nick Begich
According to the authors, the U.S. government has a new ground-based "Star Wars" weapon in the remote bush country of Alaska. This new system, based on Tesla's designs, can disrupt human mental processes, jam all global communications systems, change weather patterns over large areas, cause environmental damage and more. The military calls this atmosphere zapper HAARP for High-frequency Active Auroral Research Program which targets the electrojet—a river of electricity that flows thousands of miles through the sky and down into the polar icecap. The device will be used to x-ray the earth, talk to submarines, more.
233 PAGES. 6x9 PAPERBACK. ILLUSTRATED. $14.95. CODE: ADPH

OCCULT ETHER PHYSICS
Tesla's Hidden Space Propulsion System & the Conspiracy to Conceal It
by William Lyne
Pentagon Aliens author Lyne says that there is a "Secret Physics" with a different set of rules hidden away from us earlier in this century by a powerful elite who fear that technology based on it will strip away their power and wealth. Chapters on: The Occult Ether Theory and Electro-propulsion; Wireless Transmission of Energy; Tesla's Teleforce Discoveries; J.J. Thomson's "Electromagnetic Momentum"; Ether and "Ponderable Matter"; Rotatory Motion and the "Screw Effect"; Tesla's Dynamic Theory of Gravity; Tesla's Secrecy; The Atomic Hydrogen Furnace; more.
106 PAGES. 7x10 PAPERBACK. ILLUSTRATED. REFERENCES. $8.00. CODE: OEP

OCCULT ETHER PHYSICS: TESLA'S HIDDEN SPACE PROPULSION SYSTEM AND THE CONSPIRACY TO CONCEAL IT

NIKOLA TESLA'S EARTHQUAKE MACHINE
with Tesla's Original Patents
by Dale Pond and Walter Baumgartner
Now, for the first time, the secrets of Nikola Tesla's Earthquake Machine are available. Although this book discusses in detail Nikola Tesla's 1894 "Earthquake Oscillator," it is also about the new technology of sonic vibrations which produce a resonance effect that can be used to cause earthquakes. Discussed are Tesla Oscillators, Vibration Physics, Amplitude Modulated Additive Synthesis, Tele-Geo-dynamics, Solar Heat Pump Apparatus, Vortex Tube Coolers, the Serogodsky Motor, more. Plenty of technical diagrams. Be the first on your block to have a Tesla Earthquake Machine!
175 PAGES. 9x11 PAPERBACK. ILLUSTRATED. BIBLIOGRAPHY & INDEX. $16.95. CODE: TEM

STRANGE SCIENCE

UNDERGROUND BASES & TUNNELS
What is the Government Trying to Hide?
by Richard Sauder, Ph.D.
Working from government documents and corporate records, Sauder has compiled an impressive book that digs below the surface of the military's super-secret underground! Go behind the scenes into little-known corners of the public record and discover how corporate America has worked hand-in-glove with the Pentagon for decades, dreaming about, planning, and actually constructing, secret underground bases. This book includes chapters on the locations of the bases, the tunneling technology, various military designs for underground bases, nuclear testing & underground bases, abductions, needles & implants, military involvement in "alien" cattle mutilations, more. 50 page photo & map insert.
201 PAGES. 6X9 PAPERBACK. ILLUSTRATED. $15.95. CODE: UGB

KUNDALINI TALES
by Richard Sauder, Ph.D.
Underground Bases and Tunnels author Richard Sauder's second book on his personal experiences and provocative research into spontaneous spiritual awakening, out-of-body journeys, encounters with secretive governmental powers, daylight sightings of UFOs, and more. Sauder continues his studies of underground bases with new information on the occult underpinnings of the U.S. space program. The book also contains a breakthrough section that examines actual U.S. patents for devices that manipulate minds and thoughts from a remote distance. Included are chapters on the secret space program and a 130-page appendix of patents and schematic diagrams of secret technology and mind control devices.
296 PAGES. 7X10 PAPERBACK. ILLUSTRATED. BIBLIOGRAPHY. $14.95. CODE: KTAL

LOST SCIENCE
by Gerry Vassilatos
Secrets of Cold War Technology author Vassilatos on the remarkable lives, astounding discoveries, and incredible inventions of such famous people as Nikola Tesla, Dr. Royal Rife, T.T. Brown, and T. Henry Moray. Read about the aura research of Baron Karl von Reichenbach, the wireless technology of Antonio Meucci, the controlled fusion devices of Philo Farnsworth, the earth battery of Nathan Stubblefield, and more. What were the twisted intrigues which surrounded the often deliberate attempts to stop this technology? Vassilatos claims that we are living hundreds of years behind our intended level of technology and we must recapture this "lost science."
304 PAGES. 6X9 PAPERBACK. ILLUSTRATED. BIBLIOGRAPHY. $16.95. CODE: LOS

THE TIME TRAVEL HANDBOOK
A Manual of Practical Teleportation & Time Travel
edited by David Hatcher Childress
In the tradition of *The Anti-Gravity Handbook* and *The Free-Energy Device Handbook*, science and UFO author David Hatcher Childress takes us into the weird world of time travel and teleportation. Not just a whacked-out look at science fiction, this book is an authoritative chronicling of real-life time travel experiments, teleportation devices and more. *The Time Travel Handbook* takes the reader beyond the government experiments and deep into the uncharted territory of early time travellers such as Nikola Tesla and Guglielmo Marconi and their alleged time travel experiments, as well as the Wilson Brothers of EMI and their connection to the Philadelphia Experiment—the U.S. Navy's forays into invisibility, time travel, and teleportation. Childress looks into the claims of time travelling individuals, and investigates the unusual claim that the pyramids on Mars were built in the future and sent back in time. A highly visual, large format book, with patents, photos and schematics. Be the first on your block to build your own time travel device!
316 PAGES. 7X10 PAPERBACK. ILLUSTRATED. $16.95. CODE: TTH

MAPS OF THE ANCIENT SEA KINGS
Evidence of Advanced Civilization in the Ice Age
by Charles H. Hapgood
Charles Hapgood's classic 1966 book on ancient maps produces concrete evidence of an advanced world-wide civilization existing many thousands of years before ancient Egypt. He has found the evidence in the Piri Reis Map that shows Antarctica, the Hadji Ahmed map, the Oronteus Finaeus and other amazing maps. Hapgood concluded that these maps were made from more ancient maps from the various ancient archives around the world, now lost. Not only were these unknown people more advanced in mapmaking than any people prior to the 18th century, it appears they mapped all the continents. The Americas were mapped thousands of years before Columbus. Antarctica was mapped when its coasts were free of ice.
316 PAGES. 7X10 PAPERBACK. ILLUSTRATED. BIBLIOGRAPHY & INDEX. $19.95. CODE: MASK

PATH OF THE POLE
Cataclysmic Pole Shift Geology
by Charles Hapgood
Maps of the Ancient Sea Kings author Hapgood's classic book *Path of the Pole* is back in print! Hapgood researched Antarctica, ancient maps and the geological record to conclude that the Earth's crust has slipped in the inner core many times in the past, changing the position of the pole. *Path of the Pole* discusses the various "pole shifts" in Earth's past, giving evidence for each one, and moves on to possible future pole shifts. Packed with illustrations, this is the sourcebook for many other books on cataclysms and pole shifts.
356 PAGES. 6X9 PAPERBACK. ILLUSTRATED. $16.95. CODE: POP.

One Adventure Place
P.O. Box 74
Kempton, Illinois 60946
United States of America
Tel.: 815-253-6390 • Fax: 815-253-6300
Email: auphq@frontiernet.net
http://www.adventuresunlimitedpress.com
or www.wexclub.com/aup

ORDERING INSTRUCTIONS

✓ Remit by USD$ Check, Money Order or Credit Card
✓ Visa, Master Card, Discover & AmEx Accepted
✓ Prices May Change Without Notice
✓ 10% Discount for 3 or more Items

SHIPPING CHARGES

United States

✓ Postal Book Rate { $3.00 First Item
50¢ Each Additional Item

✓ Priority Mail { $4.00 First Item
$2.00 Each Additional Item

✓ UPS { $5.00 First Item
$1.50 Each Additional Item

NOTE: UPS Delivery Available to Mainland USA Only

Canada

✓ Postal Book Rate { $4.00 First Item
$1.00 Each Additional Item

✓ Postal Air Mail { $6.00 First Item
$2.00 Each Additional Item

✓ Personal Checks or Bank Drafts MUST BE
USD$ and Drawn on a US Bank
✓ Canadian Postal Money Orders OK
✓ Payment MUST BE USD$

All Other Countries

✓ Surface Delivery { $7.00 First Item
$2.00 Each Additional Item

✓ Postal Air Mail { $13.00 First Item
$8.00 Each Additional Item

✓ Payment MUST BE USD$
✓ Checks and Money Orders MUST BE USD$
and Drawn on a US Bank or branch.
✓ Add $5.00 for Air Mail Subscription to
Future *Adventures Unlimited* Catalogs

SPECIAL NOTES

✓ RETAILERS: Standard Discounts Available
✓ BACKORDERS: We Backorder all Out-of-
Stock Items Unless Otherwise Requested
✓ PRO FORMA INVOICES: Available on Request
✓ VIDEOS: NTSC Mode Only. Replacement only.
✓ For PAL mode videos contact our other offices:

European Office:
Adventures Unlimited, Panewaal 22,
Enkhuizen, 1600 AA, The Netherlands
http: www.adventuresunlimited.nl
Check Us Out Online at:
www.adventuresunlimitedpress.com

Please check: ✓

☐ This is my first order   ☐ I have ordered before   ☐ This is a new address

Name	
Address	
City	
State/Province	Postal Code
Country	
Phone day	Evening
Fax	

Item Code	Item Description	Price	Qty	Total

Please check: ✓

☐ Postal-Surface
☐ Postal-Air Mail
(Priority in USA)
☐ UPS
(Mainland USA only)

Subtotal ➡	
Less Discount-10% for 3 or more items ➡	
Balance ➡	
Illinois Residents 6.25% Sales Tax ➡	
Previous Credit ➡	
Shipping ➡	
Total (check/MO in USD$ only) ➡	

☐ Visa/MasterCard/Discover/Amex

Card Number

Expiration Date

10% Discount When You Order 3 or More Items!

Comments & Suggestions	Share Our Catalog with a Friend